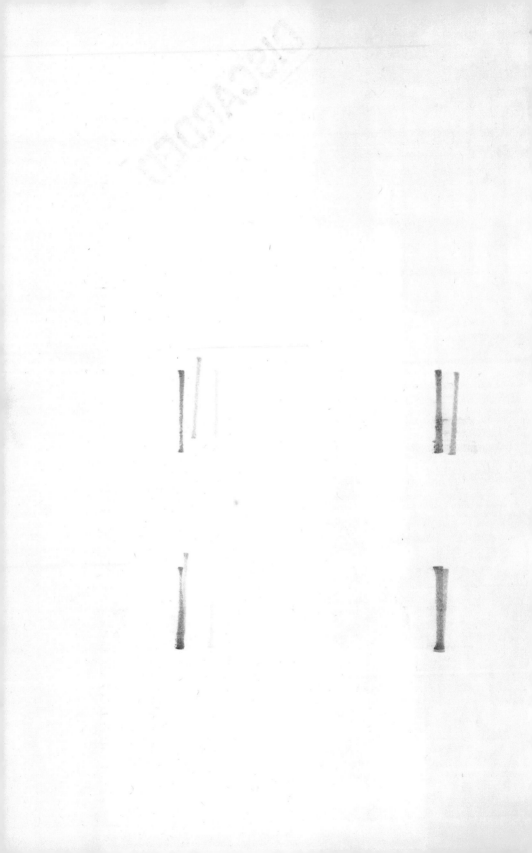

Marx's Politics

The king and queen
Strapped down! to a board!
That's against all respect
And all etiquette!
Heinrich Heine, *Deutschland,*
Ein Wintermärchen, 1844

The second curse for the king of the rich
Whom our distress could not soften or touch
The king who extorts the last penny from us
And sends his soldiers to shoot us like dogs
We are weaving, weaving!
Heinrich Heine, "The Weavers," 1844,
translated by Engels for the Chartist
journal, *The New Moral World*

Marx's Politics

Communists and Citizens

Alan Gilbert

Rutgers University Press

New Brunswick, New Jersey

Portions of previously published articles by the author have been adapted and incorporated in this work: "Marx on Internationalism and War," *Philosophy and Public Affairs* 7(Summer 1978): 346–369 is reprinted by permission of Princeton University Press; "Salvaging Marx from Avineri," *Political Theory* 4(February 1976): 5–34 is reprinted by permission of the publisher, Sage Publications, Inc.; "Social Theory and Revolutionary Activity in Marx," *The American Political Science Review* 73(Summer 1979): 521–538, is reprinted by permission of the American Political Science Association. Translations from Karl Marx, *On Revolution*, copyright © 1971 Saul K. Padover, are used with the permission of McGraw-Hill Book Company.

Library of Congress Cataloging in Publication Data

Gilbert, Alan, 1944–
  Marx's politics.

  Bibliography: p.
  Includes index.
  1. Marx, Karl, 1818–1883—Political science.
I. Title.
JC233.M299G54   320.5′315′0924   80–23254
ISBN 0–8135–0903–3

Illustration adapted from an etching by Käthe Kollwitz,
Storming the Owner's Mansion (1897), from her series The Weavers.

For Richard and Emma Gilbert

Contents

Acknowledgments

I HAVE GAINED MANY INSIGHTS into Marx's political activity from my own participation in the anti-Vietnam war movement of the late 1960s and the multiracial working-class antiracist movement of the 1970s. I would especially like to thank Barbara Hertz, Epifanio Camacho, Marianne Gilbert, Milt Rosen, Victor Guerrero, Floyd Banks, Finley Campbell, and many other members of the International Committee against Racism.

Conversations over many years with my friend Bob Leonhardt have contributed strongly to my understanding of Marx. When I began working on this project at Harvard, Michael Walzer and Stanley Hoffmann provided kind encouragement and sound advice. To Judith Shklar, I owe a variant of the title of her book *Men and Citizens: A Study of Rousseau's Social Theory*. Charles Tilly's guidance in French history helped me to understand the acuteness of Marx's analysis of political countercurrents among the French peasantry. Benjamin Barber organized a debate with Shlomo Avineri in *Political Theory* and later urged me to draw out some of the broader implications of this argument. Professor Avineri has always responded graciously to our serious disagreements. Richard Boyd made important suggestions concerning Marx's theory and realism in the philosophy of science. When I came to the Graduate School of International Studies of the University of Denver, Josef Korbel's friendship, wisdom, and example aided me greatly.

Marianne Gilbert and Jonathan Adelman read and criticized the final draft. Marlie Wasserman and Leslie Mitchner of Rutgers University Press were very helpful in the preparation of the manuscript for publication. Members of the American Political Science Association and of the Southern California and Rocky Mountain chapters of the Conference for the Study of Political Thought responded to papers on Marx's politics with useful queries and counterarguments.

Of many others who contributed questions and suggestions at various stages along the way, I would like to thank David Crocker, Arthur DiQuattro, Timothy Fuller, Richard Gilbert, Howard Hertz, Nannerl Keohane,

Harvey C. Mansfield, Jr., Horst Mewes, Ralph Miliband, Richard Miller, Barrington Moore, Jim Prickett, Robert Schulzinger, Michael Schwartz, Peter Steinberger, Peter Stern, Paul Thomas, and Tom Weston.

I have usually used available English translations, but where not otherwise indicated, the translations are my own.

Abbreviations

Address—Marx and Engels, *Address of the Central Committee to the Communist League* in *MESW*, 1:106–117.

Bund Dokumente—Förder et al., ed., *Der Bund der Kommunisten: Dokumente und Materialen, 1836–1849.*

CM—Marx and Engels, *Manifesto of the Communist Party* in *MESW*, 1:21–65.

Condition—Engels, *The Condition of the Working Class in England.*

CS—Marx, *The Class Struggles in France, 1848 to 1850* in *MESW*, 1:188–242.

CW—Marx and Engels, *Collected Works.*

Diskussionen—"Diskussionen im Kommunistischen Arbeitersbildungsverein in London. 18. Februar 1845–14. Januar 1846" in *Bund Dokumente*, pp. 214–238.

EB—Marx, *The Eighteenth Brumaire of Louis Bonaparte* in *MESW*, 1:247–344.

GI—Marx and Engels, *The German Ideology* in *CW*, vol. 5. I also cite (as *The German Ideology*) the edition edited by S. Ryazanskaya (Moscow, 1964).

IWA—International Workingmen's Association.

MESW—Marx and Engels, *Selected Works*, 2 vols., Moscow, 1962. I also cite (as *Selected Works*) the one-volume *Selected Works* (New York, 1974).

NRZ—*Neue Rheinische Zeitung.*

PW—Engels, *The Peasant War in Germany.*

SC—Marx and Engels, *Selected Correspondence*, Moscow, 1965.

"Seventeen Demands"—Marx and Engels, "Demands of the Communist Party in Germany," in Appendix to this volume.

Werke—Marx and Engels, *Werke.*

ZAV—*Die Zeitung des Arbeiter-Vereines zu Köln.*

Marx's Politics

— I —

Introduction

1–1. Economic Determinism and Marx's Politics

AT MARX'S GRAVESIDE, Engels stated: "Marx was before all else a revolutionist. . . . Fighting was his element." To ears attuned to economic determinist or contemporary humanist accounts of Marx's thought, Engels's words sound strange. As economic determinist interpreters have long told us, Marx cloistered himself in the British Museum and studied the grand economic forces propelling society forward. He discounted any major role for revolutionary activity in general and personally shunned politics. A more sophisticated economic determinist account might acknowledge the importance of revolutionary politics; given certain conditions of production (for example, the emergence of a bourgeoisie or an advanced level of capitalism) and some definite political activity (for example, a republican movement or a socialist party), a democratic or communist revolution will ultimately ensue. Yet for most commentators on Marx as a determinist theorist, if one knows the economic forces, one knows the politics.[1]

More recently, a humanist reinterpretation has focused on Marx's early unpublished manuscripts or on his notebooks for *Capital*. This view identifies the "real" Marx as a philosopher of men who collectively alienate themselves in production and politics, but who have the potential to subject these activities to their collective guidance. While making an important contribution to Marx scholarship, these interpreters have sometimes fabricated an arcane Marx "before" or even "against Marxism." They have noticed that active men alienate themselves in creating the productive forces; yet once forged, these alien forces govern the dynamics of society and politics in a fashion reminiscent of ordinary economic determinism. Despite Marx's insistence on revolutionary practice, these writers implicitly counterpose the

1. Karl Marx and Friedrich Engels, *MESW*, 2:168. G. V. Plekhanov, "Socialism and the Political Struggle" in *Selected Philosophical Works* 1:80–92. Martin Bober, *Karl Marx's Interpretation of History*, pp. 107–112, 363–388.

philosophical shadow of action to real political activity. Like the "true socialists," whom Marx satirized in the *Manifesto,* they have written fancy but
inexact phrases over the classical determinist text, leaving the older account
of Marx's politics perfectly intact.[2]

Yet Marx's extensive political activity repeatedly fails to jibe with economic determinist preconceptions. In the 1840s, Marx helped to found the
Communist League and led the radical wing of the German democratic revolution. An economic determinist might contend that at this time, socialism
could attain power only in advanced capitalist England, then nearing a proletarian majority; in Germany, only a vigorous democratic revolution catapult-
ing the bourgeoisie to power could succeed. Yet in the *Manifesto,* Marx
looked to backward Germany as the setting for both a democratic and an
"immediately following" proletarian revolution. The economic determinist
"knows" that Marx dismissed the peasantry as a regressive and reactionary
force. But in 1848 Marx organized his first communist rally in Germany
among peasants in rural Worringen; his strategy pivoted on unity between
rural and urban democrats and communists. According to the determinist,
the internal dynamics of capitalism should have provoked a strong English
socialist movement by the 1860s, and the unexpected decline of Chartism
must have derived from temporary economic improvement. Yet, following
Gladstone, Marx argued that English capitalists had purchased their dazzling
prosperity entirely at the expense of workers; the English proletariat had
made no substantial gains since the 1840s. To explain socialism's poor following in England, Marx pointed to the racist division between English and
Irish laborers which he called the "secret of the impotence" of English workers despite their relatively high level of unionism. According to Marx, the
rulers knowingly spawned degrading images of the Irish "through press, pul-
pit and comic papers." At Marx's initiative, the IWA (International
Workingmen's Association) spearheaded the campaign for the freedom of
Ireland and the overcoming of this hostility within the working class.[3]

Glimpsing these paradoxes for an economic determinist interpretation,
many scholars have ignored Marx's politics or considered his activity mere
atheoretical "shuffling."[4] Even the recent work on Marx's early conception

2. Shlomo Avineri, *The Social and Political Thought of Karl Marx.* Alan Gilbert, "Salvaging Marx from Avineri."

3. Marx to Kugelmann, November 24, 1869, Marx to Engels, December 10, 1869, and
Marx to Meyer and Vogt, April 9, 1870, in Marx and Engels, *SC,* pp. 230–232, 236–237.

4. Oscar J. Hammen, "Marx and the Agrarian Question," p. 680.

of working-class "self-emancipation" omits Marx's strategy for Germany in 1848 or distorts his activity to fit an underlying determinist preconception.[5] But no view that plays down the role of politics or attempts to deduce strategy in a simple fashion from the level of productive forces within a country can adequately account for Marx's historical analyses. Such scholarship offers no insight into the frequent disjunction between Marx's political activity and its conception of his theory; it merely conceals an important problem. At Marx's graveside, Engels justly identified the thrust of Marx's lifework as revolutionary politics. From his first to his last writings, Marx condemned the dead scholasticism that isolated theory from practical activity and did not aim to "change the world." [6] Taking Marx at his word, we should try to discern the theory in his political activity. Furthermore, Marx's politics may cast new light on the character of Marx's general theory. Perhaps scholars have begrudged Marx his own complex mode of historical theorizing and of formulating political strategy.

1–2. Marx's Two Types of Theorizing and the Concept of Auxiliary Statements

IN HIS GENERAL MATERIALIST THEORY, Marx pursued two "guiding hypotheses." First, in the *Manifesto,* he argued that "the history of all hitherto existing society is the history of class struggles." [7] Second, to explain these political clashes, Marx looked to an underlying material foundation in the modes of production. In each entire social epoch, he argued, a determining relationship exists between the way men (and women) produce material wealth and their forms of political and intellectual life. Furthermore, contradictions between new forces of production (the mental and physical activities of the producers using existing raw materials and implements) and older social relations of production (the relations between exploiters or nonproducers and producers) generate new relations of production and new forms of class conflict, and ultimately, new forms of society. Analytically, these general materialist hypotheses provided criteria for discerning the fundamental features of the emerging capitalist society: its enormous expansion of pro-

5. Michael Lowy, *La Théorie de la révolution chez le jeune Marx.* Richard N. Hunt, *The Political Ideas of Marx and Engels.* Ralph Miliband, *Marxism and Politics.*

6. Marx, *Theses on Feuerbach* in Marx and Engels, *Selected Works,* p. 30.

7. In 1888, Engels, *MESW,* 1:34, n. 6, added the qualification "all *written* history." Early communal society had neither classes nor class struggle.

duction, its vast uprooting of small property holders and dissolution of traditional customs, its revolution against feudalism. Beyond this, capitalist factories brought large numbers of workers together and forced them to associate. Marx's study of this material underpinning indicated the type of class struggle and new society that would probably spring from capitalism. Politically, Marx's theory provided an insight into the historical process through which small groups of radicals or isolated working-class movements could hope, despite immediate appearances, to become decisive revolutionary forces.[8]

In articulating this broad pattern of history, Marx occasionally offered very general, abstract formulations as in his *Preface* of 1859:

> No social order ever perishes before all the productive forces for which there is room in it have developed; and new, higher relations of production never appear before the material conditions of their existence have matured in the womb of the old society itself. Therefore mankind always sets itself only such tasks as it can solve; since, looking at the matter more closely, it will always be found that the task itself arises only when the material conditions for its solution already exist or are at least in the process of formation.[9]

To interpret this statement, however, one would want to know exactly how Marx applied it to specific historical situations. If a social order develops "all the productive forces for which there is room in it" before it generates a new one, did the first major crisis of capitalism in 1857 already indicate that this system had grown old? Did Marx offer any guideline about how large a bourgeoisie must exist prior to a democratic revolution or whether a majority proletariat must exist prior to a socialist one? If not, Marx overstated his case. To say that the relevant productive forces for socialism are "at least in the process of formation" (and hence that class conflict and the relations of production, influenced by international economic and political circumstances, have a wide latitude in determining potential courses of development) is not to argue in any strong sense that capitalism must develop "*all* the productive forces for which there is room in it."

Astutely comparing Marx's basic hypothesis to some theories in the natural sciences, Richard Miller has argued:

8. I offer a further elaboration of these themes as they appear in the first part of the *Manifesto* in section 8-2.

9. Marx, *Preface to a Contribution to the Critique of Political Economy* in *Selected Works*, p. 183.

One needs to understand to what extent and in what ways his [a scientist's] statements are meant to hold in order to decide whether the description is true as intended or is an invalid oversimplification . . . a geologist might say, "The history of the earth's surface is the history of continental drift." If he meant to explain "the general idea guiding his studies in plate-tectonics," we would accept his statement as a legitimate simplification of reality. This is true even though the earth was once entirely covered with water (hence, there were no continents), and, before that, was molten (hence, there was nothing like a continent).[10]

Marx elaborated his guiding hypotheses in two distinct, only partially related directions. In the first, he produced a new, remarkably sophisticated analysis of the general tendencies of an ideal capitalism in *Capital*. In the second, he worked out explanations and strategies for events and movements within definite historical settings.

The first reinforced the insights into the oppression of the proletariat and its political struggle to emancipate itself already noted. In forging this theory, Marx studied capitalist tendencies "abstracted" from any specific capitalism, even that of England. Thus, in volume 3 of *Capital*, he explained recurring capitalist crises in terms of a sharply qualified "law" or "tendency" of the rate of profit to fall. This tendency depended on a sufficiently rapid rate of introduction of machinery to offset increases in productivity (the rate of exploitation). Counteracting tendencies such as cheapening of constant capital (machinery), foreign trade to countries with a lower level of productivity, relative overpopulation, and so forth could retard or offset this tendency. As Marx stressed, many real circumstances, including the economic and political struggle of workers against the capitalists, intervened between the idealized structure to which the abstract "law" applied and an actual falling rate of profit.[11]

Marx's second type of theory zeroed in on specific situations: what strategy should German communists adopt in the democratic revolution of 1848? How might one explain the victory of the second Napoleon in France in 1851? In analyzing these situations, Marx never concluded that general economic causes necessarily determined one political outcome rather than another. Instead, he appealed to a specific combination of economic and politi-

---

10. Richard W. Miller, "The Consistency of Historical Materialism," p. 392.

11. Karl Marx, *Capital*, 3:229. Ronald L. Meek, *Economics and Ideology and Other Essays*, p. 142.

cal factors to define the alternatives in each upcoming case or to explain retrospectively a unique result. Over time, different political strategies of the contending forces might lead to dramatically different outcomes. While this second type of theorizing made use of arguments drawn from the first (criteria for beginning to analyze classes, for example), it examined a different, more complex object: the actual political setting for a revolutionary movement as opposed to the internal dynamics of capitalism (or earlier social systems). When applying the general theory to formulate explanations or strategies, Marx always modified it in certain characteristic, mainly political, ways.

Marx distinguished these two types of theoretical activity. In *Capital,* he underlined the vast array of "empirical" conditions that the general theory left out:

> The direct relationship of the owners of the conditions of production to the direct producers—a relation always naturally corresponding to a definite stage in the development of the methods of labor and thereby to its social productivity—reveals the innermost secret, the hidden basis of the entire social structure, and with it . . . the corresponding form of the state. This does not prevent the same economic basis—the same from the standpoint of its main conditions—due to innumerable different empirical circumstances, natural environment . . . external historical influences, etc. from showing infinite variations and gradations in appearance, which can be ascertained only by analysis of the empirically given circumstances.[12]

As Marx moved from the general theory to the formulation of historical explanations or strategies, he took account of these "innumerable different empirical circumstances," external influences, and the like. In 1877 in his famous letters on the communist potential of the Russian *mir* (agricultural commune), Marx compared dispossessed Roman peasants who became a "mob of do-nothings" to postenclosure English farmers who became wage earners, and noted:

> Events strikingly analogous but taking place in different historical surroundings led to totally different results. By studying these forms of evolution separately and then comparing them, one can easily find the clue to this phenomenon, but one will never arrive there by using as one's master key a general

12. Marx, *Capital,* 3:772.

historico-philosophical theory, the supreme virtue of which consists in being superhistorical.[13]

Historical reality disciplined Marx's materialist political analysis; no abstract account of social forces can legitimately override actual history.

In the 1870s, Marx thought that a proletarian revolution in advanced Europe might precede a direct communist revolution in Russia. Thus, minimally, if one country passed through certain definite stages of production, it would condition the future development of others; followers on the international scene would not have to repeat the first country's history step by step. The productive dynamic of Marx's general theory in *The German Ideology* or the *Preface* of 1859 indicated a broad trend without specifying the course that any given country must pursue. In interpreting the *Preface,* one should emphasize that socialism requires not a distant "ripeness" of productive forces, but only that such forces, broadly speaking, "are at least in process of formation." Therefore, in 1848 Marx could expect a socialist outcome to a protracted German revolution and still defend his general pattern of history.[14]

In a letter to Zasulich in 1885, Engels also insisted that Marx's strategies required attention to particular circumstances: "To me the historical theory of Marx is the fundamental condition of all *reasoned* and *consistent* revolutionary tactics; to discover these tactics one has only to apply the theory to the economic and political conditions of the country in question." [15] Yet this "only" is not so simple. Though Marx and Engels always followed the procedure that Engels described, they never closely analyzed the difference between these two types of theorizing.

The concept of auxiliary statements as used in the philosophy of science may clarify the relation between Marx's general theory and his specific strategies and explanations. According to Hilary Putnam, a general scientific theory gains acceptance through certain striking successes, as when Newton derived Kepler's laws from his theory of universal gravitation. Yet even a successful theory confronts many problems it has not yet solved, and some that may simply be too difficult to solve. In tackling these problems as well as in the original successes, scientists never apply the general theory by itself, but only in conjunction with auxiliary statements that enable them to spec-

13. Marx to the editorial board of the *Otechestvenniye Zapiski,* November 1877, *SC,* p. 313.
14. William H. Shaw, *Marx's Theory of History,* pp. 79–81.
15. Letter of April 23, 1885, *SC,* p. 384.

ify the context. Scientists sometimes regard these statements as much less certain than a well-established general theory. To explain other phenomena, however, they may use well-established facts or well-tested laws from other scientific theories—the appropriate auxiliary statements will vary according to the context of inquiry. To apply Newton's theory, Putnam argues, astronomers use several simplifying assumptions (auxiliary statements) such as: no bodies exist except the earth and the sun; these bodies exist in a hard vacuum; they are subject to no forces except mutually induced gravitational forces. In making predictions or explanations, scientists often do not spell out such auxiliary statements. When they use the word "theory," they hardly consider such statements to be part of it—a rough analogy to Marx's formulation of his guiding hypotheses and general laws.[16]

According to Putnam, general theories do not imply obvious predictions, and scientists rarely try to falsify an accepted theory that has had striking practical successes. They discard an old theory as untrue only when glaring anomalies emerge, and someone offers a better alternative theory to explain them. Until then, scientists usually seek new auxiliary statements within the given paradigm.

Analogously, when applying his theory, Marx also used certain kinds of auxiliary statements to specify the context. To explain the weakness of English socialism in the 1860s, for instance, Marx stressed two kinds of auxiliary statements: the specific international political setting characterized by England's colonial domination of Ireland and the role of political traditions, in this case, racist attitudes among English workers. Engels's letter to Bloch in 1890 attempted to mark off specific configurations of factors uncovered through historical analysis from "ultimate" economic causation in precisely this way. In explaining the rise of Prussia, Engels emphasized the importance of religious innovation and the Reformation, as well as of Prussia's international "entanglement" with Poland.[17]

Putnam notes a general dialectic of prediction and explanation in science, which also exists in Marx. When astronomers observed the deviant orbit of

16. Hilary Putnam, "The Corroboration of Theories" in *Collected Philosophical Papers*, 1:254–259. Philosophers of science often call such statements "auxiliary hypotheses." Carl Hempel, *Philosophy of Natural Science*, pp. 22–25. This term is misleading since it suggests that such statements must be tentative, while they may include not only well-established facts but theories fully as complex and well tested as those to which they serve as auxiliary. For an interesting discussion, see Richard N. Boyd, *Realism and Scientific Epistemology*, pp. 79–81.

17. Letter of September 21–22, 1890, in *Selected Works*, p. 692.

Uranus, for example, they did not doubt the theory of universal gravitation. Instead Adams in England and Leverrier in France simultaneously predicted the existence of another planet whose gravitational pull would account for the deviation. Astronomers subsequently discovered Neptune. A failure of explanation led to successful prediction; the existence of Neptune then served as a new auxiliary statement to correct the general theory's explanation of the orbit of Uranus.

In the 1840s and 1850s, Marx predicted that English workers would soon form a strong socialist movement. Despite the continuing oppressiveness of capitalism, they did not. Confronted with this failure, Marx examined the social and political divisions within the English working class more closely and offered a new auxiliary statement on the political consequences of English colonialism. Marx now envisioned internationalism on the Irish question not only as a moral obligation for the English working class but also as a political necessity: the continued thralldom of Ireland presented the chief obstacle to socialism in Britain. Marx's changed explanation led in turn to a refined strategy on Ireland in the IWA and had general anticolonial implications for his political theory.[18] This dialectic of strategy and explanation, given fresh political experience, illustrates Marx's 1845 thesis on Feuerbach that revolution involves "practical-critical activity." [19]

Yet Putnam's characterization of auxiliary statements in Newtonian astronomy seems to differ from a description appropriate to Marx's argument. Putnam treats such statements as rough counterfactual idealizations which

18. Lenin would later extend Marx's particular strategy for the English working class with respect to Ireland to a general recommendation for the proletariat of any imperialist power to campaign against the power's acts of colonial domination. Here we may see a different dialectic between specific historical explanation and general theory. Concurring with Hegel's critique of Kant's unknowable "thing-in-itself," Lenin would later speak of the "living movement, deeper and deeper, of our knowledge about things." V. I. Lenin, "Conspectus of Hegel's *Science of Logic,*" *Collected Works,* 38:91.

19. That Marx's theory yields more successful explanations than predictions or strategies is not an argument against comparing historical materialism and mature theories in the natural sciences. Some mature theories, notably Darwin's account of the origin of species, offer no specific predictions at all but simply compelling explanations. In such a comparison, Marx's theory (explanation, relatively difficult though frequently successful strategy or prediction) lies somewhere between Darwin's biology (explanation, no prediction) and Newtonian and contemporary astronomy (explanation, relatively exact prediction). Michael Scriven, "Explanation and Prediction in Evolutionary Theory." For some examples of Marxian predictions, see sections 8–3, 10–5, 11–1, 11–2 and Chapter 14.

identify only the main contextual features needed for explanation (suppose for explanatory purposes that only two bodies count . . .). Marx's auxiliary statements, on the contrary, include detailed accounts of the relevant economic and political facts—for instance a specific international situation, the relation of economic and political forces within a country, particular ideological traditions—which a general or abstract theory of modes of production and class struggle cannot include. Looked at more closely, however, Marx's statements also exhibit an element of abstraction in order to emphasize a main contextual feature. For example, to explain the decline of English socialism, Marx stressed the significance of British colonialism in Ireland rather than in India mainly because so large an Irish proletariat existed in England itself. Similarly, his concentration on English racism toward Irish workers abstracted from other important differences or divisions—of Manchester textile workers and Welsh miners, skilled and unskilled, male and female—any one of which might have proved significant in that historical situation.[20] Thus, in the event itself, a political or economic facet other than those Marx had emphasized beforehand might be decisive. Where a specific strategy or prediction failed, Marx could often change or add an auxiliary statement to explain the unexpected outcome without putting the general theory in question. In such cases, the historical salience of the aspect involved, say of racist divisions between English and Irish workers in the 1850s, would make the new explanation compelling. A realist in the philosophy of science today might see these changes or refinements as bringing Marx's general analysis into closer approximation to reality rather than overthrowing his earlier theory.

Marx's historical arguments exhibited three levels—a general theory of modes of production and class conflict, the analysis of specific international and national circumstances, and the study of new political movements. While the auxiliary statements did not contradict Marx's general theory, Marx did not deduce them from it but rather elicited them from his study of the given historical situation. The conjunction of the general theory with a set of auxiliary statements could generate different strategic estimates from those that the general theory seemed to predict. Furthermore, Marx often arrived at his strategies from the evaluation of particular political move-

20. Mao Tse-tung's stress on a principal contradiction in any given historical situation captures this feature of Marx's strategies and explanations. Mao, *On Contradiction* in *Selected Readings,* pp. 89–95.

ments. For example, Marx would base his interpretation of the dynamic of a German revolution in 1848 on the emergence of Babeuf's communism in the French Revolution. Thus, in the interplay of the three levels of Marx's analysis, particular historical circumstances and revolutionary political experience had a special impact. In this context, the economic determinist, who ignores such circumstances and movements and focuses on Marx's general theory interpreted apolitically as all important, wholly misunderstands the character and derivation of Marx's politics.

Marx's use of auxiliary statements presented no immediate difficulties for his general theory. Yet given the differing objects of the general theory and specific explanations, a category error—substituting some general economic cause ("Germany in 1848 had too low a level of productive development for socialism") for a specific combination of economic and political factors—may easily occur within Marxian theorizing. Except for a brief reaction to the defeat of revolution between 1850 and 1852, Marx himself never made this error. Nonetheless, his own general formulations have sometimes facilitated such economic determinist misreadings of historical experience.

1–3. Tensions in Marx's Strategies

MARX'S STRATEGIES had three aspects: (1) a specification of those classes that communists could win over to support democracy or socialism through the experience of class conflict (thus, in a democratic revolution, Marx would expect workers, peasants, artisans, and in some circumstances the bourgeoisie to combat the aristocracy and monarchy; in a socialist revolution, peasants, insofar as usury and mortgages oppressed them, might ally themselves with workers against the capitalists); (2) a delineation of the configuration of historical circumstances and political movements in which revolution might occur; and (3) an emphasis on certain political insights—internationalism, the need to end, not just reform, capitalism—that communists must interject into a radical movement. As a strategist, however, Marx recognized the internal tensions in communist politics. The power of ideology, habit, and divisions among the masses played upon by the old ruling class as well as the military force at the rulers' disposal rendered history opaque.[21] Though capitalist oppression weighed on the workers, they would not simply organize themselves to secure socialism in obedience to some proto-Lukacsian "im-

21. Marx, *Capital,* 1:71–83.

puted consciousness" (*zugerechnetes Bewusstsein*). In Marx's view, real relations of production and power stood out most distinctly in political conflicts in which working people strove to rectify specific injustices. Workers' struggles for higher wages or shorter hours, and democratic revolts against feudal princes provided the arenas in which the oppressed classes could acquire revolutionary awareness. Such conflicts became political "locomotives of history." [22] In these "real" but nonsocialist movements, Marx contended, communists must participate energetically. Yet they must not confine themselves to the role of resolute unionist or avid democrat. As the *Manifesto* put it, though defending the "momentary interests" of the proletariat, they must also "take care of the future of the movement." They must advocate internationalism—the "common interests of the proletariat regardless of all nationality"—and ceaselessly instill the perspective of socialism. [23]

These two aspects of communist activity may clash. A vigorous strike might reveal the full array of political and cultural weapons at the disposal of the capitalists, such as injunctions, police, army, and press. It could suggest the systemic character of capitalist exploitation. Yet unions, as reform organizations, claim only a "better rate of exploitation" from the workers' point of view, not the abolition of the wage system. [24] Similarly, a victorious democratic revolution would propel the bourgeoisie into power; it would not topple the capitalists along with the aristocrats. Given this tension, Marx regarded advocacy of internationalism and socialism within these movements as a fundamental principle.

Upholding the communist future of the movement often drew fierce attacks from the bourgeoisie and even from hesitant radicals. For Marx's vehement support of the 1848 Paris June insurrection, he lost half the financial backing for his paper, the *Neue Rheinische Zeitung* (*NRZ*). In 1871 Marx and the IWA defended the Paris Commune's "storming of heaven." As Marx exulted in a letter to Kugelmann, the rulers retaliated by disturbing Marx's "twenty years' idyll in my den" and made him "the best calumniated and most menaced man in London." [25] All accounts of Marx's strategy that portray the working class riding the crest of an economic wave to power or

22. Marx, *CS, MESW*, 1:217.
23. Marx and Engels, *CM, MESW*, 1:46, 65.
24. Marx, *Wages, Price and Profit, MESW*, 1:446.
25. Letter of June 18, 1871, in Marx, *Letters to Kugelmann*, p. 126.

project its "self-emancipation" in slow motion miss Marx's fiery spirit of internationalist daring and defiance.

In the absence of favorable circumstances, political activity alone will not result in revolution; revolutionary situations, often induced by war, are unusual. Yet over long periods, before such circumstances coalesce, the character of radical political efforts becomes an important, even a decisive, variable in determining the ultimate outcome. Recent scholarship, notably E. P. Thompson's *The Making of the English Working Class,* Charles, Louise, and Richard Tilly's *The Rebellious Century,* and Michael Schwartz's *Radical Protest and Social Structure,* has fatally undermined conservative "breakdown" or "deviance" explanations of "social disorder" and uncovered the rationality and originality of popular movements as responses to social and political grievances. As Schwartz suggests, constant "practical-critical" activity characterizes such movements. Over time, the tenants of the southern United States whom he studied responded to unexpected attacks by the elite with such varied moves as cooperative buying and selling, boycotting of merchants including militant picketing, lobbying in state legislatures, running candidates, and finally, attempting to create an entire countereconomy. These tactics reflected changing understandings of their opponents' nature and resources.[26] In the history of such a movement, the alternative social and political interpretations available to participants play a crucial role; they determine the movement's response to setbacks, the character of renewed attempts to invigorate it, and its ultimate flourishing or defeat. If these understandings prove persistently wrong or inadequate (for instance, the Farmers' Alliance's insufficiently thorough rejection of racist divisions between black and white tenants), the movement may founder. Even if these movements do not dissolve, they may become incapable of defending their members' interests, or, in the case of nationwide forces, of taking power, let alone of transforming society. A variety of economic determinism, often found in social scientists' notions of "modernization," "affluence," and "technocracy" tends to reduce such failure to circumstances alone. In contrast, a Marxian explanation would illustrate the notion that men *make* their own history, though not under circumstances of their own choosing. It would highlight the impact of alternative political understandings and strategies within the context of these social and political conditions. On a more subtle level, the

26. Michael Schwartz, *Radical Protest and Social Structure,* pp. 157, 193–196.

political consequences of a particular Marxian socialism or communism are hardly transparent. Tensions between the present and future movement have troubled every Marxian organization, as they did Marx himself.[27]

1–4. Citizens and Communists

Marx's politics derived in the 1840s from his study of French political and social republicanism as well as of ancient Greek citizenship. During this period, much of his writing drew its irony from contrasts between those who adhere to a common or public interest and those sunk in merely private "vegetative" pursuits, between energetic revolutionary heroism as shown at times by the Jacobins and doddering German parliamentary senility, between thinking translated into vigorous political action and empty talk. On the one hand, Marx looked toward a new, social process of liberation, a revolt of the slaves, of those forcibly removed from the old political spotlight. In this sense Marx in 1844, briefly criticized the republican "political" viewpoint as an idealistic politics of the will alone and suggested that a social movement of modern wage slaves, led by the inheritors of Spartacus, would simply put an end to the old Rome. Yet Marx also thought that the reactionary politics of the modern state, in the service of an exploiting class, dehumanized and denatured men. Following modern social republican as well as ancient politics, he thought that citizens should bear arms and share in political institutions. Within the proletarian movement, he hailed a sharp, heroic sense of the common interest, of internationalism, breaking down all social divisions and political borders. While the ancients would have feared the Paris Commune of 1871 as a paradoxical "republic of labor," Marx saw within it a new intrinsic enthusiasm for nonexploitative political activity. The worker-officials, he rhapsodized, discharged their tasks not for the modern capitalist motivation of making money, but to forge genuinely cooperative social relationships. For the first time in history, these workers took the affairs of society in hand. Internationalism played an integral part in this new community; the Commune elected Hungarians and Poles to serve among its leaders. Profoundly transforming the old social order, it enlisted the aid of the working women of Paris, "heroic, noble and devoted, like the women of antiq-

27. Sidney Tarrow, *Peasant Communism in Southern Italy.*

uity." [28] Thus, Marx's conception of politics derived its force from a tension between older republican views of citizenship and proletarian communism. Throughout his activity in the German revolution of 1848, Marx wove this more general theme into his analysis of the practical strategic tension between mere citizenship in a capitalist-led democratic movement and internationalist adherence to the common interest of the European democratic and socialist movements.

To discern the relations between Marx's theory and practice, I have followed the path of Marx's own activity between 1843 and 1852 and divided this book into three sections. The first, "Marx's Strategy and Organizing before 1848," traces the origins of Marx's strategies in his study of great political movements, the French Revolution and English Chartism, analyzes how Marx worked, often against opposed radical conceptions, to forge a new communist movement, and reinterprets the *Communist Manifesto* in this context (Chapters 2–8). The second section, "Marx in the German Revolution," focuses on Marx's attempt to apply his strategy in 1848–1849 (Chapters 9–10). The third, "Reevaluations after the Revolution," shows how he altered or deepened major aspects of his theory in response to defeat (Chapters 11–13). The book examines Marx's derivation of his strategy from previous political experience and follows his activity before and during the revolution—a movement from practice to theory to practice. It then explores his reworking of theoretical positions in the aftermath—a return to or refinement of theory. Methodologically, its contextualism attempts to mirror the elegant dialectic of practice and theory in Marx's own organizing.

In the early chapters, I summarize the relevant features of the French Revolution and Chartism to ease the path for the general reader. For the same reason I have added a chronology, a list of historical figures, and an appendix containing Marx's important, but not widely known, program for Germany in 1848. In a second volume, I will examine *Capital* in the context of Marx's activity in the International Workingmen's Association and in the formation of the first socialist parties, and compare German Social Democracy and Bolshevism as interpretations of Marx's politics. On certain issues, for in-

---

28. Marx, *The Civil War in France* and *First Draft* in *Writings on the Paris Commune,* pp. 84, 169. In the first draft, Marx had hailed these women as part of "manly, stern, fighting, working, thinking Paris"; in the final draft, he deleted this ancient but chauvinist characterization of courage.

stance Marx's attitude toward the peasants, some scholars have disputed the continuity of Marx's activity; in such cases, I sometimes employ examples drawn from a later period to illustrate his consistency. In addition, to show the devastating effects of different conceptions of Marx's theory on descriptions of (or stereotypes about) Marx's activity, I occasionally indicate in the text or notes certain typical misunderstandings.

PART ONE

Marx's Strategy and Organizing before 1848

— II —

The French Revolution and
Marx's Strategy

2–1. French Republicanism and Communism

MARX'S "INTRODUCTION TO THE *Critique of Hegel's Philosophy of Right*" of 1843 recognized the unique character of the French Revolution as the most international, radical, and thoroughgoing revolution of the broad epoch that had included the English Puritan Revolution, the American Revolution, and rebellions in Ireland, Holland, and Belgium.] In the 1840s, German liberalism and radicalism moved in the shadow of that great and complex political experience.

The prerevolutionary French aristocracy, growing wine on great estates, lived on relatively fixed revenues in an era of soaring expenses. Unlike English yeomen who enclosed the common lands to engage in the wool trade, French aristocrats increasingly repressed the producing population without dispossessing it. By driving off and demoralizing the peasants, English landlords had curbed the threat of radical revolt. By maintaining the peasants while exploiting them more severely, the French nobility had generated an explosive agrarian radicalism.[2]

In the eighteenth century, wars with the British in North America spurred the French monarchy's growing hunger for funds and drastically increased its pressure on the aristocracy and in turn the peasantry. This expenditure accelerated the inflation and eroded the worth of previous revenues. As the lords' demands increased, the peasants visualized the nobility ever less as protectors and more as parasites. They identified with the rising third estate.

Over previous centuries, the monarchy had undermined the warrior nobility and created a *noblesse de robe* of officials in finance and administration. In the eighteenth century, however, the old nobility recaptured positions in the

---

1. Karl Marx, *Writings of the Young Marx on Philosophy and Society*, pp. 251, 260–261. E. J. Hobsbawm, *The Age of Revolution, 1789–1848*, p. 75.

2. Barrington Moore, Jr., *Social Origins of Dictatorship and Democracy*, pp. 48, 52–56, 63–65.

administration and clergy and antagonized the professional bourgeoisie.³ Meanwhile a commercial bourgeoisie flourished. France had become England's major international economic competitor; its trade quadrupled between 1720 and 1780, and its colonial system rivaled Britain's. Yet the third estate's leadership confronted an entrenched monarchy which opposed the bourgeoisie's political ambition but granted it economic subsidies.⁴

The third estate included urban artisans and the laboring poor as well as the peasants. While the commercial and professional bourgeoisie claimed to represent these forces against the nobility, its zeal for free trade, the banishing of guild regulations, and unrestricted speculation in grain would generate acute tensions within the revolutionary movement.

The Enlightenment's vast intellectual turbulence reinforced this new radicalism. To summarize its effect rather cursorily, the materialism and atheism of such writers as Diderot and Bayle undermined the sanctity and power of the Catholic Church and even contributed to a brief "dechristianization" campaign at the height of the Revolution. In *The Holy Family* (1845), Marx and Engels would stress Bayle's contention that a society of atheists could govern itself reasonably, justly, and honorably: "[Bayle] heralded the atheistic society which was soon to come into existence by *proving* that a society consisting only of atheists is possible, that an atheist *can* be a man worthy of respect, and that it is not by atheism but by superstition and idolatry that man debases himself." ⁵ Bayle had explored and mocked the crafty political uses of fantastic popular beliefs about eclipses and comets. Starting from his essay, Marx opposed the religiosity that sanctified the exploitativeness of privileged classes. As against the Church and an overarching aristocracy and monarchy, the French radical movement admired the republican equality of ancient citizens brilliantly though cautiously delineated in the writings of Montesquieu and Rousseau.⁶ Rousseau had also castigated those "atrocious

---

3. Hobsbawm, *Age of Revolution*, pp. 78–80. For an alternative view, see Colin Lucas, "Nobles, Bourgeois and the Origins of the French Revolution" in Douglas Johnson, ed., *French Society and the Revolution*, pp. 104–106.

4. Hobsbawm, *Age of Revolution*, p. 77. Moore, *Social Origins*, pp. 56–57.

5. Denis Diderot, *Lettre sur les aveugles* in *Oeuvres philosophiques*, pp. 118–124. Pierre Bayle, *Pensées diverses sur la comète* in *Oeuvres diverses*, pp. 66–70. Albert Soboul, *The French Revolution, 1787–1799*, 2:345–350. Karl Marx and Friedrich Engels, *CW*, 4:127.

6. Both Montesquieu and Rousseau analyzed the social conditions, including a small territory and population, relatively equal property holding, and commonality of customs, in which the ancient republics had flourished. A large modern state, however, did not offer a likely analogue to these conditions.

men" who "weep at the possibility of a fertile year" and corner the market in grain while thousands starve, and celebrated peasant citizens deliberating about their own affairs. In addition, Montesquieu had satirized the slave trade and the grotesque consequences of European colonialism.[7] The French revolutionaries would judge all social institutions by a standard of reason, based on the natural rights of the individual, and oppose those practices that did not measure up. As Hegel would later argue, this revolution appeared as a "sunrise" of reason that "stood the world upon its head," for men claimed to remake human association on the basis of rational principles, and furthermore, overturned the feudal reality, which had contradicted those principles.[8]

In 1789 the third estate's representatives to the Estates General, drawn mainly from the professional bourgeoisie, challenged the other two estates, the clergy and the nobility. Along with a section of the clergy, the third estate constituted a new National Assembly. Simultaneously, a popular movement burgeoned and drove on these representatives from below. The bad harvests of 1788 and 1789 threatened starvation for peasants, as well as for the urban sans-culottes (artisans, shopkeepers, and the laboring poor; sans-culottes meant literally those without breeches). In late April, artisans and workers in the faubourg St. Antoine sacked the factories of the saltpeter manufacturer Henriot and the wallpaper maker Réveillon. They seized grain shipments and attacked tollbooths. Faced with the threat of counterrevolution against the Assembly, the sans-culottes stormed the Bastille on July 14. Similarly, responding to the "great fear" of aristocratic reaction, peasants rose up in July and August, burned the châteaus, and dispossessed the nobility.[9] As a result of these explosive movements, the new legislature abolished all feudal privileges. When the revolutionary wave receded, however, the legislature set stiff redemption payments for the peasants.

Subsequently, the National Assembly passed a liberal reform program that included the enclosure of common lands to encourage rural entrepreneurs at the expense of the poor peasants, the banning of unions, and the elimination of guilds. These measures drove apart the classes composing the third estate.

7. Roger D. Masters, ed., *Jean-Jacques Rousseau, The First and Second Discourses,* p. 194; *Jean-Jacques Rousseau, On the Social Contract,* p. 108. Montesquieu, *De l'esprit des lois,* 1:257–259, 261–262.

8. Denis Diderot, "The Encyclopedia" in *Rameau's Nephew and Other Works,* pp. 287, 292. G. W. F. Hegel, *The Philosophy of History,* pp. 446–447.

9. Albert Soboul, *A Short History of the French Revolution, 1789–1799,* pp. 58–59. George Rudé, *The Crowd in the French Revolution,* pp. 179–180.

The Assembly tried to satisfy the majority of peasants only by the sale of church lands as well as those of the emigrant nobility. This Assembly also proclaimed the pioneer emancipation of the Jews, and in 1791, established a constitutional monarchy.[10]

But the sans-culottes, meeting in their own political clubs, articulated independent demands and called for a republic. Externally, the duke of Brunswick, as Engels would note in the *Neue Rheinische Zeitung*, vowed to raze Paris. Stung by the Revolution's radicalism and fearing republican repercussions at home, counterrevolutionary armies from monarchical Germany and parliamentary England invaded France. The National Assembly, led by the moderate Girondins, a group affiliated closely with the commercial bourgeoisie, declared war on the invaders in April 1792. Yet this leadership rejected any popular mobilization, and its armies met quick defeat. The counterrevolution soon conquered sixty out of eighty French provinces, and prospects for the revolutionaries seemed bleak. But this appearance belied the revolution's underlying dynamism. Radical artisans and peasants attributed these defeats to royalist sabotage and perfidy.[11] On June 2, the radicals toppled the monarchy and proclaimed a republic. They celebrated the Year I of a new era in human history, one that would attempt to revive ancient republican virtue.

The Jacobin Committee of Public Safety displaced the Girondins and conscripted three-quarters of a million men, the famous *levée en masse*, to vanquish its enemies. In language reminiscent of Rousseau's images of Sparta, the decree summoned republicans to all-out war:

> The young men will go forth to fight; married men will forge weapons and transport provisions; the women will make tents and uniforms and serve in the hospitals; the old men will be carried to public places to rouse the warriors' courage, preach hatred for kings and uphold the unity of the republic.[12]

Within fourteen months an astonishing reversal occurred. The French revolutionary army repelled all invaders, occupied Belgium, and initiated twenty years of almost unbroken military success. The Committee of Public Safety, led by Robespierre, imprisoned and later executed the king. The

10. Hobsbawm, *Age of Revolution*, pp. 86–87.
11. Ibid., p. 89.
12. Soboul, *Short History*, p. 93; *French Revolution*, 2:328–330. See also Danton's speeches of March 10, 1793, in Paul H. Beik, ed., *The French Revolution*, pp. 250–255.

regime's new laws favored the poor peasant by dividing emigré lands into small plots and allowing the new owners ten years to pay (yet the rich peasants still made headway at the expense of the poor). Finally, the Jacobins abolished slavery in the French colonies and supported the great Haitian slave revolt led by Toussaint L'Ouverture.[13]

In 1792 the antislavery agitator Frossard had strikingly articulated the internationalism of this revolution in a pamphlet to the Assembly: "The trade in Blacks, this bloody invention of avarice, must disappear before the regenerative aspect of liberty. Its proscription is the only way to announce to Guinea that France has no more tyrants." The vigor of this movement awakened support among radicals in Germany, Great Britain, notably Ireland and Scotland, Poland, and Haiti; the French Revolution granted citizenship to some of these sympathizers. Both in its international impact and in the universality of its principles, this revolution transcended national parochialism.[14] Its example would galvanize the internationalism of later democratic, socialist, and communist movements.

In 1792 and 1793, the Parisian artisans, fearing steep rises in basic commodity prices, once again took the initiative and demanded that a maximum be set on the price of bread. They clashed with the commercial bourgeoisie. The mobilization for war coupled with this internal crisis drove the revolution even further to the left. Popular leaders like Jean-Paul Marat and Jacques Roux stressed the social question. Mere proclamation of formal republican citizenship would put no bread into the mouths of the poor. For Marat, speculators and profiteers with "their shameless system of pillage and exploitation" had transmogrified the republic into an "imposture": "Nothing has changed but the decorations on the National Tribunal . . . the actors, the masks, the intrigues—these have remained the same." In 1792, Marat called for mass revolutionary action:

> In all countries in which the rights of the people are not mere phrases, . . . the plundering of a few shops and the hanging of the shopkeepers at their door would soon put an end to these corrupt manipulations which reduce millions of persons to despair and starve thousands to death. Will the

13. Soboul, *French Revolution*, 2:315, 331–333.

14. Benjamin-Sigismond Frossard, "On the Abolition of the Trade in Negroes" in Beik, ed., *French Revolution*, p. 235. Imperial interests and racist ideology would later make a farce of these republican principles in the French colonies.

representatives of the people not finally do a little more than merely babble about the distress, without proposing any remedy to alleviate it? [15]

Though the government had hunted Marat, Charlotte Corday, a monarchist, murdered him in 1792. His assassination reinvigorated the popular movement to strike at its enemies.

As Jacques Roux argued ominously before the Convention,

> The Constitution [of June 24, 1793] is about to be presented before the sovereign people for their assent. Have you anywhere in that document outlawed speculation? No. Have you imposed the death sentence for hoarders? No. . . . Liberty is no more than a vain shadow of its real self when one class of men can with impunity starve another. . . . So hand down a further judgment. The *sans-culottes* are ready with their pikes to enforce your decrees.[16]

From June 26 to 28, simultaneous with the passage of the Jacobin constitution, the artisan washerwomen of Paris rioted against the soaring price of soap. They unloaded ships' cargoes along the quays, set prices, and divided the soap among themselves. As Marx would reiterate in 1848, throughout the radical phase of the revolution, the vigorous sans-culottes acted and dragged the hesitant Jacobins haltingly in their wake. On July 26, the Convention reluctantly passed a death penalty for hoarders (it defined a hoarder as any merchant who refused to list his stock of basic commodities on the door of his establishment). Yet the revolutionary authorities would not act on this law.

As food prices skyrocketed, demonstrations by construction and armament workers on September 4 and 5 again proclaimed "War on Tyrants! War on Aristocrats! War on Hoarders!" and stormed the Convention itself. They forced the Jacobins to pass laws requiring grain requisitioning, the arrest of suspected hoarders, and a general maximum on basic commodity prices. The Convention also passed a law—later called the law of suspects—against those who might have collaborated with the counterrevolution. These measures instigated the terror of 1793–1794.[17]

15. Jean-Paul Marat, "Nothing Has Changed" and "Guard against Profiteers" in *Writings,* 2:41–43, 58–59.

16. Soboul, *French Revolution,* 2:322–323. Beik, ed., *French Revolution,* pp. 261–263.

17. Soboul, *French Revolution,* 2:325, 332–338. Rudé, *Crowd in the French Revolution,* pp. 126–127, 205–206.

Though a strictly political republican viewpoint subordinated all others, the moderate and radical bourgeoisie and artisans wrestled for power behind the abstract phrases of liberty, equality, fraternity, and virtue. The guillotine, reflecting this social turbulence, cut now against aristocrats, now against radical leaders of the sans-culottes like Hébert and Roux, now against moderates like Danton, and finally against Robespierre himself. The terror, directed against the leaders of the sans-culottes, chilled political discussion in the clubs. In Saint-Just's phrase, "The Revolution [had] frozen solid."

By suppressing the sans-culottes, however, the Jacobins had destroyed the social basis of their revolutionary energy. Foreign victories also made this rule of "virtue" seem less necessary to its former bourgeois supporters. Ultimately, a conservative bourgeois regime triumphed on 9th Thermidor (July 24, 1794).[18] It licensed an extralegal white terror against the sans-culottes and former Jacobins as a vehicle to restrain any resurgent radical movement from below and to consolidate its power. Under its aegis, inflation raged, and the bourgeoisie, notably the *jeunesse dorée,* flaunted its contempt for the austere egalitarianism of the revolution at its height.[19]

But the revolutionary cycle continued. As Marx would emphasize, the dynamic of formal republican equality under capitalism engendered the first communist movement, led by François Noel Babeuf. The Babeuvists contrasted the division of land into private plots and the oppression of the majority of the peasants with their own vision of common landholding—"the earth belongs to no one"—and its use for the benefit of all. They sought a "community of goods." In the "Manifesto of the Equals," Babeuf proclaimed:

> The French Revolution is but the forerunner of another revolution far more grand, far more solemn, and which will be the last. The people has marched over dead bodies against the kings and priests coalesced against it. It will do the same against the new political Tartuffes [the hypocrite in Molière's play of that name] who have usurped the places of the old.
>
> Long enough and too long have less than a million of individuals disposed of what belongs to more than twenty millions of men like themselves—of men

18. Hobsbawm, *Age of Revolution,* pp. 93–95. Moore, *Social Origins,* p. 91. Soboul, *Short History,* p. 115.

19. Soboul, *French Revolution,* 2:424–428. Albert Soboul, *The Sans-Culottes,* pp. 2–3, 47–52. Gwynne Lewis, "The White Terror of 1815 in the Department of the Gard" in Johnson, ed., *French Society,* pp. 286–287.

in every respect their equals. . . . Away for ever with the revolting distinctions of rich and poor, of great and little, of master and servant.

Though the Babeuvists foresaw some resistance from those formerly privileged as well as those influenced by "old habits, old prejudices," they expected a rapid triumph of communism.[20]

Inflation renewed radical sentiment. In the cafés, the sans-culottes sang Babeuf's song, "Dying of Hunger, Dying of Cold." Babeuf, however, did not attempt to lead a mass movement and instead formed an isolated conspiracy. Nonetheless, Marx would comment in the *Manifesto* that he "gave voice to the demands of the proletariat" in the French Revolution. In 1796, the regime arrested and subsequently executed Babeuf and his main followers. It finally quelled the revolution.[21]

During the French Revolution, artisan and peasant radicalism had stemmed from different sources and moved in different phases. When these classes marched together, they pushed the revolution to the left. When the rich peasants gained rural predominance over the poor, however, the movements separated, and ultimately, the revolution declined.[22] Thus, study of French experience would provide fertile material for Marx's conception of an artisan-peasant-proletarian alliance in the struggle for German democracy and socialism.

Subsequently, Napoleon rose to power and ignited the suppressed but still present enthusiasm of revolutionary republicanism in a new mobilization to extend French rule. His empire also consolidated small peasant landownership and created political memories that would haunt the politics of the 1850s. The triumph of these peasant property holders along with the preservation of small shops and businesses contributed to the relatively undynamic French capitalism of the nineteenth century. Yet French conquests spread the Code Napoléon and liberalized several parts of Europe including the German Rhineland. Napoleon's vast military effort, penetrating deep into Rus-

---

20. Philippe Buonarroti, *Babeuf's Conspiracy for Equality*, pp. 315–317. "On the day that follows the real revolution, they will say to one another in amazement—'What—universal happiness depended on so little! We had but to will it. Ah, why had we not willed it sooner?'"

21. Soboul, *Short History*, pp. 140–141; *French Revolution*, 2:487–492.

22. Moore, *Social Origins*, pp. 77, 91–92, 109–110.

sia, eventually met defeat at the hands of an Austrian, Prussian, English, and Russian coalition.[23]

This alliance restored a weakened French monarchy. Though favoring the bourgeoisie, the new monarchy compensated the remnant aristocracy for its losses.[24] But in 1830 and again in 1848, popular forces regained their revolutionary vigor and renewed their attacks, first for a different monarchy and then for a republic. During this period, the ideas of Babeuf, recorded in 1828 in a manuscript of his comrade Buonarroti, *Babeuf's Conspiracy of Equals*, instigated a new French communist movement. Organized mainly as conspiracies of intellectuals and proletarians, led by men like Louis Auguste Blanqui and Armand Barbès, these revolutionary movements sought to establish a community of goods. They initiated isolated and unsuccessful putsches as in 1839. On May 15, 1848, however, they also helped to spur on the mass movement to achieve a second republic. In addition to these conspiracies, the silk weavers of Lyons staged insurrections in 1831 and 1834. Their songs captured the mass sentiment against exploitation:

> We weave for you, great ones of the earth,
> And we, poor *canuts*, one buries us without a shroud . . .
> We are all naked

> But when our reign arrives . . .
> We'll weave the shroud of the old world . . .
> It's us, the *canuts*
> We'll no longer go all naked.[25]

Observers as diverse as Tocqueville, Balzac, and Marx remarked that the great swell of republican egalitarianism swept onward toward communism. Within the movement for political equality, the lineaments of a movement for social equality had become visible.[26]

---

23. Hobsbawm, *Age of Revolution*, pp. 93, 212–213, 109–113.

24. Robert Forster, "The Survival of the Nobility during the French Revolution" in Johnson, ed., *French Society*.

25. Hobsbawm, *Age of Revolution*, p. 238, cites this song. The translation is mine.

26. Alexis de Tocqueville, *Recollections*, pp. 10–11. Honoré de Balzac, *Les Paysans*, p. 155.

2–2. The French Revolution, German Democracy, and Communist Politics

THUS, THE FRENCH REVOLUTION, that "lighthouse of all revolutionary epochs" as Marx hailed it in 1848, electrified Europe. It demonstrated the radical potential of demands for political equality and impelled a movement for social equality. When Marx first conceived a strategy for Germany in the 1840s, he did not look mainly to the impact of the steam engine and the future unfolding of capitalism. Instead he examined and then reexamined this towering political experience. In the French Revolution, the class forces projected in Marx's general theory (*The German Ideology* or the *Manifesto*) – the bourgeoisie, workers, and peasants who opposed the aristocracy and monarchy, or proletarians, declining artisans, and poor peasants who opposed the capitalists and aristocrats—intertwined in actual battle. The Revolution revealed the political logic of these conflicts within a definite setting. With proper adjustment for new circumstances, this experience would serve as a model for Marx's strategy in 1848.[27] Throughout the 1840s Marx moved back and forth between current German realities, his new materialist theory, his conception of ancient political community, and the French Revolution as he sought to discern Germany's revolutionary possibilities.

In 1843, Marx admired French republicanism in comparison with the apolitical, self-concerned "zoology" of German feudal life. Between 1843 and 1845, he criticized the Jacobin notion of ancient community, virtue, and equality as a "merely political" viewpoint in the light of the Revolution's own internal dynamic toward social equality. He envisioned the 1844 Silesian weavers' uprising as the forerunner of a direct German communist revolution. After 1845, Marx reanalyzed the French Revolution on the basis of his new historical materialist hypothesis and concluded that, in Germany, a democratic revolution would have to precede a proletarian one. This new assessment stressed the changing impact of revolutionary experience on the participants. In each case, a more thorough examination of the French Revolution led to an alteration in Marx's strategy.

Marx sketched the first view in 1843 in an exchange of letters with the philosopher Arnold Ruge concerning the formation of a new journal, the·

---

27. Moore, *Social Origins*, p. 69.

Deutsch-Französische Jahrbücher (German-French Annals).[28] The glorious achievements of the French Revolution, according to Marx, dwarfed the lifeless, perverted "spiritual animal kingdom" of Prussian despotism. The Revolution "restored man to himself"; it reworked a social world to replace an "order of dead things" with an order of free and equal men. At this time, Marx believed that feudal monarchy more than capitalism manifested the "horrible logic of self-interest" and philistinism; it stratified men as unequal beings.[29] The noble German princes subjugated the people like a trainer a herd of horses and transformed them into political animals. In an elaborate pun, Marx invoked the Aristotelian image of ancient citizenship in which man, a political animal, rules and is ruled in turn: "A German Aristotle, who would derive his politics from our conditions, would start by stating, 'Man is a social, but completely apolitical animal.' " [30] Like the young Hegel and French radical republicans, Marx had studied and admired ancient political life (he had written a doctoral dissertation on Epicurus and Democritus); though Marx opposed Greek slavery and parasitism, he always looked to ancient political community as one, sometimes unstated, touchstone in his evaluation of modern politics.

Hegel's philosophy had attempted to grasp the principles of objective reason and freedom unfolding through the myriad of seemingly meaningless passionate individual actions in human history. In his *Philosophy of Right,* he had celebrated the Prussian monarchy as the consummation of a genuine ethical universality or modern political community through which the individuals composing civil society could seek their private and competitive purposes. Feuerbach had already criticized Hegel's idealism. As we shall see in Chapter 6, Feuerbach denied that any objective idea or spirit realizes itself in history; rather, he insisted, God or the philosophical idea exists only as an alienated projection of human species-capacities and dreams. Hegel had thus

---

28. The name of the journal embodied an early unity of theory (German philosophy) and practice (French politics).

29. Hegel created the image of an apolitical "spiritual animal kingdom" (geistige Tierreich) in his *Phenomenology of Spirit,* pp. 237–252. Marx, letter to Ruge, May 1843 in Marx, *Writings,* pp. 205–209. Marx, *Frühe Schriften,* p. 235. Horst Mewes, "On the Concept of Politics in the Early Works of Karl Marx," p. 279. For a useful discussion of Marx's reading on the French Revolution, see Paul Kägi, *Genesis des historischen Materialismus,* pp. 169–189, 196–197, 289–292.

30. Letter to Ruge, May 1843 in Marx, *Writings,* p. 206.

inverted subject (God) and predicate (nature, history, man), and Feuerbach sought to stand them right side up (in other words, for Feuerbach, man the subject creates God, the imaginary object, not the reverse).[31] Applying Feuerbach's philosophy, Marx criticized contemporary German political reality as a similar inversion of subject and predicate: the monarchy, created and sustained by citizens, acted, while dominated men groveled before their own creature. Instead of an integrated ethical and political life shared by equal men and women, this social realm ultimately contracted into the will of the despot alone. Turning again to the *polis,* Marx commented:

> Freedom, that feeling of man's dignity, will have to be awakened again in these men. Only this feeling, which disappeared from the world with the Greeks and with Christianity vanished into the blue mist of heaven, can again transform society into a community of men to achieve their highest purpose, a democratic state.[32]

A quickened sense of the common interest, of public greatness and man's dignity rather than self-seeking and servility, could resuscitate a genuine political community.

Consistent with his early vision of the centrality of political life, Marx insisted that philosophical criticism must start by "taking sides in politics." In 1842, Marx, still under Hegel's influence, studied the Prussian wood-theft

---

31. In some important respects, Feuerbach's and Marx's critiques of religion derived from Hegel's own dialectical insights. For instance, in the *Phenomenology,* Hegel criticized a particular "faith" in the beyond which grew out of the divisions of the cultured "self-alienated spirit." Feuerbach's critique accentuated the "this-sided" or earthly divisions in Hegel's exploration of faith (of course Hegel distinguished faith from religion in general). Hegel, *Phenomenology of Spirit,* pp. 321–322, 348–349. Similarly, in criticizing Hegel's *Philosophy of Right,* Marx strengthened Hegel's emphasis on the danger that capitalist differentials of wealth and poverty might undermine the ethical universality of the modern state. Hegel, *Philosophy of Right,* pp. 148–150.

32. Marx, *Writings,* p. 206. In "Debates on Freedom of the Press" in the *Rheinische Zeitung, CW,* 1:137, Marx argued, "A country which, like the old Athens, treats boot-lickers, parasites, toadies as exceptions from the general standard of reason as public fools, is the country of independence and self-government. A people which, like all people of the best of times, claims the right to think and utter the truth only for the court fool, can only be a people that is dependent and without identity." Though she rightly stresses the influence of the ancients on Marx's political thought, Arendt wrongly criticizes Marx for lacking a concept of political action or political community. Hannah Arendt, *The Human Condition,* pp. 165, 133, 159, 209, 321. Arendt, *On Revolution,* pp. 55–58.

laws, which not only fined the peasants, a modern punishment, but exacted labor services, a feudal one. He also investigated the Moselle vintners' "cry of distress," denounced as "insolence" by Prussian bureaucrats. This oppression of the peasants rather than of urban workers brought the tension between social inequality and citizenship to the fore. During these legal debates, however, Marx conceived these peasants as passive and suffering and believed them incapable of changing their own conditions. From this study, however, Marx by 1843 had already concluded that the "real presupposition" of the political state, namely private property, fatally undermined "the control of man." Only socialism, "the abolition of private property," could realize the fundamental principle of republican equality. Thus, given the reality of an exploitative, class-riven society, Marx dialectically grasped the limitations of republican consciousness. He identified private property as the source of the modern state's oppressiveness and egotism in contrast to Hegel's vision of the state as a corrective for the misery engendered by private property.[33]

Between 1843 and 1845, Marx pursued his study and criticism of the French Revolution and arrived at a second characterization of an upcoming German one. Marx sought to surmount the limitations of politics or revolutionary will as a point of view. In "On the Jewish Question," Marx argued that the French Revolution had not resurrected freedom, but had produced a profound cleavage between man as an individual member of civil society, pursuing private aims in conflict with others, and man as a modern citizen, cooperating in an "illusory" universal, "the political state." Marx's "Introduction to the *Critique of Hegel's Philosophy of Right*" (1843) asserted that a new German revolution might transcend this cleavage.

The French Revolution's ardor had already influenced a future German one. In France, a single class, the nobility and clergy, had "ruthlessly" crystallized "the notorious crime of society as a whole." Their negative significance, concentrating numerous defects, had determined the "positive general significance of the bourgeoisie." Faced with so clear and offensive an enemy, the French bourgeoisie dared to make political revolution, arousing "an impulse of enthusiasm in itself and in the masses, an impulse in which it frater-

33. Marx, "Justification of the Correspondent from the Mosel" and "Debates on the Law on Thefts of Wood," *CW*, 1:358, 224–263. Letter to Ruge, September 1843 in Marx, *Writings*, pp. 214–215. Marx, *Preface to a Contribution to the Critique of Political Economy, Selected Works*, p. 181. Halting his account before Marx's activity in the revolution of 1848, Lowy mistakenly argues that Marx saw the peasants only as a suffering class, not as a potential radical ally. Lowy, *Théorie de la révolution*, pp. 42–43.

nizes with society at large . . . and is experienced as its general representative." Marx still celebrated the political temper, the public spiritedness, the "breadth of soul," and "revolutionary boldness" of the French bourgeoisie, "which flings at its adversary the defiant words, *I am nothing and I shall be everything.*" [34] This very energy spurred on a popular movement led by the sans-culottes and Babeuf, which vehemently proclaimed social equality.

In Germany, however, a stronger aristocracy and monarchy confronted a timorous, egotistical bourgeoisie striving for a share of power, yet already fearful of a more conscious proletariat. Though the German middle classes had fought the French invader during the Napoleonic wars, they had discovered that in France, a social and political order could flourish without aristocratic domination. Like his counterpart in the original French Revolution, the ambitious Cologne manufacturer or Berlin banker often found the political system of the German confederation intolerable. In France, the July Monarchy, established after the revolution of 1830, had endorsed the capitalist principle *enrichissez-vous*. In Great Britain, bourgeois representatives had entered the House of Commons after the electoral Reform Act of 1832. But in Germany the monarchs still excluded the bourgeoisie from political office and hampered its financial affairs by constant bureaucratic supervision. Despite the Zollverein (customs union) of 1834, the monarchies confused the merchant with the intricacies of a dozen monetary systems and curbed trade with heavy tolls. Given these restrictions, the German bourgeoisie found in English and French experience fuel for its grievances. [35]

But the radical dynamic of the French Revolution—the role of the sans-culottes, the *levée en masse,* the terror, and Babeuf's communism—frightened the bourgeoisie. Jarred by the French Revolution, Prussia had instituted the Stein-Hardenberg agrarian reforms of the early nineteenth century, which granted some peasants—those with oxen and a share in the regular village fields—formal title to their land, though the reforms forced even these peasants to cede one-third to one-half of their property to the lord. For poorer peasants excluded by the law, feudal services remained. As Marx would contend in 1848, the peasantry had acted as a strong radical ally of the French bourgeoisie, and German peasants would also rebel. The timorous German bourgeoisie, however, pushed the peasants away. As early as 1830, the liberal

34. Marx, *Writings,* p. 261.

35. In the Rhineland, the 100,000 inhabitants of Cologne and Aachen sent three delegates to the diet while the nobility, numbering less than 7,000, sent twenty-five. Theodore S. Hamerow, *Restoration, Revolution, Reaction,* p. 59.

merchant David Hansemann, who would briefly become Prussian finance minister in 1848, warned that, "By majority . . . we are never to understand the one determined by counting heads, but rather the true strength of the nation which . . . by its better education, greater insight, and its property . . . has a larger stake in the maintenance of a stable, vigorous and good government." [36] No part of the German bourgeoisie would seek to ignite the political dynamite of peasant, artisan, and proletarian radicalism and root out the aristocracy. In addition, the German bourgeoisie feared its French counterpart's pre-revolutionary philosophical militancy, its widespread materialism, atheism, and republicanism (Marx and the German communists would take up this radical philosophical tradition). Thus, the shadow of the French Revolution paralyzed the German bourgeoisie. As Marx put it in his "Introduction," "The middle class hardly dares to conceive the idea of emancipation from its own [political] perspective. The development of social conditions and the progress of political theory show that perspective to be antiquated or at least problematic." [37] The German bourgeoisie had merged its fate with the older ruling classes; the German governments fused the "civilized deficiencies of the modern political order (whose advantages we do not enjoy) with the barbarous deficiencies of the *Ancien Régime* (which we enjoy in full)." Marx scathingly foretold a Germany that would reach the "level of European decadence" (capitalism) before attaining "European emancipation" (political revolution), and likened German social life to "a fetishist wasting away from the diseases of Christianity." [38]

Revolution by the dispossessed proletarians—a class with universal chains—offered the only alternative: "In Germany no brand of bondage can be broken without every brand of bondage being broken." Though trailing England and France in economics and politics, Germany was relatively advanced in philosophy; a German revolution, fusing philosophy and the proletariat, might outleap previous European development. [39]

Marx's new analysis of the German revolution elevated the social (the role of the proletariat) over the political (his earlier conception of French republicanism). Like the French bourgeoisie's revolutionary defiance, however, the image of the proletariat's energetic shattering of all bondage retained a political resonance. Marx's analysis differed profoundly from an economic deter-

36. Ibid., pp. 46, 61, 65.
37. Marx, *Writings*, pp. 261–262.
38. Marx, *Writings*, p. 259. See also Marx, "Thefts of Wood," *CW*, 1:230–231.
39. Marx, *Writings*, pp. 264, 251, 253–254.

minist one. Instead of envisioning an economic stage theory of revolution, valid for every country (first capitalism replaces feudalism, then socialism supersedes capitalism), Marx focused on the special combined oppression that would propel the German revolution toward communism. In this, his argument prefigured the revolutionary dynamic of societies like twentieth-century Russia.[40] Marx's account also stressed the specific international setting of the revolution, the impact of an earlier revolution on the prospects for a later one, and the role of uneven development between countries and between different social activities. It simultaneously highlighted the bourgeoisie's historic vigor in the Puritan and French revolutions and showed why, after these revolutions, that vigor must decline and a new pattern of development emerge. Marx envisioned an interrelated historical sequence of revolutions with dramatic and less dramatic variations rather than a uniform repetition in each new setting of a single abstract prototype. Marx's subsequent strategies and historical explanations would always invoke accounts of such political and economic causes or, as I have called them earlier, auxiliary statements. Although these statements accorded with and were discovered by the application of Marx's general materialist outlook (thus, the German bourgeoisie's timidity stemmed from its economic weakness and from fear aroused by the intense class conflict of the French Revolution), Marx's strategy, shaped by the given configuration of circumstances, could lead to new and unusual results.

The Hegelian image of the proletariat as a passive force ("the heart") which theory or philosophy ("the head") must galvanize, still influenced Marx's "Introduction" of 1843. Despite his critique of politics, Marx had not fully reworked his image of the social as a sphere of suffering, not of action; "theory" must still seize the proletariat. But in Germany, a new proletariat existed. English industry with its cheap textiles had already undermined the skilled but slow production of the German hand-loom weaver. Furthermore, new German mechanized factories, though less advanced than those of the English, still outcompeted and dispossessed these artisans as well as exploiting their own workers. Driven by the impact of the "hungry forties," thousands emigrated to France, England, or the United States. Many others, close to starvation, strove to change conditions in Germany itself.

Though the weavers' wrath could not reach the English capitalists, they

---

40. Marx, *Capital*, 1:9. See also V. I. Lenin, *The Development of Capitalism in Russia, Collected Works,* vol. 3.

found German manufacturers nearer to hand. In 1844, thousands of weavers in Silesia, a province in eastern Germany near Poland, rebelled against textile manufacturers in Langebielau and Peterswaldau, and Marx reexamined his image of a passive proletariat.

Marx's former collaborator Ruge condescendingly dismissed the weavers' rebellion, asserting that the "all penetrating political soul" of republicanism had neglected it. Marx defended the uprising from the need for such "penetration." Following Moses Hess and Engels, Marx suggested that where the French workers appeared as the politician and the English as the economist of the European proletariat, the Silesian weavers had emerged as its theoretician, as its most thoroughgoing opponent of private property. The weavers' song "Das Blutgericht" indicted the rich who tore the bread out of the poor's mouths; this song surmised that "one fine day, the money of the rich will disappear like butter in the sun." Marx celebrated "that bold *call* to struggle, [embodied in this revolt] in which there is not even a mention of hearth and home, factory or district, but in which the proletariat at once, in a striking, sharp, unrestrained and powerful manner, proclaims its opposition to the society of private property." [41]

In Langebielau, the weavers sang "Das Blutgericht" while they sacked and burned the Zwanzigers' mansion. As in most popular rebellions, these artisans distinguished their cruelest oppressors, the Zwanzigers, from the nearby manufacturer Wagenknecht who, according to Wilhelm Wolff, treated them more "humanly." In Peterswaldau, the weavers destroyed machinery and ownership records at the Dierig Brothers works. For Marx, this demolition of titles of property indicated a theoretical opposition to capitalism, not a mere lashing out at the machine. On the first day of fighting, the weavers liberated prisoners from the police in Peterswaldau and routed the Prussian militia. They succumbed to superior force only on the second. In all, the army killed eleven weavers and wounded twenty-four. Bitter experience had burned the link between monarchy and capitalist into the consciousness of these artisans. According to "Das Blutgericht,"

> The hangmen are the Zwanzigers,
> The constables serve their graces,

---

41. Hal Draper, *Karl Marx's Theory of Revolution,* 1:177, cites "Das Blutgericht." Marx, "Critical Marginal Notes on the Article 'The King of Prussia and Social Reform. By a Prussian,' " *CW*, 3:201.

How brave they crack the whip, the curs,
They should find hiding places.[42]

Heine's famous poem, "The Weavers," influenced by Marx, fused the image of these rebellious workers with sinister fates, weaving the shrouds of Germany's capitalists, princes, and priests.[43]

As Ruge saw it, these "weak" weavers had not shaken the monarchy. Marx, however, insisted on their strength. To stifle a liberal festival at Düsseldorf in 1843, the Prussian monarchy had merely issued a cabinet order and not even fired a shot. Yet the weavers had forced Prussia to engage in a major military operation. In the uprising's aftermath the liberal press suddenly concerned itself with the "organization of labor." To head off potential revolt, many masters set up joint committees with apprentices. Thus, the weavers had forced the issues of poverty and capitalism from social obscurity into the spotlight of public debate.[44] Prefiguring economic determinism, Ruge suggested that "industry in Germany is not yet so developed as in England" to account for the weavers' alleged weakness. Marx, however, stressed the importance of learning from such revolts rather than "playing the schoolmaster" to them: "This, of course, requires some scientific insight and some love of mankind, whereas for the other operation a glib phraseology, impregnated with empty love of oneself, is quite enough." [45] Paradoxically, as Marx criticized narrow "political" revolutions most severely, he discerned a great capacity for original public action in the weavers' regenerative "social" movement. In responding to the June insurrection and the Paris Commune, Marx would retain this admiration of and willingness to learn from energetic political revolt.

During 1844 in Paris, Marx came into direct contact with German and French artisan communist secret societies. In these gatherings, he perceived a human need not just for instruction or for propaganda, but for society itself and for a transformed but almost Aristotelian *philia*. Here alone he saw a "nobility of man [*Adel der Menschheit*] shine through to us from these work-

42. Draper, *Marx's Theory of Revolution,* 1:175, 177. Wilhelm Wolff, "Das Elend und der Aufruhr in Schlesien" in Carl Jantke and Dietrich Hilger, eds., *Die Eigentumslosen,* p. 170.

43. Nigel Reeves, *Heinrich Heine, Poetry and Politics,* p. 155.

44. *CW,* 3:189–190.

45. Ibid., 3:201–202.

hardened figures." [46] This union or coming together of the workers revealed the brotherhood of man or Marx's "species-being." Thus, Marx criticized the "illusory" universality of the modern republican state, separated from civil society, by the standard of a unified social and political life in which all worker-citizens might participate. In contrast to contemporary exploitative European politics and government, Marx fused an ancient vision of the political life of free men with the experience of modern working-class political action. Marx's vision of "social" union commemorated the old politics while it denounced the new.

In 1844, Marx temporarily identified the term "politics" itself with oppressive state activity. He argued that government policy could not wipe out poverty. In capitalist England, charity and administrative measures from on high had not stemmed the increase of pauperism which aloof politicians ultimately blamed on the poor themselves. Similarly, Napoleon failed to abolish French poverty by decree. For Marx, the Jacobins perfectly illustrated the defects of this political point of view:

> The mightier the state, and the more political therefore a country is, the less it is inclined to grasp the general principle of social maladies and to seek their basis . . . in the present structure of society, the active, conscious and official expression of which is the state. . . . The *classic* period of political intellect is the *French Revolution.* . . . *Robespierre* saw in great poverty and great wealth only an obstacle to *pure democracy.* Therefore he wished to establish a universal Spartan frugality. The principle of politics is the will.[47]

The Jacobins, at war with the very civil society they proclaimed in the rights of man, paradoxically sought to resurrect ancient civic virtue and equality with the guillotine. As they cut off the heads of individual citizens, however, civil society, hydralike, grew them anew. Ancient republican virtue, based on slavery, could not flourish in a modern capitalist society; politics by itself offered no solution. Though terrorism alone would ultimately founder, Marx argued, the state could assert itself violently in opposition to civil society. But genuine transformation could only come from within society through the direct action of the oppressed classes.

In his reply to Ruge on the Silesian weavers, Marx even criticized the

---

46. Marx, "Ökonomisch-Philosophische Manuskripte" in *Bund Dokumente*, pp. 190–191.
47. *CW*, 3:195, 197, 199. Marx and Engels, *The Holy Family*, *CW*, 4:122–124.

Lyons silk weavers' partially republican understanding, which had "deceived their social instincts" in the revolts of 1831 and 1834 (Marx may have misunderstood these uprisings).[48] Yet, despite this vigorous condemnation of politics, Marx still averred that only political revolution (certainly an act of will, though hardly the creation of will alone) would cast off the old society's oppressive husk. Marx temporarily envisioned that a nearly anarchist regime would follow such a revolution: "Where its [socialism's] own organizing activity begins, where its proper object, its soul, comes to the fore—there socialism throws off its political cloak."[49] By the *Communist Manifesto* of 1848, however, Marx would foresee a substantial period of political activity by a proletariat "organized as the ruling class" and the creation of a new state before a classless society could emerge. Yet even the *Manifesto*'s arguments continued to display an ambiguity about the role of politics: the *Manifesto* hailed the dissolution of the old exploitative politics and was in that sense antipolitical, yet it instigated the formation of a new social and political association of workers to replace the old structure. Only in the later stage of communist dissolution of classes would the new "public power," functioning as a state, disappear. As in the case of the *polis,* war, in this case class war, conditioned Marx's new social and political community. Whether, in Marx's later view, any politics would survive this war seems unclear. Yet some form of association, friendship, and public consideration of issues would probably characterize that full communism in which "the free development of each is the condition for the free development of all."

In Marx and Engels's *The German Ideology* (1845), they first sketched the fundamental historical materialist hypothesis that modes of production determine the basic forms of social life, and that fundamental social and political changes emerge from a conflict between old relations of production and new forces of production. In a brief reference to Germany, they applied this argument flexibly, taking account of the impact of the international situation, notably English competition, on the emerging German proletariat:

> To lead to collisions in a country, this contradiction [between the productive forces and the form of intercourse] need not necessarily come to a head in this particular country. The competition with industrially more advanced coun-

---

48. *CW,* 3:204.

49. Ibid., 3:206, 205. Exaggerating even Marx's 1844 critique of politics, Avineri has made Marx out as an opponent of revolutionary violence. Avineri, *Social and Political Thought of Karl Marx,* p. 218. Gilbert, "Salvaging Marx from Avineri," pp. 15–18.

tries, brought about by the expansion of international intercourse, is sufficient to produce a similar contradiction in countries with a backward industry (e.g. the latent proletariat in Germany brought into view by the competition of English industry).[50]

Marx used his new theory to comprehend and enhance the Silesian weavers' revolt, not to dismiss it because of Germany's economic backwardness. Thus, class conflict disciplined the application of the theory. The famous opening sentence of the *Manifesto,* "The history of all hitherto existing society is the history of class struggles," served as Marx's most fundamental "guiding hypothesis." Given the disastrous effects of English competition and the beginnings of an indigenous capitalism, Marx and Engels saw Germany as a likely setting for a successful communist uprising.

In *The German Ideology,* Marx and Engels envisioned simultaneous revolution in the dominant European countries (England, France, Germany). Once again, practical experience, the evolution of the differing democratic movements toward communism, and their increasing internationalism, provided the underpinning for this conception. Thus, in 1845, Engels reported on the Festival of Nations in London to a Rhenish journal. At this gathering, nearly one thousand European democrats and communists commemorated the founding of the French Republic on September 22, 1792. The English Chartists, the first radical movement largely composed of factory workers, identified its demand for universal male suffrage with Continental democratic movements; these movements, in turn, supported it. Chartist spokesman George Julian Harney defined "the grand question" of the French Revolution as the "destruction of inequality and the establishment of institutions which would guarantee to the French people that happiness which the masses are and ever have been strangers to." Though the privileged classes still shuddered at "terrible and hellish" Jacobinism, Harney condemned La Fayette and the Girondins as traitors by the stern standard of social equality, and saluted Robespierre, Saint-Just, Marat, and especially Babeuf as genuine democrats:

> That conspiracy [Babeuf's] had for its object the establishment of a veritable republic, *in which the selfishness of individualism should be known no more—* (cheers); in which private property and money, the foundation and root of all

wrong and evil, should cease to be—(cheers); and in which the happiness of each should be based on the *common labor* and *equal enjoyments of all* (Great cheering).[51]

Engels generally concurred with this speech and rejected political democracy: "The French Revolution was a social movement from beginning to end and after it a purely political democracy became a complete absurdity." Engels praised this celebration of the French Revolution first for its internationalism ("all the nations which were stupid enough to let themselves be used to fight against the Revolution have owed the French a public apology"); second, because the French Revolution had cleared the way for a general European social revolution; and third, because the "iron energy" and determination of the revolutionary era overshadowed the current "cowardly, selfish, beggarly, bourgeois epoch." Engels concluded, "Democracy nowadays is communism." [52] This procommunist evolution among radical democrats illustrated Marx's and Engels's notion of the political consequences of capitalism's universal economic tendencies; Marx's theory in turn would spur on more vigorous internationalist organizing.

In *The German Ideology* and *Theses on Feuerbach,* Marx stressed not only capitalist oppression but the mass experience of revolutionary "practical-critical activity" in instigating the working class to shake off "all the traditional muck" and prepare itself to regenerate society. Marx criticized the old materialism which looked down on history from above and called for a benevolent, but miraculous transformation. This doctrine, Marx argued, "forgets that circumstances are changed by men and that the educator must himself be educated. . . . The coincidence of the change of circumstances and of human activity or self change can be comprehended and rationally understood only as *revolutionary practice.*" [53] After 1845, Marx reconsidered the overly contemplative element in his previous critique of the French Revolution and came up with his final strategy for 1848. Despite the inherent limitations of democratic revolution, Marx argued, communists should not, like the old materialists, preach social transformation as an aloof sect. Instead,

---

51. Ibid., p. 49. Engels cited Harney's speech in "The Festival of Nations in London," *CW,* 6:8–11, 14.

52. *CW,* 6:3, 5, 391–392. Contrary to Nietzsche's critique, Marx and Engels envisioned no tame, philistine epoch of the "last men."

53. *GI,* p. 47. Marx, *Theses on Feuerbach, Selected Works,* p. 27.

they should expose democracy's inadequacies as active participants in this real movement.

Marx's new approach adopted Aristotle's insight in Book III of the *Politics* that radical democracy might lead to the expropriation of the rich (Aristotle of course considered this the height of injustice).[54] For Marx, the communists would consistently imbue the spontaneous struggle against absolutist oppression with deeper insight into its social causes and heightened energy in overthrowing it.

In 1847 in his critique of the radical democrat Karl Heinzen, "Moralizing Criticism and Critical Morality," Marx noted that German liberal merchants like Hansemann and Camphausen feared a democratic revolt in which "the rabble gets insolent and lays hands on things." In Germany, only such a revolution could unmask capitalist exploitation, still concealed by monarchical oppression. Contrasting England and the United States with Germany, Marx suggested that "social questions . . . increase in importance in proportion as we leave behind us the realm of absolute monarchy." Thus Marx stressed the transition from a monarchy to a capitalist republic rather than a further unfolding of productive forces as the key to Germany's socialist potential. He identified the appearance of an active communist movement in the French Revolution more precisely:

> The first manifestation of a truly active communist party is contained within the bourgeois revolution, at the moment when the constitutional monarchy is eliminated. The most consistent republicans, in England, the Levellers, in France Babeuf, Buonarroti, etc., were the first to proclaim these "social questions." *The Babeuf Conspiracy,* by Babeuf's friend and party comrade Buonarroti, shows how these republicans *derived from the "movement" of history* the realization that the disposal of the social question of rule by princes and republic did not mean that even a single "social question" has been solved in the interests of the proletariat.[55]

In the France of 1794, this newborn communist movement, lacking deep roots in the masses, an industrial proletariat, and a comprehensive revolutionary theory, could not succeed. Despite the sans-culottes' vigor, the Terror "with its mighty hammer blows could only serve to spirit away the remains of absolutism." But fifty years later, on the eve of 1848 in Germany,

54. Aristotle, *Politics,* 1281a 15–22, 1281b 16–22.
55. Marx, "Moralising Criticism and Critical Morality," *CW,* 6:323, 321–322.

"more advanced conditions" might create a stronger dynamic toward communism.[56] Marx and Engels envisioned an alliance of the proletariat, the petite bourgeoisie including the artisans, and the peasants as the linchpin of democratic revolution. While they did not spell out this projected alliance in detail until 1848 itself, they already believed that the proletariat could win these nonproletarian forces to socialism through their own experience and interests.

Thus, Marx's strategy for the German revolution of 1848 evolved through a series of studies of the French Revolution. Pursued in the light of Marx's new materialist hypothesis, these studies led to a broad framework for communist policy: to transform a protracted democratic revolution into a socialist one. Yet Marx could predict neither when the revolution would break out nor the changing dispositions of the contending forces. In these limitations, Marx tacitly acknowledged the elements of risk and chance inherent in all political action.[57]

Responsive to new circumstances, Marx's and Engels's strategy had an intentionally tentative, fluid character. Thus, in early 1848, Engels suggested that a democratic revolution in Germany might usher in "a few years" of capitalist domination before socialism could triumph:

> They [the bourgeoisie] are so shortsighted as to fancy that through their triumph the world will assume its final configuration. Yet nothing is more clear than that they are everywhere preparing the way for *us*, for the democrats and the Communists; than that they will at most win a *few years* of troubled enjoyment only to be then immediately overthrown.[58]

---

56. *CW*, 3:319. Ignoring the intervening fifty years, Richard N. Hunt mistakenly projects Marx's arguments about the sans-culottes into the new circumstances of 1848 to justify his arcane economic determinist reading of the *Manifesto*. Hunt argues that Marx simply cannot have meant his strategy of a linked democratic and proletarian revolution in Germany. Hunt, *Political Ideas of Marx and Engels*, pp. 180–181.

57. Marx to Kugelmann, April 17, 1871, *SC*, p. 264.

58. Engels, "The Movements of 1847," *CW*, 6:528. Hunt, *Political Ideas*, pp. 179–180, reads Engels's comment on "at most . . . a few years" of troubled capitalist rule (hardly an endorsement of a substantial period of capitalist economic development) as a reference mainly to Germany, and uses it to argue against Marx's and Engels's strategy in the *Manifesto*. But Engels made this argument for all of Europe, placing Italy and Switzerland in the most backward category (the most likely candidates for the few years), France which had already undergone two revolutions and Germany in the second category (more likely to experience democratic and proletarian revolution in immediate succession), and finally, Britain and the United

If the bourgeoisie refused to act in so confident but shortsighted a fashion, however, Engels asserted that the proletariat would immediately push them aside: "They [the bourgeoisie] must conquer—or already go under." [59] In this first exuberance of the communist movement, he (and Marx) overestimated the German proletariat's revolutionary vigor.

States in a third (socialism): "Behind them [the bourgeoisie] stands everywhere the proletariat sometimes participating in their endeavors and partly in their illusions as in Italy and Switzerland, sometimes silent and reserved, but secretly preparing the overthrow of the bourgeoisie, as in France and Germany; finally, in Britain and America, in open rebellion against the ruling bourgeoisie." Engels's draft of the *Manifesto* foresaw simultaneous communist revolution in England, America, France, and Germany, though he argued that this revolution would prove most difficult to complete in Germany. "Principles of Communism," *CW*, 6:352.

59. *CW*, 6:528.

— III —

Chartism and Marx's
Second Revolutionary Strategy

3–1. English Capitalism and the Working-Class
Movement

VIBRANTLY EXPANSIONARY ENGLISH CAPITALISM, the predominant world-transforming economic power of the early nineteenth century, engendered the first radical working-class movement. Manufactured exports, the trade in slaves, and commercial wars had spurred the first wave of English industrialization. After 1780, cotton textile production expanded rapidly. By 1805, this industry exported roughly two-thirds of its output and absorbed an increasing part of the work force. Machine weaving not only dispossessed the independent hand-loom weavers in England but also undermined calico production and deprived the skilled artisans in India of their livelihood. It drove Silesian weavers to starvation and to the revolt of 1844. With the aid of the English government, the cotton manufacturers destroyed the textile industry of Egypt which had employed 30,000 to 40,000 workers.[1] Built on the undoing of so many, this burgeoning industry created the city of Manchester which multiplied tenfold in population between 1760 and 1830 (from 17,000 to 180,000). This textile center gave its name to the predominant nineteenth-century school of liberal economics.[2] In *The Condition of the Working Class in England,* Engels would depict its brutal housing and working conditions.

Following the French Revolution, the English ruling class sought to suppress the widespread republican sentiment among artisans and workers, but the "dark Satanic mills" of capitalist production fostered new forms of mass revolt. In the Peterloo massacre of 1819, the militia fired on a Manchester meeting of 60,000 workers, killing ten and wounding several hundred. Peter-

---

1. E. J. Hobsbawm, *Industry and Empire,* pp. 32–34, 40–51; *Age of Revolution,* pp. 216–217. Between 1750 and 1770, for example, the output of home industries increased 7 percent while that of export industries jumped 80 percent.

2. Hobsbawm, *Industry and Empire,* pp. 40–41, 67–68.

loo revealed for the first time a dialectic of concentrated capitalist and government repression opposed to mass working-class rebellion. Shelley's "Mask of Anarchy" summoned the workers to:

> Rise like lions after slumber
> In unvanquishable number
> Shake your chains to earth like dew
> . . . Ye are many, they are few.

The revulsion against the Peterloo massacre among workers and others forced parliamentary recognition of unions in 1824–1825.[3]

Inspired by the French July Revolution of 1830, the English middle classes agitated for extension of the suffrage. Massive working-class demonstrations supported this demand. Furthermore, a wave of burnings of hayricks and destruction of threshing machinery swept the agricultural areas. But even the urban working-class movement lacked an independent leadership, and no coordination existed then or for the next twenty years between industrial and agrarian working-class revolt. Thus, the Reform Bill of 1832 granted the vote and seats in Parliament only to the propertied middle classes; it deliberately excluded urban and rural workers.[4]

Capitalism had slowly torn apart the hard but relatively independent lifestyle of the artisan who owned his tools and of the peasant who held his land, subjected these laborers to home work (putting out manufacture) for merchants, and finally, ransacked every moment of a family's time including the traditional "short holiday of childhood" (in 1838, men would compose only 23 percent of all textile workers; the rest were women and children). It engendered a fundamental sense of grievance. In addition, immigrants, previously victimized by English colonialism in Ireland, joined in every aspect of unionism and the struggle for reform.[5]

This English and Irish working class, stymied by middle-class leadership, evolved its own movement called Chartism. Its founders drew up a People's Charter in 1838—hence its name—which demanded universal suffrage for

---

3. Marx and Engels, *The Birth of the Communist Manifesto*, pp. 21–22.

4. E. J. Hobsbawm and George Rudé, *Captain Swing*, pp. 17–19, 282–283, 297–298. Donald Read, "Chartism in Manchester" in Asa Briggs, ed., *Chartist Studies*, p. 38.

5. E. P. Thompson, *The Making of the English Working Class*, pp. 331–349. Hobsbawm, *Age of Revolution*, p. 255. G. D. H. Cole, *A Short History of the British Working Class Movement 1789–1947*, pp. 66, 70–72.

men, a secret ballot, annual parliaments annually elected, abolition of the property qualification and payment for members of Parliament, and equal electoral districts rearranged after each decennial census. Chartists advocated a shorter working day and special restrictions on the working hours of women and children. Though Chartists organized women's political unions and opposed capitalist oppression of women and dissolution of the family (advanced positions for the time), they neither included women in the demand for the vote nor in the political leadership of the movement.[6] Many Chartist activities had also combatted the new Poor Law which had separated husbands, trapped in the workhouses, from wives. In addition, radical Chartist leader Feargus O'Connor raised the issue of the return of unemployed workers to the land and opposed the oppression of agrarian workers.[7]

The mass Chartist campaigns dialectically united working-class and Jacobin styles of radical activity:

> Working class experience gave the laboring poor the major institutions of everyday self-defense, the trade union and mutual aid society and the major weapons of such collective struggle, solidarity and the strike. . . . Conversely the methods of political agitation which belonged to Jacobinism and radicalism in general but not specifically to the working class proved both their effectiveness and their flexibility: political campaigns by means of newspapers and pamphlets, public meetings and demonstrations, and where necessary riot and insurrection. . . . [Without this campaigning], there would have been no even modestly effective legislative control of factory conditions or working hours. . . . The Jacobin tradition in turn drew strength and an unprecedented continuity and massiveness from the cohesive solidarity and loyalty which were so characteristic of the new proletariat.[8]

The movement's leaders at first consisted of skilled craftsmen such as painters, hatters, and tailors. Factory workers, however, like John Doherty,

6. J. T. Ward, *Chartism*, p. 25. Some Chartists strongly advocated women's suffrage. See R. J. Richardson, "The Rights of Woman" in Dorothy Thompson, ed., *The Early Chartists*, pp. 115–127.

7. Cole, *Short History*, pp. 98–99. Joy MacAskill, "The Chartist Land Plan" in Briggs, ed., *Chartist Studies*, pp. 304–309, 340–341. Hobsbawm and Rudé, *Captain Swing*, pp. 283, 15–17. O'Connor's program, however, had little influence among rural proletarians who did not rebel to acquire land.

8. Hobsbawm, *Age of Revolution*, pp. 250–251.

the Irish cotton spinner, and miners like Tony Hepburn and Martin Jude, soon came to the fore.[9]

In 1838, workers endorsed the Charter in thousands of meetings; 1,280,000 signed the petition to Parliament. A conflict emerged between a moral-force wing of Chartism centered in Birmingham and London and a physical-force wing concentrated in the factories of the North and Midlands as well as in Wales and Scotland. Faced with growing repression, the latter led an abortive insurrection at Newport in Wales in 1839.[10] By 1840, the English government had imprisoned most Chartist leaders.

During the subsequent depression, however, the repression failed. Chartism grew stronger, and the antagonism between working-class and middle-class politics intensified. The middle-class Anti-Corn Law League, led by Cobden and Bright, sought to unite master and men against the gentry by agitating for the removal of tariffs on imported corn. The Chartists repelled their efforts. They even disrupted League meetings in working-class districts, viewing them as a diversion from the struggle for the Charter. The 1842 petition gathered 3,500,000 signatures, and the Chartist movement reached a membership of 40,000. During the summer, a spontaneous Chartist general strike, the "plug riots" (so named because strikers pulled the plugs on the boilers to halt work in Lancashire and Yorkshire), spread widely. The magistrates and local police feared to attack this movement. Nonetheless, for lack of coordinated leadership, the strike failed.[11]

In the later 1840s, Chartism declined from this peak. Given vigorous Chartist activity, however, a split between gentry anticapitalists and pro-Manchesterites allowed the passage of the Ten Hours Bill in 1847. Responding to the French February republican revolution of 1848, the Chartists launched a new petition and called for a massive demonstration in April. The government feared a simultaneous revolt in Ireland, and Irish leaders hoped that the Chartists could provide a military diversion in England to make their own campaign successful.[12] Yet the Chartist leadership as a whole had never made the central and politically explosive issue of Irish independence a

9. Ibid., pp. 251, 254. Thompson, *Making of the English Working Class*, pp. 431, 432.

10. Cole, *Short History*, pp. 97, 103–110. Alex Wilson, "Chartism in Glasgow," and David Williams, "Chartism in Wales" in Briggs, ed., *Chartist Studies*, pp. 278–279, 237–240.

11. Read, "Chartism"; F. C. Mather, "The Government and the Chartists"; and Asa Briggs, "National Bearings" in Briggs, ed., *Chartist Studies*, pp. 35–37, 385–386, 297–298.

12. Mather, "Government" in Briggs, ed., *Chartist Studies*, pp. 394–395.

focus of its program, nor had it underscored to English workers the connection between their destiny and that of the Irish. Some radical Chartist leaders like Ernest Jones and George Julian Harney had participated in the Fraternal Democrats composed of European republicans and communists including Marx and Engels. These leaders saw the importance of international solidarity as well as of victory within England. They agitated for militant action to win the Charter.

Given the tradition of mutual antagonism between Chartism and the two governing parties, Jones and Harney had a considerable reservoir of experience and class hatred to draw on. Chartism had always denounced those "robber factions," the "tyrannical plundering Whigs" and "tyrannical plundering Tories," as upholders of class legislation; these parties helped strip the workers of the fruits of their toil and suppressed them if they fought back. Yet the Chartist leadership had not prepared its followers for parliamentary reaction in the face of Continental revolutions and the threat of Irish rebellion. When Parliament scornfully rejected the workers' demands, the Chartists, despite some local uprisings, offered no energetic response. The government jailed militant leaders like Jones, and the movement declined.[13]

External factors such as the defeat of the European revolutions and the revival of the English economy after 1849 undermined Chartism, but the movement's internal weaknesses, its failure to oppose divisions between English and Irish workers sufficiently, as well as its inadequate preparation for rebellion against Parliament, strongly contributed to its downfall. This second political experience, that of a spontaneous movement of factory workers, forged by modern industry, yet making its own political consciousness, profoundly influenced Marx's formulation of strategy.[14]

3–2. Engels's *The Condition of the Working Class in England* and Marx's Study of Chartism

In the 1840s, Marx had already characterized the new German proletariat not only as suffering but also as subversive. As we have seen, he did not base this judgment simply on a philosophical notion of a universal propertyless class. Instead, he saw this subversive potential precisely in the proletariat's actual political movement, notably the Silesian weavers' revolt.

Marx now turned to societies in which a democratic revolution had al-

13. Ibid., pp. 372, 397.
14. See especially Thompson, *Making of the English Working Class.*

ready occurred, and in which capitalism flourished; he again sought to discern the real movement, or type of political experience through which masses of workers could acquire a revolutionary outlook. In Marx's *The Poverty of Philosophy* (1847), he would note that historians had thoroughly traced the origin and history of the bourgeoisie; yet "when it is a question of making a precise study of strikes, combinations and other forms in which the proletarians carry out before our eyes their organization as a class, some are seized with real fear and others display a *transcendental* disdain." [15] Engels's *The Condition of the Working Class in England* (1845) had provided the "first precise study" of this proletarian movement.[16]

In *Condition*, Engels combined an investigation of living conditions in the great towns like Manchester with an industry by industry survey of capitalist oppression. He also delineated the stages of the new working-class movement that waged a "social war" against these conditions. The first and "least successful" manifestation of the workers' hostility to exploitation—theft—had left individual workers at the mercy of the government. The workers therefore turned to a second more collective form of resistance, Luddite machine smashing, which erupted in separate industries and localities, but resulted in severe punishment. With the repeal of the Combination Acts in 1824, Engels contended, a third stage emerged, consisting of union organizing against the capitalists in specific trades. Composed mainly of skilled workers, these unions restricted the number of apprentices in each trade to prevent competition, opposed wage slashes caused by the introduction of new machinery, offered financial assistance to the unemployed, and created a "tramping system" through which traveling workers could receive subsistence and information about job openings from any branch. Engels also explored union tactics: sending deputations to the employer to demand higher wages, circulating petitions, initiating strikes against all the capitalists in a given area, intimidating scabs, and the like. Although union history "is the story of many defeats and of only a few isolated victories," Engels saw strikes as a standing protest against the pressures of capitalism and a training ground in revolution:

> The incredible frequency of strikes affords the best proof of the extent to which the social war now rages in England. Not a week passes . . . without

15. Marx, *The Poverty of Philosophy*, p. 173.
16. Lowy, *Théorie de la révolution*, pp. 91–94, stresses the influence of Buret's studies of Chartism on Marx.

a strike occurring somewhere . . . these strikes are often nothing but skirmishes in a social war . . . and a preparation for the great campaign which draws inevitably nearer. Strikes are the manifestos by which particular groups of trade unionists pledge their adherence to the cause of the working classes.[17]

While Engels condemned individual acts of terrorism, he thought they flowed from the bitterness of this war: "In times of exceptional unrest, individual trade unionists . . . are guilty of deeds [vitriol throwing, shooting, or bombing] which can only be explained by the existence of hatred nourished in the depths of despair." But Engels advocated strikes, which forged collective solidarity and became a school for socialism. According to Engels, the enduring heroism of the English striker, who daily "sees his family in the grip of slow starvation" outstripped the militancy of the French barricade fighter; "men who are prepared to suffer so much to break the will of a single obstinate factory owner will one day be able to smash the power of the whole bourgeoisie." [18] This insight into the revolutionary potential of unionism would distinguish Engels and Marx from both utopians and most union leaders. In a letter to Bebel in 1875, Engels pointed out that all French socialists in the 1840s shunned "combinations" (unions) and strikes as did most Continental revolutionaries, "with the exception of us two, who were unknown in France." [19]

Yet capitalism still divided workers by region and industry, and even militant unions often went down to defeat. Thus, English workers had seen the need for a "purely" political movement, Chartism, which could unite all workers against their oppressors. The aims of this party, as we have seen, included legislation for universal suffrage and shorter working hours:

> Since the workers do not respect the law, but merely submit to it when they are not strong enough to change it, it is natural that . . . they should aim at replacing the law of the middle classes by the law of the working classes. This proposed law of the proletariat is the People's Charter.[20]

Through the suffrage, the proletariat could bridle the bourgeoisie's lust for profit. Eventually, socialism, at that time a middle-class movement in Eng-

---

17. Friedrich Engels, *Condition,* pp. 244–246, 254.
18. Ibid., pp. 249, 255–256.
19. Marx and Engels, *SC,* p. 300.
20. Engels, *Condition,* pp. 258–259.

land, would fuse with Chartism.[21] In *Poverty of Philosophy* and the *Manifesto,* Marx condensed the last three stages of Engels's account of Chartism—unionization, formation of a radical party to fight for a shorter work week by legal enactment and the vote, and finally, socialist revolution—into a new strategy for the working-class movement. Under predemocratic, capitalist conditions, a revolutionary movement could potentially combine such a strategy with a worker-peasant alliance, though, as we shall see, Marx did not attempt this in 1848.[22]

In reaching this first evaluation of a working-class political movement, however, Engels's argument exhibited four important contradictions: first, the view that unions could not force wages above the subsistence level clashed with his support for unions; second, his advocacy of internationalism contradicted his acceptance of derogatory English stereotypes about Irish immigrants; third, his awareness that class struggle tends toward violent revolution conflicted with his opposition to violence; and fourth, his conception of women as politically passive undercut his opposition to the capitalist oppression of women. The first contradiction arose from Engels's adoption of the "iron law of wages" from the radical political economy of the time; the last three reflected conflicts within Chartism itself. Marx and Engels would quickly overcome one of these contradictions in their theory or strategy; the others, however, would linger into the 1860s or longer.

First, in *Condition,* Engels adopted the theory that under capitalism, wages must inevitably fall to a level only sufficient for "bare existence," a "wage minimum," and questioned the effectiveness of unionism: "All these efforts on the part of trade unionists cannot change the economic law by which wages are fixed according to supply and demand in the labor market. Consequently, trade unions are helpless in the face of the major factors influencing the economy." [23] Engels stated that depressions (a major factor) force unions to submit to wage slashes, while in prosperity, unions can force wages up. These points are generally true. From them, however, Engels concluded that unions "are not in a position to secure for their members higher wages than those which they would in any case obtain as a result of free competition between capitalists for skilled men." [24] Following many radicals of the 1840s, one might ask: why have them?

21. Ibid., pp. 268–270.
22. Marx to Engels, April 16, 1856, *SC,* p. 92.
23. Engels, *Condition,* p. 246.
24. Ibid.

But Engels then contradicted himself: "If the manufacturers did not have to face mass organized opposition from the workers, they would always increase their own profits by continually reducing wages." Thus, unions *can* significantly alter the level of wages. In any case, Engels disliked the implication that strikes and unions made no difference. It coincided too neatly with "often heard" capitalist arguments against unionism and opposed a method of fighting that the workers themselves had so clearly adopted.[25] In the *Manifesto,* Marx and Engels would stress the role of strikes and unions in their revolutionary strategy; yet they retained a "bare subsistence" theory of wages. They would not resolve this contradiction between practical working-class movements and their general analysis of capitalism until Marx formulated his new theory of labor power, subsistence, and surplus value toward the end of the 1850s.

Second, in the "Dedication" to *Condition,* Engels celebrated the incipient internationalism of English workers, their political self-understanding as men, not just Englishmen:

No working man in England . . . ever treated me as a foreigner. With the greatest pleasure I observed you to be free from that blasting curse, national prejudice and national pride, which after all means nothing but *wholesale selfishness.* . . . I found you to be more than mere Englishmen, members of a single isolated nation, I found you to be MEN, members of the great and universal family of Mankind.[26]

Yet when Engels turned to the fate of Irish immigrants in England, he discerned only their suffering and degradation. Unlike the English workers, they lacked potential subversiveness. Though blaming the alleged Irish character on "society," Engels simply rehashed racist prejudices:

The poor devil [the Irishman] must get some pleasure out of life and so he goes and drinks spirits. Society has debarred him from other pleasures. Two things make life supportable to the Irishman—his whisky and his lively, happy-go-lucky disposition. . . . Everything combines to drive the Irishman to drink—his light-hearted temperament akin to that of the Mediterranean peoples, his coarseness which drags him down virtually to the level of a savage, his contempt for all normal human pleasures which he is incapable of

25. Ibid.
26. Ibid., p. 8.

appreciating because of his degraded condition, combined with his dirty habits and his abject poverty.[27]

At this time, Engels saw only the negative influence of Irish immigration in driving down the English workers' standard of life, and providing an "uncivilized" moral example. He delineated only the forces that undermined internationalism among English and Irish workers, not the common oppression which might unite them. His description of the Irish workers flagrantly contradicted his depiction of the Chartists. Yet the English press often trumpeted similar stereotypes about the subhumanity of English workers, and many missionary reformers, who sympathized with the workers' misery, nonetheless believed them. Engels supported the workers' movement in England but did not see that movement's special need to defend those most oppressed by English capitalism.

The Chartists had recruited many Irish workers and an Irishman, Feargus O'Connor, had emerged as Chartism's most renowned, militant leader. In subsequent articles on Chartism and Ireland written before 1848, Engels recognized the role of Irish workers in the English working-class movement and adopted a far more consistent internationalist position. Reviewing the effects of the potato famine in driving the Irish to emigrate, he recognized the greater daring that the Irish workers, given their more severe oppression, might bring to the class struggle in England: "British democracy will advance more quickly when its ranks are swelled by two million brave and ardent Irish." [28] The earlier stereotypes had abruptly disappeared. Throughout the 1840s, Engels and Marx believed that the liberation of Ireland would only come through the victory of socialism in England. In the 1860s, however, as I noted in Chapter 1, Marx would drastically alter this way of looking at the political relationship between colonizer and colonized and argue that the liberation of Ireland provided the key to the advance of English socialism.

Third, in considering the issue of violent revolution, Engels hailed the "full-blooded vigor of this [the Chartists'] agitation": "The Chartists incited the people to take up arms and rise in revolt. The days of the French Revolution were recalled when the making of pikes became a popular hobby." Engels cited a speech made in 1838 by a Methodist minister, J. R. Stephens,

27. Ibid., pp. 106, 107.
28. Engels, "The Coercion Bill for Ireland and the Chartists" in Marx and Engels, *Ireland and the Irish Question*, p. 47. Thompson, *Making of the English Working Class*, pp. 442–443.

who urged workers at a Manchester meeting to resist the capitalists violently:

There is no need for you to fear the power of the Government. . . . You have something which is mightier than them all. . . . All you need to do is to take a bundle of straw dipped in pitch and take a few matches, and we shall see what the Government and its hundreds of thousands of soldiers will be able to do when this weapon is boldly used.[29]

In the "Conclusion" of *Condition,* Engels argued that exploitation would impel the workers to frenzied violence: "Popular fury will reach an intensity far greater than that which animated the French workers in 1793." [30]

Yet remnants of "true socialist" philosophical pacifism and fear of the workers lingered in Engels's analysis and made him ambivalent about revolution. Communism, he thought, should tame this working-class violence and render social transformation "less bloody, less violent and less vengeful." Though Engels's argument otherwise focused on what he and Marx would later call the "self-emancipation" of the English workers, he separated communism from the proletariat and identified it with an overarching "humanity." Engels vividly documented the rulers' daily oppression of the workers, yet he ascribed the need for revolutionary violence solely to the workers' stored-up bitterness over past exploitation rather than to self-defense against foreseeable capitalist efforts to stamp out revolution. At times he attempted to scare bourgeois readers with the workers' "ungovernable passions." On the one hand, he advocated "social war" against the exploiters; on the other, he sought to moderate the workers' fury. Actually, as Marx and Engels would emphasize in examining future nineteenth-century uprisings like the June revolt and the Paris Commune, the workers, far from taking bloodthirsty revenge, would defend themselves insufficiently against the sheer murderousness of the threatened bourgeoisie. In the English case, Engels's position in 1845 echoed the ambivalence of the Chartist movement. Unprepared to rebel, as we have seen, they would cave in before parliamentary rejection in 1848, despite their millions of followers. Marx would soon argue in *Poverty of Philosophy* and the *Manifesto* that the proletariat must institute

29. Engels, *Condition,* p. 260.
30. Ibid., p. 334.

its "sway" over the bourgeoisie by force and persuade Engels to abandon these survivals of "true socialism." [31]

Fourth, Engels depicted and bitterly condemned the special exploitation of women, embodied in long hours of work under brutal physical conditions, segregation in specific categories of employment, lower wages for the same work as men, subjection to sexual harassment by employers, and most notably, the undermining of child care.[32] In examining the splitting up of families, Engels focused on cases in which the wife found work while the husband was jobless. Beyond the general despondency caused by unemployment, however, the unemployed man suffered a reversal of roles. Engels perceived that the sudden desolation of the man, forced by circumstance to do housework and look after children, reflected a fundamental selfishness and domination in the "normal" family structure:

> We shall have to accept the fact that so complete a reversal of the role of the two sexes can be due only to some radical error in the original relationship between men and women. If the rule of the wife over her husband—a natural consequence of the factory system—is unnatural, then the former rule of the husband over the wife must also have been unnatural. If the family as it exists in our present-day society comes to an end then its disappearance will prove that the real bond holding the family together was not affection but merely self-interest engendered by the false concept of family property.[33]

Here Engels pressed toward a first critique of the denial of political and legal rights to women and their consignment to a "natural" destiny of solely minding house and children. Like most Chartists, however, Engels remained uncritical of the demand for universal male suffrage. More important, he stressed only the suffering of women at work and ignored their potential or actual militancy on the job and in the general movement for socialism.

---

31. Ibid., pp. 334–336. Hunt, *Political Ideas*, pp. 145–146, fails to observe that Engels soon abandoned this argument from *Condition*.

32. Engels, *Condition*, pp. 158–162, 167. Drawing upon the reports of factory inspectors, Engels probably overemphasized the "moral depravity" of factory life.

33. Ibid., pp. 164–165. In his conception of this "natural consequence of the factory system," Engels (and Marx) overestimated the need capitalism would have to rely mainly on the labor of women and children once working-class protest against this form of special oppression emerged. *CM* in *MESW*, 1:41.

Yet women participated vehemently in the struggle for the Charter. As the Women's Political Union of Newcastle upon Tyne contended,

> We have been told that the province of woman is her home, and that the field of politics should be left to men; this we deny. . . . Is it not true that the interests of our fathers, husbands, and brothers, ought to be ours? If they are oppressed and impoverished, do we not share those evils with them? . . . We have searched and found that the cause of these evils [from the slave trade to the impoverishment of working-class families] is the Government of the country being in the hands of a few of the upper and middle classes, while the working men who form the millions, the strength and wealth of the country, are left without the pale of the Constitution, their wishes never consulted, and their interests sacrificed by the ruling factions.[34]

Though the Chartists placed women in a subordinate role, Chartist women joined with their husbands, brothers, and sons in directing their hatred at the common capitalist oppressor, not at men in general. A hostile description of a demonstration in Wales that seized a hotel, freed three Chartist prisoners, and attacked the police, singled out the women who had taken the lead in the fighting: "Some of the women who had joined the crowd kept instigating the men to attack the hotel—one old virago [vowed] that she would fight till she was knee-deep in blood" to prevent the prisoners from being taken out of Llanidloes. In organizing for the suffrage and in leading demonstrations, the political activity of Chartist women went far beyond what Engels had recognized. During the Paris Commune, Marx would later hail the militancy of working women, similarly described as "Megaeras and Hecates" by the terrified French bourgeoisie.[35] Engels and Marx always supported the general working-class solidarity of men and women against their oppressors. Yet in their lifetimes, they never worked out an approach to overcoming the lesser status of women within the revolutionary movement.

In *Condition*, Engels had drawn from a spontaneous working-class movement the first formulation of a communist strategy under fully developed capitalism. His conclusions would cohere straightforwardly with Marx's overall theory of class struggle though he and Marx would strengthen and

---

34. Thompson, *Early Chartists*, pp. 128–129.

35. Ibid., pp. 222–225. Marx, *Civil War in France* and 1871 speech at the London Conference of the IWA on organizing women workers in Marx and Engels, *Writings on the Paris Commune*, pp. 92, 224.

transform the concepts of working-class internationalism and violent revolution that Chartism had foreshadowed. Engels's argument posed unresolved questions about the nature of subsistence and exploitation and about the political role of women in Marx's general theory. Study of political experience, then, provided a vehicle for refining theory and strategy.

In an introduction written in 1892, Engels referred to *Condition* as a phase in the "embryonic development of modern socialism." He drew a striking analogy between the human fetus which in its first stages "still reproduce[s] the gill arches of our fish-ancestors" and socialism as represented by *Condition*, which retained "traces of descent from . . . German philosophy." [36] He recognized that the theoretical and practical inconsistencies in *Condition* had served as a starting point for the working out of "modern socialism." Yet Engels's analogy breaks down in its suggestion that socialism had reached final maturity, especially since Engels himself had become severely critical of late nineteenth-century German Social Democracy. Though Marx's full theory provided definite strategies for proletarian revolution and a vision of a new society, it exhibited important internal tensions that affected its application in new situations. From its outset, "modern socialism" has required constant elaboration and even transformation in the light of fresh experience.

36. Engels, *Condition*, p. 364. Contrary to those of today's scholars who neglect the influence of classical German philosophy on Engels, he frequently employed philosophical arguments about alienation during this period. Engels, *PW*, p. 153; "The Condition of England: *Past and Present* by Thomas Carlyle"; and "The Condition of England. The English Constitution," *CW*, 3:463, 465–466; 512.

— IV —

Marx's Organizing and the League of the Just

4–1. Marx's Political Debates

ONCE MARX HAD ELABORATED his two revolutionary strategies, he entered upon a period of intense political and organizational activity. As Engels later put it,

> We were both of us already deeply involved in the political movement, and possessed a certain following in the educated world, especially of Western Germany, and abundant contact with the organized proletariat. It was our duty to provide a scientific foundation for our view, but it was equally important for us to win over the European and in the first place the German proletariat to our conviction. As soon as we had become clear in our minds, we set about the task.[1]

Marx attempted to win other radicals—intellectuals and artisans alike—to his point of view. With those who disagreed, resounding clashes sometimes ensued. In the next chapters, I trace Marx's combative efforts to win other radicals to his political strategy or to isolate his political opponents. This activity would set the stage for Marx's impact in the revolution of 1848.

Influenced by an economic determinist account of Marx's theory, many scholars have dismissed Marx's political activity as insignificant and attributed the issues that separated Marx from other radicals to some external psychological or social cause. Werner Blumenberg's *Portrait of Marx* provides a classic example. For Blumenberg, Marx, with his "off-putting manner" could not engage in effective political organizing:

> With Marx, the unconditional quality and ruthless logic that characterize his thought took the form of intransigence in political activity. In this respect he was never very successful. It is difficult to imagine Marx and Engels as leaders

---

1. Friedrich Engels, "On the History of the Communist League," *MESW*, 2:345.

of a party; for this they lacked the most important requirement: the art of handling men. There was something curt and off-putting in their manner.

Blumenberg's critique presupposes a peculiar image of a successful politician: a bland, unprincipled conciliator, specializing in the manipulative art of "handling men." From the start, Blumenberg fails to consider the more long-term, political vision or strategy needed to forge a serious revolutionary movement; he also ignores the possibility of nonmanipulative political activity. Having asserted Marx's hopelessness as a politician, Blumenberg jumps to the conclusion that somehow Marx "won" all his political debates: "It goes without saying that in these disputes Marx naturally triumphed over all his opponents." [2] Blumenberg employs the rhetorical crutches, "it goes without saying," "naturally," as a substitute for explaining what Marx won or how Marx, the ineffectual politician, accomplished this feat. In fact, Marx did not convince most of his major radical adversaries, but his clear political arguments attracted an important group of followers. Blumenberg, however, ignores the role of Marx's and his followers' activism in galvanizing nineteenth-century socialism. Instead Blumenberg holds the theory, which he never defends, that Marx's ideas alone exerted overwhelming power and somehow compensated for Marx's unappetizing qualities (he calls this chapter: "The Power of New Ideas: Communism").

The accuracy of Marx's analysis of capitalism certainly made it effective but not so easily as Blumenberg believes. Many of Marx's most striking formulations did not see the light of publication during his lifetime (the economic and philosophical manuscripts, *The German Ideology*) or lapsed into temporary obscurity after 1850 (the *Manifesto*). Not only the conflict between capitalists and workers, which Marx foresaw, but also Marx's own vigorous organizing gave these ideas their first political foothold. In contrast, Blumenberg's view and the tradition it represents, reduce Marx's exchanges with other radicals to a personality defect, a mere querulousness or arrogance.

Similarly, Jerrold Seigel's *Marx's Fate: The Shape of a Life* offers a psychohistorical castigation of Marx's "hostility," "aggressive style," and more oddly, his "excluding others from the personal space he occupied." Seigel notes that, "politically, Marx was often able to cooperate with people whose views differed from his," a point that would appear to necessitate an investigation of the political reasons why Marx cooperated in some cases but not in

2. Werner Blumenberg, *Portrait of Marx,* pp. 72, 75.

others. Instead, Seigel accepts the crass character descriptions provided by Marx's opponents and even interprets a misrepresentation of Marx's arguments by Weitling as an account of what Marx actually said.[3]

Many situations, however, call for some degree of hostility as a rational response: hatred by a democrat for an oppressive autocracy for example, or hostility toward someone who slanders a friend. A justification for Seigel's reductionism requires an assessment as opposed to mere assertion of the irrationality of Marx's actions for if Marx's strategies and arguments make political sense, then this type of psychological explanation becomes superfluous. Yet Seigel obscures the rationality of Marx's position by offering only a brief account of Marx's role in 1848, which focuses on Marx's views on events in France rather than his vigorous activity in Germany. Seigel translates Marx's life into psychodrama: Marx is "not merely a revolutionary" (perhaps a "parochial" vocation though clearly Marx's own) but rather "an exemplary presence in the development of the modern consciousness. . . . His life exemplifies the link that joins thought to action [which Seigel does not explore] and the gap that separates them."[4]

Other scholars have depicted these conflicts as stratum based. In his *Marxism and Totalitarian Democracy,* Richard N. Hunt, for instance, concludes that artisan communists usually endorsed immediate proletarian revolution in Germany because of their anxiety to regain their lost status as independent property holders. The intellectuals within the Communist League, looking down on the artisans, tended to adopt a Marxian or economic determinist point of view.[5] In a more subtle variant of this argument, Michael Lowy sees Weitling as a representative artisan theorist, or in Gramsci's phrase, an "organic intellectual" endorsing immediate socialist uprising, Moses Hess as a typical intellectual leaning toward "true socialism," and Marx as moving beyond these partial points of view to "totalize" a picture of a proletarian movement that would ultimately emancipate itself.[6] Here sociological arguments that have some general plausibility—dispossessed artisans may often have adopted an immediate communism, radical German intellectuals may

3. Jerrold Seigel, *Marx's Fate,* pp. 181–184. See section 4–4.

4. Ibid., pp. 197–200. Seigel offers occasional flashes of insight into Marx's later activity, for instance into Marx's strategy in the IWA which relied on a gradual resolution of explicit political differences based upon common experience in the real movement. Seigel, pp. 236–237. See also Saul Padover, *Karl Marx,* pp. 229–237.

5. Hunt, *Political Ideas,* pp. 148–152, 157–158, 189–190.

6. Lowy, *Théorie de la révolution,* pp. 20–21, 89.

sometimes have favored the sentimental "true socialism" because of an antipathy to class struggle–distort the complexities of these political debates and their implications. The array of German and European social forces and the participants' psychological dispositions influenced these political conflicts, but did not in any simple sense determine them.

In these debates, Marx's new theory and strategy stood out in stark contrast to other conceptions of political republicanism and immediate proletarian or social uprising. Marx's own position drew its coloration at this time from his critique (and sometimes self-criticism) of competing conceptions of the relation between theory and practice. When Ruge and Marx founded the *Deutsch-Französische Jahrbücher* in 1843, they had envisioned the linking of German philosophy and French revolutionary politics. Ruge maintained this sheerly political democratic vision throughout the 1840s and never understood the evolution of Marx's point of view.[7] When Hess, Engels, and Marx first foresaw the merging of philosophy (the head) and the proletariat (the heart), they thought of joining the philosopher Feuerbach, the representative critic of Hegel, with the artisan Weitling, the "prophet of his class" as Feuerbach had called him.[8] Yet this fusion would supposedly lead to direct social or proletarian revolution as Marx conceived it between 1843 and 1845. Moses Hess, not Marx, would retain this conception in the later 1840s. Between 1845 and 1852, Marx gave new meaning to the *Theses on Feuerbach*'s famous concept of "practical-critical activity."

4–2. Schapper against Weitling: The Decline of Conspiracy

IN SEEKING POLITICAL INFLUENCE, Marx first turned to the German artisan communist movement, the League of the Just. Breaking away from republican secret societies, radical German artisans had founded this communist conspiracy in the 1830s. They had boldly disseminated communist ideas and shaped the views of substantial numbers of German craftsmen. Their ideas had influenced Marx as well as other radical philosophers like Feuerbach and Hess. Marx's activity with the League was his first attempt to win working people, either those who retained their own tools or those recently dispossessed, to his new strategy.

7. Sidney Hook, *From Hegel to Marx,* pp. 162–164.
8. Lowy, *Théorie de la révolution,* p. 87.

In the 1830s, the main leaders of the League, Karl Schapper, a former forestry student, and Wilhelm Weitling, a tailor, had adopted the fundamental insight of the French communists that formal political equality alone would not lead to genuine social equality. In the League's manifesto of 1838, *Die Menschheit wie sie ist und wie sie sein sollte* (Mankind as it is and as it ought to be), Weitling noted that the "beautiful names," republic and constitution, would not clothe or feed the ever-troubled poor: "To improve their [poor people's] conditions, the next revolution must be social." [9] Weitling and Schapper hoped to achieve the "community of goods," not just the equality of independent peasants and artisans, through violent revolution. [10]

Located mainly in Paris, the League appealed to the massive German emigrant artisan community (70,000 out of a total Parisian population of 900,000). From the outset, the League responded to the vibrancy of French social republicanism and adopted a relatively internationalist outlook. According to a Paris leader, Hermann Ewerbeck, the League recruited Flemings, Hungarians, and Scandinavians as well as Germans. Weitling's "Mankind" advocated the breaking down of "all narrow-minded concepts of nationality." Schapper also identified the German fight for freedom and equality with a vague, overarching "humanity." Nonetheless, article 1 of the League's 1838 rules formally restricted membership to those who spoke German and practiced German customs. [11]

Beyond its insight into the corrosive effects of social inequality on political community, however, German communism, like French social republicanism, had learned little from its great French predecessors. Where Rousseau or Montesquieu had envisioned relative egalitarianism among the citizens of small, slaveholding republics, and teased apart the subtle relationships between the nature and principle of different forms of government, the French and German artisans of the 1830s had no clear idea of the social and political setting in which communism might flourish. To establish the community of goods, they thought that communists needed simply rage at injus-

9. *Bund Dokumente,* p. 108. On the evolution of previous republican societies, the Deutscher Volksverein and the Bund der Geächteten, in a radical egalitarian direction, see Werner Kowalski, *Vorgeschichte und Entstehung des Bundes der Gerechten,* pp. 38–39, 41–48, 64–72, 183–184.

10. Karl Schapper, "Gütergemeinschaft," *Bund Dokumente,* pp. 98–107.

11. *Bund Dokumente,* pp. 109, 93. Samuel Bernstein, *Auguste Blanqui and the Art of Insurrection,* p. 81. Though unusually attentive to the issue of internationalism, Lowy overemphasizes the early nationalism of the League, *Théorie de la révolution,* p. 151.

tice and optimism rather than social theory. They looked to a sudden successful uprising rather than patient political education and the recruitment of a
broad base of support.

Following an age-old tradition, Weitling's "Mankind" attacked the role of
money rather than that of private property in the means of production as the
root of social oppression. In addition, Weitling and Schapper transfigured
Christianity to suggest that the rich, who formerly could not slip through
the eye of a needle into heaven, would soon face similar obstacles on earth.
Suffused in a Christian atmosphere, speeches in League meetings habitually
began with "My Brothers in Christ" and concluded with "Amen"; a League
song looked to the forthcoming inauguration of "the kingdom of heaven on
earth." In "Mankind," Weitling foresaw a new Messiah, prefigured by Thomas Münzer, leader of the peasant war of 1525, and Felicité de Lamennais,
the radical priest. According to Weitling and Schapper, a law of nature mandated a communal society rather than the contemporary selfish and competitive one. Thus, once enthroned, the new Messiah would not face a difficult
task.[12] Though these German artisans had learned from nineteenth-century
French communism, they had yet to adopt the materialism and atheism of
eighteenth-century French radical republicanism. In a striking example of
uneven development, they fused an advanced post-French Revolution politics with their own social interpretation of German Christianity.[13]

In the 1830s, German conspiratorial communism shared with its French
counterpart a fresh, undeveloped character which it soon lost through defeat.
French insurrections in 1834 and 1839, based on a clique of revolutionaries
and out of phase with any broad political movement, quickly collapsed. The
League of the Just stood aside from the 1839 uprising, led by Barbès's Société
des Saisons. Nonetheless, the Parisian authorities attacked the League. A military patrol arrested Schapper for possession of a knife but later released him
for lack of evidence. In the subsequent repression, the main leaders of the
League dispersed. Schapper, Bauer, and Moll emigrated to London, and
Weitling to Switzerland, leaving Ewerbeck in Paris.[14]

12. Kowalski, *Entstehung des Bundes der Gerechten,* p. 166. Wolfgang Schieder, *Anfänge der
deutschen Arbeiterbewegung,* p. 244.

13. For example, Blanqui, the leader of the French communists, made atheism the first
principle of his movement.

14. Wilhelm Weitling's introduction to the third edition of *Garantien der Harmonie und
Freiheit,* pp. 293–294, romantically depicted the wounding of Austen, a shoemaker from Dan-

Faced with this setback, the former unity of viewpoint among the leaders dissolved. While Weitling drew hardened conspiratorial conclusions from the French experience, the London leaders and Ewerbeck shied away from insurrection and embraced Cabet's idyllic Icarian communism.

In Switzerland, Weitling launched a network of workers' clubs and singing societies, and recruited members to the League. He edited a newspaper, *Der Hülferuf der deutschen Jugend* (The Call for Help of German Youth), and a monthly journal, *Die junge Generation* (The Young Generation), and wrote two major books, *Garantien der Harmonie und Freiheit* (Guarantees of Harmony and Freedom) and *Das Evangelium des armen Sünders (The Poor Sinner's Gospel)*. "Guarantees" exerted an especially powerful influence on the growing communist movement in Germany. Confronted with Weitling's vigorous organizing and his subversive interpretation of Christ, the Swiss authorities arraigned, tried, and convicted him on charges of blasphemy and inciting to riot in 1843. After a year's imprisonment, Weitling emigrated to England, where an enthusiastic meeting of democrats and communists welcomed him as a persecuted leader of the communist movement.[15]

Between 1840 and 1844, Schapper, Bauer, and Moll had formed the German Workers' Educational Society and forged a London branch of the League with 250 members. As they had once learned from French communism, so they now, like Engels, studied Chartism, the first mainly industrial working-class movement. In this context, Bauer noted that "the progress of industry pushes the social question powerfully into the foreground."[16] Given defeat, the London leaders paid even keener attention to international revolutionary experience than before.

At this time, the London leaders favored Chartism's moral-force rather than its physical-force wing. In 1843 in a letter to Cabet, they strenuously denied their previous advocacy of violence: "The German communists . . . want only peaceful propaganda, and . . . have never thought of employing physical force to make their principles triumphant because they know too

---

zig, on the barricades next to Barbès himself. But Austen belonged to the Société des Saisons, not to the League of the Just. Contrary to previous scholarly opinion, Schieder argues persuasively that the League of the Just did not join in the 1839 insurrection. Schieder, *Anfänge*, pp. 160–161. *Bund Dokumente*, p. 999, n. 16.

15. The London leaders had sent funds to support Weitling's papers. Schieder, *Anfänge*, p. 66. *Bund Dokumente*, pp. 180–182.

16. Herwig Förder, *Marx und Engels am Vorabend der Revolution*, p. 57.

well that truth and justice will never reign by the force of bayonets, but only by the force of reason." [17] Conspiracy no longer satisfied them.

4–3. Lumpenproletarian Uprising versus Peaceful Propaganda

IN A SERIES OF MEETINGS between 1845 and 1846, the London leaders and Weitling clashed constantly. Because the London leaders eventually concurred with Marx whereas Weitling fell out with him in 1846, scholars have tended to overlook Marx's earlier differences with Schapper, Bauer, and Moll and ignore some important similarities between Marx's outlook and Weitling's. Marx's "Critical Notes on 'The King of Prussia and Social Reform' " (1844) had argued that Weitling's "Guarantees," the "vehement and brilliant literary debut of the German workers," dwarfed the "faint-hearted mediocrity" of German bourgeois political writing.[18] Specifically, Marx sympathized with Weitling's views on the importance of social as opposed to solely political revolution, the oppression of women, and internationalism. Marx would agree, however, with the Londoners' skepticism toward isolated conspiratorial plotting; eventually, after a complex political debate, Marx persuaded them to emphasize class conflict as well as democratic and proletarian revolution.

Unlike the London leaders, Weitling had continued to advocate social revolution. His contrast between a social and "merely political" uprising laid the basis for Marx's early strategy in his "Introduction to the *Critique of Hegel's Philosophy of Right*" of 1843 and his exchange with Ruge in 1844. Though Weitling had attacked private property in "Guarantees," he still stressed the ancient struggle between the rich–the "money aristocracy" and sometimes the aristocrats of learning, the *"Gelehrten"* as well–and the poor whom he identified closely with artisans and thieves. In "Guarantees," Weitling's conception of social revolution included an initial vision of the liberation of women. Following Fourier, he condemned the marriage market of the status-seeking rich and the financial dependence of wives upon husbands, which sustained empty, loveless relationships.[19] His critique incorporated an ancient conception of natural justice–that human activities should

17. Ibid., p. 56, n. 20. See also "Brief des Kommunistischen Korrespondenzkomitees in London an Karl Marx, June 6, 1846," *Bund Dokumente,* pp. 347–349.

18. *CW,* 3:201–202.

19. Charles Fourier, *Textes Choisies,* pp. 127, 125–126. Weitling, *Garantien,* pp. 200–201.

take place for the appropriate reasons. In the case of marriage, genuine affection provided the proper foundation rather than the corrupt, or, as Feuerbach or Hess would say, "alien" motives of gaining money or currying favor with the powerful.

Opponents had accused communists of advocating an animallike "community of women" that would force each woman to accept any man–a universal extension of the empty relationship. Weitling disowned any such view.[20] Yet, he never offered any sociological analysis of the function of the oppression of women in maintaining exploitative societies, or of the harsher effects of this oppression on women workers or peasants as opposed to upper-class women. He also never envisioned any active political role for women (nor during this period did other communists including Marx and Engels). In "Guarantees," however, Weitling prefigured the *Communist Manifesto's* famous attack on the role of adultery and prostitution in bourgeois marriage.

For Weitling, the power of the rich as a class did not pervade the government. Instead, the contradiction between social inequality and formal political equality led to the "rule of personal interests." Bribery and individual enrichment, not strategic responses of a ruling class based on common economic and political interests, led to reactionary policies. At times, Weitling even hoped to convert the privileged to communism. He argued that the Christian or charitable rich who gave their "superfluity" to the needy or even the king or prince whose laws provided for the welfare of the poor, had already become communists "without knowing it." Weitling saluted the noble prerevolutionary politician or dictator (a Prussian Frederick II or Emperor Joseph of Austria) and envisioned an incorruptible ruler even in the first stage of communism: "If we call forth communism through revolutionary means, then we must have a *dictator.* . . . The dictator shall not have more than anyone else; we need not begrudge him this place if he works only for the common good." [21] Weitling expected revolution to spring forth from the lumpenproletariat. In the debates of 1845–1846 he argued: "Everyone is ripe for communism, even felons. . . . Mankind is necessarily always ripe, or it never will be." [22] Where Marx had traced the birth of French communism in the political experience of the French Revolution, Weitling

20. Waltraud Seidel-Hoppner, *Wilhelm Weitling,* pp. 129–130.

21. *Diskussionen* in *Bund Dokumente,* pp. 230–231. Werner Kowalski, ed., *Vom Kleinbürgerlichen Demokratismus zum Kommunismus,* pp. 150–151. Weitling, *The Poor Sinner's Gospel,* p. 186.

22. *Diskussionen* in *Bund Dokumente,* p. 218.

overlooked the real mass movements of his time and offered the paradoxical vision of a spontaneous uprising of thieves from below combined with the miraculous descent of a noble dictator from on high.

In their meetings with Weitling, the London leaders (and Ewerbeck in Paris) condemned this conception of "founding the kingdom of heaven with the furies of hell." Schapper asserted that "a communist revolution is nonsense—it totally contradicts the principle of communism. Truth needs no physical force." Discounting the "ripeness" of thieves as well as their desirability as supporters, Schapper saw little chance for any uprising in the near future. His argument prefigured economic determinism (though without the subsequent Marxian "sophistication"): "In Europe, not even half the population can read." The bourgeoisie would first battle against the monarchy while "we proletarians stand in the background." Through peaceful agitation, however, the German proletariat would fare better in this new revolution than the French proletariat had in the July Revolution of 1830. Concurring with the "true socialists," Schapper argued that communists must "hold back the young" and headstrong, and that gradual enlightenment, not hunger or material oppression, would provide the motivation for community. Without such enlightenment, new oppressors would thrust mankind back into slavery. At best, after a considerable period of peaceful propagation, communism would triumph only in the next generation.[23]

Reacting to Weitling's vision of a dictatorship of a Messiah, Bauer responded fiercely that the proletariat, once enlightened, would enforce its demands "with lightning speed." Contrary to Hunt's appraisal of Schapper's relation to Marx, Schapper and the "impatient artisans" of 1845 advocated a far more extended stage theory of democratic revolution and subsequent enlightenment in Germany than Marx did.[24] They correspondingly proposed a far less vigorous, almost passive political role for communists in the democratic revolution and even in the projected transformation to the community of goods.

To these arguments, Weitling made some telling rejoinders: "The phrase about unripeness [*Nichtreife*] is always the nearest weapon of opponents of every forward step." Thus, Weitling foretold the role of this conception in full-blown economic determinism. (Schapper would shortly abandon this

23. Ibid., pp. 217, 220–221, 225–227.

24. Ibid., p. 231. Hunt, *Political Ideas,* pp. 150–151, asserts that whereas Marx foresaw a long period of capitalism preceding the triumph of communism, the London leaders impatiently sought immediate communist uprising.

phrase in the democratic revolution of 1848.) Weitling also noted the rapidity of change in social and political movements and observed that "what is not happening today may take place tomorrow." He compared revolution to a sudden storm whose coming one could not reckon beforehand. In a nearly Marxian materialist vein, he argued that hunger and oppression drove men to revolt and that men must educate themselves in the process of making revolution. In an oppressive society, peaceful enlightenment alone could not succeed.[25] Weitling vitiated the force of all these points, however, by focusing on an insurrection of criminals.

In these debates, Hermann Kriege shared Weitling's position. Responding to them both, Schapper stated: "Kriege's speech is a mirror for me," and recalled that he had spoken the same way as recently as 1839. After so many bitter experiences, however, he declared that " 'men are not yet ripe'; for if they were ripe, there would be nothing more to say." Like Weitling's conception of lumpenproletarian uprising, Schapper's hope for the realization of communism rested on an ultimate miracle—the transition from peaceful propaganda to that sudden and perfect ripeness of which "there would be nothing more to say." Unlike Weitling, however, Schapper would not stake everything on this miracle. Whatever his desire for change, he would stick with nonviolent "true socialist" formulations until he could find a more realistic alternative than Weitling's.

> Personally speaking, yes, I would still be for revolution. It was my highest wish to die on the field of battle; but I must suppress my private wish; I belong to mankind, and in its interest, I must fight for truth, equality, justice. And now, would Kriege really want to live in a society with felons, thieves, whores, and murderers? [26]

In subsequent discussions, Schapper hailed every means of achieving communism except Weitling's pet *Diebstahlstheorie,* which he dismissed as nonsense.[27] Thus, his temporary commitment to "true socialism" flowed mainly from a distaste for Weitling's strategy. In his belief in the importance of agitation and the working-class movement, his personal sympathy for violent conflict, and his tentative hopes for a German democratic revolution, Schapper favored the position that Marx would put forward.

25. *Diskussionen* in *Bund Dokumente,* pp. 221, 223–224.
26. Ibid., pp. 220–221.
27. Ibid., pp. 229–230.

Weitling's emphasis on internationalism among the poor influenced Marx at least as strongly as his espousal of social revolution. In "Guarantees," Weitling confronted the false patriots who argued that war endangered fatherland, nobility, religion, and property. Instead, Weitling averred, war threatened our wages, our health and that of our children, everything after which "you [the rich] reach your unclean, rapacious hand." "Now, we have no fatherland," he continued. Proletarians would gain a homeland only after a social revolution that creates a society "that cares equally about the maintenance of all its members." Only this new society could wage a just war against a counterrevolutionary invasion. In *Hülferuf,* Weitling satirized the "young Germany" movement racists like Arndt and Jahn "for whom what is not German . . . is repugnant." [28] At the 1845 Festival of Nations in London, Weitling derided any conception of the common interests of rich and poor:

> National rulers represent our brethren as cruel and rapacious; but who are more rapacious than they . . . who for their own privileges excite and conduct us to war? Is it really our common interest that necessitates war? Is it the interest of sheep to be led by wolves to fight against sheep likewise led by wolves? [29]

Inspired by this fraternal gathering of democrats at the festival, he envisioned a similar mingling of soldiers of many nationalities on the very field of battle to oppose their masters. Then "we should soon have done with all those blood and marrow sucking interests who now oppress and plunder us." [30]

In their increasing advocacy of internationalism, the London leaders concurred with Weitling. Their efforts to contact English radicals like Harney gave rise to the Festival of Nations as well as to the founding of the Fraternal Democrats. The German artisans propagated the idea that democratic and communist movements should stick together. In this, they strongly influenced Marx who derived his internationalism from previous revolutionary practice.[31] This artisan communist movement, along with the experience

28. Seidel-Hoppner, *Weitling,* pp. 39, 113, 116–118. Weitling, *Garantien,* pp. 88–91. Schieder, *Anfänge,* pp. 259, 256. Kowalski, ed., *Vom Kleinbürgerlichen Demokratismus zum Kommunismus,* pp. 158–159.

29. Engels cited Weitling's speech in *CW,* 6:12.

30. Ibid., 6:13. Weitling's internationalism coexisted with stereotypical attitudes toward Slavs. Weitling, *Gospel,* p. 82.

31. *Bund Dokumente,* p. 182.

of the French Revolution, provided a starting point for Marx's transformation of theory and strategy, which would soon influence many members of
the League of the Just and spur its metamorphosis into the Communist
League.

While the London leaders had abandoned Christianity in the early 1840s,
Weitling increasingly adapted religion to the cause of communism. His
"Guarantees" hailed the "Second Messiah" who would come to "realize the
teaching of the first. He will destroy the corrupt edifice of the old social
order . . . and transform the earth into a paradise." Weitling's *Gospel* described Jesus as a carpenter's illegitimate son, and a worker himself, formed
in the image of God and yet with human failings. This artisan Christ taught
equality for the poor and scourging of the rich. In a review of Zimmerman's
book on the sixteenth-century peasant wars for *Die junge Generation*, Weitling also sought to bend Lutheranism to the cause of revolution. Though
Weitling attacked Luther for calling upon the princes to "strike down the
peasants like cattle," he argued that Luther, with a true Christian change of
heart, might have led the poor. Unlike Weitling's "Mankind," this review
ignored the actual leader of the peasant revolt of 1525 and precursor of German communism, Thomas Münzer.[32]

Weitling also modeled the image of Christ the artisan martyr closely on
his own experience. The *Gospel* strongly implied that Weitling himself
would become proletarian dictator and second Messiah. Though he hailed
Feuerbach's *Wesen des Christentums* (*Essence of Christianity*) which transformed
theology into anthropology and called for human action to change society,
Weitling increasingly cast his vision of communism in a religious, not a
republican idiom. Though admitting somewhat self-consciously that he had
not studied German philosophy, Weitling peremptorily dismissed it as a
"muddle." [33]

During this period, the London and Paris leaders' statements took on an
increasingly secular cast. They made Feuerbach's *Essence* the basis of biweekly
discussions throughout the League. These leaders opposed Weitling's and
especially Kriege's use of Christianity. In their debates of 1845–1846, Kriege

32. Kowalski, ed., *Vom Kleinbürgerlichen Demokratismus zum Kommunismus*, pp. 213–214.
Weitling, *Gospel*, p. 10. Lowy, *Théorie de la révolution*, p. 91. Seidel-Hoppner, *Weitling*, p. 143.
Carl Wittke, *The Utopian Communist*, pp. 74–75.

33. Kowalski, ed., *Vom Kleinbürgerlichen Demokratismus zum Kommunismus*, p. 166, overesti-
mates Weitling's "atheism." Christianity was far more for Weitling than a cloak for communism. Weitling, *Gospel*, pp. 182–183.

had gibbered, "Away with reason whenever it suppresses feeling." Schapper and Bauer hailed the potential contribution of the philosophers who had adhered to the communist cause since 1842. Hunt's interpretation overstresses the distrust of these artisans for intellectuals and omits the great hopes that the London leaders in their "true socialist" as well as Marxist phases placed in philosophy.[34]

In "Guarantees," Weitling sketched an image of a future communist society that would replace money with a new currency based on commerce or work hours. The new society would guarantee necessities for all workers as well as the elderly, the sick, and children; it would distribute nonnecessities according to commerce hours. Thus, Weitling looked to a distribution governed at least partly by need. But Weitling lacked any background in classical economics. In his account, productivity (or what Marx would call socially necessary labor) did not affect the value of labor time. This system militated against efficiency by counting the labor time of more and less productive workers equally. It therefore provided no coherent method to regulate production in the new society.[35]

Despite Weitling's condemnation of German philosophy, "Guarantees" evinced a great respect for science and the rule of experts. A ruling "trio," chosen from the three main branches of science, would guarantee equality and productivity. Panels of experts, not the people, would choose among inventions submitted by prospective leaders; the three winners would assume power. As Weitling's conception of revolution banished politics, omitting any attempt to persuade the masses on the basis of their own experience of the need for communism, so his ultimate regime excluded politics as well. In galvanizing his communist society, Weitling eliminated not only economic but also political motivations. Eventually the technocratic rule of the enlightened would supersede the new Messiah of the revolution, and the formal structure of government and law would dissolve. Weitling's technocracy contrasted markedly with Marx's idea that the working class must emancipate itself. In the discussions of 1845–1846, Schapper expressed the

---

34. *Diskussionen* in *Bund Dokumente*, pp. 216, 232, 236. Hunt, *Political Ideas*, pp. 151–152, 157–158.

35. Weitling, *Garantien*, pp. 165, 170, 179–180. Marx defined socially necessary labor time as the time needed for a worker to produce a commodity under normal conditions of production with the average level of skill and intensity prevailing in a society. Marx, *Capital*, 1:39. See also Marx's *Critique of the Gotha Program*, *MESW*, 2:22–24.

hope that the new philosophers would supply a guarantee of individual freedom under communism which Weitling's system undermined.[36]

4–4. Weitling and Marx

AFTER FALLING OUT with the London leaders, Weitling went to Brussels, and in March 1846 met with Marx's Communist Correspondence Society. Predictably, Weitling and Marx clashed. In a letter to Hess, Weitling presented an opaque account of the differences. He attacked Marx as merely an "encyclopedic" intellectual with connections among the wealthy and summarized Marx's position:

1. An examination must be made of the Communist Party.
2. This can be achieved by criticizing the incompetent and separating them from the sources of money.
3. This examination is now the most important thing that can be done in the interest of communism.
4. He who has the power to curry authority with the money men also has the means to displace the others and would probably apply it.[37]

Translating Weitling's interpretation, we can see Marx's concern with forming a group of communists who agreed with his strategy in the democratic revolution ("criticizing the incompetent") and wanted to organize for it. To Weitling, however, this "separation" appeared mainly as an effort to please the money men.

Weitling's final two points indicated the differences between them more directly:

5. "Handicraft communism" and "philosophical communism" must be opposed, human feeling must be derided; these are merely obfuscations. No oral propaganda, no provision for secret propaganda, in general, the word propaganda not to be used in future.
6. The realization of communism in the near future is out of the question; the bourgeoisie must first be at the helm.[38]

---

36. Weitling, *Garantien*, pp. 152–153, 164–165. Wittke, *Utopian Communist,* p. 62. *Diskussionen* in *Bund Dokumente,* p. 236.

37. Weitling to Hess, March 31, 1846, in Karl Marx, *On Revolution,* p. 130.

38. Ibid., p. 131.

The unity of artisan and philosophical communism ("philosophy and the proletariat") that Weitling envisioned led to immediate communist uprising or at least to socialist agitation against German democracy. For Marx, however, the unity of theory and practice—the self-emancipation of the workers—could only arise from the real movement of the class struggle, not from utopian reveries ("artisan communism," "philosophical communism"). In Germany, this class struggle involved two linked stages, the bourgeois democratic revolution immediately preceding a proletarian one. As Weitling saw it, Marx's political realism simply undercut communism. In this sense, Weitling spoke bitterly of "human feeling derided." According to the observer P. V. Annenkov's account of the clash, Marx responded angrily to Weitling's disdain for political clarification or debate among the workers by suggesting that Weitling acted like an "inspired prophet" without a serious program and treated the workers like "donkeys." Marx concluded vehemently, "Ignorance never benefited anyone." [39]

In 1846, Marx's strategy and the theory it embodied seemed novel and strange. Like the democrats Ruge and Heinzen, Weitling offered an external criticism not of Marx's full position, but of certain fragments seen through the distorting lens of Weitling's own politics. Though Marx strongly disagreed with Weitling, he accurately appraised Weitling's argument; Weitling, however, had little grasp of Marx's.

As Weitling stressed religious sentiment, one of his biographers, Wittke, mistakenly identifies religion as the main issue between Weitling and Marx. Wittke dismisses Marx as a heartless, atheist economic determinist and avers, "He [Weitling] saw clearly that a system which eschewed all considerations of morality, social ethics and religious emotionalism and frankly proceeded on the amoral principle that the end justifies the means, might be turned into the devil's own philosophy leading to a new form of tyranny." [40] As a justification for violent revolution, Marx endorsed the goal of a society that would eliminate exploitation and permit a wide flowering of human activities. Yet Marx protected himself against the negative, perhaps terrorist or conspiratorial consequences of an "end justifies the means" view by emphasizing the necessary role of the masses. No revolution could occur without their participation; no movement that attacked them, like Weitling's uprising of thieves, could flourish. Thus, Marx condemned Weitling's crude utili-

39. *Bund Dokumente*, pp. 304–305.
40. Wittke, *Utopian Communist*, p. 120.

tarian and dictatorial view as counterproductive and foolish. Ironically, Weitling's cult of feeling and humanitarianism, so much admired by Wittke against Marx's "heartlessness," accompanied calls for unlimited banditry as the vehicle for revolution.

Weitling continued to meet with the Brussels Committee. The political conflict intensified around the activities of Weitling's former ally Kriege, who had recently emigrated to the United States. Previously a supporter of Weitling's *Diebstahlstheorie*, Kriege had reversed himself. He filled his New York newspaper, the *Volkstribun*, with sentimental phrases about love and appealed to representatives of all classes, particularly the rich. Kriege effusively concluded an open letter to John Jacob Astor: "Tell me that you have a heart for the poor, downtrodden children of man, and I will love you as you have never been loved; I will work for you as no one has worked for you. I await your answer with feverish anxiety." [41] To Kriege, concern for the plight of "humanity" justified such groveling: "We have other things to do than worry about our *miserable selves; we* belong to mankind." [42] Since "mankind" suffered, the more fortunate must respond either as missionaries or as philanthropists.

In the Brussels Committee's "Circular against Kriege," Marx contrasted Kriege's Christian "slavish self-abasement" with the political self-confidence and revolutionary defiance of a serious movement to remake the world: "Such a doctrine [Kriege's], preaching the voluptuous pleasure of cringing and self-contempt, is entirely suited to valiant—*monks,* but never to men of action, least of all in a time of struggle." As opposed to a missionary radicalism, which patronized the poor, Marx upheld the dignity, courage, and intelligence of political action, which the workers needed "more than their bread." [43]

In the United States, the National Reform Association had promulgated an agrarian program of dividing the land into farms of 160 acres, abolishing slavery, instituting a ten-hour working day, and the like. Marx and Engels supported this real movement to make most men into private owners as a

41. Ernst Schraepler, *Handwerkerbünde und Arbeitervereine, 1830–53,* p. 160.
42. Marx and Engels cited Kriege in "Circular against Kriege," *CW,* 6:49.
43. Ibid. In "The Communism of the *Rheinischer Beobachter,*" Marx argued, "The social principles of Christianity preach cowardice, self-contempt, abasement, submissiveness and humbleness, in short all the qualities of the rabble, and the proletariat which will not permit itself to be treated as rabble, needs its courage, its self-confidence, its pride and its sense of independence even more than its bread." *CW,* 6:231.

step forward in the American context. Yet Kriege, bewilderingly, transformed it into a fantastic movement for communism. Though Kriege asserted that the soil must remain "inalienable communal property," Marx noted that Kriege paradoxically demanded an immediate start on "dividing it up." According to Kriege, land division would bring about equality. Marx showed that, on the contrary, if this movement succeeded, differentiation into large capitalists and hired laborers would soon occur:

> [Kriege] considers 160 acres of land as an ever constant measure, as if the value of such an area did not vary according to its quality. The "farmers" will have to exchange, if not their land itself, then at least the produce of their land, with each other and with third parties, and when this juncture has been reached, it will soon become apparent, that one "farmer," even though he has no capital, will simply by his work and the greater initial productivity of his 160 acres, reduce his neighbor to the status of his farm laborer.[44]

If Kriege advocated communism, what then was capitalism? For Marx, the agrarian movement provided an arena for masses of people to fight for reforms, win limited victories, and learn through their experience that they must overthrow the bourgeoisie. But this temporary "historical justification" of the National Reform Association rested entirely on political clarity about the strengths and weaknesses of such a movement. Just as communists could not drive a democratic revolution toward a proletarian one by hailing republicanism or political equality as the final goal, neither could they metamorphose a movement for agrarian small property holding into an effort by a phantom "mankind" to institute "communal property" for "all eternity." In effect, Kriege mocked communist principles under pretense of advocating them. The Brussels Committee unanimously adopted the "Circular" condemning Kriege and expelled him from the German communist movement.[45]

In contrast, Weitling believed that even the rich might embrace communism and that Kriege had merely tailored communist principles to suit American conditions. Weitling wrote to Kriege that Marx, the nihilist, would first cut off Weitling's head, then the heads of Weitling's friends like Kriege, and finally, Marx's own: "The critic devours everything that exists." As Marx's "Circular" defended the agrarian movement, deflated Kriege's

44. *CW*, 6:42.
45. Ibid., 6:41–45. Wittke, *Utopian Communist*, p. 118. Förder, *Marx und Engels*, pp. 68–76.

communist posturing, and criticized his truckling before the rich, Weitling's criticism seems off the mark.[46]

Shortly after this controversy, Weitling emigrated to the United States. During the revolution of 1848, he returned briefly to Cologne to speak before the Democratic Society on July 21. Weitling's strategy made him irrelevant to the struggle for democracy. His call for an immediate communist dictatorship of the enlightened inspired little enthusiasm. At this meeting, Marx distributed copies of the *Communist Manifesto*. At the next meeting on August 4, Marx stressed that "political and social interests" (the republican and socialist revolutions) must interpenetrate; he opposed Weitling's separation of these interests and his one-sided denunciation of democracy. According to Marx, the democratic movement had to rely on the masses to succeed. In the revolution's first stage, Marx foresaw a government composed of representatives of the heterogeneous classes within the democratic movement rather than Weitling's dictatorship of an individual. This exchange in the midst of revolution pointed up their fundamental differences strikingly.[47]

4–5. Marx's Differences with the London Artisans

IN 1846, the Brussels Committee had notified the London leaders about the clash between Marx and Weitling and sent them the "Circular against Kriege." The Londoners then invited the committee to work more closely with them. To inflame the "barely suppressed hatred" between intellectuals and workers, they noted, Weitling had spread the lie among German artisans that the Brussels Committee excluded workers and envisioned the domination of the "aristocrats of learning" (*Gelehrten-Aristokratie*).[48] They then

46. Schraepler, *Handwerkerbünde,* p. 161, cites Weitling's letter.

47. *CW,* 7:556. Hunt, *Political Ideas,* pp. 197–198 rightly stresses that Marx foresaw a mass democratic revolution, not a conspiratorial putsch resulting in a dictatorship. Hunt argues that Soviet scholars consider Marx's speech garbled. Actually, these Soviet editors hold the same economic determinist views as Hunt and obscure Marx's thinking on the connection between democratic and proletarian revolution in 1848. They argue, "Like Gottschalk, Weitling ignored the bourgeois democratic character of the revolution and called for immediate and revolutionary fulfillment of utopian plans for social transformation. . . . In his speech, Marx dealt especially with the peculiarities of the German revolution and its vital task: to eliminate the remnants of feudalism." *CW,* 7:650, n. 346.

48. In the light of Weitling's "trio" of scientific experts, this charge, peculiarly enough, captures the spirit of his own ultimate position rather than Marx's.

offered a penetrating estimate of Weitling's disposition: "Weitling can endure no one except those who blindly obey his commands and find no book interesting if he has not written it." Weitling fantasized that he alone "could save the world." Previously the main theoretical leader of the League, he had emerged from prison to discover himself "one among equals." Weitling could not accept this new status. The Londoners dismissed Weitling's "religious nonsense" and "ridiculous system of commerce hours" and found his opposition to any scientific study in the League particularly irritating. They again rejected conspiracy and called for a "spiritual revolution" as a prerequisite for an ultimate "physical" one, which would come spontaneously if the powerful would not give in.[49]

In this letter, the London leaders judged Marx's indictment of Kriege "too harsh" and suggested that a "friendly warning" might have produced better results. They hoped to win over Kriege and others like him—"he is young and can still learn." Their next letter, however, disagreed with the content of the Brussels "Circular" rather than its style. They criticized Marx's stress on the development of capitalism and mechanization, and on the increasing distress of the workers not as wrong but as one-sided. They saw nothing "bastardlike" in philosophical arguments that attempted to discern the true nature of man and did not want to "damn the sentimentalists." [50] To them, Marx's combative efforts at political clarification did not convince his opponents but insulted them and drove them away. Though they themselves had grasped the implications of Marx's controversy with Weitling (fanciful conspiracies and uprisings based on the lumpenproletariat versus a real proletarian movement), they obscured the consequences of other differences, even of impassioned appeals to John Jacob Astor, in a mist of brotherliness. In part, this "softness" about political strategy flowed from their own internal ambivalence. On the one hand, they wanted a realistic movement that could lead to an ultimate communist transformation and saw Weitling's approach as a clear threat to such a movement's seriousness. On the other, they foresaw a long period of peaceful propaganda without revolu-

49. *Bund Dokumente*, pp. 347–348. In a letter to Bebel in 1888, Engels noted that Weitling had treated every political disagreement as a sign of others' envy. He even opposed Engels's and Marx's plan to issue an edited collection of the great utopians with a commentary as "unfair competition against his own system." Lost in dogmatic reveries, Weitling dreamed of creating a universal language in which the dative case, "an aristocratic discovery," would disappear. Marx and Engels, *Werke*, 37:118.

50. Letters of June 6 and July 17, 1846, *Bund Dokumente*, pp. 350, 379.

tionary action and believed that protracted ironing out of differences would not prove too costly. In short, they considered the effects of the debate only on the restricted group that already considered itself socialist or communist. While Marx sought to win over radicals who disagreed with him like the London leaders, he kept his eye on the broad movement of workers and peasants. He refused to compromise on fundamental divergences over participation in this "real movement" or the advocacy of internationalism, and would not treat such issues of principle as a private matter. Without splits on these issues, in his view, communists would hang themselves up in futile internal debate and make little headway among the masses. A confused communist movement that "sincerely" pledged to serve John Jacob Astor and yet proclaimed "defiantly" that "all history is the history of class struggles," would make a curious impression on ordinary workers and peasants. Yet such people and not just the handful of contemporary radicals would make any eventual revolution.

Because the Londoners did not fully concur with Marx's aim of vigorous, consistent activity to spur on the mass movement and infuse it with communist politics, they attributed his "harshness" solely to tensions between intellectuals and artisans, to "damned *Gelehrten-Arroganz*." They conjured up a sentimental image of Kriege, the real friend of the workers, in contrast to Marx, the standoffish intellectual. They improbably suggested that in his few months in America, Kriege had made "thousands of friends" among German artisans. The Brussels "Circular" perceptively commented that Kriege had not organized workers but rather "pressed the popgun of love to the chests" of the rich.[51] Though the Londoners otherwise praised the Brussels Committee's activities, these important differences remained.

Shortly afterward, Marx and Engels clashed again with the Londoners over the efforts of a movement in Schleswig-Holstein to overthrow Danish rule and reunite with Germany. In an address to the Schleswig-Holsteiners, the Londoners condemned this "nationalist" movement and astutely pointed out the oppressive role of Germany in Italy and Poland. Though Engels shared this judgment, he wrote to Marx that unity with the Zollverein (or later with the German democratic movement) would represent a forward step for the Schleswig-Holsteiners. He held that the Londoners' address ignored all historical development and current relationships. Engels wondered

---

51. Ibid., p. 380. Marx and Engels, *CW*, 6:50.

if the Londoners would deem any oppressed nation worthy of support.[52] In the 1840s, Marx and Engels opposed surviving precapitalist economic and political arrangements in Europe, and particularly, the influence of tsarism. In this context, they identified some national democratic movements, for example in Germany, Poland, and Italy, as progressive. In perhaps their most strained judgment of the period, they also supported the attempt to unite Schleswig-Holstein with Germany.

To arrive at these political judgments, Marx and Engels analyzed the international situation and the configuration of capitalist and precapitalist powers. They also emphasized the importance of further capitalist development in many parts of Europe (for example, they never argued that Poland could undergo proletarian revolution in the 1840s). In pursuing their internationalist humanism, the London leaders avoided such specific evaluations and confined themselves to vague counsels: "All men are brothers, and love is their bond." [53] In the next two years, Marx and Engels would strive to win the London artisans to the general historical materialist theory and to its novel strategic implications.

52. *Bund Dokumente,* pp. 407–409, 413–414.
53. Ibid., p. 408.

— V —

Marx and Proudhon

5–1. Marx, Engels, and the German Artisans in Paris

BY THE END OF 1846, Marx and Engels had already achieved considerable influence with the London communists. They ran into more resistance, however, from Parisian radicals including German artisans. On May 5, 1846, Marx wrote to Proudhon, asking him to become the committee's main correspondent in Paris. Marx emphasized the role of correspondence committees in furthering international communication and cooperation among different communist movements, especially those of Germany, England, and France.

While these movements pursued the common goal of transforming European feudalism and capitalism into a nonexploitative social system, Marx expected strong "differences of opinion" to emerge. As in the later IWA, he looked to a protracted process of experience and debate to achieve agreement and did not make adherence to his own theory a precondition of unity. Through this correspondence, he suggested,

> one can attain an exchange of ideas and impartial criticism. This is a step the socialist movement has to take . . . in order to get rid of nationalistic limitations. And at the moment of action it is certainly extremely useful for everyone to be informed about affairs abroad as much as about those in his own country.[1]

On May 17, 1846, Proudhon agreed to be a correspondent, but criticized the idea of revolution: "This sham means [to social reform] would be simply an appeal to force, to arbitrariness, in brief, a contradiction. . . . I prefer then to burn Property over a low flame rather than give it new force by making a Saint Bartholomew's massacre of the property holders." [2] Proud-

1. Marx, *On Revolution*, p. 132. See also "Rundschreiben des ersten Kongresses des Bundes der Kommunisten an den Bund," June 9, 1847 in *Bund Dokumente*, p. 477.

2. Pierre-Joseph Proudhon, *Confessions d'un révolutionnaire*, p. 435. This volume reprints the exchange of letters between Proudhon and Marx in an appendix.

hon's attack on revolution seems out of place. Marx had not even mentioned revolution in his original letter. Since Marx had met Proudhon in Paris in 1844, Proudhon might simply have been taking up an earlier debate. More likely, however, Proudhon knew Marx's views through the reports of the "true socialist" Karl Grün whom Proudhon defended. Marx's collaborator Philippe Gigot had attacked Grün in a postscript to Marx's letter: "The man is nothing more than a literary swindler, a type of charlatan, who would like to traffic in modern ideas." To the charge that Grün sought to exploit modern ideas, Proudhon answered fatalistically that Grün, living in exile with his wife and two children, had no alternative: "What would you have him exploit in order to live, if not modern ideas? . . . Ah, if we were all millionaires, things would go better." To the charge that Grün had depicted himself as Proudhon's "preceptor," Proudhon replied that if Grün had done so, he had acted presumptuously, and "I am sure he regrets it." In Proudhon's view, Grün worked to "keep the sacred flame going among the Germans who reside in Paris." Proudhon called upon Marx to reconcile himself with Grün and transcend "the minor divisions which, it appears, already exist in German socialism." He closed with a proposal that Marx might help distribute Grün's translation of Proudhon's new book, the *Système des contradictions économiques ou philosophie de la misère* (System of Economic Contradictions or Philosophy of Poverty).[3]

Proudhon's letter angered Marx who opposed the growing influence of "true socialism" among German artisans in Paris. The Brussels Correspondence Committee exchanged letters with Ewerbeck, and in August 1846, Engels himself moved to Paris to found a branch of the Communist Correspondence Committee and work in the League of the Just. Engels soon won over Ewerbeck and Adolf Junge, but generally made slow progress against "true socialism" in the Paris League. During this period, Engels's correspondence with the Brussels Committee described the debate over the necessity of violent revolution and satirized Proudhon's influence: "What these

3. Ibid., pp. 433–434, 436–437. A discussion of "true socialism" appears in Chapters 6 and 7. Oscar J. Hammen, *The Red '48ers,* p. 142, evokes an image of Proudhon the innocent as opposed to Marx the hatchet man: "Proudhon without knowing it, was to become the target of Marxian attacks. For the next twenty years Marx fought to destroy Proudhon's influence." In one paragraph, Hammen describes Proudhon's denunciation of Marx's views on revolution; in the next, he suggests that Proudhon "without knowing it" brought out Marx's "spiteful" communist "urge to destroy." Hammen ignores all the theoretical and political issues between the two men.

people have in mind is nothing more or less than to *buy up the whole of France* for the time being and later perhaps the whole world by dint of proletarian savings." [4] Engels called the artisans under the influence of this dream "blokes who cannot manage to keep six sous in their pockets to go to a wine saloon on the evenings they meet" and disparaged the more resistant ones as *Straubinger* (traveling artisans). Engels's depiction of these artisans smacked of the intellectual snobbery feared by the London leaders and illustrates the class tensions in the German communist movement of the 1840s as well as in all subsequent radical movements. [5]

To some extent, however, Engels vented an anger in these letters that he did not manifest directly to the artisans. Despite their "true socialist," Weitlingian, or Proudhonist views, Engels engaged in an extremely patient political effort to persuade them. After lengthy discussions, he won a majority vote (13 to 2) on three essential points: "(1) The interests of the proletariat are to be put through in opposition to those of the bourgeoisie; (2) to do this through the abolition of private ownership and its replacement by a community of goods; (3) to recognize no other means to realize these objectives than forcible, democratic revolution." [6] The Paris League later elected Engels as its delegate to the 1847 congresses of the Communist League, which mandated the drafting of the *Manifesto.*

As described by one scholar, given the small numbers involved, Engels's attitude towards these craftsmen seems faintly ridiculous, "as if the destiny of the world would be decided by a meeting of fifteen or twenty craftsmen from among the eighty to one hundred thousand Germans in Paris." [7] Engels had relatively little success in Paris in recruiting vigorous communist activists. Yet this patient organizing, especially among German artisans in London and democrats in Brussels, made Marx's viewpoint into a force in 1848 and, over the next forty years, into a worldwide movement. Small beginnings and very sharp uphill political battles have characterized every significant Marxian movement just as they did the very first. An economic determinist interpretation may mock such organizing, but given the enormous historical impact of Marxian political activity, this easy ridicule misses the point.

4. *SC,* p. 30. Förder, *Marx und Engels am Vorabend der Revolution,* p. 121.
5. Engels to Marx, December 1846 and January 14, 1848, *Werke,* 27:70, 111. In 1885, Engels acknowledged this weakness. "On the History of the Communist League," *MESW,* 2:340.
6. Letter of October 23, 1846, *Werke,* 27:61. Förder, *Marx und Engels,* p. 123.
7. Hammen, *Red '48ers,* p. 143.

5–2. Mutualism versus Class Conflict

TOWARD THE END OF 1846, Proudhon published "Philosophy of Poverty," which elaborated his analysis of the peaceful evolution of a just mutualist society. More profoundly than Grün's, his views would influence German artisans in Paris as well as French working people. At every point, Proudhon's argument and strategy resoundingly clashed with Marx's.

Proudhon had written to Marx that he awaited "the lash of your criticism." As Marx put it in a letter to Schweitzer in 1865, "this [Marx's criticism] soon fell upon him in my *Misère de la philosophie,* etc. [*Poverty of Philosophy*] in a fashion which ended our friendship forever." [8] Proudhon envisioned a new society in which individuals could exchange their products without becoming victims of usury. In other words, he took the form of commodity exchange under capitalism, an apparent exchange of equal values, and made it his criterion of justice (he would later define justice as "social order established on a system of free transactions and reciprocal guarantees").[9] Then he evaluated capitalist exchange from this point of view and found it wanting. Usury represented the typical unfair or unequal exchange. Fair exchanges, Proudhon argued, occurred at cost of production, and the labor time embodied in the product determined this cost. In "Philosophy of Poverty," he called for establishing the "sincerity of exchanges" at these costs of production (or the "proportionality of values") which he would also refer to as mutualism: "Equality is produced between men by the rigorous and inflexible law of work, by the proportionality of values, by the sincerity of exchanges and the equivalence of functions; in one word, by the mathematical solution of all antagonisms." [10] But the subjective arbitrariness of the participants in exchange undermined equality. Proudhon offered the example of the advantage derived by a capitalist who employs a group of laborers (a "collective force") with productivity superior to that of any unorganized collection of workers. But the capitalist pays them only as individuals. The employer deserves a reward, Proudhon argued, for foresight in organizing

8. Karl Marx, *Poverty of Philosophy,* pp. 197, 199. In this letter, Marx also noted: "When I declared his book to be the petty-bourgeois code of socialism and proved this theoretically, Proudhon was still being branded as an extreme archrevolutionary alike by the political economists and by the socialists. That is why even later on I never joined in the outcry about his 'treachery' to the revolution. It was not his fault, that, originally misunderstood by others as well as by himself, he failed to fulfill unjustified hopes."

9. Pierre-Joseph Proudhon, *De la justice dans la révolution et dans l'église,* 1:206.

10. Proudhon, *Système des contradictions économiques ou philosophie de la misère,* 1:256.

production, but in fact he takes more than his share: "The point is to know if the sum of individual salaries paid by the entrepreneur is equivalent to the collective effect of which I speak; because if it is otherwise, Say's axiom, *Each product is worth what it costs,* would be violated." [11] Proudhon argued that monopoly by the entrepreneur perverts this collective force, robs the workers, and reduces them to misery. But like the "true socialists," Proudhon did not oppose all capitalists. He regretted that the workers identified the word "capitalist" with "idleness" and argued that profit (a "net product") stems from the abstinence of a worker-producer who chooses not to consume all of his output. [12]

Proudhon condemned the general confidence in political action of French radicalism ranging from plain republicanism to Blanqui's "dictatorship of Paris." Instead, given the "sincerity of exchanges," he argued, a new mutualist form of social association would spring up among men, and the superfluous political structure would wither away. Politics would become an inactive authority of laws. [13] Proudhon envisioned an egalitarian society, especially one composed of peasants and artisans, in which everyone would own a small piece of property and justice would represent the "balance" or reciprocity among the competing interests of the property-holding participants (this criterion would stigmatize as unjust any system that combines control of the means of production by the few with propertylessness for the many). In brief, he sought to forestall the tendency to concentration and dispossession inherent in modern capitalism.

On a practical level, Proudhon ran for representative from the Doubs in 1848, a paradoxical venture given his theoretical hostility to politics. In his campaign, Proudhon called for reconciling the principle of social reform with that of bourgeois conservatism and urged the workers to "extend your hand to your bosses" and capitalists to accept this offer of peace. [14] In 1848, Proudhon also founded a People's Bank to supply free credit. He quickly obtained a membership of over 20,000. Yet because of the competing political influence of the more collectivist Luxemburg delegates, Proudhon's ar-

---

11. Proudhon, *Philosophie de la misère,* 1:271. Proudhon, *General Idea of the Revolution in the Nineteenth Century,* p. 81.

12. Proudhon, *Philosophie de la misère,* 1:271–273.

13. Michael Oakeshott, *On Human Conduct,* p. 319, n. 1, rightly interprets Proudhon in this way.

14. Proudhon, *Confessions,* p. 187.

rest, and the failure to reach his goal of 50,000 francs in capital, Proudhon dissolved the bank a few months after its foundation.[15]

Even in "Philosophy of Poverty" itself, Proudhon's use of the criterion of equal labor times incorporated in commodities to liberate the workers and create a new social world ran into serious difficulties. As Marx argued, Ricardo had already identified the determination of value by labor time as the economic law of existing, capitalist society, "the formula of the present enslavement of the worker," not "as M. Proudhon would have it, the 'revolutionary theory of the emancipation of the proletariat.'" Marx contrasted the explanatory power of Richardo's scientific theory with Proudhon's ethical illusions:

> Ricardo establishes the truth of this formula [his theory of value] by deriving it from all economic relations, and by explaining in this way all phenomena, even those like ground rent, accumulation of capital and the relation of wages to profits, which at first sight seem to contradict it; it is precisely that which makes his doctrine a scientific system: M. Proudhon, who has rediscovered this formula of Ricardo's by quite arbitrary hypotheses, is forced thereafter to seek out isolated economic facts which he twists and falsifies to pass them off as . . . beginnings of realization of his regenerating idea.[16]

Marx then traced out how Proudhon confused two separate points: the value of the specific commodity labor and measuring the value of any commodity by the labor time embodied in it. Since Proudhon identified these two things, he argued that the worker should receive the value of his product instead of poverty wages. But as Richardo had already pointed out, the value of the worker's commodity, labor, is "the cost of subsistence of men." At this time, Marx still argued that "the natural price of labor is no other than the wage-minimum."[17] Any value of the commodities produced by the workers' "labor" above this minimum would yield profits for the capitalist. Thus the capitalist system constantly engenders, by the Ricardian law of value, riches and impoverishment, capitalists and workers.

Later, in *Capital,* Marx would make this criticism of Proudhon in a partic-

15. Stewart Edwards, ed., *Selected Writings of Pierre-Joseph Proudhon,* p. 75, n. 2. Bernard Moss, *The Origins of the French Labor Movement,* pp. 43–44. The Luxemburg Commission sought to guarantee by political means the right to work.

16. Marx, *Poverty,* pp. 49–50.

17. Ibid., pp. 50–51. Marx would later use the term "labor power" rather than "labor."

ularly penetrating way. Commodity production starts with the premise of independent property owners who exchange commodities. But as it develops, capitalism generalizes commodity production and transforms it into its opposite: production based on a vast, propertyless proletariat. The form of circulation under capitalism remains the same, an apparent exchange of equals (wages from the capitalist for labor power from the laborer); yet the capitalist extracts surplus value or unpaid labor time. Marx noted: "We may well, therefore, feel astonished at the cleverness of Proudhon, who would abolish capitalistic property by enforcing the eternal laws of property that are based on commodity production." [18]

In Marx's view, Proudhon misunderstood capitalist exploitation and reduced a characteristic feature of this system of production, its regular engendering of profit, to mere individual acts of swindling. Ricardian socialists like Bray and Hodgskin and French radicals from Proudhon to Blanqui had all adopted this inaccurate conception of exploitation which had its origin in the Aristotelian and Catholic critique of usury. Marx would comment sarcastically in *Capital*:

> What opinion should we have of a chemist, who instead of studying the actual laws of the molecular changes in the composition and decomposition of matter and on that foundation solving definite problems, claimed to regulate the composition and decomposition of matter by means of the eternal ideas of *'naturalité'* and *'affinité'*? [19]

Proudhon sustained his immanent conception of justice by the circularity of his moral intuitions: "I derive the laws of my understanding from the dictates of my conscience; in my conscience I find sanctions for my opinions and proof of my certainty." Where his conscience did not seem a sufficient guide, Proudhon sometimes played ventriloquist and allowed "the impersonal reason of humanity" or a fantastic Prometheus to propose some economic category vital to Proudhon's argument.[20] Just as theologians hailed Christian revelation as "divine" and stigmatized all other religions as "heathen," so Proudhon and the classical economists found commodity production "natural" and dismissed all other forms as "artificial." Proudhon took

18. Marx, *Capital*, 1:587, n. 1.
19. Ibid., 1:84, n. 1.
20. Proudhon, *De la justice*, 4:492–493.

over the egalitarian appearance of commodity exchange and hoped for a restoration of its "natural basis" in independent artisans. Similarly, he adopted the prevailing views on the subordinate status of women and extolled their exclusion from public life.[21]

In an inadvertent parody, Proudhon had appropriated Hegel's dialectics not to exemplify but to stifle conflict. His "Philosophy of Poverty" stated the advantages and drawbacks of the categories of existing political economy (division of labor, competition, monopoly, and the like), their "good side" and their "bad side." Proudhon saw the negative side only as a "problem" that the "impersonal reason of humanity" must peacefully resolve either by eliminating it or by jumping to a new set of categories to complete "a serial relation in the understanding." For Marx, Proudhon's method of reasoning had "nothing of Hegel's dialectics but the language. For him the dialectic movement is the dogmatic distinction between good and bad." Hegelian (and Marxian) dialectics proceed through the struggle of opposites which results in a qualitative break or metamorphosis. Proudhon's dialectics gloss over this struggle and transformation. As Marx noted, it is always the bad side that in the end triumphs over the good side. "It is the bad side that produces the movement which makes history." [22]

Feudalism generated a bad side, the capitalist mode of production, which overthrew it; capitalism in turn produces an impoverished working class. Marx viewed science as the analysis and fostering of the proletariat's development as a revolutionary force:

So long as they [utopians] look for science and merely make systems, so long as they are at the beginning of the struggle, they see in poverty nothing but poverty, without seeing in it the revolutionary subversive side, which will overthrow the old society. From this moment [when theorists grasp the subversive side], science, which is a product of the historical movement, has associated itself consciously with it, has ceased to be doctrinaire and has become revolutionary.[23]

---

21. In ibid., 4:278, Proudhon asserted that "by refusing the woman equality ["isonomie"– the Greek term for ruling and being ruled in turn], society does her no wrong; it treats her according to her aptitudes and prerogatives. In the political and economic order, the woman truly has nothing to do; her role only begins beyond [these orders]." See also Jacques Freymond, ed., La Première International, 1:76.

22. Marx, Poverty, pp. 112, 121.

23. Ibid., pp. 125–126.

Unlike those who attempted to refashion society according to dogmatic standards, Marx always emphasized the "practical" or spontaneous character of the workers' movement. Proudhon's mutualism, "true socialism's" love, Weitling's trio of experts, and later Lassalle's cooperative production based on Prussian state aid and Bakunin's equalization of classes all skirted or opposed this class struggle springing from capitalism itself. Yet Marx's general formulations on the "real movement" frequently neglected two features of his theory and strategy. Within this real movement, leaders already existed who sought to dull its energy and reconcile it with the existing system (in 1848, the Frankfurt parliamentarians would compromise with the monarchy, and many German democrats would shun the Paris June insurrection). Only the propagation of internationalist and socialist politics and the emergence of revolutionary leadership with a serious following among the masses could defeat these conservative leaders. Furthermore, a process of "practical-critical" activity always characterized Marx's politics; the real movement had to learn from its experiences and defeats.[24] As in several formulations of his general theory, Marx's argument against Proudhon stressed the objective process of class conflict and played down his strategy's distinctive political character. He thus left open an interpretation of his general theory that de-emphasized or excluded politics. Only a close study of the connection between Marx's theory and activity can reveal the exact bearing of such broad theoretical statements.

In *Poverty of Philosophy,* Marx traced the general role of strikes and working-class politics in forging a revolutionary movement. Proudhon had argued that increases in wages would result in increases in prices, in lessened demand, and finally, in diminished production and scarcity of goods. For him, unions and strikes would harm production without bettering the workers' conditions:

> Every upward movement in wages can have no other effect than a rise in the price of corn, wine, etc., that is, the effect of a dearth . . . to double wages . . . is to attribute to each one of the producers a greater share than his product, which is contradictory, and if the rise extends only to a small number of industries, it brings about a general disturbance in exchange; in a word, a dearth. . . . It is impossible, I declare, for strikes followed by an

24. Marx, *EB, MESW,* 1:250–251.

increase in wages not to culminate in a *general rise in prices;* this is as certain as that two and two make four.[25]

Marx responded, "We deny all these assertions, except that two and two make four." First, if the price of goods doubles at the same time as wages, real wages do not change; the rise in prices does not lead to dearth. Second, under competitive conditions, a general rise in wages would result in lower profits, but not in a change of prices. In those industries with a higher ratio of machinery to labor, which would temporarily make higher profits, new firms would move in, output would increase, and prices would fall until the rate of profit returned to normal.

In "Philosophy of Poverty," Proudhon condemned strikes as antisocial and unjust: "A workers' strike is *illegal,* and it is not only the Penal Code that says so, it is the economic system, the necessity of the established order . . . that workers should undertake by combination to do violence to monopoly, is something society cannot permit." [26] In *Idée générale de la révolution au XIXe siècle (General Idea of the Revolution in the Nineteenth Century),* Proudhon also argued: "It [association] is equally opposed to the advantageous use of labor and to the liberty of the workman." [27] As Marx pointed out, however, the development of modern industry itself continually "calls forth and strengthens" the association of workers and leads to organization and strikes; Marx rightly predicted that workers would ultimately force capitalism to legalize unions.

In Proudhon's *Capacité politique des classes ouvrières* (Political Capacity of the Working Classes), he even justified the French government's shooting down of striking miners:

To apply force against the employers and landowners, to disorganize the workshops, to stop work, to threaten capital really means to conspire to cause *general ruin.* For the authorities who shot down the miners in *Rive-de-Gier,* it was a great misfortune. But here the authorities acted like ancient Brutus, who had to choose between fatherly love and his duty as consul; it was neces-

25. Marx cited Proudhon in *Poverty,* p. 166.
26. Marx cited Proudhon in ibid., p. 170.
27. Proudhon, *General Idea,* p. 85. Proudhon, *De la capacité politique des classes ouvrières,* p. 388.

sary to sacrifice his children in order to save the republic. Brutus did not hesi-
tate, and the generation that followed did not dare to condemn him for it.[28]

Of the many paradoxes in Proudhon, the combination, as Lozovsky suggests,
of asserting on the one hand "property is theft" and on the other "shoot
down the miners" is the strangest. Marx in his "Indifference to Politics"
(1873), would satirize Proudhon's assimilation of bourgeois graspingness to
republican selflessness: "As long as the proletariat has existed, one cannot
recall a single case of a bourgeois having hesitated to sacrifice his workers to
save his own interests. What Brutuses the bourgeois are!" [29] Some accounts
of Marx that acknowledge his political activity, like those of Hammen,
Ryazanov, and Lewis, omit any discussion of Proudhon's antipathy to strikes
and miss one of the great issues in the debate between Marx, defender of the
new working-class movement, and most European radicals into the later
1860s.[30]

Proudhon and later Proudhonists in the IWA used these same arguments
to oppose the struggle for shorter hours and all political activity stemming
from the "veritable civil war" between capital and labor. Against them, Marx
insisted that until the abolition of classes, political revolution would mark
each step of social evolution. Echoing George Sand, the final words of social
science would remain: *"Le combat ou la mort; la lutte sanguinaire ou le néant.
C'est ainsi que la question est invinciblement posée."* [31]

5–3. Proudhon's Analysis of European Politics

MARX DIFFERED WITH PROUDHON not only about the nature of social theory
and the general strategy and consequences of working-class revolt; his estimate of the contemporary European situation opposed Proudhon's at every
turn. Proudhon hoped to reverse the course of modern history. In his
Carnets, he condemned the English as the main enemy not only of the French
but of all workers. This "gigantic power" embraced the globe, spreading the
"canker of pauperism" everywhere. Until the dawning of the new mutualist

---

28. Proudhon, *De la capacité,* pp. 377–380, 384–385.

29. A. Lozovsky, *Marx and the Trade Unions,* p. 31. Marx, Engels, Lenin, *Anarchism and Anarchosyndicalism,* p. 98.

30. Hammen, *Red '48ers,* pp. 144–148. David Ryazanoff, *Karl Marx and Friedrich Engels,* pp. 81–85. John Lewis, *The Life and Teaching of Karl Marx,* pp. 91–95.

31. Marx, *Poverty,* pp. 173–175. Freymond, *Première International,* 1:382.

age, Proudhon advocated the alliance of "second order" powers (France, Belgium, Switzerland, Italy, Portugal, Spain, Prussia) against English competition. Even the tsar could help. "In this regard, never show hostility to this [the Russian] government," Proudhon wrote to himself, "make common cause with it against England." Contrary to Marx, Proudhon sought to strengthen the precapitalist powers against capitalism.[32]

Ignoring the oppressiveness of slavery and serfdom, Proudhon also endorsed such systems as appropriate tutors for "inferior races." Where Marx, Engels, and other European democrats identified with the struggle for Polish independence, Proudhon regarded the tsar as necessary for "the education of Poland." Where most radicals defended abolitionism in North America, Proudhon contemptuously dismissed the "vulgar opinion that takes no account of the difference of races." In a manner parallel to the English gentry's anticapitalism in the early nineteenth century, or that of the slaveholders before the American Civil War, Proudhon criticized English factory owners: "One complains that servile labor is unproductive—enfranchise your workers, then, you miserable hypocrites." [33]

Proudhon had no well defined or effective political strategy. At times he would emphasize the spontaneity of an apolitical, social movement for free credit; at other times, for instance, when faced with the victory of reaction in 1851, he would look to the second Napoleon to institute social reform through dictatorial means. Paradoxically, Proudhon's anarchism resisted capitalist authoritarianism far less vigorously than Marx's communist vision that the workers must emancipate themselves.[34]

Some writers have taken Proudhon's dislike of Marx as an indication of Marx's spleenful character. In his letter of 1846, Proudhon had insisted on a "tolerant" radical movement that might encompass all views. (These writers neglect Proudhon's muttering in his *Carnets: "La Révolution, c'est moi.* If 35 million men offend me, I will not pardon them—I will be better than 35 million men.") Stung by Marx's criticism, and disdaining to provide a serious reply, Proudhon interpreted Marx simply as a Jew:

> Write an article against this race which poisons everything. . . . Demand its
> expulsion from France except individuals married to French citizens. . . . It

---

32. Proudhon, *Carnets,* 2:19, 183–184.
33. Ibid., 2:81, 184.
34. Edwards, ed., *Selected Writings,* p. 166, n. 58.

is not for nothing that Christians have called them murderers of God. The Jew is the enemy of the human race. It is necessary to send this race back to Asia or exterminate it.

H. Heine, A. Weil, and others are only secret spies; Rothschild, Crémieux, Marx, Fould, mischievous beings, spiteful, envious, bitter, etc., etc., who hate us.[35]

Except from a racist standpoint, Proudhon's analysis of Heine, Marx, and the rest lacks credibility. The psychological reductionists have not always scrutinized their "more tolerant" sources. Whether or not Marx would have made a jolly dinner companion, the standard indictment of Marx's character obscures the fundamental theoretical and political issues that divided Marx from many radicals of the 1840s.

Though Marx wrote *Poverty of Philosophy* in French, these novel ideas had a limited impact in a France that was industrializing slowly.[36] Proudhon's conceptions would continue to influence the French radical movement through the IWA and the Paris Commune. But Marx aimed to found a strong movement of the future, not to curry immediate favor. Though he did not foresee the time or difficulty involved before his strategy would gain acceptance, he could look forward to the further unfolding of capitalism and to vigorous political organizing to forge a working-class movement. If the upcoming democratic conflicts led to socialism, well and good; he would drive them forward as rapidly as possible. If not, he already had a firm perspective for future action.

35. Proudhon, *Carnets*, 3:39–40; 2:337–338. Hal Draper's useful article, "A Note on the Father of Anarchism," exaggerates a connection between Proudhon's unpublished notes and Nazism.

36. Blanqui and his followers read *Poverty of Philosophy* and liked its emphasis on revolutionary politics but never agreed with Marx about the real movement. Bernstein, *Auguste Blanqui and the Art of Insurrection*, pp. 144, 301–302.

— VI —

Philosophy and the Proletariat:
A Dual Path

6–1. Feuerbach's Anthropology and
Communism

THOUGH MARX HAD BEGUN to win over the London leaders and secure some following in Paris, he had to contend with a major opposed radical trend in Germany, "true socialism," which looked to a transformed, "human" monarchy to eliminate poverty. Like Marxism, "true socialism" had emerged from Feuerbach's critique of Hegel. The first formulations of philosophical communism paralleled each other in Hess and Marx, and at times their paths seemed to join. "True socialism" took off from Hess; it influenced Kriege, the London leaders, and even some of Engels's formulations in *The Condition of the Working Class in England.* Much recent scholarship on Marx's early writings, stressing his humanist critique of alienation, has fastened on what these two views had in common. Yet these two socialisms found themselves by and large on opposite sides of the barricades in the democratic revolution of 1848. From 1845 on, Marx undertook a major political campaign to defeat this opposing view.

Hegel's philosophy criticized abstract conceptions of the relationship between human consciousness and the world. Starting with an examination of "sense-certainty" in his *Phenomenology of Spirit* (1807), Hegel discovered that all attempts to point out the "here and now" could not get beyond the bare universals of language. As day changes to night, this "here and now" suddenly gives way to a different one. Thus, all "here and nows" were equally distant from the fully grasped richness of a particular reality. Through a dialectical investigation of successive modes of consciousness and their relation to the world, Hegel arrived at a comprehensive self-consciousness or absolute knowledge, which claimed to discern an objective reason at work in the particulars of the modern state, art, and religion.

Starting as a Hegelian, Feuerbach eventually refused to take the very first step of the *Phenomenology of Spirit.* He criticized Hegel for leaping away too quickly from the immediate "here" into thought:

> The "here" of [Hegel's] *Phenomenology* is in no way different from another "here" because it is actually general. But the real "here" is distinguished from another "here" in a real way; it is an exclusive "here." "This 'here' is, for example, a tree. I turn around and this truth has disappeared" [says Hegel]. This can, of course, happen in the *Phenomenology* where turning around costs nothing but a little word. But, in reality, where I must turn my ponderous body around, the "here" proves to be a very real thing even behind my back.[1]

In effect, Feuerbach agreed with Hegel that the real tree, the particular, escaped the universal. But Feuerbach founded his own philosophy in trying to stick with this material particular; he regarded any universal concepts in religion or metaphysics as ideal projections (this insistence created serious difficulties for his conception of a general human nature). As Marx Wartofsky has properly stressed, Feuerbach's *Essence of Christianity* attacked the alienation of human capacities not only in theology but in philosophy and language as well. For Feuerbach, "all determinations of the Divine Being are, therefore, determinations of the being of man." Theological abstractions, the alleged "actions" of God, simply inverted subject and predicate:

> Because the positive and essential basis of the conception or determination of God can only be human, the conception of man as an object of consciousness can only be negative, that is, hostile to man. In order to enrich God, man must become poor; that God may be all, man must be nothing. But he also does not need to be anything for himself, because everything . . . he takes from himself is not lost, but preserved in God.[2]

Acting and dreaming men created God in their own image. *Essence* offered a psychological as opposed to a historical critique of Christianity and argued, for example, that an imaginary divine love derived from the frustrations of human love: "The more an ideal, imagined woman was the object of their real love [the Virgin Mary for monks], the more easily could they dispense

1. Ludwig Feuerbach, *Towards a Critique of Hegel's Philosophy* in Zawar Hanfi, ed., *The Fiery Brook: Selected Writings of Ludwig Feuerbach*, p. 78.

2. Feuerbach, "Introduction to the *Essence of Christianity*" in Hanfi, ed., *Fiery Brook*, pp. 111, 124. See also Feuerbach, *Principles of the Philosophy of the Future* in Hanfi, ed., *Fiery Brook*, pp. 188–189.

with woman in flesh and blood." [3] This concept of the projection or alienation of human capacities in religion inspired Marx and Engels as well as
Hess. Furthermore, Feuerbach argued, Hegelian or "speculative philosophy"
also "transforms the passive attributes [of God] into active ones—the entire
being of God into action, which, however, is . . . human action." Objective reason did not drive history forward or even reveal itself in an unin-
tended pattern of human action; human action gave rise to any pattern that
appeared. Thus, Feuerbach resolved religion and the old philosophy into anthropology, into human social (or "species") practice, and called for a new
materialist philosophy. He sardonically underlined the weakness in the old
idealism (even objective idealism), which exhausted reality and reached its
final stage in the philosopher's mind:

> The maxim of all hitherto existing speculative philosophy, "All that is mine I
> carry with me," . . . I unfortunately cannot apply to myself. There are so
> many things *outside myself* that I can carry neither in my pocket nor in my
> head, and yet I must look upon them as belonging to me; that is, belonging
> to me not as an ordinary human being—with him we are not concerned in the
> present context—but as a philosopher.[4]

Feuerbach's critique moved cautiously from metaphysics and religion to
politics. The Protestant, Feuerbach said, discerns in the pope or the king "a
man just like me" and strives to create a religious republic. Feuerbach criticized this alien, heavenly republic, and looked instead to political republicanism: "In the Christian religion, you have your *republic in the sky:* which is
why you need no real one on *earth.* On the contrary, you must be a slave on
earth so that heaven will not be superfluous." [5] His *Lectures on the Essence of
Religion* aimed to transform "theologians into anthropologists . . . candidates for the next world into students of this world, religious and political
flunkeys of heavenly and earthly monarchs and lords into free and self-reliant
citizens of the earth." [6] Contrary to Hegel, a monarchy coexisting with a
competitive and selfish civil society could not unite the Greek ethical universality and the spirit of individuality brought into the world by Christianity.

3. Feuerbach, "Introduction" in Hanfi, ed., *Fiery Brook,* p. 124.
4. Feuerbach, "Preface to the Second Edition of the *Essence of Christianity*" in Hanfi, ed.,
Fiery Brook, pp. 252–254.
5. Feuerbach, *Notwendigkeit einer Veränderung* in Feuerbach, *Kleine Schriften,* p. 235.
6. Feuerbach, *Lectures on the Essence of Religion,* p. 23.

Self-reliant and nonobsequious citizens must live in a republic. Marx's early conception of citizenship adopted Feuerbach's critique of an animallike, enslaved world of inequality, sanctified by religion. In Marx's "Introduction to a *Critique of Hegel's Philosophy of Right*," he concurred with Feuerbach's principle that "man is the highest being for man" and envisioned a "categorical imperative to overthrow all conditions in which man is a debased, forsaken, contemptible being, forced into servitude, conditions which cannot be better portrayed than in the exclamation of a Frenchman at hearing of a projected tax on dogs: Poor dogs! They want to treat you like men." [7]

Feuerbach often mentioned the caution imposed on German philosophy by the Prussian censor. The nonexistent "German liberty of science . . . stretch[ed] just up to the truth," he noted sarcastically. It paralleled German liberty of navigation which extended "just up to the sea." Under the monarchy, when science comprehended and expressed the truth, it became "an object for the police." [8] Despite Feuerbach's continuing hopes of receiving a professorship, he gradually went further than republicanism and called for a unity of the human species: communism. Though he praised Weitling's social critique of republicanism in "Guarantees," he never examined the obstacles to such a community in any detail.

In 1844 in a letter to Feuerbach, Marx hailed the *Principles of the Philosophy of the Future* and the *Lectures on the Essence of Religion* as the most significant works of contemporary German literature. For radicals, Marx suggested, these books provided "a philosophical basis for socialism." Marx summarized Feuerbach's fundamental contribution to this new movement's conception of the human species, composed of what Marx would later call "social individuals": "The unity of man with man, which is based on the real differences between men, the concept of the human species brought down from the heaven of abstraction to the real earth, what is this but the concept of society?" [9] Following Hegel and to a lesser extent Aristotle as well as Feuerbach, Marx conceived man as a political animal, that is, as one who can only individualize him (or her) self in his relations with others. An exploitative society, one characterized by great inequalities, could not provide a basis for true individuality for most of its members; it would suppress many of the

7. Marx, *Writings of the Young Marx*, pp. 257–258.
8. Feuerbach, "Preface" in Hanfi, ed., *Fiery Brook*, p. 249.
9. *CW*, 3:354. Marx, *Grundrisse*, p. 84.

"real differences" among human beings through their subordination to an oppressive or alienated work process. The concept of a human species, rightly understood, pointed toward communism.

Yet Feuerbach never reexamined history nor propounded even a broad analysis of how a communist society might function. Instead he strove to comprehend the psychological and sometimes the physiological basis of static human relationships. As Engels later pointed out, Feuerbach's critique of idealism stripped away the conceptual richness of Hegel's interpretation of history and left a thin reductionist psychological (and in a weak moment digestive—"man is what he eats") view of society.[10]

Feuerbach's analysis of community never transcended an emphasis on love and feeling. In his *Principles of the Philosophy of the Future* (1843), Feuerbach argued:

> Only in feeling and love has the demonstrative *this*—this person, this thing, that is, the particular—absolute value. . . . In this and this alone does the infinite depth, divinity and truth of love consist. . . . The Christian God himself is only an abstraction from human love and an image of it. . . . Love is passion, and passion alone is the distinctive mark of existence.[11]

Unlike Hegel, who in Feuerbach's view canceled in his *Logic* the difference between being and thought, Feuerbach insisted on love as the essential expression of the need for a being outside oneself and cast the prototypical species relationship in a sexual idiom: "Two human beings are needed for the generation of man—of the spiritual as well as the physical man; the community of man with man is the first principle and criterion of truth and generality." For the old idealism, "that which is not thought does not exist"; for the new materialism, "that which is not loved . . . does not exist." [12] Far from overturning the old philosophy's categories, however, Feuerbach's apotheosis of love retained the vision of an active, idealist, and manly Ger-

---

10. Engels, "Ludwig Feuerbach and the End of Classical German Philosophy" in *MESW*, 2:385. Marx Wartofsky, *Feuerbach*, pp. 411–417, 152–159. Feuerbach had previously provided a sophisticated criticism of Dorguth's crude reductionist materialism.

11. Feuerbach, *Philosophy of the Future* in Hanfi, ed., *Fiery Brook*, p. 225.

12. Ibid., pp. 231–232, 227.

man theory (the head) and a passionate, feminine, materialist French practice (the heart).[13]

Aiming toward an epochal philosophy, a philosophy expressing and transforming the current condition of men, Feuerbach ironically claimed that only one vestige of idealism clung to his conception of practical philosophy. Against those who sought to restrict humanity by its past and present, Feuerbach contended that many things that now "appear to myopic and timorous men as dreams, as unrealizable ideas, as pure chimeras, would come to exist in the future." [14] Feuerbach's critique of alienation and his increasing political boldness pointed toward Marx. Yet he never transcended this vague communism or the bare assertion that the future would bring the political victory of "truth and virtue." His sentimental celebration of love flowed easily into "true socialism."

6–2. Hess: Marx's Materialism and Love

Moses Hess, the main philosophical founder of "true socialism," extended Feuerbach's critique of alienation to political republicanism and to money. As Babeuf had foreseen, the French Revolution had foundered on the continued social hierarchy of master and servant. For Hess, the similarities between the older feudal or slave regimes and the modern democratic one outweighed the differences. Following Proudhon, he contended that the people merely aped the king and priests—democracy enthroned the arbitrariness and selfishness of many individuals rather than replacing these destructive qualities with genuine community. At times, Hess seemed to consider older societies preferable to a capitalist one. He distinguished slavery as a "natural form of robbery and murder" from the "unnatural" and "inhuman" character of modern commerce. Hunger drove men to submit to this contemporary, alien domination of money. The essence of this new "shopkeeper's world"—neediness, isolation of each man from his fellow men, deprivation of all man's capacities, universal servitude to money—belied its appearance of independence, security of individual property, and freedom. As a remedy for

13. Feuerbach, *Preliminary Theses on the Reform of Philosophy* in Hanfi, ed., *Fiery Brook*, pp. 164–165. Engels, "Feuerbach" in *The German Ideology*, p. 660. As Wartofsky properly stresses, Feuerbach's own philosophy never matched his astute dialectical critique of previous philosophies.

14. Feuerbach, "Preface" in Hanfi, ed., *Fiery Brook*, p. 252. Feuerbach, *Notwendigkeit* in *Kleine Schriften*, p. 220.

these practical deficiences in modern democracy and capitalism, the greatest democrat, Robespierre, had wrongly conjured up a supreme being.[15]

Unlike the French communists, however, Hess condemned not only the domination of rich over poor but any form of social hierarchy or leadership. Hess criticized Saint-Simon's faith in a scientific hierarchy that merely mimicked the existing one. Only Proudhon's attack on authority itself and on politics represented the true French counterpart to German philosophical atheism. Heine had drawn an analogy between definite phases of the French Revolution and German philosophy: Robespierre and Kant, Napoleon and Fichte, the Restoration and Schelling, the July Revolution and Hegel. Though he partially agreed with Heine, Hess discerned a closer relation between a German trend toward atheism in speculative philosophy and a French trend toward communism in social philosophy. He linked somewhat curiously Fichte and Babeuf, Schelling and Saint-Simon, and Hegel and Fourier.[16] (Heine and Hess prefigured Marx's dictum that Germany had experienced modern political history only in thought.) Following Feuerbach, Hess insisted that "the time has come for the philosophy of spirit to become the philosophy of action."[17] A new movement would fuse German theory (Feuerbach and Hess) and French practice (Proudhon).

Hess sought the simultaneous abolition of all dualisms, of the domination of state, religion, and money over men. Given this aim, democratic revolution meant merely the elevation of money, and Hess opposed it. Instead, he advocated a kind of moralism in which a cursory social and political analysis pivoted around abstract demands for justice and the realization of "humanity" and love. He called upon all classes to adhere to these values. Only a direct communist movement could substitute a society based on love for the current egotistical one. In 1844, Engels, still under Hess's influence, wrote enthusiastically to the Chartist *New Moral World* of the spread of communism in Elberfeld among the well-to-do. Judging from the sizable meetings, communism had emerged as a real force there, though, Engels noted regretfully, no workers had attended.[18]

15. Moses Hess, *Philosophie der That, Über das Geldwesen,* and *Kommunistisches Bekenntniss in Fragen und Antworten* in Auguste Cornu and Wolfgang Mönke, ed., *Moses Hess, Philosophische und Sozialistische Schriften 1837–1850,* pp. 216–218, 336–337, 344, 366.

16. Hess, *Philosophie* and *Socialismus und Communismus* in Cornu and Mönke, eds., *Moses Hess,* pp. 217–218, 199–200.

17. Ibid., p. 219.

18. *CW,* 4:230–231, 238.

Hess's vision of a direct communist uprising prefigured Marx's "Introduction" of 1843; Hess, however, did not foresee Marx's focus on the proletariat, that "class with radical chains." In 1843–1844, Marx applied the concept of alienation to the categories of English political economy. He directed his analysis at capitalism as a specific social formation rather than restricting himself, as Hess had, to a more abstract, transhistorical critique of money and commerce. Within the philosophical framework of Feuerbach and Hess, Marx moved as far as possible toward isolating the labor process and distinct modes of production as the foundation of other social activities.

When Marx and Engels first conceived the new historical materialist theory, they enlisted Hess's peripheral collaboration on *The German Ideology*. In his contribution to this book, Hess vituperated against the "true socialist" Kühlmann who had "painted the transition from present social isolation to communal life in truly idyllic colors." Kühlmann had substituted a process of peaceful, quasi-religious conversion for the "terrible social upheaval" of the real movement. Against this "prophet," Hess, influenced by Marx and Engels, insisted on the need to "take up the *real* sword and hazard one's *real* life" in the political battle for socialism. On July 28, 1846, Hess wrote to Marx that he eagerly awaited Marx's new theoretical work. At first, communist ideas had flowed from German philosophy; any further advance, however, depended on the analysis of "historical and economic prerequisites." [19]

At this time, Hess had seemingly drawn close to Marx's position. Yet despite his participation in the Communist League, Hess retained his earlier moralistic conception of socialism. In 1847, in a first draft for what became the *Communist Manifesto*, Hess, following Marx, distinguished forced labor under capitalism from human labor resulting from an inner need. In this communist "Catechism," however, Hess omitted politics and strategy. He concluded not with a call to action but with a paean to human love as the newly deciphered foundation of religion.

> 67. Is God in heaven anything besides love?
>   No, nothing else.
> 68. What comes from love?
>   The entire creation or the cosmos, which, like love, is eternal, infinite, immeasureable . . .

19. *GI*, p. 538. Hess, *Briefwechsel*, p. 165.

70. What is life?
    Love itself, which unites everything and makes everything capable of begetting.[20]

Hess, who engendered "true socialism," did not adopt Marx's strategy of communist participation in the democratic revolution. Though Hess flirted with Marx's general materialist theory of history, he never transformed his earlier German philosophical framework. Where Hess projected broad philosophical concepts and hopes, Marx applied his new theory to particular German circumstances and discerned the conditions under which masses of working people might adopt communism.

While Hess himself did not strongly oppose the democratic movement, a new socialism, spreading rapidly among German intellectuals, suddenly discovered redeeming features in a "human" monarchy. Karl Grün, a follower of Hess, indicted the formal freedom of representative government under capitalism and supported the king:

> We *never* had the political freedom that France and Belgium possess. But when *Fichte* and *Hegel* can teach in Berlin . . . when Goethe can be minister in Weimar . . . when Feuerbach can destroy Christianity without being banned by any conclave or synod and live peacefully in the kingdom of Bavaria, look, that is *human* freedom.[21]

The predominantly "true socialist" *Triersche Zeitung* also celebrated the feudal monarchy as a more genuine precursor of socialism than the money economy and representative government. After the Saxon army bloodily suppressed democratic demonstrations in 1845, the "true socialist" Semmig recalled the French July Revolution of 1830, which had merely set a bourgeois monarch, Louis Philippe, on the throne, and warned the workers away from political action: "You, the poor, workers . . . who formerly let yourselves be set in motion and seduced into riots by the liberal bourgeoisie (remember 1830), take care! Do not support their strivings and struggles which yield profit only for them . . . before all else, never take part in *political*

---

20. Hess, *Bekenntniss* in Cornu and Mönke, eds., *Moses Hess*, p. 367.
21. Förder, *Marx und Engels*, p. 147, n. 20.

revolutions." [22] Urging proletarian passivity, the "true socialists" embroidered the monarch's shooting down of democrats with rhetorical flowers of humanity, community, and love.

Between 1845 and 1848, Marx and Engels changed the thrust of their attack on the "true socialists." In *The German Ideology,* they (and Hess) criticized the "true socialists' " preference for monarchy and sentimental glossing over of class struggle from the point of view of immediate communist revolution. After 1845, and particularly in the *Manifesto,* they concentrated their fire on "true socialism's" opposition to the democratic revolution.

According to *The German Ideology,* the "true socialists" began their analysis not from class struggle and the antagonistic social structure that spawns it, but from ideals of humanity and love. The "true socialists" condemned the usurer, but not the large owner of the means of production; they hoped to restore the "true property" of artisans and shopkeepers. As they had no clear conception of capitalist social relationships, their justification of small property could easily slide into an apology for industrial capitalism. Though "true socialists" regarded the monarchy as "human," they disdained French working-class communism as "crude" and "narrow." Instead of a class interest, they eulogized the "eternal" cause of "humanity": "The very name of communism, the contrary of competition, reveals its one-sidedness; but is this bias, which may *very well* have value *now* as a party name, to *last for ever?*" [23]

Marx contended, on the contrary, that the "true socialists" could not exorcise the fierce class collisions in France by chanting magical phrases about humanity and love. He likened them to the naive "honest" fellow, who believed that men drown only because the nefarious idea of gravity holds them in its spell. Banish this conception, the fellow thought, and all will be well. This fellow saw a real problem—actual drownings provided fresh empirical evidence daily to feed his concern.[24] Like the "true socialists," however, he adopted an eccentric solution—the banishing of reality and of science.

For Marx, the "true socialists' " "human" condescension toward French communism turned into pompous, philistine patriotism. He invoked Heine's merciless satire:

22. Ibid., pp. 147, n. 21, 154.
23. *GI,* p. 462.
24. Ibid., p. 24.

Swim not, brothers, against the stream,
That's only a useless thing!
Let us climb up to Templow Hill
And cry: God save the King![25]

Seeing the proletariat not only as a suffering class but as a revolutionary one, Marx rejected the appeals to the goodwill and higher interests of all mankind, including the exploiters, which in differing ways characterized the "true socialists," Weitling, and Proudhon. When Rudolph Matthäi poetically conjured up the biblical lilies of the field as an emblem of a future, untroubled human existence, Marx mused: "Yes, consider the lilies of the field, how they are eaten by goats, transplanted by 'Man' into his buttonhole, how they are crushed beneath the immodest embraces of the dairy-maid and the donkey driver!" [26] For Marx, communism could only emerge dialectically through class struggle, and he aimed to sweep aside "all phrases" that hushed up this antagonism.

So far, Hess might have agreed with Marx. As Marx forged his new strategy for German democracy, however, he saw more clearly the irony of this ghostly "German" translation of vibrant French revolutionary experience. According to Marx, the German petite bourgeoisie had "shuddered" at the political energy of the original French revolutionaries. Kant's moral philosophy offered a transcendental, politically futile interpretation of the interests and powers that had impelled this great revolutionary movement. Though French communism now haunted the European regimes, the "true socialists" had fashioned a far tamer, more ineffectual, and incoherent ideal spook:

To the absolute governments with their following of parsons, professors, country squires and officials, it [the "true socialist" criticism of democracy] served as a welcome scarecrow against the threatening bourgeoisie.

It was a sweet finish after the bitter pills of floggings and bullets with which these same governments just at that time, dosed the German working class risings.[27]

25. Ibid., p. 467.
26. Ibid., p. 472.
27. *CM*, pp. 58–59.

In 1848, Marx would attempt to drive the democratic revolution to destroy absolutism utterly. Correspondingly, the "true socialists" decried even the bourgeoisie's limited revolutionary actions and defended the monarchy. This practical division between Marxian communism and one form of socialism demonstrates that seemingly small differences in viewpoint can often grow into profound antagonisms during actual political conflicts. From the beginning, Marx saw this link between theory and practice and its consequence, the need for rigorous political demarcation or disunity among radicals. A consistent struggle against those sects that opposed the real movement or those radicals who failed to advocate internationalism within it, characterized Marx's politics throughout his career.[28]

Hess himself had great respect for Marx, and saw the possible abuse in the "true socialists' " espousal of Hess's point of view. After 1845, he eschewed the older philosophical phrases and turned more decisively toward Marx's materialism to replace his earlier humanism. In 1847, he criticized the eclecticism of Proudhon's "dialetical" rephrasing of classical economics. Instead of producing real oppositions, he asserted, Proudhon simply "fell between two stools." In 1847 in his "Die Folgen einer Revolution des Proletariats" (Consequences of a Proletarian Revolution), Hess offered a nearly Marxian formulation:

> A revolution of the proletariat . . . presupposes a struggle not only about abstract principles but about immediate and tangible interests . . . presupposes that the very existence of the great majority of workers is threatened, that these workers know who the enemy is they have to fight and that they have the means in their own hands to vanquish him.[29]

Foreshadowing the *Manifesto,* Hess stressed the role of foreign trade, the development of large-scale industry which "must" reach a "peak," and the inevitability of crises caused by overproduction. These economic conditions would impel the workers to make revolution. So far, as Hook and Lichtheim emphasize, he concurred with Marx's general theory. Unlike Marx in 1847,

28. As Marx wrote to Bolte on November 23, 1871, "The International was founded in order to replace the socialist and semi-socialist sects by a real organization of the working class for struggle . . . the history of the International was a *continual* struggle of the General Council [led by Marx] against the sects and amateur experiments which sought to assert themselves within the international against the real movement of the working class." *SC,* p. 269. See also Engels to Bebel, June 20, 1873, ibid., pp. 283–284.

29. Cornu and Mönke, eds., *Moses Hess,* p. 430.

however, he believed not only that capitalist contradictions affected Germany and made socialism possible, but also that capitalism would drive German workers like a tidal wave to overwhelm monarchy, Junkers, and bourgeoisie together.[30] He adopted a radical economic determinist version of Marxism without sufficient exploration of German conditions. In contrast to Hess's abstract economic process culminating in crisis, Marx saw a worker-peasant alliance and the political experience of democratic revolution as prerequisites for a German proletarian revolution. In an inversion of the typical approach of the "true socialists" who scrawled abstract philosophical phrases over the real political categories of French communism, Hess wrote Marx's general materialist analysis of capitalism over his old "true socialist" philosophy, leaving the latter intact. Hess's new position strikingly reveals the insufficiency of Marx's general theory, in the absence of specific historical analysis and the appropriate auxiliary statements, as a predictor of Marx's strategy. Hess transformed Marx's general theory into its opposite, an ideal framework to which German reality must conform. It did not. In the revolution of 1848, Hess played no significant role.

Yet Hess still trailed after Marx at a distance. In his "Red Catechism" (1850), Hess finally attributed limited importance to democratic revolution as a prelude to a proletarian one, so long as the proletariat fought alongside but not for the bourgeoisie.[31] By the time he caught up to Marx's strategy in the *Manifesto,* however, the German revolution had passed him by. From the early 1840s, Marx's and Hess's paths crisscrossed in a peculiar pattern. Marx followed and then went further than Hess in analyzing alienation. Hess trailed behind Marx on materialism and never fully adopted it. Finally, Hess briefly endorsed Marx's strategy for German democratic and socialist revolution, but never appreciated the cutting edge of Marx's new historical analysis.

Contrary to Hunt's status reductionism, intellectuals like Hess and later Gottschalk and not the artisan leaders of the Communist League strongly

30. Ibid., pp. 430–431, 444. In "Consequences," Hess envisioned a direct proletarian revolution as possible only in England. He argued, however, that a shock from outside, caused by such a victory, would trigger proletarian revolution in Germany. Hook, *From Hegel to Marx,* pp. 203–205. George Lichtheim, *The Origins of Socialism,* pp. 178–183, mistakenly argues that after 1845, "if there remained a divergence [between Hess and Marx], it was philosophical rather than political."

31. Hess, *Rother Katechismus für das deutsche Volk* in Cornu and Mönke, eds., *Moses Hess,* pp. 448–450.

opposed democratic revolution. Class background at most makes individuals more rather than less likely to adopt a given standpoint among alternatives in a particular situation. In actual political conflicts within a movement, however, an individual's views (Hess's or Schapper's or Marx's for that matter) evolve in a far more complex manner, often heavily influenced by fresh experience, than this simple notion will allow.

Looking at the clash between Marx and Weitling in 1846, Hess himself fell back on a psychological explanation. Ignoring Weitling's bitter conflict with the London leaders of the League, Hess blamed Marx for Weitling's anger and confusion. "You have made him completely crazy," he wrote to Marx. Self-consciously reducing his own political and philosophical differences with Marx to a matter of style, he wrote, "You are a dissolver. I am a natural conciliator." Hess empathized with Weitling who had fallen from his lofty position as ideologue of the League. Hess formally resigned from the "Marx party," although he promised to keep up his personal relationship with Marx. He raised money for Weitling who had left Brussels in a huff. In these money matters, Weitling treated him badly. More perceptively, Hess wrote to Marx that his relationship with Weitling inverted his relationship with Marx. Personally, he considered Weitling a "low fellow" and found him repugnant; he felt bound to Weitling only by "party affairs." Hess never fully agreed with Weitling who made no gesture toward Marx's analysis of capitalism. Yet Hess hoped for a direct communist uprising. Caught in a conflict of friendships, political hopes, and theoretical positions, Hess, the "natural conciliator" as he himself put it, or the great "Konfusionarius" as Jenny Marx once nastily wrote, vacillated. He disliked precisely that atmosphere of crisp political debate that clarified differences, dispelled confusion, and resulted in common action. Contrary to the psychological reductionists, Hess found Marx likable and enlightening rather than arrogant. He simply did not agree with his strategy. Politics, not personality, provided the key to Marx's clash with Hess and Weitling as well as with other radicals. After resigning from the Brussels Correspondence Committee, Hess soon reconsidered and joined the newly formed Communist League.[32]

6–3. Historical Materialism and Alienation

In *The German Ideology* and afterward, Marx used his new materialist hypothesis to analyze the general tendencies of capitalism as well as to ferret

32. Hess to Marx, May 20, May 29, and June 5, 1846. Hess, *Briefwechsel*, pp. 155–158.

out the political alternatives in specific historical situations. These later writings no longer employed the concept of alienation in a central analytic role. Marx eschewed moralism as a pivot for social theory and sought to diminish any element in his own argument that others might use in this way.

Yet Marx continued to indict those creations of human activity such as capital (dead labor or accumulated surplus value) and the parasite state that dominated living men. Modifying the ancients, especially Aristotle, he viewed social activities done and enjoyed for their own sakes as the basis of a good or just society. His analysis of alienation and exploitation consistently illustrated this criterion for a good society by negative example. Following Shakespeare's *Timon of Athens,* Marx attacked the corrupting influence of money, that "equation of incompatibles," which enabled the rich to counterfeit the qualities they lacked:

> Gold, yellow, glittering, precious gold!
> Thus much of this, will make black white; foul fair;
> Wrong right; base noble; old young; coward valiant.
> . . . Why, this
> Will lug your priests and servants from your sides;
> Pluck stout men's pillows from below their heads;
> This yellow slave
> Will knit and break religions; bless the accurs'd;
> Make the hoar leprosy ador'd; place thieves
> And give them title.[33]

Here Marx endorsed Aristotle's notion that the ablest flute player, not the wealthiest, most beautiful, or virtuous incompetent, should get the best supply of flutes.[34]

In Marx's lectures "Wage Labor and Capital," delivered to workers in Brussels and Vienna in 1847 and 1848, he emphasized the perversion of human labor involved in the capitalist form of production. Under capitalism, working men and women conduct their activities not to create the object but merely to secure the means to exist: "What he [the worker] produces for himself is not the silk that he weaves, not the gold that he draws from the mine, not the palace that he builds." Though Marx never used the word

33. Marx, *Capital,* 1:132. Marx, *Economic and Philosophical Manuscripts of 1844* in *CW,* 3:323–324. Marx, *Grundrisse,* p. 163.

34. Aristotle, *Politics,* 1282b 30–1283a 4.

"alienation" in these lectures, he characterized this activity to the workers as "unnatural," as done for motives alien to the activity itself. To drive this point home, Marx employed an unusual metaphor: "If the silkworm were to spin in order to continue its existence as a caterpillar, it would be a complete wage worker." [35] Like silkworms who never become butterflies, the workers can never achieve their own purposes or realize their potential multiple competencies under capitalism. Thus, Marx's later arguments on abolishing the division between mental and manual labor and the emergence of "social individuals" grew out of this perspective. [36]

In subsequent writings, Marx would return to this silkworm metaphor. In *Theories of Surplus Value,* he argued that Milton produced *Paradise Lost* not for a few pounds but as an activity of his own nature, just as the silkworm spins the gaudy silk. In the *Civil War in France,* the workers who collectively took over the political arena and instituted the Commune, like Milton, carried on their activity for its own sake. [37] A new political community, aiming to abolish exploitation, inspired its own motivations for action.

Marx's descriptions of nonalienated activity drew their force by and large from examples of individual artistic activity or scientific achievement. The Commune provided Marx's first collective example. Given the absence of any practical socialist experience, Marx never fully discussed the changes that would occur in the sphere of "necessary labor" in the early stages of communism. Nonetheless, the notion of nonalienated or nonexploitative production influenced his celebration of the revolutionary class itself as the "greatest productive power." Under communism, workers would engage in productive activities more vigorously and with greater happiness. Production for social needs as well as production based on the aims of the producers themselves would increasingly supplant production for exchange. Marx's argument prefigured a fundamental (and much vexed) issue in twentieth-century communism: political understanding, based on agreed-upon collective purposes and not only material incentives, might play a vital role in the productive power of a socialist system. Without his theory of the consequences of exploitation or alienation, Marx's basic concept of "productive force" would

35. *MESW,* 1:82–83.

36. Marx, *Critique of the Gotha Program* in *MESW,* 2:24; Marx, *Grundrisse,* pp. 161–164, 325, 487–488, 540–542, 611–612, 705–706, 712, 749, 832. Marx, *Capital,* 1:431–432, 571, 573, 607, 608, 615, 618, 621.

37. Karl Marx, *Theories of Surplus Value,* p. 186. Marx and Engels, *Writings on the Paris Commune,* p. 153.

have an altogether different, much more narrowly technological and nonrevolutionary character.[38] Marx turned away from the ancient idealization of philosophy and looked to creative activities more closely linked to work. Yet an almost Aristotelian notion of activities carried on for their own sakes reverberates throughout Marx's indictment of capitalist exploitation.

As political alternatives play a vital role in historical materialism, so too, despite Marx's persistent warnings against the misuse of moral rhetoric, do conceptions of alternative orderings of human society. To be meaningful, according to Marx, such conceptions must be materially realizable given specific historical circumstances and political movements. Moral anger cannot substitute for a mainly nonmoral mode of historical explanation. But this concern over the accuracy and realizability of moral judgments does not eliminate the role of such judgments in Marx's own approach.[39]

Despite Marx's overt critique of moralism, his own theory consistently appealed to concepts loaded with at least a rough ethical argument. In a quasi-Hegelian fashion, Marx had superseded his earlier philosophical framework based on Feuerbach and Hess, and yet retained, suspended in his new one, an important component of his earlier understanding. Marx's new linking of theory and practice kept an ethical, though not a political touch with Hess's notion of the unity of philosophy and the proletariat.

38. Marx, *Capital*, 3:799–800. Marx, *Critique of the Gotha Program* in *MESW*, 2:22–24. Shaw, *Marx's Theory of History*, p. 15, misreads Marx's concept of productive force in this way.

39. See Richard W. Miller, "Aristotle and Marx: The Unity of Two Opposites." Miller, "Reason and Commitment in the Social Sciences." Alan Gilbert, "Historical Theory and the Structure of Moral Argument in Marx."

— VII —

Marx's Organizing in Brussels and Germany

7–1. Communist Correspondence and Democracy

BETWEEN 1845 AND 1847, Marx played a decisive role in the transformation of the League of the Just into the Communist League. In addition, he forged a network of activists in London, Brussels, and Germany who agreed with his point of view and would fight for it during the democratic revolution of 1848.

In Brussels, Marx engaged the Communist Correspondence Committee in many-faceted political activity, prefiguring his organizing in Cologne in 1848. Its members participated in the Brussels German Workers' Educational Society which had recruited 105 members by late 1847. Marx also involved the committee in joint activities with the Brussels Democratic Association. As a member of the Democratic Association's executive committee, Marx correspondingly encouraged it to concentrate its efforts on the Belgian working class and to uphold internationalism. As part of a democratic delegation, he journeyed to Ghent, the chief Belgian manufacturing center, to set up a branch among French-speaking workers. After a first meeting in early 1848, the Walloon organization attracted 3,000 people to its second meeting (the newly formed Communist League also initiated contact with the Walloon workers). Pursuing internationalism, the Democratic Association corresponded with the Fraternal Democrats in London and saluted the Chartists' efforts to unite English and Irish workers:

> We [the Democratic Association] have seen that there is a better chance now than ever before to break down that prejudice which prompted the Irish people to confound in one common hatred the oppressed classes of England with the oppressors of both countries. We hope to see very shortly united in the hands of Feargus O'Connor the direction both of the English and the Irish popular movement . . . and consider the approaching alliance of the op-

pressed classes of both countries, under the banner of democracy, as a most important progress of our cause in general.[1]

Marx and Engels also spoke at a Brussels democratic meeting commemorating the Cracow uprising of 1846, which demanded Polish independence, the freeing of the peasants, and the emancipation of the Jews. Russian and French conservatives had stigmatized the uprising as "communist"; Marx noted that it had sought only the abolition of the "political distinctions between classes," not the abolition of classes altogether. This political revolution might merely have issued "naturalization papers" to Polish lords in place of foreign ones: "This political change will have altered nothing in his [the peasant's] social position." Following the example of the French Revolution, the Polish movement would have to take up the "social question" and transform former serfs into free proprietors. Even in this case, however, the Polish workers and peasants would have achieved a radical democracy rather than communism.[2]

In addition to these broad activities designed to affect the mass movement, Marx worked closely with a small number of activists in the Communist Correspondence Committee: Philippe Gigot, Edgar von Westphalen, Ferdinand Wolff, Louis Heilberg, Sebastian Seiler, Georg Weerth, Joseph Weydemeyer, and especially Wilhelm Wolff (or "Lupus" as Marx and Engels habitually referred to him). Though Wilhelm Wolff had managed to acquire a university education at Breslau, he vividly recalled the burdens of his Silesian peasant family which supplied the lord not only with rent, but with four chickens and four rolls of spun flax per year, with a payment on the birth of each calf or pig, and with compulsory labor service at harvest "as long as it lasts." Between 1834 and 1840, the Prussian government had imprisoned Wolff for participation in an illegal student revolutionary organization (*Burschenschaft*). Upon his release, he had joined the incipient democratic movement. During the Silesian weavers' uprising, he had written of the justice of the weavers' cause and indicted private property. In Brussels, he quickly took up Marx's strategy and established contacts for the Correspondence Committee in Silesia. Wolff counseled Silesian communists to set up

1. *CW*, 6:641–642, 549, 630.

2. Ibid., 6:545–552. Marx, "On the Jewish Question" in *Writings of the Young Marx,* pp. 218–223. Though Marx occasionally used crass anti-Semitic and other racist stereotypes, he and Engels vigorously opposed the political consequences of anti-Semitism. Marx to Engels, July 31, 1862, in Marx and Engels, *Gesamtausgabe,* pt. 3, 3:82, 84.

reading and discussion clubs, modeled on the Brussels Correspondence Committee and the German Workers' Educational Society.[3]

Marx strove to establish other branches of the Communist Committee in Germany itself. He corresponded with Weydemeyer who had returned to Westphalia and disseminated Marxian ideas in Otto Lüning's *Westphälische Dampfboot* (Westphalian Steamboat) and in the *Triersche Zeitung*. In suppressing some of Weydemeyer's articles for the *Triersche Zeitung*, the Prussian censor emphasized Weydemeyer's "hateful descriptions of the contrasts that separate the propertied and the propertyless," his attacks on the monarchy, and his insistence on a "complete transformation of the present mode of acquisition." Lüning's paper mixed Marxian communism with "true socialist" appeals to inaugurate a community based on love. Weydemeyer saw this confused patchwork of ideas as a reaction to the novelty of Marx's theory of the economic foundation of democracy and socialism. Along with Dr. Roland Daniels of Cologne, Weydemeyer urged Marx to publish his book on "national economy" which they believed would have a comparable impact to Feuerbach's *Essence of Christianity*.[4]

At this time, Marx did not undertake such a work, and even *The German Ideology* remained unpublished. In Brussels, however, Marx strongly influenced a new journal, the *Deutsche Brüsseler Zeitung*, which Weydemeyer and others circulated in Germany. Weydemeyer also strove with little success to raise funds for a new German periodical.

Contending mainly with the "true socialists," Marx and Engels urged their correspondents in Elberfeld and Cologne to participate in the democratic revolution as a prelude to a proletarian one. In May 1846, the Elberfeld communist G. A. Köttgen circulated a call for mutual contacts among communists in preparation for a congress. In June, the Brussels Committee responded that communists should call such a meeting only as leaders of a strong, nationwide movement. They suggested that in the interim Köttgen should form a correspondence committee similar to their own. Köttgen had

---

3. E. P. Kandel, ed., *Marx und Engels und die ersten proletarischen Revolutionäre*, pp. 305, 169–170. Wolff corresponded with Hermann Sandler, a teacher from Landshut, and with Franz Springer, the bookseller, and his brother Hermann from Striegau. Richard W. Reichard, *Crippled from Birth*, pp. 91, 224. Auguste Cornu, *Karl Marx et Friedrich Engels*, 4:39. Wilhelm Wolff, "Das Elend und der Aufruhr in Schlesien" in Jantke and Hilger, eds., *Die Eigentumslosen*.

4. Schraepler, *Handwerkerbünde und Arbeitervereine*, pp. 165–166. Cornu, *Marx et Engels*, 4:45, n. 1. Weydemeyer to Marx, April 30, 1846, *Bund Dokumente*, p. 314.

proposed that the German communists circulate a petition to the king of Prussia; the Brussels Committee noted that unless a "compact and organized mass" of at least 500 workers stood behind it, such a petition would underline the communists' disorganization and expose their names to the enemy. Instead, they suggested, the communists should organize a petition for a progressive tax along with the Trier bourgeoisie. The Brussels letter mocked German moralism. If the bourgeoisie dragged its feet, the Elberfeld communists should still "join them for the time being in public demonstrations, proceed jesuitically, put aside Teutonic probity, trueheartedness, and decency, and sign and push forward the bourgeois petitions for freedom of the press, a constitution, and so on. When that has been accomplished, a new era will dawn for communist propaganda." [5]

Infected with a heavy dose of moralism, the "true socialists" abstained from the democratic movement where they did not oppose it. In contrast, Marx and Engels judged alternative tactics by whether or not they accelerated the democratic movement, not by "tiresome moral scruples." As we have seen, this realistic standard ruled out Weitlingian reliance on criminals as counterproductive rather than immoral (though on deeper examination, perhaps a genuine moral disgust among the workers for the lumpenproletariat would be found to lead to the ineffectiveness of Weitling's strategy).

As the German bourgeoisie feared a radical democratic revolution, however, this policy of participation ran two dangers. If communists submerged themselves and failed to provide vigorous leadership, the democratic movement might sputter. If they provided simply democratic leadership and failed to win mass support for communist ideas, then they would arrive in the "new era for communist propaganda" on a very weak footing, and the bourgeoisie might be able to drive them underground. Marx and Engels hoped to initiate a broad movement against the old regime. The class struggle itself would teach the participants important new understandings and open up a wide arena for communist organizing. But the Elberfeld communists, internally divided, failed to implement their suggestions.

Marx concentrated his attention on Cologne where a small communist circle consisting of Heinrich Bürgers and the doctors Roland Daniels and Karl d'Ester had gathered. D'Ester and Bürgers had cooperated with Marx on the earlier *Rheinische Zeitung* and had also joined in a discussion group on the "social question." In 1845, d'Ester edited two radical papers that circu-

5. *Bund Dokumente*, pp. 351–353, 342–344.

lated among Cologne artisans and workers. D'Ester excoriated "free competition" where capitalists derived their profits entirely from the misery of others, condemned philanthropy as fruitless, and hailed universal suffrage and the Silesian weavers' revolt. According to d'Ester, only workers' associations could break the power of capital. In June 1846, d'Ester and Daniels along with Dr. Andreas Gottschalk, took part in a Rhenish doctors' congress. Following Marx's strategy, they proposed resolutions to emancipate doctors from military and judicial control, to secure greater medical care for the poor, and to eliminate poverty among the doctors themselves.[6]

Subsequently, d'Ester and Bürgers participated in a series of Cologne election meetings. At first, they avoided any reference to the economic clashes between workers and capitalists; such arguments would in their view have ruined the chances of electing a communist to the town council. Instead they offered a democratic program to divide the petite bourgeoisie from the liberal merchants like the Camphausens. A coalition including the cigar maker Franz Raveaux, leader of the radical democrats, and d'Ester won the election. D'Ester and Bürgers did not altogether submerge communist politics. At one meeting, Bürgers instigated a spirited debate by proposing that concentration of capital led to increased poverty; eventually, the meeting passed a resolution to that effect.[7]

Though d'Ester and Bürgers galvanized the democratic movement in Cologne, the communist circle failed to grow. Meanwhile, a second communist group, influenced by "true socialism" and especially by Moses Hess, formed around Gottschalk and the officers August Willich and Friedrich Anneke. Gottschalk opposed the political liberalism of Ruge, and like Hess, concurred with Marx's socialist critique of Proudhon. Gottschalk worked with Bürgers to secure the translation of *Poverty of Philosophy* which Marx had written in French, to publish Hess's translations of the French communists Dézamy and Buonarroti, and to raise funds for a new communist journal. When Marx and the Brussels Committee joined the Communist League in 1847, Hess recruited Gottschalk.[8] Thus, both communist groups had founded a Cologne branch of the League by early 1848. Though Marx strove from afar to initiate communist organizing for democracy in Cologne,

6. Dieter Dowe, *Aktion und Organisation*, pp. 114–115.

7. Ibid., pp. 115–118. Cornu, *Marx et Engels*, 4:45–46. Schraepler, *Handwerkerbünde*, p. 168.

8. Dowe, *Aktion*, pp. 126–129.

Gottschalk and his allies who disagreed with Marx's strategy would play a far more active role at the revolution's outset.

7–2. The Communist League

THROUGH ORGANIZING the Brussels and Cologne Correspondence Committees and initiating exchanges with the London League of the Just, Marx became a driving force in founding the new Communist League which would adopt a Marxian program, the *Manifesto*. According to Engels's later account, he and Marx did not actually join the League of the Just until the spring of 1847. Yet they already exerted great influence upon it, and Moll visited Brussels and Paris in 1847 as much to inform them about the political situation inside the League as to solicit their formal membership.[9] In their addresses to the League of November 1846 and 1847, the London leaders had dramatically shifted from peaceful Cabetian agitation for communist colonies to Marxian preparation for democratic revolution. They condemned Russian tsarism—"the devil in human form"—for its oppression of Poland, and argued that communists must prepare to fight tsarist barbarism with "muskets as well as words." In the upcoming "political revolution," they expected that the proletariat might cooperate with the insipid liberals. Given these circumstances, they stressed the importance of a communist newspaper and a program or catechism in order to expose the bourgeoisie's attempts to substitute the despotism of money for that of the princes. The draft catechism, discussed at the June conference, endorsed "the political liberation of the proletariat through a democratic state-constitution" as the first prerequisite for the transition from the present society to the community of goods. Given the League's traditions, the term "political liberation" (*politische Befreiung*) had an especially Marxian resonance.[10]

At the first Communist League Congress in London, Wilhelm Wolff represented Brussels and Engels, Paris. This congress adopted new statutes which, as Engels put it, removed "whatever remained of the old mystical names dating back to the conspiratorial period." These statutes made the

---

9. The London leaders had ignored Marx and Engels in their first soundings in the League about a congress. Schraepler, *Handwerkerbünde*, pp. 194–196. Without any other evidence, Hunt, *Political Ideas*, p. 187, overinterprets personal unfamiliarity and caution as a sign of fundamental political disagreement.

10. *Bund Dokumente*, pp. 452–453, 432, 435–436, 474. Förder, *Marx und Engels*, pp. 266, 268. Engels, "On the History of the Communist League," *MESW*, 2:347.

organization completely democratic, "with elective and always removable boards" as against conspiracy which required dictatorial leadership. At this congress, the League of the Just changed its name to the Communist League and, according to Engels, adopted explicitly Marxian revolutionary aims: "the overthrow of the bourgeoisie, the rule of the proletariat, the abolition of the old, bourgeois society based on class antagonisms and the foundation of a new society without classes and without private property." [11]

The June congress issued a "Circular," drafted by Schapper and Wolff, which emphasized the League's renewed political energy and its victory over hostile internal elements. It mentioned the Paris branch's exposure of Grün, again criticized as a frivolous "exploiter of communist ideas," and of Proudhon, as well as its expulsion of the Weitlingians. The Paris League had lost some members. But, the "Circular" argued, "through the struggle, minds have been quickened to renewed activity." Schapper, like other London leaders, had criticized Marx's harsh "Circular against Kriege" in 1845; now, however, Schapper saw a connection between theoretical clarity and bold, persistent revolutionary activity. This "Circular" also underlined the case of Mentel, a Berlin tailor of "true socialist" views, who, when arrested, suddenly converted to Christianity and told the Prussian authorities everything he knew about the League. The "Circular" attributed his cowardice to the general vacuity and enervating sentimentality of "true socialism." [12]

The "Circular" stressed that proletarian struggle against the bourgeoisie had grown throughout Europe and that revolution would soon become a real possibility. Given this situation, it called forth the redoubled political energy of its proletarian members, who, though bitterly oppressed by capitalism, had supported the League with their time, effort, and funds. It celebrated the virtue of consistent participation in the political struggle itself and suggested that the upcoming revolutionary times would "reveal what our League was and how it worked":

> Even if we should not live to see *all* the fruits of the great struggle, even if hundreds of us fall under the grapeshot of the bourgeoisie, all of us, even the fallen, have lived to be in the *struggle,* and this struggle, this victory alone is worth a life of the most strenuous work. [13]

11. Engels, "History," *MESW,* 2:348.
12. *Bund Dokumente,* pp. 477–478, 479–480, 238–240, 258–272.
13. Ibid., pp. 486–487.

In the next "Circular," the League leaders outlined the obstacles the League faced; they insisted that difficulties would not deter "real men" but would spur them to greater efforts (the League's critique of the oppression of women did not yet extend into an attempt to elicit their participation). Class war and growing political understanding would produce a new political community.

In September, the Communist League issued its only number of the *Kommunistische Zeitschrift* (Communist Journal). This document again illustrated the transition from older true socialist and conspiratorial tendencies to Marxian socialism. The League of the Just had sounded the republican slogan, "All Men Are Brothers!" The *Kommunistische Zeitschrift* did not see capitalists as the workers' brothers and proclaimed "Proletarians of All Lands, Unite." Karl Schapper's first article, "Proletarians," envisioned machinery as a progressive social force. It criticized only the use of machinery by capitalists to oppress the workers.

According to Schapper, the journal aimed "to work for the emancipation of the proletariat, and . . . to encourage the unity of all the oppressed." [14] It advocated the primacy of the working class within any alliance of the oppressed and bluntly opposed other radical tendencies, starting with utopian "retailers of systems": "We know from experience how senseless it is to discuss and brood over the exact arrangements of a future society, and thereby to neglect all the means that may lead us to it." Prefiguring the *Manifesto,* it indicted "true socialist" "lovesickness" with its alternating artificial (one might almost say Kleistian) "moonlit" ecstasies and depressions as a form of mental and political "self-enervation." [15]

No longer propagandists for peaceful transition nor conspirators, the editors

> are not those communists who preach eternal peace while in every land our enemies arm for war . . . we at least will throw no sand in the eyes of the people but tell them the truth and make them aware of the approaching storm. . . . We know well that between the aristocratic and democratic elements on the European continent, it must come to armed conflict.[16]

14. Ibid., pp. 501–503. The "Probeblatt der '*Kommunistischen Zeitschrift,*' September, 1847," is reproduced in ibid., pp. 501–524.

15. Ibid., pp. 504–505.

16. Ibid., p. 505.

The article also distinguished the Communist League from those communists who believed that a successful revolution could institute the community of goods without a transition. Foreshadowing the ten regulations in part two of the *Manifesto,* the article argued that communists would transform private property into social property "only gradually." [17]

Another article in the journal on Cabet's emigration plan underlined the break between the London leaders and Cabet. Cabet had enlisted European workers to set up an Icaria in North America. Because many workers, driven by the famine of the mid-1840s, had planned to emigrate in any event, Cabet's proposal gained considerable support. The article praised Cabet's previous efforts "in the cause of suffering humanity" but urged revolutionaries to remain in Europe and transform society there, not to escape in search of paradise. In Europe, it argued, the most favorable conditions existed for the introduction of the community of goods. "If upright men, fighters for a better future, emigrate and abandon the field to obscurantists and thieves, then Europe must decline . . . and poor mankind will be forced to undergo trials of suffering and fire for another century." Instead, another article on German emigrants sardonically suggested, why not put an end to the "Christian-German nonsense" and send their "superiors by the manifold grace of God" packing for Texas? [18]

The article offered a subtle materialist rejection of utopianism. Utopian colonies would fail because the emigrants had absorbed "all the failings and prejudices of contemporary society" and would not lose them merely by opting to voyage to Icaria. A selfish European upbringing would issue in tensions between colonists, which the European as well as the "powerful and hostile external" American society would exacerbate to undermine the colony. While artisans would emigrate, only farmers could make Icaria work. "A worker cannot be transformed into a peasant so easily as many imagine." Lack of the "little amenities of civilization which even the poorest European worker can at times secure" and sickness resulting from change of climate, would further dissolve community. But even should the colony succeed, it would "take on an exclusive or sectarian character." [19] Far from furthering an internationalist movement for working-class communism, this dream opposed it. To measure Marx's ascendant influence, we may recall that only two

17. Ibid., p. 506. Hunt, *Political Ideas,* pp. 185–186, peculiarly insists that Schapper was "more impatient" for communism than Marx.

18. *Bund Dokumente,* pp. 509, 524.

19. Ibid., pp. 509–510.

years before, the editors of this journal had criticized Weitling from Cabet's point of view.

In another article, "The Prussian Diet and the Prussian Proletariat, together with the Proletariat throughout Germany," Wilhelm Wolff urged workers' participation in the German democratic revolution. While the argument in Schapper's "Proletarians" had potentially exempted England and the United States from violent revolution, Wolff envisioned a protracted life-and-death struggle to destroy every bourgeoisie, "a war not merely of words, but of fists and muskets." The author warned, however, of "another enemy, nearer than the bourgeoisie, who must be vanquished first . . . the absolute unlimited monarchy that calls itself 'graced by God' and robs us in heaven's name, that imprisons us in the talons of medieval landlords, strangles us in the 'Christian-Germanic' state, and regularly sends its police, gendarmes, priests, and guns to the aid of capital." Because absolutism still survived, the democratic revolution must precede socialism. Wolff recalled the "Christian" monarch's suppression of the Silesian weavers: "The 'merciful' sovereign had the weavers stuck with bayonets and shot down like dogs." The proletariat had an interest in "political freedoms" and should unite with the bourgeoisie to destroy the monarchy, "thus far and no farther." [20]

According to Wolff, the workers underestimated their substantial collective power. A bread riot had just erupted in Berlin. Though only a few hundred workers had taken part without a common plan or previous organization, "the whole city trembled": "Have not two highly placed officials declared that Berlin, despite all of its troops, would have fallen under proletarian control if the workers had only known how to use their power and act in concert?" [21] With greater forces and better organization, the proletariat could have overthrown the monarch and by implication, the bourgeoisie as well.

7–3. Marx's Strategy and Political Conflict among Radicals

HUNT WRONGLY DEPICTS a split in the Communist League between artisans who longed for immediate proletarian revolution, and economic determinist intellectuals like Marx who supported democracy but compromised on the

20. Ibid., pp. 517–520.
21. Ibid., p. 521.

strategy for Germany in the *Communist Manifesto.* This neat social division ignores the subtle political evolution of the London artisans, of Marx and Engels, and of other intellectuals like Hess. To sustain it, Hunt has to ignore the artisans' vigorous participation in the democratic revolution of 1848; he also has to reinterpret their earlier endorsement of democracy as somehow opposing Marx's stress on industrialization and on alliance with the bourgeoisie: "Artisan impatience to find some escape from their doomed world expressed itself positively as the desire for immediate communism and negatively as an implacable hostility toward the bourgeoisie and all its works. . . . [In their writings] one does not find hostility toward the industrial revolution *per se,* just indifference." [22]

Yet in the *Kommunistische Zeitschrift* Schapper hailed the progressive aspect of machinery under capitalism and its usefulness under socialism in straightforwardly Marxian terms; another leading article called on workers to unite with the bourgeoisie to defeat absolutism.[23] As the *Kommunistische Zeitschrift* strikingly demonstrated, Marx had won some artisans, notably leaders like Moll, Bauer, and Schapper, to his perspective on the need for democratic revolution as a political prerequisite for a subsequent socialist one, while impatient intellectuals, like Hess and Gottschalk, longed for immediate workers' uprisings and scorned democracy as merely bourgeois (Moll and Schapper would lead the fight against Gottschalk in the Cologne Worker Society on precisely this issue). A status reductionism like Hunt's confuses these complex political relationships.

Between 1845 and 1848, Marx adopted a multifaceted political approach to his differences with other radicals, including careful efforts to win over the London artisans, recruitment of new forces like Weydemeyer and Wolff, repeated attempts to work with less decisive communists like Moses Hess, and outright rejection of "true socialists" and others who opposed the real movement. Offering a new theory, Marx took a long-term strategic view and openly disdained immediate popularity. Marx wanted socialist political results as rapidly as possible, not temporary personal favor based on an unworkable program. Marx's views differed fundamentally from those of more short-sighted democrats, anarchists, or communists who demanded instant

---

22. Hunt, *Political Ideas,* pp. 185–186.

23. In a footnote, Hunt dismisses the significance of this leading article on overthrowing absolutism before taking on the bourgeoisie simply because a member of the "Marx circle," Wilhelm Wolff, wrote it. Ibid., p. 186, n. 28. The London artisans who edited the *Kommunistische Zeitschrift,* however, not only printed this article but saw no need to contradict it.

victory (Weitling, Heinzen, Bakunin, Kriege, Ruge). Such radicals often did not understand Marx's argument or vehemently rejected its consequences.[24] Others like Hess, torn between allegiance to older political ideas and forces and the seductive elegance of Marx's conception, moved back and forth. Since Marx combined a highly theoretical analysis of capitalist dynamics with a new, practical strategy, realistic revolutionaries, like Moll, Schapper, and Bauer, who had experienced the abysmal failure of conspiracy, found his view most compelling. A psychological approach might tell us more about someone like Kriege, to whom success meant everything, philosophy and politics nothing, than about Marx himself.

In 1873, Engels would summarize his and Marx's attitude toward such political conflicts within the radical movement in a letter to Bebel. At that time, Bebel's Eisenach Social Democrats who leaned toward Marxism were considering a merger with the Lassalleans who hoped that Prussian state aid to cooperatives would overcome the misery of capitalism. Engels warned Bebel that both groups constituted only a tiny minority of the German workers and urged the Social Democrats to keep their eye on the masses rather than on the already radicalized Lassallean sect. Engels and Marx had always tried "not to entice a few individuals . . . from one's opponent, but to work on the great mass, which is not yet taking part in the movement." Winning over the Lassalleans, Engels suggested, might prove counterproductive: "A single individual whom one has oneself reared from the raw is worth more than ten Lassallean turncoats, who always bring the germs of their false tendencies into the party with them." The former Lassalleans would insist on the validity of their previous program and bend the new movement toward it. "Rearing" fresh revolutionaries, on the other hand, would require intense political discussion and work with nonradicals as well as constant willingness to learn from the real movement.[25] Engels's remarks again reveal the non-elitist character of his and Marx's strategy which aimed not at setting a tiny cluster of radical cognoscenti in opposition to everyone else but at inspiring a vast revolutionary movement of the workers themselves. Whether such a movement could flourish or gain power depended mainly on external condi-

24. In January 1847, Bakunin wrote to Herwegh of Marx's alleged "vanity, malice, gossip, theoretical haughtiness, and practical cowardice," and stated that he physically could not draw "a free, full breath of air" in the Brussels artisan communist correspondence society. Heinzen likened Marx to an argumentative "ape who hopped from one Hegelian thesis and antithesis to another." Schraepler, *Handwerkerbünde,* pp. 179–180, 173, 177.

25. *SC,* p. 283.

tions, but, Engels argued, the party regardless of its numbers must always maintain this broad perspective.

Furthermore, Engels noted, changing historical situations often required new tactics, strategies, or even organizations. Many radicals, like Weitling, did not draw lessons from such historical shifts; they "get stuck and do not join in the further advance." Citing "old man Hegel's" dialectics, Engels insisted that "a party proves itself victorious by splitting and being able to stand the split." Political conflict between those who sought to advance a revolutionary movement and those who would reduce it to an isolated clique, assumed a "life and death character"; the solidarity of the proletariat, in this sense, would realize itself only in bitter struggle like that of "the Christian sects in the Roman Empire . . . amidst the worst persecutions." Even under enemy attack, an internal conflict over principles might lead to the movement's greater flowering, whereas unity around a nonrevolutionary or watered-down program might result in its demise. Engels contrasted "dialectical" division, and a consequent revolutionary clarity and vigor, with enervating "unity." Lenin would subsequently adopt a similar attitude toward political conflict in the radical movement.[26] Among political nonstarters like many of Marx's opponents, one might easily dismiss such a view. But despite the setbacks and reversals of later socialist and communist movements, the formidable historical influence of Marx's theory testifies to Engels's insight.

---

26. Ibid., p. 285. Hegel, *Phenomenology of Spirit*, pp. 350–351. Krupskaya's *Memories of Lenin*, 1:102–103, cited a famous statement from *One Step Forward, Two Steps Back* about the first controversy between the Bolsheviks and the Mensheviks: "I [Lenin] cannot help remembering a conversation of mine at that Congress with one of the 'Center' delegates. 'What a depressing atmosphere prevails at our Congress,' he complained to me. 'All this fierce fighting, this agitation one against the other, these sharp polemics, this uncomradely attitude!'–'What a fine thing our Congress is,' I replied to him. 'Opportunity for open fighting. Opinions expressed. Tendencies revealed. Groups defined. Hands raised. A decision taken. A stage passed through. Forward! That's what I like! It is something different from the endless wearying intellectual discussions, which finish, not because people have solved the problem, but simply because they have got tired of talking.' The comrade of the 'Center' looked at me as though perplexed and shrugged his shoulders. We had spoken in different languages." Unlike Lenin, the delegate of the "Center" looked only at the internal squabbling among radicals and disregarded the political consequences for the mass movement that such differences might entail.

— VIII —

The Communist Manifesto
and Marx's Strategies

8–1. The Paradoxes of the *Manifesto*

THE COMMUNIST LEAGUE'S FIRST CONGRESS had mandated a program in the form of a catechism. After early drafts by Schapper and Hess, Engels rewrote it. His draft served as a basis for discussion at the second League congress in November which Marx attended as the representative of the Brussels branch. According to Engels, the "fairly long debate" on the new theory took up ten days; the congress commissioned Marx and Engels to produce the final program. Engels then urged Marx to drop the catechism form, include more history, and recast the document as a manifesto.[1] By February 1848, on the eve of revolution in France, Marx finished this task.

As its name implies, the *Manifesto* issued a defiant call to overthrow capitalism. Transforming a "specter" into the program of a living movement, it boldly proclaimed the communist aim to abolish exploitation and classes based upon it, and to found a new society run by the associated workers themselves: "Let the ruling classes tremble at a Communistic revolution. . . . Working men of all countries, unite!" Yet many scholars have interpreted the *Manifesto* as a narrowly determinist argument, sketching the ineluctable impact of new productive forces on successive forms of human society. Such an interpretation submerges the role of politics and strategy and misses the *Manifesto*'s distinctive character as a revolutionary program. Even so, a sophisticated determinism, including a strong component of political activity, almost captures the argument of the *Manifesto*'s first sections. Yet such an interpretation founders on the fourth section's seemingly paradoxical program for a socialist revolution in backward Germany. Though the early sections depicted the peasantry mainly as a doomed and "reactionary" class, the fourth section envisioned a major revolutionary role for German and Polish peasants. Where the early sections described the dissolution of

---

1. Engels, "History of the Communist League," *MESW*, 2:348. Boris Nicolaievsky and Otto Maenchen-Helfen, *Karl Marx*, pp. 137–138.

European national attachments, the fourth insisted on international support for the "national emancipation" of Poland. In the *Manifesto,* Marx combined a theory of the general historical trends of capitalism with a communist program for the specific circumstances of upcoming democratic revolutions.

8–2. The *Manifesto*'s General Theory

MARX'S THEORY BEGAN with the hypothesis that all history, outside of early communal arrangements, "is the history of class struggles": "Freeman and slave, patrician and plebeian, lord and serf, guild-master and journeyman, in a word, oppressor and oppressed, stood in constant opposition to one another, carried on an uninterrupted, now hidden, now open fight." These struggles culminated either in the revolutionary transformation of society or in the "common ruin" of the combatants, an aside already pointing to the possibility of a stunted or eccentric historical development. As roughly stated in the *Manifesto,* changing modes of production underlie these conflicts; shifts in methods or forces of production sometimes give rise to new classes, stimulate profound intellectual and political changes, and lead to new historical forms. Even in the *Manifesto,* Marx sketched a complex materialism. For instance, the bourgeoisie unleashes new forces of production in an intellectual as well as a material sense; the process of production incorporates new scientific discoveries and stands revealed as a "mental as well as material metabolism" with nature.[2] Marx's materialism does not play down the impact of science, religion, or politics in production; instead it provides broad hypotheses about the interplay of these differing activities, given the predominance of the mode of production over an entire historical epoch. Marx emphasized that an individual's consciousness or will does not shape these relationships; rather, each individual is born into the midst of these already given, alien relations which restrict his or her personal alternatives as well as the larger potentials for future social transformation.

The *Manifesto* placed in bold relief the new capitalist era, which had reduced older class relations to a dichotomy between a small class of property holders owning the means of production and a vast propertyless proletariat.[3] In the first sections, Marx traced the bourgeoisie's rise as a "product" of

2. *CM,* pp. 35–37. Marx, *Grundrisse,* p. 161. Shaw, *Marx's Theory of History,* pp. 20–22.
3. *CM,* p. 35.

emerging productive forces: from the burgesses and guild masters of the early towns through a manufacturing middle class stimulated by the discovery of America and colonization of other lands into an industrial middle class based on the steam and machinery of modern industry and operating in a world market. At each economic "step," the bourgeoisie had dialectically made a corresponding political advance:

> An oppressed class under the sway of the feudal nobility, an armed and self-governing association in the medieval commune; here independent urban republic (as in Italy and Germany), there taxable "third estate" of the monarchy (as in France), afterwards, in the period of manufacture proper, serving with the semi-feudal or the absolute monarchy as a counterpoise against the nobility, and in fact, cornerstone of the great monarchies in general, the bourgeoisie has at least, since the establishment of Modern Industry and the world market, conquered for itself, in the modern representative State, exclusive political sway. The executive of the modern State is but a committee for managing the common affairs of the whole bourgeoisie.[4]

Concentrating the productive forces in its hands, the bourgeoisie forged politically centralized modern nations. Marx's argument made the productive forces the main engine of social development and treated other activities, including political changes, as secondary.

In these sections, Marx celebrated the bourgeoisie's demonstration of "man's power" in transforming nature: "It [the bourgeoisie] has accomplished wonders far surpassing Egyptian pyramids, Roman aqueducts, and Gothic cathedrals; it has conducted expeditions that put in the shade all former Exoduses and crusades." This modern system of production impelled a dizzying pace of social change unlike that in previous epochs, an "uninterrupted disturbance of all social conditions, everlasting uncertainty and agitation." The bourgeoisie extended its powers on an international scale, "batter[ed] down all Chinese walls" with its cheap commodities, ferreted out raw materials in the "remotest zones," and finally, "create[d] a world after its own image."[5]

Yet, like the ancient Tibetan gods that fed off the skulls of the slain, capitalism displayed its productive capacities at the expense of the pro-

4. Ibid., p. 36.
5. Ibid., pp. 37–39.

ducers.[6] Tracing the peak of bourgeois achievement, Marx then sketched the trends that would lead to its demise.

According to the *Manifesto,* capitalism would engender a spontaneous proletarian understanding of its oppressor. In place of feudal exploitation "veiled by religious and political illusions," the bourgeoisie had instituted "naked shameless, direct, brutal exploitation." Like the corrupt metamorphosis of Balzac's Lucien de Rubempré from an ambitious provincial poet into a Parisian journalist and "merchant of words," capitalism's "cold cash nexus" reduces the motivations of diverse human activities to a uniform striving for money. Capitalism reveals official law, morality, and religion as "bourgeois prejudices" behind which the worker might detect bourgeois interests "lurking in ambush." [7] Here again, Marx used a criterion of old and new types of human activities, conducted for their own sakes, to criticize contemporary capitalist corruption. A powerful underlying ethical argument led to his dismissal of conventional bourgeois morality.

Furthermore, capitalism concentrates workers in large factories and inadvertently spurs association of workers to achieve their economic and political purposes. This same process tends to dissolve older differences in skill, displace the remnant independent artisan and peasant property holders, and reduce the new working class to one homogeneous mass: "The various interests and conditions of life within the ranks of the proletariat are more and more equalized, in proportion as machinery obliterates all distinctions of labor." Concentration enhances the arbitrary despotism of capital, placing the worker-privates of the industrial army "under the command of a perfect hierarchy of officers and sergeants." Foreshadowing the horrible perfection of twentieth-century Taylorism, Marx suggested that "not only are they [the workers] slaves of the bourgeois class and of the bourgeois state; they are daily and hourly enslaved by the machine, by the over-looker, and above all, by the individual bourgeois manufacturer himself." [8]

Impoverishment compounds these tendencies. The *Manifesto* contrasted the individual artisan who sometimes rose to become a bourgeois with the modern laborer who sinks into ruin. It denounced the bourgeoisie's incompetence "to assure an existence to its slave within his slavery." Stripping the workers of any stake in existing nations, capitalism creates common revolu-

6. Marx, "The Future Results of British Rule in India" in *Karl Marx on Colonialism and Modernization,* pp. 138–139.

7. *CM,* pp. 36–37, 44. Honoré de Balzac, *Illusions perdues,* p. 356.

8. *CM,* pp. 42, 41.

tionary interests across all borders. Like the sorcerer's apprentice, it conjures up forces beyond its control, culminating in baffling crises in the midst of its overwhelming productivity:

> For many a decade past, the history of industry and commerce is but the history of the revolt of modern productive forces against modern conditions of production. . . . Society suddenly finds itself put back into a state of momentary barbarism; it appears as if a famine, a universal war of devastation had cut off the supply of every means of subsistence; industry and commerce seem to be destroyed; and why? Because there is too much civilization, too much means of subsistence, too much industry, too much commerce.[9]

Given these combined tendencies of capitalism, the bourgeoisie generates its own gravediggers. To complete a classic determinist image, Marx asserted: "Its [the bourgeoisie's] fall and the victory of the proletariat are equally inevitable." [10]

Drawing on Engels's *Condition,* Marx recapitulated the political stages of working-class revolt that accompany the advances of modern industry: from Luddism to the formation of unions to a working-class political organization battling for shorter hours and the suffrage to violent revolution sweeping away the bourgeoisie and inaugurating "the sway of the proletariat." Though capitalism would drive this proletarian party to make revolution, Marx nonetheless staked out a definite political role for communists throughout this process. In the *Manifesto's* second section, Marx responded to numerous bourgeois objections that communism would abolish freedom, culture, and marriage; in the third, he scathingly criticized other radicalisms of the 1840s. Despite the dynamics of capitalism, Marx did not expect these political "frozen prejudices" to "melt in air." In addition to countering such ideas, communists must infuse the existing movement with internationalism, a defense of "the common interests of the proletariat independently of all nationality" (despite the great importance placed on internationalism in the *Manifesto,* Marx provided no real explanation of its basis; he argued only that capitalism created dispossessed proletariats in each separate country). Communists must also advocate the abolition of private property in the means of production "as the leading issue" in every movement.[11] In other

9. Ibid., pp. 45, 39–40.
10. Ibid., p. 45.
11. Ibid., pp. 46, 65.

words, the workers should protest against low wages and capitalism, not against inadequate wages alone.

The *Manifesto* offered a striking dialectical picture of the communists' political role. Though they represent the proletariat's "most advanced and resolute section" in the current struggles for unions or democracy, they also see "the line of march . . . and the ultimate general results of the proletarian movement." They defend the "present" movement, the "momentary interests" of the proletariat, and simultaneously look to the movement's "future," illuminating particular victories and defeats from the overall perspective of socialism. Thus, in France, Marx argued, communists would support the defenders of "democratic-socialism" (the Mountain) in the present; yet they would criticize all the Mountain's republican "phrases" or "illusions" that blunted the clash between the capitalists and the workers (the proletariat's June insurrection which the Mountain opposed would disrupt this particular communist tactic).[12] The *Manifesto* suggested that the immediate movement would not, in and of itself, generate these necessary communist activities. Yet given the overriding impetus of capitalist dynamics in the *Manifesto*'s early sections, Marx's dialectical insights did not seem to indicate any strong tensions among these communist tasks. In political practice, however, as we shall see, such aims often at least partially conflict.

Unlike the previous minority revolutions, the *Manifesto* argued, an "independent, self-conscious movement of the immense majority" would make the proletarian revolution in its own interest. In a vigorous image, Marx suggested that when the most oppressed social class rises, it will "spring the whole superincumbent strata of official society into the air." After the revolutionary movement had destroyed the old political apparatus, it would create a new form of rule combining democracy for the majority and dictatorship—the gradual "despotic" rooting out of private property—for the exploiters. After 1850, Marx would call this regime a "dictatorship of the proletariat."[13] Following an epoch of proletarian rule which would culminate in the abolition of classes, the "public power" would ultimately "lose its political character." Even so, the *Manifesto* envisioned a wider latitude for a transformed political or public power than Marx had foreseen in 1844 in his exchange with Ruge. As Marx's later analysis of the Paris Commune would

---

12. Ibid., p. 64.
13. *CS*, pp. 162, 217. See Gilbert, "Salvaging Marx from Avineri," pp. 23–24.

indicate, this new "republic of labor," run by the workers, would display an original political character.

Thus far, the *Manifesto* exuberantly anticipated the coming proletarian society. It greatly exaggerated the nearness of proletarian victory on such a model in many barely capitalist European societies. According to Engels's early draft, "in the civilized countries almost every branch of industry has fallen under the sway of the factory system." Modern industry had "outgrown" capitalist relations, which had now become "a fetter on production" that the workers must break. Realizing that Engels had overstated the pervasiveness of capitalism, Marx and Engels deleted this argument from the final draft. Yet a general expectation of imminent victory remained. On rereading Engels's *Condition* in 1863, Marx reached an unpalatable conclusion that might equally apply to the *Manifesto*:

> How freshly and passionately, with what bold anticipations and no learned and scientific doubts, the thing is still dealt with here! And the very illusion that the result will leap into the daylight of history tomorrow or the day after gives the whole thing a warmth . . . compared with which the later "gray [on] gray" makes a damned unpleasant contrast.[14]

8–3. The *Manifesto*'s Political Impact

SOME OF TODAY'S READERS might find these sections of the *Manifesto* antiquated. Proletarian revolutionary movements have so far failed to win power in highly industrialized settings; European working-class misery did not increase; capitalism did not level all distinctions of skill; women and children did not remain the most suitable objects of modern capitalist exploitation. Making these points so starkly, however, one might overlook the *Manifesto*'s main political significance. Unlike the other radicals of the 1840s, Marx envisioned a new international working-class struggle springing from the terrain of capitalism itself. Since Marx wrote, every capitalist country has witnessed great, often violent battles over unions and the eight-hour day. Significant socialist and then communist parties have appeared, which have affected, sometimes decisively, each country's destiny. Three international movements

14. Marx and Engels, *The Birth of the Communist Manifesto,* pp. 171, 177. Marx to Engels, April 9, 1863, *SC,* pp. 140–141. Hunt, *Political Ideas,* pp. 187–190, ignores Marx's and Engels's belief that capitalism had already exhausted its potentialities.

have come into being (the IWA and the socialist and communist interna-
tionals). If they did not achieve all of their goals, for instance blocking
World War I or revolutionizing Europe, perhaps the forces arrayed against
them were too great, or their own strategies insufficiently perceptive and
flexible to meet new challenges. Given the frequently acute oppressiveness of
capitalism, manifested in depression or war, the true measure of the *Manifesto*
is what it foresaw and instigated rather than what it did not. Ignored by
most intellectuals until after the rise of Social Democracy, the working-class
movement that the *Manifesto* had prophesied made it a great modern political document and a subject of eventual academic controversy. Forty years
after Marx and Engels wrote the *Manifesto,* Engels properly characterized it as
"the most widespread, the most international production of all socialist literature, the common platform acknowledged by millions of working men
from Siberia to California." [15]

The *Manifesto* erred not in its appreciation of class struggle under capital
ism, but in its belief that such conflict would culminate quickly in revolutionary socialism. As Marx wrote to Engels in 1863, practical as well as
scientific doubts soon crept in. Marx eventually qualified every one of the
basic tendencies of capitalism and took note of opposing economic or political forces that might abate a common European revolutionary storm.

In *Capital* he argued that though the bourgeoisie proclaimed its exploitation to the "sober senses," it also dizzied these senses with a commodity
fetishism that camouflaged the real extraction of surplus value from the
workers under an appearance of equal exchange (wages for labor power).
Hence many workers' struggles demanded a "fair day's pay for a fair day's
work," determined by a balance of forces under capitalism, rather than seeking the "abolition of the wages system." [16] Much more strongly than in the
Manifesto, Capital suggested that the nature of class conflict between capitalists and workers required constant revolutionary illumination.

In part four of the *Manifesto,* Marx stressed the persistence of the European peasantry as an impediment to proletarianization and as a potential radical force in its own right (even in the first section, he had noted that peasants
might become radical by adopting a political stance as future proletarians).
Marx's *Capital* depicted the division of the workers between skilled and un-

15. *CM*, pp. 31–32.
16. Marx, *Capital,* 1:71–83, 167–198; *Wages, Price and Profit, MESW,* 1:446.

skilled, employed and unemployed.[17] In the IWA, he stressed above all the social divisions caused by the politics of divide and rule, between, for example, English and Irish laborers, as the chief obstacle to socialism. Given the social and political divisiveness of capitalism, the communist policy of unification and internationalism, highlighted in the *Manifesto* and Marx's *Inaugural Address of the IWA,* would play a decisive role; the leveling economic tendencies of capitalism alone would not lead to revolution.

Marx's lectures on "Wage Labor and Capital" (1847) already envisioned a relative rather than an absolute working-class impoverishment. Growing potential for realizing individual needs coupled with the corruption resulting from capitalist inequality would stimulate a communist movement:

> A house may be large or small; as long as the surrounding houses are equally small it satisfies all social demands for a dwelling. But let a palace arise beside the little house, and it shrinks from a little house to a hut. The little house now shows that its owner has only very slight or no demands to make; and however high it may shoot up in the course of civilization, if the neighboring palace grows to an equal or even greater extent the occupant of the relatively small house will feel more and more uncomfortable, dissatisfied and cramped within its four walls.[18]

Marx's analysis, of course, did not juxtapose workers and capitalists as individuals; instead, capitalist "palaces" arise from the exploitation and limited claims of workers. As noted in Chapter 1, *Capital* also depicted a "tendency of the rate of profit to fall," counteracted by other tendencies; capitalism inescapably leads to economic crises, but these countertendencies may postpone such breakdowns, or once the breakdowns have occurred, may breathe new life into the old economic system. While the "perennial gale" of capitalist destruction may relent or temporarily die down to a whisper, capitalism never reaches final economic collapse. Marx also pointed to war rather than economic crisis as a harbinger of revolution.

Using Hilary Putnam's criteria, the predictive successes of the *Manifesto* and *Capital,* particularly concerning the significance of working-class struggle and its international potential, have made Marx's general theory an im-

---

17. Marx, *Capital,* 1:44, 635–637, 640–712.

18. Marx, "Wage Labor and Capital," *MESW,* 1:93–94.

portant, if highly disputed, paradigm for the analysis of capitalist societies.[19] Indeed a sophisticated Marxian analysis, paying close attention to politics and sharply qualifying the arresting basic image of the *Manifesto*'s early sections or of *Capital*'s "Historical Tendency of Capitalist Accumulation," might provide a framework for interpreting the defeats and potentials of radical movements in twentieth-century capitalist societies without commitment to any empirical absurdity. While such a study lies beyond the scope of this book, I will return briefly to this issue in the conclusion.

8–4. The *Manifesto*'s Strategy for Germany

THE STRATEGIC SECTION OF THE *Manifesto* already indicated Marx's unstated but acute analysis of historical and political realities. Here the issue of peasant emancipation in precapitalist, tsar-dominated Poland superseded the general image of the vanishing, reactionary peasant. The revolt of the Polish peasants could ignite revolutionary democratic movements throughout Europe. Marx envisioned a working-class internationalism that would support these democratic as well as socialist uprisings. As a likely setting for socialist revolution, he focused on backward Germany rather than England:

> The Communists turn their attention chiefly to Germany, because that country is on the eve of a bourgeois revolution that is bound to be carried out under more advanced conditions of European civilization, and with a much more developed proletariat, than that of England was in the seventeenth, and of France in the eighteenth century, and because the bourgeois revolution in England will be but the prelude to an immediately following proletarian one.[20]

Though Marx did not retrace the dynamic of the French Revolution, this political experience, coupled with "much more advanced conditions of European civilization," provided the key to his conception of socialist revolution in the last section of the *Manifesto*.

In the democratic upsurge, communists would sustain the bourgeoisie in order to gain better conditions in which to overthrow it. If bourgeois rule lasted for any substantial period, an expansion of industry and commerce,

---

19. Shaw, *Marx's Theory of History*, p. 166. Putnam, "The Corroboration of Theories," *Collected Philosophical Papers*, 1:259, 268–269.

20. *CM*, p. 65.

notably the railroads, would enlarge and unify the proletariat. A single republic would demolish the provincialism of the thirty-nine German principalities and facilitate a nationwide socialist movement. Finally, the workers would gain universal suffrage and freedom of speech; communists could defend their principles under "less arduous" conditions and unite the proletariat into a "closely knit, militant and organized class." [21] On these counts, communist instigation of democratic revolution would benefit the proletariat.

Yet the triumphant bourgeoisie would immediately move to suppress communist activity as a mortal danger to its social predominance. Thus, Marx argued, in the democratic revolution, communists must "never cease for a single instant to instil into the working class the clearest possible recognition of the hostile antagonism between bourgeoisie and proletariat." [22] They must quickly acquire a well-organized political following to stave off bourgeois attacks and to pursue the potential for "an immediately following" proletarian victory. As we examine the *Manifesto*'s specific guidelines for communist activity in the German democratic revolution, the tension in Marx's political strategy leaps to the fore. This tension flowed from and mirrored the class divisions in the democratic movement itself. In 1848, Marx strove to overcome this conflict not in thought alone, but in action.

21. Engels, "Principles of Communism" in Marx and Engels, *Birth*, p. 189. Marx and Engels, "Demands of the Communist Party in Germany" in Appendix.
22. *CM*, p. 65.

PART TWO

Marx in the German Revolution

— IX —

Marx's Internationalism

9–1. The June Revolt

MARX'S ANALYSIS of the international situation provided the framework for his strategy in 1848, and internationalist policies characterized his activity throughout the revolutionary period. As the Paris June insurrection overshadowed all other events in 1848, Marx's response to it can serve as a starting point for examining his strategy and activity in the German revolution.

Following the February republican uprising in France, the new National Assembly espoused the "right to work" and set up "national ateliers." Though these ateliers provided some jobs for the unemployed, these "socialist" institutions differed only in the rhetoric surrounding them from the English poorhouses and became engines to exploit cheap labor. Adding insult to injury, a June 21 decree ordered married men to engage in public works projects in the provinces, in particular, draining marshes in the Sologne. It also required "the forcible expulsion of all unmarried workers from the . . . ateliers or their enrollment in the army." The republican Executive Commission responded to the complaints of a workers' delegation: "Obey the orders of the government; [if] the workers do not wish to go to the provinces, we will compel them by force . . . by force, do you understand?" After February, however, the monarchy no longer towered above the capitalists as the "lightning rod" for proletarian discontents. Illuminating the basic conflict of modern society, the Parisian workers responded to this decree with the first massive insurrection directed against the bourgeoisie.[1]

From June 25 on, the *NRZ* supported this insurrection. Engels's first articles emphasized its "purely proletarian character." The slogans "Bread or Death" and "Work or Death" were emblazoned on the flags on its barricades; republican catchwords, the *Marseillaise,* and other "memories of the

---

1. *CS*, p. 160. Roger Price, *The French Second Republic*, pp. 156–157, 159, 162. Charles Tilly and Lynn M. Lees, "The People of June, 1848" in Roger Price, ed., *Revolution and Reaction*, pp. 201–202. Price, ed., *1848 in France*, pp. 107–111. Marx, "Die Pariser 'Réforme' über die französischen Zustände," *Werke*, 5:449.

great revolution" had "disappeared." Engels called this June insurrection a "revolution of despair" at the unexpectedly oppressive nature of a bourgeois republic, a conscious life-and-death struggle analogous in all previous history only to the Roman slave war and the Lyons uprising of 1834. June had revived the cry of the Lyons silk weavers, "Live Working or Fighting Die." [2]

Faced with this profound threat, the bourgeoisie had cast aside the settled etiquette of barricade warfare: brief fighting and a change of regime. It responded with a brutal "war of extermination" against the workers. When the bourgeoisie mobilized the National Guard to suppress the revolution, it drove out the guard's proletarian membership. Only fifty guardsmen, according to Engels, reported from the working-class faubourgs of St. Antoine, St. Jacques, and St. Marceau. As a representative of the military commission of inquiry later noted, many guardsmen took part in the uprising. "Belleville," he wrote to the *procureur général* at Paris, ". . . has been one of the principal centers of insurrection, the struggle there has been most bitter. Of 7,000 National Guards, at least 3,000 took part in the insurrection." Thus the bourgeoisie had to seek military support from the provinces. Unlike the republican fighters of July 1830, or February 1848, the bourgeoisie offered no laurels to these Parisian workers to celebrate their courage. Yet, Engels suggested, history would specially honor this first decisive proletarian battle.[3]

On June 29, Marx's famous editorial "The June Revolution" conceived the uprising as a long-term victory for the workers. For "they [the Parisian workers] are *beaten,* but their opponents are defeated." The harsh reality of class struggle had exposed all republican "illusions or phrases" to which Marx had referred in the *Manifesto.* The Ecole Polytechnique students sided with the bourgeoisie; the medical students refused to treat wounded workers; the reputable republican papers, the *National* and the *Réforme,* decried the uprising; Lamartine's poetic "star shells" had viciously metamorphosed into "Cavaignac's incendiary rockets." As in the French Revolution, the workers and artisans had anticipated a new age of common citizenship; yet the new republic had distinguished among unequal beings as unerringly as Louis Philippe:

> The *fraternité,* the brotherhood of the opposing classes, of which the one exploits the other . . . proclaimed in February, written in big letters on the face of Paris, on every jail and on every barracks—has for its true, unadulter-

2. *Werke,* 5:112, 118–119.
3. Ibid., 5:128, 132. Price, *Second Republic,* pp. 178, 182, 184, 186–187, 190.

ated, prosaic expression *civil war,* . . . war of labor against capital. This brotherhood flamed from all the windows of Paris on the evening of June 25, illuminating the Paris of the bourgeois while the Paris of the proletariat burned, bled and moaned.[4]

In January, Marx had written in the *Manifesto,* "The history of all hitherto existing society is the history of class struggles." June exemplified this thesis with a vengeance.

In *The Social and Political Thought of Karl Marx,* Shlomo Avineri contends that Marx disavowed the June insurrection and depicts Marx's standpoint as economic determinist. According to Avineri, the rebels fell victim to "Jacobin-Blanquist" illusions and illustrated the "impotence of politics" where economic conditions have not yet "ripened":

> Despite his [Marx's] seeing in the political upheavals of this year a chance to create the circumstances for a socialist revolution, he consistently opposes all radical attempts at armed insurrection. A political revolution cannot bring down the walls of social reality. At the end of June 1848, Marx concludes his observations on the failure of the Jacobin-Blanquist *émeutes* in Paris by calling it not a defeat of the proletariat but a defeat of the republican Jacobin illusions, which fooled the workers into thinking that the failure of 1793 could become the success of 1848.[5]

Avineri omits Marx's estimate of the historical setting of French and European democratic revolution, and Marx's hope that a successful Parisian insurrection could spur it forward. In place of this estimate, Avineri superimposes on French history Marx's general thesis that advanced capitalism alone would undermine the "walls of [current] social reality." Without a fully developed capitalism, Avineri (but not Marx) concludes, working-class rebellion could accomplish nothing.

Yet Marx vehemently supported the June insurrection. He pointed out that the workers did not impotently "surrender" under attack. Instead they won a long-term victory by exposing the bourgeois ideology of republicanism. This insurrection had deepened into a conflict about the social order itself. As Feuerbach's philosophy criticized the heaven of religion and discov-

---

4. Marx, *On Revolution,* pp. 147, 148. On the class composition of the June rebels and the role of the intellectuals, see Price, *Second Republic,* pp. 187–188, 164–166, 171–176, 182–184. For the role of women, see Tocqueville, *Recollections,* p. 161.

5. Avineri, *Social and Political Thought,* p. 194. Avineri never explains this "despite."

ered its source in "man," so this struggle defeated the "hazy, blue sky of republican ideology" and exposed the "opium of 'patriotic' feelings." It did this not merely in books, but in the lives of thousands of fighting French workers. Unlike Joshua at Jericho, this first uprising did not bring down the walls of bourgeois domination, but it trumpeted communist consciousness widely among the masses and brought socialism one step nearer.[6]

Avineri contends that "republican-Jacobin" illusions goaded the workers to rise up; he turns Marx's critique of republican ideology into a condemnation of a working-class rebellion against unemployment and governmental deception. But Marx argued that the workers had republican illusions only about their common citizenship with the bourgeoisie. June proved irrevocably that the proletariat could expect no help or even mercy from that quarter:

> The brotherhood lasted only so long as the interest of the bourgeoisie fraternized with the interest of the proletariat. . . .

> The February Revolution was the beautiful revolution, the revolution of universal sympathy, while the contradictions that burst forth against the monarchy remained undeveloped and slumbered side by side in harmony. . . . The June Revolution is the ugly revolution, the repulsive revolution, because reality took the place of the phrase.

> . . . Order! cried Cavaignac, the brutal voice of the French National Assembly and of the republican bourgeoisie.

> Order! thundered the grapeshot as it tore the bodies of the proletariat.[7]

In summarizing this experience, Engels argued that the workers had not expected Cavaignac to use such "Algerian methods of war" in Parisian barricade fighting. They had not responded with the only weapon available to

6. Marx, *On Revolution*, pp. 153, 148–149. Friedrich Engels, *Revolution and Counterrevolution in Germany*, p. 72. Many organizers of the IWA and the first socialist parties learned the lessons of class war from June.

7. Marx, *On Revolution*, p. 148. Etienne Cabet, who responded to the ferocity of class war by leaving France to found a communist colony in Indiana shortly after June, underlined Marx's point: "It's . . . the government, it's the *National*, it's the *Réforme*, it is above all Ledru-Rollin and Lamartine who have lost everything." Christopher H. Johnson, "Etienne Cabet and the Problem of Class Antagonism," pp. 440–442.

them, "incendiarism," because this tactic violated "their sense of right." Placed on the defensive, the workers went down to defeat. Thus, against the bourgeoisie's sheer murderousness, the proletariat had acted in too decent and humane a fashion. According to Marx, future proletarian uprisings should expect to bear the brunt of bourgeois hatred, a point he would reiterate during the Paris Commune.[8] Throughout 1848–1849, Marx looked to a renewed Parisian insurrection as a catalyst to revolution throughout Europe.

9–2. Internationalism and German Democracy

TO MARX AND ENGELS, support for June exemplified the internationalism that they had stressed in the *Manifesto*. This internationalism cut not only against conceptions propagated by the aristocrats and monarchy, but also against current prejudices in the democratic movement. Their stand disturbed the German bourgeoisie and petite bourgeoisie, and the NRZ lost numerous shareholders because of it. In response to Marx's editorial, the *Kölnische Zeitung* declaimed:

> The *Neue Rheinische Zeitung* calls itself an *Organ of Democracy*. We call it an *Organ* of the Red Republic. No one who preaches riot and anarchy is a supporter of democracy. Is the *Neue Rheinische Zeitung* perhaps interested in the social question and takes the part of the insurgents because of an exaggerated friendship for the human race? [9]

In Engels's "The *Kölnische Zeitung* on the June Revolution," he mocked these editors who defended the bourgeoisie as "the honest men," castigated the workers as "thieves," and poured "sulfuric acid" on the workers' wounds. Engels responded vigorously to the charge of "criminality" as an inversion of the truth: "They [the workers] looted! But what did they steal? Weapons, ammunition, surgical dressings, and the most necessary items of food." Engels contrasted a tradition of popular justice, legitimizing the reappropriation of necessities in times of crisis and starvation, with the *Kölnische*

8. Engels, "Die Junirevolution," *Werke*, 5:149. In 1871, Marx would criticize the insufficient aggressiveness of the Communards who should have marched on Versailles. Marx to Kugelmann, April 12, 1871, *SC*, p. 263.

9. Nicolaievsky and Maenchen-Helfen, *Karl Marx*, pp. 168–169. Hammen, *Red '48ers*, p. 250. Marx's and Engels's steadfast adherence to the cause of the Parisian workers, despite a breach with more conservative forces, prefigured their later conflict with the more conservative union leaders of the IWA over the Paris Commune.

Zeitung's attempt to reduce a great historical uprising to individual acts of criminality. The rebels had dialectically written their own idea of justice boldly on the shop windows: "Death to the thieves!"(*Mort aux Voleurs!*), that is, to the exploiting class, the bourgeoisie.[10]

Marx and Engels contrasted the *Kölnische Zeitung*'s timid "republicanism of the day before yesterday," recoiling at proletarian politics, with the austere nobility of the ancient citizen. Engels ironically referred to the "Spartan Cologne paper," and to its editor Wolfers, in the biting phrase of Shakespeare's Mark Antony, as "an honorable man." For Marx and Engels, the new solidarity of workers, the social republicanism of a nonexploitative society, paradoxically inherited and transformed classical political virtue. The modern proletarians fused the just audacity of Spartacus, leader of the Roman slaves, and the adherence to common interest and political vigor of the republican citizen. As Marx put it, a genuine democratic press should elegize the June revolutionaries' heroism, reminiscent of the ancients, and their prefiguring of a galley-slave republic, a "republic of labor":

> The plebeians, torn by hunger, reviled by the press, abandoned by the physicians, cursed by the respectable thieves as firebrands and galley slaves, their women and children plunged into boundless misery, their best survivors deported overseas—for them the laurels on the darkling brow, that is the *privilege,* that is the *right of the democratic press.*[11]

The June insurrection demarcated the class divisions within the German democratic movement. Only the Cologne Worker Society paper, and Stephan Born's *Das Volk,* journal of the Berlin Workers' Brotherhood, joined the *NRZ* in supporting the Paris workers.[12]

In contrast to his indictment of bourgeois editors, Marx praised

10. Engels, "Die 'Kölnische Zeitung' über die Junirevolution," *Werke,* 5:142–143. On popular conceptions of justice, see Edward P. Thompson, "The Moral Economy of the English Crowd," and James Scott, *The Moral Economy of the Peasant,* ch. 6.

11. Engels, "Kölnische Zeitung," *Werke,* 5:140–142. Marx, "The June Revolution" in *On Revolution,* p. 150. In 1871, Marx would hail the Commune as a "republic of labor" and frequently invoke the imagery of ancient heroism.

12. Even before June, Born emphasized internationalism: "We have the right to take sides with our oppressed brothers, be they German, French or English. . . . They all have only one interest, liberation from the chains of the rule of money; they all have only *one* oppressor." P. H. Noyes, *Organization and Revolution,* p. 144. Unlike Marx, Born discouraged the Workers' Brotherhood from participating in the democratic revolution.

Proudhon's speech in the French National Assembly of July 31, 1848. In this case, Proudhon had boldly defended the real proletarian movement and highlighted the property question. In Proudhon's own words, he had become *"l'homme-terreur."* "By recognizing the right to work in the constitution, you [the bourgeoisie] have also recognized the abolition of property," Proudhon said to the other deputies. "Place yourselves eternally under the protection of bayonets, prolong eternally the state of siege: capital nonetheless will still be afraid, and socialism has its eyes riveted upon it." [13]

Contrary to Proudhon's theory of class harmony, actual French revolutionary antagonisms had driven him first in one direction, then in another. After February, in the first flowering of popular sentiment for classless political citizenship, Proudhon won an election in the Doubs on a social platform of class reconciliation and a people's bank. In June, though empathizing with the workers' hunger, Proudhon did not regard the expulsion of unmarried workers from the ateliers as a sufficient reason to oppose the republic. Influenced by classic antiradical or anticommunist ideology, he swallowed the rumors that foreigners had instigated the June insurrection. (Later, he would comment critically on the "imbecility" of his own view and conclude that misery had impelled the revolt.) Though shocked by the bourgeoisie's ferocious response, he still did not fully support the rebels but considered them victims of an "odious lack of faith" who had unfortunately given way to indignation. The February Revolution had made in the name of governmental power "a promise that power could not keep." [14] Instead of forming a mutualist association and absorbing the old political structure, the June rebels had erroneously looked to government for help.

In June's aftermath, the consolidation of the fear of revolution, described so vividly by Tocqueville, impressed Proudhon. As the French Assembly shifted right, so Proudhon moved to the left: "It is necessary to teach the victors of June that they have not finished with it as they suppose . . . that the only fruit they have reaped from their victory is a surplus of difficulties." To avenge June, Proudhon averred, radicals must "pose the social question with redoubled energy" or even with "a sort of terrorism." Thus, in his National Assembly speech, he sometimes invoked a proletarian socialism, producing an almost continuous uproar and even horror among the other repre-

13. Marx, "Proudhons Rede gegen Thiers," *Werke*, 5:307–308. Proudhon had a different though still menacing recollection of the speech's last line: "capital will not return; socialism has its eyes on it." Proudhon, *Confessions*, pp. 201–202.

14. Proudhon, *Confessions*, pp. 167–170.

sentatives. While his analysis of June still differed from Marx's, his reaction to its defeat temporarily pushed him toward a similar stand. Far from pursuing a personal vendetta, Marx saluted Proudhon's changed position, especially his defense of June in the Assembly, as an "act of great courage." [15]

The *Kölnische Zeitung*'s Parisian correspondents had praised Proudhon's economics and philosophy. Taking a less dialectical view of Proudhon than Marx did, the editors now turned on him viciously for his defense of June, prompting Marx to question ironically: is Mr. Proudhon no longer Mr. Proudhon? Marx lost sight neither of Proudhon's shifting relationship to the class struggle nor of his general views. After the nightmare of June, however, history did not count for the *Kölnische Zeitung*. Proudhon's malignant mask (after June) metaphysically replaced his benign visage (before June) with no trace of memory between them. [16]

During this period, the *Kölnische Zeitung* turned many of its other judgments topsy-turvy. Before the revolt, this paper had seen French society as a model of class harmony, England as a model of class strife. But June reversed these roles. Wolfers asked, "Where is it possible in England to discover *any trace of hatred* against the class which *in France is called the bourgeoisie?*" Engels noted that Wolfers not only dismissed the "social civil war" of the preceding eighty years as "nothing but a long demonstration of the love of the English proletariat for its bourgeois employers," but also characterized France as the "classic country as regards hatred of the bourgeoisie." Engels sarcastically continued:

> For the last ten years English agitators, applauded by the entire proletariat, have tirelessly preached burning hatred of the bourgeoisie whereas the French working class and socialist literature has always advocated reconciliation with the bourgeoisie on the grounds that the class antagonisms in France were far less developed than in England. [17]

Louis Blanc, Cabet, Caussidière, Ledru-Rollin, men at whose names the *Kölnische Zeitung* currently made "the triple sign of the cross," had urged peace between proletariat and bourgeoisie. The swiftness and utterness of the

15. Tocqueville, *Recollections*, pp. 160, 168–170, 195. Proudhon, *Confessions*, p. 192. Marx, *Poverty of Philosophy*, p. 200.

16. Marx, "Proudhons Rede," *Werke*, 5:308.

17. Engels, "Die 'Kölnische Zeitung' über englische Verhältnisse," *Werke*, 5:284–286.

reversal and the inaccuracy of the judgment testify to the depth of the German bourgeoisie's shock at the Parisian workers' June insurrection.

9–3. Russia, Poland, and Germany

THROUGHOUT 1848, Marx stressed the link between the destiny of working-class social republicanism and the European democratic movements. As a June victory would have breathed new life into the entire revolution, so its defeat marked the resurgence of Russian-led, European reaction.

During this period, Marx viewed tsarism as a pivot upholding the Prussian monarchy and counterrevolution in Germany. In his *NRZ* editorial "The Russian Note," he condemned foreign minister Nesselrode's paternalistic reminder to the Prussian government that the tsar had defended Germany's "integrity and independence" against Napoleon in 1812. Marx responded sarcastically, "The Holy Alliance and its impious works, the congresses of bandits at Carlsbad, Laibach, Verona, etc., the persecutions in Russia and Germany against every enlightened word, ought evidently to have impressed upon us a profound gratitude." Nesselrode implicitly threatened Russian intervention if Germany did not remain divided into thirty-nine principalities. He urged a lofty sounding "moral unity" of Germany, meaning its subservience to Russian policy, but not a more dangerous "material unity." [18]

Contrary to Nesselrode, Marx contended that a Napoleonic victory would have eradicated the "three dozen petty kingdoms" and forged German unity. In 1848, Marx evaluated war not by German chauvinist criteria, but by whether it advanced "civilization," marked by the institution of bourgeois political and economic power, or "barbarism," marked by the strengthening of feudal and monarchical arrangements. [19] Marx's New Year's editorial for 1849 called the French bourgeoisie's suppression of June "the victory of the East over the West, the defeat of civilization by barbarism," and linked it to Russian interests: "In Wallachia the oppression of the Romance people was

18. *Werke*, 5:294, 298.

19. Applying such a criterion in different circumstances, Marx argued that colonialism, though motivated by "sordid passions" and characterized by great brutality, sometimes represented progress for the colonized peoples (he looked upon such progress as creating the conditions in which the colonized could revolt against their masters). In the 1860s, however, Marx would change his outlook in analyzing English colonialism in Ireland. Marx to Meyer and Vogt, April 9, 1870, *SC*, pp. 235–238. Alan Gilbert, "Marx on Internationalism and War."

initiated by the tools of the Russians, the Turks; in Vienna, Croats, Pandurs, Czechs, Serassaner, and such lumpen rabble strangled German freedom; and at the moment the Czar is all over Europe." [20]

Marx and Engels vehemently defended the Polish independence movement. Early in 1848, a Polish democratic uprising forced the Prussian monarchy to grant national autonomy to the Grand Duchy of Posen. Shortly afterward, the Prussian government and press began to spread the rumor that Polish democracy discriminated against the German minority. Using this excuse, Prussia reconquered Poland in a brief but ferocious conflict. In July, the Frankfurt parliament ratified this conquest.[21]

Marx and Engels saw Polish democracy as a pivot of the East European revolutionary movement. Between August 9 and September 6, 1848, Engels devoted eight articles in the *NRZ* to the Poland debate in the Frankfurt parliament. He ridiculed chauvinist arguments in favor of the conquests and mocked patriots like Lichnowski. When Russia, Prussia, and Austria divided up Poland in 1772, Engels argued, the Prussian monarchy had grown stronger internally and more dependent on the tsar. The current Polish peasant demands for "agrarian democracy" and land reform would invigorate the movement to shake off Russian as well as feudal bondage. Jarring tsarism, Polish democracy would also undermine Russia's ability to sustain feudalism in Germany; the Polish movement menaced tsar and kaiser at once. Correspondingly, success for German democracy presupposed freedom for Polish serfs: in revenge for partition, Poland "became the revolutionary party in Russia, Austria, and Prussia." Marx and Engels acted energetically on this program. On August 11, the Cologne Democratic Society, presided over by Marx, endorsed the *NRZ*'s position.[22]

---

20. Marx, *On Revolution*, p. 43. During this period, Marx condemned the tsar and his supporters, not all Russians. Despite his support for democratic elements in Eastern Europe, Marx sometimes criticized whole peoples—"Turks," "Pandurs," and "Croats"—as reactionary in a dubious, racist way. See Roman Rosdolsky, "Friedrich Engels und das Problem der 'Geschichtslosen Völker,' " pp. 241–246, 250, 265. Rosdolsky's useful account and critique of Marx's and Engels's attitude toward Austrian Slavs is marred by his omission of their vigorous pursuit of internationalist policies in 1848 as well as the later changes in their position. He thus severs the connection between Marx's views on the national question and Lenin's, undialectically treating one as all bad and the other as all good, and provides an uncritical endorsement of Lenin's position.

21. Hammen, *Red '48ers*, p. 277.

22. *Werke*, 5:355, 487, 488. See also Marx's editorial of 1849, "The House of Hohenzollern," in *On Revolution*, p. 480.

Once the Poles unleashed an insurrection, Marx and Engels hoped to mobilize German democracy to defend Poland. Tsarism would intervene, and a republican war against Russia would ensue. Once again, the French Revolution provided the great example. In an early article, Engels cited the duke of Brunswick's 1792 threat to "raze Paris to the last stone" which instigated the Convention's *levée en masse* against France's counterrevolutionary enemies. A German democratic movement, as dynamic as its French predecessor, would wage war on European absolutism and make socialism possible. Marx and Engels noted that only a war against Russia would be a *"war of revolutionary Germany."* [23]

As 1848 wore on, Marx also emphasized the reactionary role of England, "the country which has defrayed the costs of European restoration with its own money." Threatened by Chartism, England united with Russia to oppose democratic and socialist movements on the Continent. [24]

9–4. The Common Interests of the Proletariat

THE *Manifesto* HAD HERALDED but left unexplained the common proletarian interests that communist internationalism should defend. In the *NRZ*, however, Marx and Engels spelled out the character of these interests. This solidarity did not depend on an advanced level of productive forces within countries, let alone a great degree of capitalist penetration into a foreign economy. Instead, this internationalism derived mainly from a political fact: the likelihood of a common response by European exploiting classes, bourgeois and aristocratic, to a revolutionary threat affecting any one of them. If the democratic movements proceeded separately and provincially, this Holy Alliance would crush them one by one. The unity of Russia, England, and the continental monarchies drove democracy and socialism into an alliance against them. Thus, every German democrat had a vital stake in international solidarity. Marx invoked the configuration of reactionary powers as a decisive auxiliary statement that led to the strategic judgments of the *Manifesto*'s fourth section, especially its stress on German support for Polish democracy. Lacking this historical setting, the reader of the *Manifesto* sees only the abstract general theory, or, more rarely, the seemingly paradoxical applications.

23. Engels, "Auswärtige deutsche Politik" and *NRZ* editorial, "Die auswärtige deutsche Politik und die letzten Ereignisse zu Prag," *Werke*, 5:154; 202.

24. Marx, "The Revolutionary Movement" in *On Revolution*, pp. 43–44.

Yet patriotism still perverted German democracy and sustained a Prussian expansion which doubly reinforced internal reaction. Prussian military campaigns crushed potential external allies of German democracy and prepared an army to defeat revolution. Faced with this mortal threat, Marx and Engels mounted an all-out fight in the *NRZ* against racism and patriotism.

In Engels's articles on the Prague uprising and its defeat by Austria, he contended that German democracy "had to renounce [Germany's] whole past." The German monarchies had attacked democratic movements in Italy and Poland as well as among the Czechs. For this reason, other democrats bitterly identified German democracy with their oppressors: "A nation that throughout its history allowed itself to be used as a tool of oppression against all other nations must first of all prove that it has been really revolutionized." A genuine German democracy "should have proclaimed the freedom of the nations hitherto suppressed by her." [25]

Engels's article of July 2 on Germany's foreign policy argued that Prussia had distinguished itself among nations by its deceptive policy of divide and rule: "To excite peoples against each other, to use one to oppress the other and to maintain by doing so absolute power: such was the art and work of the preceding governments and their diplomats." For seventy years, Germany had sided with Britain against North American independence, with the aristocratic emigrés against the French Revolution, with the House of Orange against the Dutch republic, and with the Austrian monarchy against the Hungarians. An article of July 12, "German Foreign Policy and the Latest Events in Prague," extended this analysis. Internally, the German rulers had opposed democratic revolution with a campaign to nurture race hatred (*Stammhass*) as a diversion for the "glowing lava" of revolutionary sentiment. They had attempted to focus such hatred upon the Czechs, the Poles, and the Italians. This policy aimed to "train in race wars of unheard of horror and unspeakable barbarism a soldiery such as the Thirty Years' War could hardly produce." These "wars of restoration" as Marx and Engels called them perpetuated a counterrevolutionary army, propagated racist ideology, and undermined German democracy from within. [26]

Most of the German press supported Prussian wars of restoration. Citing the report of a German in Prague, the *NRZ*'s editorial of July 12 opposed the

25. *Werke*, 5:202, 81.
26. Ibid., 5:154–155, 202.

current slander that the Czech democratic movement aimed to suppress Czechs of German extraction. On August 27, Engels exposed the *Kölnische Zeitung's* patriotic arguments on Italy. Levin Schücking had defended the proposition that "providential affinities" had drawn Italy into Austria as part of "greater Germany." That's why, Engels replied sarcastically, the two countries had fought for 2,000 years. That's why German blood had so often reddened the streets of Milan.[27]

In the actual European clash of powers, Marx's internationalist strategy required unremitting ideological efforts. The spell of the Prussian government's patriotic appeals and a narrow attachment to putative gains from expansion enthralled many Germans. The common interest—to avoid death in a war of conquest or to make real gains by driving the democratic revolution to victory—could only win out through a political conflict. Without revolutionary organizing, Prussian power and momentum would carry its aims among the population. In the first sections of the *Manifesto,* the need for communist political campaigns seems obscure. At best, such activity would accelerate an already occurring economic process and place a political capstone, as it were, on a preceding economic foundation. In the bitter conflicts of 1848, exposing patriotism and forging democratic and socialist internationalism played an indispensable role.

Marx's stress on a common proletarian interest appealed to the political intelligence of workers and other democrats. Here more than anywhere else, he hoped to locate the "soul," electrified by great public events, of which he had spoken in his early writings.[28] Through internationalism, Marx thought, the workers would realize the social and political universality or human "species-being" that he had taken over from Hegel and Feuerbach and transformed. Ancient and modern republican theory had envisioned a small community as the locus of citizenship. Marxian communists of the 1840s looked to a much expanded political space cutting across national boundaries in which democrats and proletarians of different nationalities would unite. Marx's proletarians who knew no fatherland, would yet become the truly "political" animals. Though temporarily restricted by national divisions and expecting to triumph at first only within national boundaries, Marxian com-

27. Unsigned editorial, "Prag," and Engels, "Die 'Kölnische Zeitung' über Italien," *Werke,* 5:203–205, 370.
28. Mewes, "On the Concept of Politics in the Early Works of Karl Marx," p. 282.

munists sought to forge a social republican citizenship and a new kind of international political association.

9–5. Pan-Slavism and Civilization

In 1849, Marx and Engels condemned "democratic" Pan-Slavism as an instrument of Russian foreign policy. In their view, Pan-Slavism attempted to unite oppressed and revolutionary nations like Poland with the counterrevolutionary Slavs dominated by the Austrian monarchy, notably the Czechs. Pan-Slavism confused the claims of nations that stood at different stages of historical development and played opposed political roles. Hesitating to engage in revolutionary action until all Slavs would support it, this movement leaned toward Russia and opposed non-Slav revolutionary movements. Marx and Engels's hatred of tsarism engendered their early rift with Michael Bakunin, the leading radical advocate of a Pan-Slavist program.[29]

As Engels's article "Democratic Pan-Slavism" (1849) used the criterion of promoting civilization against barbarism to attack several future nations, some authors like E. H. Carr have reduced his and Marx's argument to mere German chauvinism. This view ignores Marx and Engels's internationalism, their clear emphasis on upholding democracy against Prussia, and their vehement defense of Poland. Yet Engels's (and by implication, his editor Marx's) quasi-utilitarian defense of revolution and capitalism as "civilizing" forces led to some peculiar judgments. Engels dismissed the Slavs under Austrian control as pseudonations which lacked histories of their own and depended for industrial, commercial, literary, and political advance on stronger peoples. This argument contradicted Engels's previous defense of the Prague uprising. Furthermore, Engels suggested that the European democratic movements should support these "counterrevolutionary" nations if they offered any sign of revolutionary stirring. Given Engels's previous acknowledgment

---

29. At the Slav Congress in Prague in May 1848, Bakunin elaborated a conception of democratic Pan-Slav unity. The following anecdote, told by Carr, illustrates the strident nationalism of his outlook: "When a former German friend taunted him with the inconvenient fact that the Slav brothers had not even a common language, he replied with spirit that there was one phrase which was understood by all Slavs from the Elbe to the Urals, from the Adriatic to the Balkans: *Zahrabte niemce!* [Down with the Germans!]" Bakunin nonetheless took part in the Dresden uprising of 1849 and did not oppose German democracy. Edward Hallett Carr, *Michael Bakunin*, pp. 156–158. Sam Dolgoff, ed., *Bakunin on Anarchy*, pp. 63–68.

of a radical potential, at least in Prague, his condemnation of these peoples because of the current political stand of their organized leadership seems hasty and overdrawn.[30]

In the same article, Engels crassly defended industrious "Yankee" expansion against stereotyped "lazy Mexicans" in the war of 1846–1848; he argued that victorious American capitalism would open up new cities and railroads in California and initiate a "world-historical" epoch of commerce with the Pacific: "The 'independence' of a few Spanish Californians and Texans may suffer because of it, in some places, 'justice' and other moral principles may be violated; but what does that matter compared to such facts of world-historical significance?"[31] Despite Engels's predominant emphasis on internationalism, some of the stereotypes of the time lingered in his and Marx's thinking.

Marx's later writings on British colonialism in India or on English original accumulation would denounce the horrible mass suffering imposed by capitalist expansion. In those first cases in which the economic and political prerequisites for radical revolution did not yet exist, Marx recognized the instrumental value of capitalist progress while condemning its exploitative consequences. He cautiously endorsed such progress only insofar as it created conditions for a just revolt against it. In such situations, he refrained from making any final moral judgments and probably believed that such judgments lacked objectivity. The capitalist era, however, had forged new means that made action to achieve a more just society possible. Only the revolt against capitalism would fuse intrinsic and instrumental goods as in international solidarity or the Paris Commune (this revolt embodied goods of character, such as heroism, and of activity, such as achieving political community; it also contributed to the goal of abolition of classes). Ultimately, Marx's ethical vision of a communist society focused on a "rich" flowering of individuality. In this perspective, Engels's (and his own) 1848 criterion of "advancing civilization" seems at best provisional and one-sided. Beyond this, by the 1860s, Marx had begun to reverse his perspective on the historical role of colonial conquests as we saw in the case of Ireland. He then condemned United States expansion into Mexico as part of the desperate effort

---

30. Carr, *Bakunin*, p. 176. Engels, *Revolution and Counterrevolution in Germany*, p. 49. Overreacting to Pan-Slavism, Engels once even called for a "war of extermination" against counterrevolutionary Slav peoples. *Werke*, 6:286.

31. *Werke*, 6:273–274.

of southern oligarchs to extend the legal domain of slavery and gain predominance over the North.[32]

9–6. German Democracy and Schleswig-Holstein

IN ONE EXCEPTIONAL CASE IN 1848, Marx and Engels supported Prussian war against Denmark for control of Schleswig-Holstein. Democratic movements in the two duchies sought an alliance with Germany; the Danish monarchy strove to reconquer them. Engels argued that the German war effort represented the "right of civilization" and would contribute to the unification of a larger, democratic Germany.[33] Unlike the unpopular German wars in Italy, Poland, and Prague, Engels noted, this war was supported by the German people: "We [Marx and Engels] therefore advocated an energetic conduct of the Danish war, from the very beginning, but this does not in any way denote kinship with the sea-surrounded bourgeois beer-garden enthusiasm." [34]

In making this somewhat difficult distinction between German chauvinism and his and Marx's defense of this war, Engels argued that the three most counterrevolutionary powers in Europe–Russia, England, and the Prussian monarchy–supported Denmark. As Prussia waged war against Denmark, Engels's inclusion of it on this list seems peculiar. But Engels saw this war as a sham: "As long as it was possible the Prussian government merely *pretended* to be waging a *war*–one recalls Wildenbruch's note, the alacrity with which the Prussian government, on the representation of England and Russia, ordered the withdrawal from Jutland, and finally the two armistice agree-

---

32. Marx, "The Future Results of British Rule in India" in *On Colonialism and Modernization*, pp. 136–137. Marx, *Capital*, 1:713–716, 760, 762. Marx, "The North American Civil War" and "The Civil War in the United States" in Marx and Engels, *The Civil War in the United States*, pp. 62–63, 66–67, 71, 78–81. Contrary to Allen Wood, "The Marxian Critique of Justice," Marx did not condemn popular demands for justice like "a fair day's pay for a fair day's work." Instead, he supported popular efforts to win better conditions and reinterpreted them on the basis of a more thoroughgoing claim: "abolition of the wages system" and exploitation. See Alan Gilbert, "Marx on Internationalism, War and Exploitation."

33. Engels, "Der dänisch-preussische Waffenstillstand," *Werke*, 5:395. Marx and Engels always sought the unity of a democratic Germany, not its fragmentation.

34. Ibid., 5:393.

ments." [35] According to Engels, Prussia feared that further war against Denmark might provoke general war, reinforce the democratic movement, and ultimately sweep away the monarchy entirely.

In any case, Russia and England threatened to intervene, and so the Prussian government concluded the Treaty of Malmö. [36] But the German democratic movement did not accept this setback. On September 5, the Frankfurt Assembly rejected the Treaty of Malmö and forced the Hansemann ministry to resign.

Friedrich Dahlmann was invited to form a new ministry to conduct the war. But the German parliamentarians feared expanded war against Russia since it would require thoroughgoing popular mobilization and might compel these representatives to provide vigorous revolutionary leadership. For just this reason, Marx and Engels urged that the National Assembly assume command of foreign policy in the name of the democratic movement.

A mass meeting in Cologne on September 7, convened at the initiative of the *NRZ,* endorsed the democratic cause in Schleswig-Holstein. Consistent with Marx and Engels's general position, the meeting explicitly opposed any forcible German annexation of "Danish speaking North Schleswig . . . against its will." In Frankfurt, democrats launched a prowar insurrection, and on September 20, another mass meeting in Cologne hailed the Frankfurt uprising. Democracy in Schleswig-Holstein had become a mass issue. [37] The Prussian government promptly placed Cologne under martial law. Despite this considerable popular anger, the monarchy survived the September crisis. It forced the Assembly to reverse its decision and ratify the armistice; it also set up a new right-wing ministry. Confronted with the armistice, Engels angrily concluded, "Lack of courage is ruining the whole German movement." Up to that time, the movement had dissipated its forces in many small and bloody encounters, yet had not acted decisively on the great issues. Engels called for greater centralization and more energetic leadership. Again he recalled past revolutionary experience; Cromwell's bold dismissal of the Long Parliament highlighted the dwarfish and timorous character of German democracy: "The National Assembly has made its decision; it has pro-

---

35. Ibid., 5:396, 529. The secret Wildenbruch note, delivered on April 8, 1848, to the Danish monarchy, disclosed that Prussia aimed not to win the war but to divert the republican movement at home.

36. Ibid., 5:396–397. Hammen, *Red '48ers,* p. 290.

37. *Werke,* 5:497–498, *CW,* 7:577–578.

nounced the *death sentence* upon itself and upon the so-called central authority created by it. If Germany had a Cromwell, it would not be long before he would say, 'You are no Parliament! In the name of God, go.' "[38] Engels worried that the German movement lacked the internal resources to push aside its current conservative leadership. He looked mainly to renewed Parisian insurrection to spark German and European revolution.

9–7. Marx's Explanation of the Counterrevolution's Successes

THE SUPPRESSION OF JUNE triggered the downfall of European democracy. Marx's subsequent article "The Victory of the Counterrevolution in Vienna" bitterly noted that the November defeat of the Vienna uprising concluded the "second act" of the counterrevolutionary drama, "the first act having been played out in Paris under the title 'the June days'." In "The Revolutionary Movement in Italy," he would note two other decisive triumphs for reaction: the defeat of the Chartists in England on April 20 and the fall of Milan to Austria on August 6.[39]

In explaining the setbacks to the revolution thus far, Marx emphasized the international impact of the defeats of specific movements coupled with insufficient democratic and working-class solidarity. He altered auxiliary statements concerned with the politics of the actual conflict rather than with economic factors. Marx believed that the political situation could change quickly. A new revolutionary effort in any of these centers might trigger a general radical resurgence. In response to defeat, Marx defied the counterrevolution and called for "red republican" insurrection in Paris and for world war: "Armies from the countryside will pour over the frontiers, and the real power of the contending parties will emerge clearly. Then we will remember June and October, and we too will cry out: *Vae Victis!*"[40] He advocated mass "revolutionary terrorism" against the enemy.

In Marx's New Year's editorial, he again called for republican war not only against Russia but also against England:

> "The country which has transformed whole nations into its proletarians, which has clasped the whole world in its giant arms . . . the country where

38. Engels, "Die Ratifikation des Waffenstillstandes," *Werke*, 5:408–409.

39. Marx, *On Revolution*, p. 42. *Werke*, 6:77.

40. Marx, "Victory of the Counterrevolution in Vienna" in *On Revolution*, p. 42.

internal class contradictions exist in their most pronounced and shameless form—England—seems to be the rock on which revolutionary waves are shattered, where the new society starves in its mother's lap." [41]

Responsive to the changing fortunes of the actual revolutionary movement, Marx did not conceive of a prolonged German democratic revolution, followed by a proletarian one, as the sole path to socialism in 1848–1849. Closer to the *Manifesto*'s first sections, he also discerned the potential for an English Chartist victory under conditions of world war.[42] English socialism would then "dictate" the revolution to the rest of Europe. In 1848, Marx did not regard socialism as "inevitable" in either Germany or England. Though his general theory of epochal economic tendencies suggested an ultimate "necessity" for socialism in Europe, the best strategic estimates for a specific country provided only guidelines, not guarantees of success. If the particular historical circumstances did not coalesce, then the revolution would fail. Neither a renewed French uprising nor a world war was to be.

In 1849, Marx and Engels continued to welcome any democratic stirrings. Engels praised the Hungarian insurrection against Austria and Russia. But the counterrevolution moved from victory to victory. Prussia eventually exiled Marx from the Rhineland and suppressed the *NRZ*.[43]

9–8. The Changing International Role of the Bourgeoisie

ON AN INTERNATIONAL PLANE, Marx studied the European bourgeoisie's mounting trepidation in the face of popular uprisings and its increasing anxiety to unite with the counterrevolution. In Windischgrätz's and Jellachich's suppression of the Vienna insurrection, the German, French, and Viennese bourgeoisies demonstrated their acutely reactionary character:

> Who fled in droves from Vienna and left to the magnanimity of the people the watch over its wealth, only to calumniate them for their services during the flight and to see them slaughtered upon its return?

The *bourgeoisie*.

41. Marx, *On Revolution*, pp. 43–44.
42. Ibid., p. 44.
43. Marx had previously renounced Prussian citizenship. Despite the revolution, the monarchy refused his application to renew his citizenship in 1848.

Whose innermost secrets did the thermometer show when it fell with every breath of the Viennese people and rose with every one of their death rattles? Who speaks in the rune language of the stock exchange?

The *bourgeoisie.*

The "German National Assembly" and its "Central Authority" have betrayed Vienna. Whom do they represent?

Above all the *bourgeoisie.*

The victory of Croatian Freedom and Order in Vienna was made possible by the victory of the "honest" republic in Paris. Who was victorious in the June Days there?

The *bourgeoisie.*[44]

The bourgeoisie had provided the ostensible leadership for the failing democratic and nationalist movements that Marx and Engels supported so vehemently in 1848. Given this experience, they concluded that the era of successful revolutions, modeled on France, had drawn to a close. Popular insurrection might still catapult the bourgeoisie into power, but the bourgeoisie would immediately seek terms of compromise with the old regime in order to bridle the emerging proletarian movement. A worker-peasant alliance frightened it more than absolutist harassment. Thus, the failure of Marx's strategy led to a revised estimate of the bourgeoisie's politics and a new strategic solution. Communists must galvanize a movement of workers and peasants and propel the democratic revolution to victory despite or even against the bourgeoisie. In addition, Marx surmised that the workers and peasants, once mobilized and armed, especially under conditions of world war, might continue to fight for socialism. In the twentieth-century, Lenin and Mao Tse-tung would reach similar conclusions.[45]

44. Marx, "Counterrevolution" in *On Revolution*, p. 41.
45. Mao of course would lead a predominantly peasant revolutionary movement.

— X —

Marx's Strategy for Germany:
The French Revolution Radicalized

10–1. Demands of the German Communists

BETWEEN MARCH 21 AND 29, 1848, Marx and Engels drafted the "Demands of the Communist Party in Germany" (hereafter "Seventeen Demands"; see Appendix). This program, originally circulated as a leaflet in Paris, represented a further step in applying the *Manifesto*'s general theory to the upcoming German democratic revolution.

Though this program served certain bourgeois interests, for instance by advocating the abolition of remnant feudal restrictions on capitalism in a unified republic, Marx mainly attempted to unite the "producers of all wealth," the proletariat, peasants, and petite bourgeoisie, who could overthrow the bourgeoisie as soon as the democratic revolution had succeeded. The program did not explicitly call for socialism; yet its implementation would have pushed strongly toward a subsequent proletarian revolution:

> It is in the interest of the German proletariat, the petite bourgeoisie, and the peasantry to work energetically to achieve the foregoing measures. For only through the realization of these demands can the millions, who have hitherto been exploited in Germany by a small number . . . attain their rights and achieve the power that rightly belongs to them as the producers of all wealth.

Marx and Engels proposed a series of democratic demands to unify the German republic, attain universal suffrage, and guarantee participation of workers in representative bodies. At the outset of the revolution, most German democrats still considered the demand for a unified republic an extreme position. Marx viewed the other demands, especially the one for universal suffrage, as creating a tension between the bourgeoisie's concentrated exploitative social power and the formal political power (the vote) in the hands of the workers and peasants. In *The Class Struggles in France* and *The Eighteenth Brumaire of Louis Napoleon,* Marx would argue that this tension would initiate, under conditions prevailing in France and Germany, a dynamic toward either socialism (which Marx thought more likely) or reaction.

In four of its seventeen demands, this program focused on the peasants. By demanding the removal of feudal burdens and the nationalizing of estates, mortgages, ground rent, and the like, it sought to forge an alliance between peasants and workers. The bourgeoisie had historically stigmatized the wealth that accrued to landed property as unproductive and the landlords themselves as extravagant. Instead of calling for division of land among the peasants, Marx's program pursued this logic and demanded the abolition of all large private estates. To prevent any misinterpretation, Marx and Engels stated, "The actual landowner who is neither peasant nor tenant has no part in production. His consumption is, therefore, a mere abuse." Marx and Engels not only envisioned the abolition of feudal properties and an enlarged state role in agriculture, but also sought to curtail private property by abolishing capitalist tenancy arrangements and private holdings of mortgages. These measures would forestall the flourishing of the usurer in the German countryside and transfer some income to the state. While these proposals would protect peasant property, they would create a system of state-owned agricultural enterprises, worked by a majority of rural proletarians. Under these circumstances, large-scale state ownership, enhanced by modern productive techniques and state title to mortgages and tenant rents, would probably outcompete and gradually abolish all private property in land. This potentially corrosive state competition would necessitate further measures to aid the peasant and ease the transition to a subsequent socialism. Thus, Marx's program would engender future tensions.

Marx and Engels's "Seventeen Demands" defended the present interests of the small peasantry and even arguably those of the urban bourgeoisie insofar as it opposed the landlords. But, Marx concluded, abolition of private property in one form (land) implied its potential abolition in another (industry). Hence, the bourgeoisie shied away from this agrarian program, which had a radical or social democratic cutting edge.

Two demands sought to concentrate other forms of property, in particular banking and communications, under state ownership as well. Nationalized banking "makes it possible to regulate credit in the interest of the *entire* people and thereby undermines the domination of the big money men." Marx argued that this measure would bind the "conservative bourgeoisie" to the revolution because the republic would control the means of exchange, gold and silver.

State ownership of communications, banking, and land would erode the power of private property. Yet even this degree of state ownership would not realize socialism. Unlike state control in agriculture, state ownership of banking and transportation would neither outcompete nor abolish large private property in industry. In the democratic revolution's aftermath, capitalists would still have considerable social leverage and would strive to dominate the state apparatus.

Therefore, the program concentrated on transforming the character of government itself; it aimed not only to streamline and "cheapen" the bureaucracy but also to bring the police and military power under popular control. The program called for "universal arming of the people" and for "worker-armies." Since for Marx the state was an instrument of violence by which one class oppressed another, arming the proletariat and peasants would boomerang, undercutting the bourgeoisie's capacity to employ force against popular revolts and developing into a vehicle for future insurrection to achieve socialism. Though Marx and Engels ultimately amended the *Manifesto* in 1872 to include the newly discerned political form embodied by the Paris Commune, their "Seventeen Demands" of 1848 already envisioned a revolutionized state structure as a decisive element in achieving democracy and socialism.

Several other demands undermined any special privileges for officialdom and provided free services to the people. Because free transportation, administration of justice, and universal education would require increased taxes, Marx called for nationalization of agricultural property, progressive taxation to replace sales taxes, limitation of inheritance, and abolition of state subsidies to the clergy. These measures would extract the additional revenues from the rich rather than from the workers, peasants, and petite bourgeoisie.

Following the Parisian proletariat's demand in the February Revolution, the program also called for national workshops. After June, Marx and Engels would expose the bourgeois use of this reform to oppress the proletariat. Still, they would urge that the revolutionary movement attempt to compel the capitalist state to employ those workers whose labor private enterprise found unprofitable.

10–2. Marx's Strategy for 1848

COUPLED WITH MARX'S ESTIMATE of the international situation, this program invoked the full array of auxiliary statements in Marx's strategy for 1848.

Following Hilary Putnam's schema, Marx's argument on the connection between democracy and socialism might have looked something like this:

1. Guiding hypotheses and general theory as outlined in the *Manifesto*
2. Auxiliary statements
   a. Because of English competition and the rise of German industry, a small proletariat existed in backward Germany.
   b. A worker-peasant-artisan alliance, modelled on the French Revolusion, would drive the German democratic revolution forward.
   c. The German bourgeoisie, given its own weakness and the experience of France, would move toward compromise with absolutism.
   d. Strong democratic revolution in Germany or Poland would trigger world war with tsarist Russia and England, further strengthening the mobilization of the German people.
   e. As in the French Revolution, a sufficiently strong democratic revolution would give rise to a communist movement.
   f. Political forces existed in the German revolution, especially Marx and his followers, who sought to propel the movement in this direction.
3. Strategy: the democratic revolution in Germany would immediately precede a proletarian revolution.[1]

Marx looked to a lengthy revolutionary process and expected to advocate socialism more strongly as the democratic revolution reached its height. Though the "Seventeen Demands" hailed the "producers of all wealth," it did not overtly advocate socialism. The *Manifesto,* however, had indicated a difficulty in this approach. The emergence of a strong communist movement in the democratic revolution required ceaseless emphasis on the antagonism between the bourgeoisie and the proletariat. Yet an overly direct socialist program might alienate the bourgeoisie, and given bourgeois agitation against socialism, the small property holders as well. Only sufficient radical political efforts and the experience of class struggle could convince peasants, artisans, and other small property holders of the need for socialism. Thus, auxiliary statement (f) on the political role of communists became the critical undefined or untested variable in the whole strategy. The "Seventeen Demands" illustrated the tension between the present movement and its future. In addition, from the point of view of an abstract strategic estimate, all

---

1. Putnam, "The Corroboration of Theories," *Collected Philosophical Papers*, 1:261.

classes would respond in somewhat unexpected ways in the actual conflict. As Lenin would argue in 1906,

> One cannot weigh with apothecary's scales the equilibrium between the new forces of counterrevolution and revolution which are growing and becoming interwoven in the [Russian] countryside. Experience alone will completely reveal this; revolution in the narrow sense of the term is an acute struggle, and only in the course of the struggle and in its outcome is the real strength of all the interests, aspirations and potentialities displayed and fully revealed.[2]

Repeated soundings of the responses of each class involved in the revolution itself would instigate further changes in Marx's strategy.

Ignoring Marx's auxiliary statements and the tensions within Marx's strategy, scholars have misinterpreted the "Seventeen Demands" in opposite ways. Avineri sees this program as simply socialist. For him the logic of universal suffrage leads smoothly to communism:

> These [demands for the establishment of a united German republic, universal male suffrage, payment of an adequate salary to all elected representatives] are not the demands of communists "in the bourgeois revolution" as the later jargon would have had it, since all these demands seek to convert and transform the (partially or fully developed) bourgeois society into a socialist one. With universal suffrage bourgeois society transcends itself.[3]

Avineri rightly suggests that Marx did not limit his "Seventeen Demands" to capitalism and foresaw a potential German socialism in 1848. But unlike the ten regulations in section two of the *Manifesto,* Marx did not set these demands in the context of proletarian overthrow of the bourgeoisie; realizing the "Seventeen Demands" would not achieve socialism. Under the definite conditions listed above and including protracted revolution, republican world war, communist instilling of hostility toward capitalism, and increasing attacks on the workers and peasants by a newly dominant bourgeoisie, Marx thought that universal suffrage might generate important tensions within a capitalist society. These conditions would not spring from universal suffrage, but would determine its impact (under other conditions, universal suffrage might lead, as in France, to the triumph of the second Napoleon).

2. V. I. Lenin, "The Crisis of Menshevism," *Collected Works,* 11:344.
3. Avineri, *Social and Political Thought,* p. 212.

Though universal suffrage would play a role in exposing social inequality, the revolution would not consist of a set of democratic demands "transcending itself." Furthermore, Avineri ignores Marx's attempts to forge a worker-peasant alliance. On the one hand, Avineri remarks that Marx foresaw a possible majority socialism in Germany; on the other, he believes that Marx ruled out, a priori, four-fifths of the German population. Avineri omits the conditions that made Marx's strategy plausible. He vacillates back and forth between an ideal projection of socialism out of universal suffrage and an economic determinist rejection of actual, "merely political," working-class revolt.[4]

Hunt, on the other hand, restricts the "Seventeen Demands" to a democratic revolution alone, sealed off from a distant, future socialism by the necessity of extensive further industrialization. Hunt cites a letter from one of Marx's sympathizers, Louis Heilberg, to Moses Hess in which Heilberg endorsed the program's "rich" content as a vehicle for "practical-revolutionary, democratic-communist" organizing for perhaps ten or fifteen years. Then, Heilberg suggested, the next generation could opt for communism.[5] But Heilberg's argument did not conflict with Marx's strategy as outlined in the *Manifesto*.

Hess had asked Heilberg to cooperate on a new journal with a vague editorial policy. The first announcement had opposed any discussion of the social question from the standpoint of definite "theories, ideas, principles, and systems" and substituted a nondescript "practical" viewpoint. Heilberg pointed to the editorial board's confusing conjunction of Hess, suspicious of democratic revolution, with Anneke, who had edited the *Deutsche Volks-zeitung* along with the plain republicans Hecker and Struve, and Hess's old

4. Avineri denies that Marx had any revolutionary strategy in 1848. Shlomo Avineri, "How to Save Marx from the Alchemists of Revolution," pp. 40, 38. Avineri sometimes argues that revolutionary praxis encompasses both objective conditions and radical political action. Avineri, *Social and Political Thought*, p. 144. By neglecting or dismissing Marx's views on the French Revolution, the peasants, internationalism, and the specific conditions of 1848, however, he fails to transcend the common apolitical determinist stereotypes. Even an unimaginative economic determinist can allow that when circumstances ripen sufficiently, say one thousand years hence, men and women will have to do something–undergo some change of consciousness and organization–to realize socialism. But no one would think this a very dialectical account of revolutionary practice. See Gilbert, "Salvaging Marx from Avineri," pp. 11–16.

5. Heilberg to Hess, April 17, 1848, in Hess, *Briefwechsel*, p. 189. Hunt, *Political Ideas*, p. 183.

opponent, Arnold Ruge. Heilberg argued that communists should speak distinctly for their own program. Unless the editors endorsed the "Seventeen Demands," he would refuse to cooperate. As the democratic revolution had already started, Heilberg wanted to drive home to Hess the policy of vigorous and persistent communist participation.[6]

In envisioning this new German revolution, Marx did not expect a quick communist denouement. Between 1789 and Thermidor, the French Revolution had taken seven years; up to Napoleon's defeat, it had lasted twenty-six. Avoiding rash, inevitably mistaken estimates, Heilberg's ten to fifteen years does not seem an overly long period for a German democratic and socialist revolution. Finally, no evidence exists that Marx, Heilberg, or any of Marx's other associates translated a revolutionary period of "civil and national wars" into one of peaceful industrialization.[7]

As Avineri relies on a general political argument to project socialism too easily in 1848, so Hunt uses a general economic determinism to limit the revolution to democracy. Superimposing these general notions on Marx, they strip away his complex analysis of historical circumstances, his awareness of the internal tension between the movement's present and future, and his persistent adaptation to new political realities. They miss the three-tiered nature of Marx's historical theory (study of new political movements, investigation of special historical circumstances, general theory of modes of production and class struggle) and the complex back-and-forth method of analysis that led to his practical conclusions. Hunt and Avineri draw opposed political conclusions from a similar misunderstanding of Marx's theory.

10–3. Marx and the Cologne Democratic Movement

AFTER THE FEBRUARY REVOLUTION, the London leaders had decided to move to Paris and made the Brussels branch of the League its executive. Fearful of a Belgian revolution, the government subjected Marx and the other German communists to vigorous harassment and expelled them from the country. The new French Republic, represented by Ferdinand Flocon, welcomed Marx in Paris. There Marx and the other League leaders made plans to return to

6. Hess, *Briefwechsel*, pp. 187–191.
7. "Sitzung der Zentralbehörde vom 15. September 1850," *Werke*, 7:614; 8:598.

Germany. In 1848, Marx, Engels, Moll, Schapper, Wilhelm and Ferdinand Wolff, and Weerth would center their activities in Cologne.[8]

On April 11, Marx arrived in Cologne with a defined political strategy, a few committed colleagues, and no mass influence. He chose Cologne for three reasons. As the most industrialized area in Germany, Cologne had the greatest concentration of bourgeois and proletarian forces; Napoleon had conquered the Rhineland and the Napoleonic Code had liberalized its press laws, especially in comparison with the rest of Germany; Marx had previously edited the *Rheinische Zeitung* there and had some reputation in and familiarity with the area. Marx anticipated a vigorous democratic movement in Cologne and the chance to disseminate his views widely through a revolutionary newspaper.

Before Marx returned, Gottschalk and others had already planned a new version of the *Rheinische Zeitung*. As the editor of the original journal, Marx seemed the natural person to edit the new one. The *Neue Rheinische Zeitung* began publication on June 1. Despite opposition from Gottschalk, Marx quickly established commanding influence. The paper's other main editors, Communist League members like Engels, Weerth, Ferdinand and Wilhelm Wolff, Heinrich Bürgers, and Ernst Dronke, had returned to Cologne with Marx or agreed with his strategy.

Engels later described the editorial policy as a "dictatorship of Marx." The paper directly expressed Marx's positions during the revolution. In contrast to many new papers that quickly died during 1848, the *NRZ* gained 6,000 subscribers and influenced democratic forces in Cologne and throughout Germany. Seeking to suppress it, the Prussian authorities would stress its especially "damaging" effect "since its impertinence and humor constantly attract new readers." [9]

In Germany, the Communist League was divided. Some members, under Marx's leadership, sought to spur on the democratic revolution. Others, like Gottschalk and Stephan Born, argued that workers should further their own separate organizations instead. Despite the League's formal adoption of the

8. Engels, "To the Editor of the *Northern Star*" and "The Situation in Belgium" and Marx, "Persecution of Foreigners in Belgium," *CW*, 6:561–563, 567–570, 649, 651–652, 658. Though Hunt conjures up deep differences, the Londoners had great confidence in Marx and agreed with his strategy. They transferred League headquarters to Brussels and temporarily acquiesced in Marx's subsequent dissolution of the League.

9. *CW*, 9:487. Jacques Droz, *Les Révolutions allemandes de 1848*, pp. 541–545.

Manifesto, many members had not committed themselves to its strategy of working for a socialist revolution by participating in the democratic one.

As the head of the Communist League, Marx had to choose between two courses of action. He could strive to win over the recalcitrant League members through protracted internal debate. If he had adopted this alternative, he would probably have played no significant public role in the German revolution. But Marx could also dissolve the League and seek to gain new followers through vigorous democratic activity.[10] Along with Engels, Schapper, Moll, Wilhelm Wolff, and a few others, Marx pursued this second course. He counted on the realism of his strategy and energetic organizing to make communism a vibrant political force.

Even before the March uprising in Berlin, the Cologne democrats had attacked the monarchy. On March 3, hoping to forestall revolutionary action from below, the Cologne municipal council dispatched the merchant Ludolf Camphausen with a petition to Friedrich Wilhelm IV. The petition asked for moderate concessions: the convening of a Prussian United Diet based on an extended franchise, the abolition of censorship, and so forth. Led by Gottschalk, Anneke, and Willich, a crowd of artisans and other democrats forced its way into the council chamber. Their demands included universal suffrage, complete freedom of press, speech, and association, a civil guard with elected officers to replace the standing army, and protection for labor including a guaranteed standard of living. Qualifying democracy, Gottschalk defended these demands "not in the name of the people–that name has been all too often misused by the privileged classes–[but] in the name of that most worthy of all estates, which receives for the sweat of its labor nothing with which it can cover its nakedness or still its hunger." Gottschalk only barely endorsed the demonstration's sentiment for a republic; he preferred "a mon-

---

10. Hammen, *Red '48ers,* p. 221, points out that League members continued to play a role in Germany in 1848 and concludes that the League never really dissolved. But this argument misses the point. The German revolution had started, and Marx had to break with some forces in the League in order to project his strategy effectively in the mass movement. Hunt, *Political Ideas,* p. 175, on the other hand, sees the dissolution of the League as the consummate antithesis between Marx the economic determinist and democrat and the "Blanquist" Lenin. He ignores Lenin's threat to resign from the Bolshevik Central Committee in the fall of 1917 unless it would lead the real movement and organize for insurrection. Like Marx, Lenin placed primary emphasis on politics, not organization. Alexander Rabinowitch, *The Bolsheviks Come to Power,* pp. 191–208.

archy with democratic foundations." The council offered to debate with Gottschalk alone if the masses would withdraw. The democrats refused. The council then summoned troops which fired into the crowd and dispersed it. Surprisingly, no one was injured.[11]

Informed about these events, by the tailor Peter Nothjung, Engels, still in exile, remarked that the democrats should have gone armed to the council meeting and that communist leadership should have encouraged the soldiers, of whom the "greater part were for it," to join the demonstration.[12] Subsequently, the municipal council established a bourgeois civic guard which formally excluded workers from membership and had Gottschalk, Willich, and Anneke arrested. But the March uprising in Berlin forced the government to release the prisoners. In this increasingly revolutionary atmosphere, Cologne workers and artisans eagerly sought to organize themselves against feudalism and capitalism. At Gottschalk's initiative, they formed the Worker Society which, after an initial meeting with 300 participants, soon burgeoned into an organization with 7,000 members.

Thus, upon his return to Cologne, Marx found a working-class organization dominated by a very different political outlook from his own. Gottschalk opposed the democratic revolution as a revolution of the workers' masters and defended only agitation or uprisings for socialism. Under Gottschalk's leadership, the Worker Society would play no important role in the democratic revolution. As this society represented the largest and best organized force among German workers, Marx either had to win it over or forget about creating a strong worker–peasant–petit-bourgeois alliance envisioned in the "Seventeen Demands." To forge this alliance, Marx did not confine himself to external agitation through the *NRZ*. His colleagues, Moll and Schapper, joined the Worker Society, and Marx joined the Democratic Society.

Conflict within the Worker Society surfaced quickly over two political questions. Faced with elections for the Frankfurt parliament, Marx argued that communists should not advocate a socialist program. They should either support democratic candidates or, where they ran themselves, defend a radical democratic program. Gottschalk opposed this approach and convinced the Worker Society to boycott the elections entirely (in 1850, Marx would

11. Noyes, *Organization and Revolution*, p. 63, and Dowe, *Aktion and Organisation*, p. 134, cite Gottschalk's speech.

12. Dowe, *Aktion und Organisation*, p. 135.

change his position and argue that workers should always run socialist candidates during a democratic revolution).[13]

The Worker Society also discussed the first attempts to resuscitate the monarchy. During the March Revolution, the main feudal leader, the prince of Prussia, had fled to England. In May, the new Camphausen government apologized for his flight claiming that the prince had gone for "educational" or "diplomatic" reasons and welcoming him back to Prussia. His return emboldened the reactionaries. The Cologne Democratic Society immediately called a demonstration against the prince and asked the Worker Society for support.

Gottschalk, however, opposed this protest. He argued that the people should not banish the prince on the basis of rumor and without a hearing. Furthermore, if the people sought to abolish the monarchy and institute a republic, he suggested that they should say so directly and not just condemn one aristocratic figure.[14] Short of the king himself, however, the returning prince seemed an appropriate target for popular hatred against feudal oppression and monarchy. But Gottschalk and his supporters again prevailed within the Worker Society. Nonetheless, participation in the democratic revolution had become the overriding political question among these Cologne workers.

Marx did not seek a public confrontation with Gottschalk by attacking him in the *NRZ*. Instead, Moll and Schapper worked energetically inside the Worker Society to promote discussion of the "Seventeen Demands" and to convince the rank and file to join the democratic movement. In June, Gottschalk himself attended the Frankfurt Democratic Congress, a change of position possibly in response to pressure from below. He also cooperated with the Cologne Democratic Society and the Society for Workers and Employers in forming a District Democratic Committee for the Rhineland composed of two representatives from each of these groups. The Democratic Society selected Marx as one of its representatives.[15]

After the defeat of the June revolt, the German governments, led by Prussia, felt sufficiently invigorated to crack down on the Democratic and Worker societies. In early July, the government again arrested Gottschalk and Anneke. The *NRZ,* along with the Worker Society paper, *Die Zeitung des*

---

13. Hammen, *Red '48ers*, p. 219.
14. Ibid., pp. 219–220.
15. Ibid., pp. 221, 241–242.

Arbeiter-Vereines zu Köln or *ZAV,* campaigned against this attack. During this time, the Worker Society elected Moll and Schapper its president and vice-president respectively. Moll and Schapper also represented the society on the Rhineland District Democratic Council.[16] Along with Marx, they constituted one-half of its members. As a result of agitation through the *NRZ* and work by Marx and his associates in the Democratic and Worker societies, communist forces had taken effective leadership of a unified Rhenish democratic movement.

But Moll and Schapper had by no means thoroughly won over the Worker Society's membership to Marx's strategy. Therefore, from mid-July on, they initiated a further systematic discussion of the "Demands of the Communist Party in Germany" in the society's central committee and in the local branches. The specific topics included the organization of labor, the agrarian question, and the role of machinery (was machinery bad in itself, as many artisans felt, or was it harmful only because of social relations that placed it in the hands of the exploiters?).[17] Marx's influence in the Worker Society inspired its agitation in the Rhenish countryside which contributed to the huge (6,000 to 10,000 people) Worringen rally on September 17. Given this successful worker-peasant alliance, Worker Society members increasingly agreed with Marx's strategy. By fall 1848, through skillful political organizing Marx and his fellow communists had not just gained positions of leadership, but inspired a substantial, vigorous democratic movement.[18] This movement's vibrancy and adherence to Marx's viewpoint grew out of Marx's previous combative yet patient political activity. Without colleagues such as Moll, Marx's outlook could not have gained significant influence within this democratic movement. Depending on the overall situation in Europe and Germany, this Rhenish movement had enormous revolutionary potential.

During 1848, Gottschalk's influence in the Worker Society deteriorated

16. Ibid., pp. 250–253.

17. Ibid., pp. 259–260. Gerhard Becker, *Karl Marx und Friedrich Engels in Köln 1848–1849,* pp. 90–100. Hunt overlooks Moll's and Schapper's intensive activity to further Marx's strategy of participation in the democratic revolution among workers.

18. Becker, *Marx und Engels,* pp. 126–130. Hammen, *Red '48ers,* pp. 301–303. Noyes, *Organization and Revolution,* pp. 7–9, holds that Marx remained aloof from the artisans in 1848 and omits his vigorous organizing in Cologne. He mistakenly asserts that workers had no interest in the democratic revolution and that Marx, a revolutionary democrat, could not have appealed to workers.

steadily. After the September crisis, the Prussian government issued warrants for the arrest of Moll and Schapper as well as several editors of the *NRZ*. Marx himself became president of the Worker Society. When Gottschalk came out of prison, he again urged indifference to democracy. But the Worker Society members no longer sympathized with his position, and he could not dislodge Marx and his colleagues from political leadership. Though Gottschalk's ally, Wilhelm Prinz, edited the society paper, the *ZAV*, they could only snipe at Marx in its columns. In desperation Gottschalk finally attempted to set up a new organization. Before abandoning the Worker Society, however, he excoriated Marx and the democratic revolution in an anonymous letter to the *ZAV*:

> What is the purpose of such a [democratic] revolution? Why should we, men of the proletariat, spill our blood for this? Must we really plunge voluntarily into the purgatory of a decrepit, capitalist domination to avoid a medieval hell, as you, sir preacher, proclaim to us, in order to attain from there the nebulous heaven of your communist creed? [19]

As Marx indicted the bourgeoisie much more strongly at this time than he had before, Gottschalk's criticism seems unintentionally ironic.

At the Frankfurt Democratic Conference, Gottschalk had alleged that he had the Worker Society in his pocket, and that the workers would support a "red monarchy" rather than a "red republic." After his imprisonment, he briefly left Germany, vowing to return if summoned by either the "people" or the "sovereign." By placing the two mortal enemies on an equal footing, Gottschalk deliberately undermined the claims of democracy. Gottschalk's attempt to treat the workers as "just boys" deeply offended the Worker Society, which condemned his antidemocratic politics. Gottschalk's attack and his new organization foundered. Revolutionary experience and Marx's organizing had convinced the workers and left Gottschalk a leader without a party.[20]

19. Nicolaievsky and Maenchen-Helfen, *Karl Marx*, p. 187. Becker, *Marx und Engels*, pp. 256–260. Hammen, *Red '48ers*, pp. 370–374.

20. "Beschluss der 1. Filiale des Kölner Arbeitervereins" and "Mitteilung über die Einberufung des Kongresses der Arbeitervereine," *Werke*, 6:585–587.

10–4. The *Neue Rheinische Zeitung* and the French Revolution

MARX SUCCESSFULLY IMPLEMENTED his initial strategy and forged a vigorous movement in Cologne to fight for democracy. In the pages of the *NRZ*, Marx fleshed out his program for the unfolding German revolution against the background of previous French experience. In the course of the conflict, he would alter some of his first estimates and stress the abjectly counterrevolutionary role of the bourgeoisie as well as the need to fight immediately for a red republic. He would then organize for this new program.

From the outset, the National Assembly refused to confirm the sovereignty of the people against the power of the counterrevolutionary German governments. Marx and Engels contrasted an energetic "revolutionary-active Assembly" like the Convention with the "schoolboy parliamentary exercises" at Frankfurt, which consisted largely of procedural discussions. In an early article, Engels placed this phenomenon—which he and Marx would later call "parliamentary cretinism"—in the context of the violent clash between citizens and Prussian soldiers in nearby Mainz and the expulsion of three Worker Society members from Frankfurt for speeches against the Prussian monarchy. Strong reactions by parliament to these events could have elicited a mass response. But the Frankfurt parliament just talked and talked. As Marx and Engels concluded on June 7, "Of what use are the best agenda and the best constitution when the governments in the meantime use bayonets as their agenda?" [21]

The new bourgeois government, led by Camphausen, elaborated its own constitutional theory. Before the popularly elected Frankfurt parliament had convened in June, the United Provincial Diet had promulgated laws (April 6 and 8) that represented a "legal basis." Camphausen called these laws an "agreement" between the monarchy and the people to institute the new constitution. Camphausen's "theory of agreement" made the monarchy and the people (or the Assembly representing the people) equally sovereign. In practice, far from erasing the basic conflict, Marx responded, this "equal" or dual sovereignty simply gave the monarchy time to rebuild its forces in order to

21. Marx and Engels, "The Program of the Radical-Democratic Party and the Left at Frankfurt," and Marx, "Freedom of Deliberations in Berlin" in Marx, *On Revolution*, pp. 430, 440–441.

crush the revolution. Throughout 1848, Marx argued that "the theory of agreement" and of "equal sovereignty" could only result in a life-and-death struggle between two powers: the monarchy, on the one hand, and either the Assembly or the revolutionary people whom the Assembly had betrayed on the other. These two powers represented the old feudal society (the princes, the Junkers, the bureaucracy, the army) and the new bourgeois society (as well as the red republic that waited behind it). According to Marx, only force could settle this conflict.[22]

Therefore, Marx's "The Crisis and the Counterrevolution" advocated "energetic dictatorship" modeled on the Jacobin Convention: "From the very beginning we blamed Camphausen for not having acted in a dictatorial manner, for not having immediately smashed up and removed the remains of the old institutions." Marx argued that only a popular uprising could instill the Assembly with determination to exercise power dictatorially against feudalism. In an article dated September 15, he looked to an army revolt in Potsdam and Nauen to initiate a struggle to save the revolution.[23]

September also marked the height of the crisis around Schleswig-Holstein. In Marx's editorial of September 17, "Freedom of Deliberations in Berlin," he stressed reliance on the revolutionary power of the people as against illusions about parliaments. The other papers, particularly the *Kölnische Zeitung*, favored abandoning Schleswig-Holstein; they complained that "8,000 to 10,000 boxing club members had 'morally' supported the pro-war left in the Berlin Assembly." The "normal" influence of Prussian bayonets did not disturb these papers, but this "exceptional" revolutionary influence allegedly upset "freedom of deliberations." Marx contended:

> The right of the democratic popular masses to exert a moral effect on the attitude of constituent assemblies by their presence is an old revolutionary right of the people, which, since the English and French revolutions, cannot be dispensed with in stormy times. To this right history is indebted for practically all the energetic steps taken by such assemblies.[24]

22. Marx, "The Crisis and the Counterrevolution" and "Speech at the Trial of Rhenish Democrats," and Engels, "The Berlin Debate on the Revolution" in Marx and Engels, *The Revolution of 1848–49*, pp. 121–123, 126–127, 241–243, 35–37.

23. Marx and Engels, *The Revolution of 1848–49*, pp. 124, 126–127, 161–162.

24. Marx, *On Revolution*, pp. 439–440.

"The scared and philistinish friends of 'freedom of deliberations' yammer[ed] against" this right, Marx argued, because they opposed energetic revolutionary decisions.

History, as illustrated in the English and French revolutions, had moved forward because the masses exerted a "moral effect" on their democratic leaders and a physical effect on their oppressors. "Freedom of deliberations" in normal times meant freedom from all influences not tolerated by law. The recognized influences, including "bribery, promotion, private interests, fear of a dissolution of the chamber," and the like, skewed such "freedom" heavily toward the existing powers. In a revolutionary struggle, the opposed influence of the masses must become the norm:

> In revolutionary times, this phrase [freedom of deliberations] is completely meaningless. . . . Either they [the deputies] place themselves *under the protection of the people* and put up with a small scolding from time to time, or they place themselves *under the protection of the crown,* move to some small town, deliberate under the protection of bayonets and cannon or even under a state of siege—and then they cannot complain when the crown and the bayonets prescribe their decisions for them.[25]

Nevertheless, the Berlin Assembly shied away from the exercise of power. Unlike the French Constituent Assembly of 1789 which moved from provincial Versailles to the "volcanic ground" of Paris and spurred on the revolution, this German Assembly retreated from Berlin to a small town: Charlottenburg.[26]

10–5. The Peasants

IN THE FRENCH REVOLUTION, the artisans, peasants and, to a lesser extent, the proletariat had driven the bourgeoisie to act vigorously. In 1848, Marx's program also sought to forge unity between German workers, peasants, and artisans, and to foresee the likely role of the bourgeoisie. The *NRZ* dealt with each of the potential allies of the proletariat.

Inspired by the French February and Prussian March revolutions, peasant uprisings did away with the feudal obligations that remained after the early

25. Ibid., pp. 440–441.
26. Ibid., pp. 441, 430.

nineteenth-century Stein reforms.[27] In his editorial of June 24, Marx enumerated some of these feudal exactions:

> Loan suzerainty, decease, capitation, Elector's metes, blood tithe, patronage money, Walpurgis rent, bees' rent, wax lease, meadow right, tithes, laudemiums, additional rentals—all this has remained until now in the "best-administered state in the world," and would have continued unto eternity if the French had not made their revolution in February.[28]

Despite the revolution, Patöw, a minister under Camphausen, had proposed in June that the Assembly extract fresh compensation from the peasants for the abolition of these exactions. Responding to Patöw's memorandum, Marx contended that the Prussian government of 1848 had taken a more reactionary stance toward the peasant uprisings than the French nobility of 1789:

> Before the [French] nobility decided on its Fourth of August [the abolition of many feudal burdens on the peasants], its castles were in flames. The [Prussian] government here represented by an aristocrat, declared for the aristocracy. It put a memorandum before the Assembly demanding that it betray the peasant revolution, which had broken out all over Germany in March to the aristocracy.[29]

In Marx's November editorials on the bourgeoisie and the counterrevolution, he also contrasted the German bourgeoisie's reactionary approach with French revolutionary energy. In an elliptical resolution, the German Assembly had viewed "an immediate abolition of compulsory peasant services to the manor" as "not urgent." Marx commented, "The French bourgeoisie began with the emancipation of the peasants. *With the peasants, it conquered Europe.* The Prussian bourgeoisie . . . has forfeited even this ally and made it a tool in the hands of the counterrevolution." [30] Once again, Marx invoked the model of the French revolutionary war against reaction. He hoped that a vigorous German democracy would ignite a similar war against Russia and England. Marx saw the peasants as a decisive force in the revolutionary struggle to make democracy (and socialism) possible in Europe.

27. J. H. Clapham, *Economic Development of France and Germany 1815–1914*, pp. 43–46, 83.

28. Marx, "Patöw's Commutation Memorandum" in *On Revolution*, p. 435.

29. Ibid., p. 436.

30. Marx, *On Revolution*, p. 474.

In 1848, Marx took practical steps to encourage the unity of workers and peasants throughout Germany. At the first Rhineland Democratic Congress on August 13 and 14, Marx and his followers proposed that all democratic societies should send emissaries into the countryside to contact peasants and organize branches among them. The Cologne Worker Society dispatched representatives to Worringen, where rural democrats, mainly peasants, founded a branch of forty members. This visit prepared the way for the rally on September 17. In organizing for this demonstration, the *ZAV* emphasized the link between workers and peasants in the fight for democracy and socialism: "The revolutionary power of Germany lies in the workers and peasants. . . . When peasants and workers unite . . . then they will quickly free themselves from the burdens of feudalism, and from the usury and oppression of capital." [31] Large numbers of democrats from Cologne attended the Worringen rally. Delegations also came from Düsseldorf, Hitdorf, Frechen, and other nearby cities. Thus, the Worringen rally embodied an incipient alliance between urban democrats, especially the workers, and peasants throughout the Rhineland.

The rally resolved to oppose any attempt, like the one in Mainz, to disarm the Cologne civic guard, and condemned the Schleswig-Holstein armistice. Led by Schapper and Engels, it firmly endorsed a "democratic social republic, a red republic," and has been called the first communist rally in Germany.[32] Even if capitalist usury and mortgages did not yet flourish in the German countryside as they did in postrevolutionary France, Marx and his colleagues thought they could win the peasants to socialism during a protracted democratic revolution. They already advocated this course. Given the relatively weak German revolution of 1848, however, Marx never spelled out practical suggestions for such a transition. Yet despite the conventional thesis that Marx condemned the peasants as reactionary, the first communist rally he initiated in Germany united workers and peasants in rural Worringen. The Worringen rally revealed the striking potential such an alliance would have had if the European and German revolutions had developed more forcefully.

At the Worker Society's first meeting after the rally (September 21), Moll saluted the peasants' fine welcome to the "human doctrine of democracy and socialism." As peasants composed the bulk of the German armies, Moll sug-

---

31. Becker, *Marx und Engels*, pp. 128–130.

32. Hammen, "Marx and the Agrarian Question," p. 689. *NRZ* article "Volksversammlung in Worringen," *Werke*, 5:496–497.

gested, this worker-peasant alliance could undermine their fealty to the princes. He urged the workers to appeal directly to the soldiers.[33] Thus, Marx and his colleagues regarded an alliance between workers and peasants as an indispensable measure in neutralizing the army or even gaining its support.

In their November campaign to withhold tax payments, Marx and Engels again looked particularly to the peasants: "Only the revolutionary vigor of the provinces can safeguard Berlin. . . . *Refusal to pay taxes* gives the countryside an opportunity to render an important service to the revolution." [34] After the Worringen rally, a warrant was issued for Engels's arrest, and he left Germany. In late 1848 he journeyed from Paris to Berne and wrote an essay, which he did not publish, based on interviews with French peasants. In an unusually conservative vein, he likened them to "barbarians in the midst of civilization." The peasants, Engels noted, had participated in the French Revolution as long as it served their private interests, that is, until it abolished feudalism. Faced with the August 1793 decrees to defend the Revolution which set maximum prices on agricultural commodities and mandated that army units equipped with guillotines be sent to deal with rural hoarders, peasant enmity swung toward the Parisian movement. The subsequent victory of Napoleon consolidated peasant property; the peasants then embraced a "fanatical nationalism" and fought "passionately" in the wars of 1814–1815. With the Bourbon restoration, the peasants again saw their property threatened by a revived aristocracy and celebrated the revolution of July 1830 against that regime. Driven by overall political changes, the peasants' politics shifted from left to right to left again on the basis of their economic interests.[35]

From 1830 on, however, the bourgeoisie launched its new exploitation of the countryside. Land parceling, mortgaging, and peasant impoverishment proceeded rapidly. In the February Revolution of 1848, the peasants demanded a lessening of taxes. They did not comprehend the newly emerging struggle between workers and bourgeoisie in Paris. But they detested the new forty-five-centimes wine tax instituted by the provisional government. Here Engels might have discerned a left-wing potential in the French peasants' hatred for the republic. But he did not. Instead, he argued that the peasants responded to both the February and the June insurrections with

33. Hammen, "Marx and the Agrarian Question," p. 690.
34. Article of November 19 cited in Marx and Engels, *Revolution of 1848–49*, pp. 277–278.
35. Engels, "Von Paris nach Bern" in *Werke*, 5:471–473.

"fanatical rage" at "revolutionary, never satisfied Paris" and blamed the urban workers as well as the rich.[36]

Bourgeois agitation against the workers as enemies of property stirred this peasant anger. "Among all the peasants I spoke to," Engels reported, "their enthusiasm for Louis Napoleon was as great as their hatred against Paris." One peasant expressed the "wish that this damned Paris would be blown sky-high." In this manuscript, Engels concluded that the peasants' "narrow," reactionary attitude flowed from their conditions of life, and was no "mistake or chance blunder." The outlook reflected the peasants' isolation, the stability and uniformity of their social relationships, and the self-enclosed character of the peasant family. Overly influenced by his conversations with conservative peasants, Engels's view coincided with economic determinism. Like Blanqui, he even suggested that "the French proletariat . . . will have to put down a general peasants' war, a war that even the writing off of all mortgage debts can only postpone for a short time." [37]

Marx, however, did not agree with this estimate, and no trace of it appeared in the *NRZ* (Engels also soon abandoned it). Instead, Marx looked to a new peasant movement, springing from this oppression, to adopt the socialist ideas of the urban workers. In his editorial "Milliard" (1849), Marx supported the French peasant and communist campaign for the return of the billion francs paid to the aristocracy in 1825 in compensation for its expropriated lands. The republic had originally rejected this demand and substituted the forty-five-centimes tax. At first, the urban workers had not grasped the counterrevolutionary impact of raising revenues from the peasants rather than from the aristocrats. Now, however, the communist Barbès, on trial at Bourges, revived this peasant claim which received urban as well as rural support.

According to the *NRZ,* a mass peasant movement demanded the return of the milliard. This rural movement emerged as a serious revolutionary alternative to peasant support for a second Napoleon:

> The demand for the milliard is the first revolutionary measure to draw the peasants into the revolution. In Cluny people demand not only the return of the milliard but also the three percent it had yielded since 1825 . . . petitions [from Agey, Ancey, Malain, St. Wibaldt, Vittaux, and other communes] have piled up . . . we shall be interested to see what the capitalists, whether

36. Ibid., 5:473–474.
37. Ibid., 5:474–475, 471.

they are called legitimists, Orleanists, or bourgeois, can counterpose to the milliard in order to push aside the democratic candidates who intend to enter the new chamber with the dowry of the milliard in order to use it for the benefit of the peasants and workers.[38]

Despite the setbacks to the urban revolutionary movement, an increasingly threatening "democratic-socialist" peasant movement sprang up, centered on the year 1852. Attending to this real movement, Marx would trace the French peasantry's revolutionary side in addition to the opposed reactionary Napoleonic current.

In 1849, this French movement inspired Marx and the other editors of the *NRZ* to instigate its counterpart in Silesia. A series of eight articles by Wilhelm Wolff called for the return of a "Silesian Billion" paid to the aristocracy for the ending of serfdom. The *NRZ* circulated reprints among the peasants. It recorded the complaint of Count Renard, one of the beneficiaries of the robbery, who told the lower house of the Prussian parliament that "the tale of the Silesian billion has affected the rural population of Silesia in an unhealthy manner." Thus, the *NRZ* contributed to the international interplay of French and German peasant radicalism. The *NRZ* also supported a petition of the agricultural proletariat in Mecklenburg, demanding a "safe and free existence," which gathered 70,000 signatures.[39] Throughout 1848–1849, contrary to the stereotype that Marx dismissed the peasants as reactionary, Marx fostered worker-peasant unity.

10–6. The Artisans

IN RECENT YEARS, scholars have emphasized the role of craftsmen, threatened by capitalist competition, in early nineteenth-century radicalism. These artisans often looked to a just social order in the past rather than to an incipient working-class socialism. Yet Marx still tried to take their interests into account in 1848.[40]

In *Restoration, Revolution, Reaction,* Theodore Hamerow stresses the importance of artisan revolt in 1848. The artisans led much of the March barricade

---

38. Marx, "Die Milliarde," *Werke,* 6:355–356.

39. Hammen, "Marx and the Agrarian Question," pp. 693–694. Kandel, ed., *Marx und Engels,* pp. 192–196.

40. For England and France respectively, see Thompson, *Making of the English Working Class* and Moss, *Origins of the French Labor Movement.*

fighting. Soon, however, they held special congresses and petitioned the Frankfurt Assembly to curtail capitalism. A Brunswick weavers' resolution conveyed the spirit of this movement:

> Through government blunders and lawlessness the capitalists were permitted to enter our trade at will and to manufacture with the aid of their financial resources the products of our trade, frequently by the use of machinery. They did not care that thousands of shops and families were ruined and thus exposed to want and starvation. Proof of this can be seen in Silesia and Saxony, for after the Silesians were deprived of their bread, were they not fed with grapeshot? . . . As for the fact that the weaver trade has until now been a free occupation, we must put an end to that . . . since from it has certainly sprung the greatest cause of our calamity.[41]

Hamerow contends that Marx and other radicals, in their "dogmatic" quest for the industrial proletariat, overlooked this real movement among the workers:

> When the mill hand remained at his machine, they [the socialists] decided that their time had not yet come. Had they but looked around them, they would have found a numerous and desperate proletariat [the artisans] ready to accept revolutionary leadership. . . . If socialism had been willing to exploit their grievances as liberalism had done, it too might have won a great victory on the barricades of a new insurrection. But the gospel of Marx had nothing good to say about the guild system, and so the handicraftsman was forced to look elsewhere, while the Pharisees of the left continued their search for the ideal working class of revolutionary orthodoxy.[42]

While Marx did not appeal to the artisans by calling for restriction of industrial freedom and restoration of the middle ages, he recognized the glaring oppression of this "latent proletariat," as he had referred to it in *The German Ideology,* and sought to win its support. In the *NRZ,* Marx's uncompromising opposition to monarchy appealed directly to the multitudes of artisans who hated feudalism—the system that by "the grace of God" rewarded the Silesian weavers with grapeshot. Furthermore, to benefit the already dispossessed, Marx demanded immediate employment by the state; he also called for tax-

41. Hamerow, *Restoration, Revolution, Reaction,* p. 149.
42. Ibid., pp. 140–141.

ing the rich to provide free education, administration of justice, and transportation. A subsequent socialism would carry these reforms further.

Contrary to Hamerow, this program for radical democracy appealed to German artisans. Marx's supporters in the Cologne Worker Society consisted of artisans as well as proletarians. This society had 7,000 members in a city of 80,000 (nearly ten percent of the total population and a considerably greater percentage of the adults). The *NRZ* also had a circulation of 6,000, again in context, an impressive figure. But Hamerow demeans the significance of this radical movement and ignores its artisan aspect:

> In vain did Karl Marx, Friedrich Engels, Andreas Gottschalk, Karl Schapper and Fritz Anneke seek to awaken the spirit of insurrection among factory workers, the bearers of the revolutionary tradition in France [*sic*] and England. In Central Europe, their arguments fell on deaf ears. The *Neue Rheinische Zeitung,* struggling to win the attention of the world, was read by at most six thousand subscribers.[43]

Hamerow does not provide membership figures for other artisan societies. Yet other historians have rightly identified this Rhenish movement as the most significant and active one in Germany.[44] In addition, Hamerow conflates the political differences that drove Marx and Gottschalk asunder. Hamerow's assertions to the contrary, Marx located and energized a significant artisan and proletarian revolutionary force in Germany in 1848. His program for the democratic revolution served as a weapon for doing so.

10–7. The Bourgeoisie

MARX COMPLEMENTED HIS ANALYSIS of the conservative international role of the European bourgeoisie, discussed in Chapter 9, with a penetrating examination of the German bourgeoisie's total lack of revolutionary vigor. Because of the bourgeoisie's vacillating leadership, the German democratic revolution soon stalled and even began to reverse. This setback and its ominous

43. Ibid., p. 139. Despite his distorted account of Marx's activity, Hamerow has provided two useful histories of Germany during this period. See also his *Social Foundations of German Unification 1858–71.*

44. Droz, *Révolutions allemandes.* For evidence of vigorous common hostility toward and action against the upper classes by Berlin artisans and workers, see Frederick D. Marquardt, "A Working Class in Berlin in the 1840s?" in Hans-Ulrich Wehler, ed., *Sozialgeschichte Heute,* pp. 193, 205–206.

international context impelled Marx to reevaluate the bourgeoisie's counter-revolutionary role. This reassessment led in turn to practical measures to reinforce the radicalism of his strategy and a new estimate of the political form ("red republic") that he expected to emerge from the democratic revolution.

Marx saw the German revolution of 1848 as a stunted version of the English and French revolutions. These archetypal "European" revolutions did not represent the victory of a particular class over the old social system. Instead, they *"proclaimed the political system of the new European society"* and reflected "the needs of the world at that time rather than the needs of those parts of the world where they occurred, that is England and France." The timorous March Revolution echoed these great events distantly as "a weak repercussion of a European revolution in a backward country," a "provincial Prussian" revolution with competitors in Vienna, Cassel, and Munich. In the perspective of these great revolutionary outbursts, the March Revolution shrank to minuscule dimensions:

> Whereas 1648 and 1789 gained boundless self-confidence from the knowledge that they were leading the universe, it was the ambition of the Berlin [revolution] of 1848 to constitute an anachronism. Its light is like that of the stars which reaches us . . . only after the bodies from which it had emanated have been extinct for a hundred thousand years. . . . Its light was that of a social body which had long since disintegrated.[45]

The French bourgeoisie had destroyed absolutism and engendered the new political struggle between itself and its enemy, the workers. Fearful of the proletariat, the German bourgeoisie could not even push aside the princes. After March, the German bourgeoisie merely compromised with the monarchy and offered the counterrevolution time to gather its forces.

Thus, in the new world context, the great bourgeois revolutions had become "antiquated." The German bourgeoisie existed as a vegetative "estate" within the old society rather than as a vigorous, history-shaping class. The new revolutionary situation of 1848 turned the bourgeoisie's seemingly revolutionary vocation into its opposite, the reactionary stumbling of a *"senile old man* . . . sans eyes, sans ears, sans teeth, sans everything." [46] The revived

45. Marx, "The Bourgeoisie and the Counterrevolution" in Marx and Engels, *The Revolution of 1848–49,* pp. 183–184.
46. Ibid., p. 185.

monarchy shielded the German bourgeoisie from the workers. In Marx's editorials on the bourgeoisie and the counterrevolution, he averred that only the masses of workers, peasants, and petite bourgeoisie could lead the democratic revolution in Germany. Marx further contended that this worker-peasant movement, led by communists, tended not just toward democracy but toward socialism.

During the revolution, Marx and Engels proposed two different goals: first, the establishing of a unified republic, and later, of a red republic. In Marx and Engels's editorial of June 7, they criticized the estimate of the so-called left and "radical democrats" in the Frankfurt parliament that. the revolution of 1848 could only result in a federal republic of the "39 little states." Unless the democratic movement could fuse these principalities into one republic, Marx and Engels argued, bourgeois production would falter and feudalism would "predominate over modern culture." The "radical democrats" drew an analogy between Germany and the United States of America. But Marx pointed out that in terms of size and resources, they should have compared the United States to an imaginary United States of Europe.[47] Marx's initial policy of fighting for a republic and expanded bourgeois production flowed from the *Manifesto*'s general argument that such conditions would promote the greatest flourishing of proletarian struggle against the bourgeoisie. Even if the radical forces in the democratic revolution could achieve no more at this time, such a republic, combining formal equality with increasing capitalist exploitation, would represent a favorable terrain on which to fight for socialism.

In the actual conflict, however, the German bourgeoisie and petite bourgeoisie hesitated to support even a unified republic. At first, Marx and Engels strove fruitlessly to win them to this goal: "We do not propose the utopian demand that a unitary, indivisible *German republic* be proclaimed *a priori,* but we ask the so-called Radical-Democratic party not to confuse the starting point of the struggle and the revolutionary movement with their end goal."[48]

Marx soon concluded that the bourgeoisie would play no revolutionary role in 1848; he therefore shifted his emphasis from a republic to a social or red republic as the movement's goal. In the dialectical balance between

47. Marx and Engels, "Program of the Radical-Democratic Party" in Marx, *On Revolution,* p. 432.
48. Ibid.

furthering the present struggle for democracy and simultaneously preparing for the "future," Marx brought socialism to the fore. In June, he posed the red republic as the political goal only for the relatively advanced class struggle in France. As the revolution continued, however, he and Engels foresaw this goal for Germany as well. In Engels's article "The Uprising in Frankfurt" (September 20 and 21), he stated that in "all civilized countries," a new type of revolution loomed:

> In Vienna and Paris, in Berlin and Frankfurt, in London and Milan the point at issue is the *overthrow of the political rule of the bourgeoisie* [*Sturz der politischen Herrschaft der Bourgeoisie*]. . . .
>
> Is there a revolutionary center anywhere in the world where the red flag, the emblem of the militant, united proletariat of Europe, has not been found flying on the barricades during the last five months? [49]

This article put the issue of proletarian revolution—at least in the sense of a republic led by workers and peasants and not by the bourgeoisie—on the immediate agenda for Germany. But the conception of socialism in the mass movement at that time did not coincide with that of the *Communist Manifesto*. While replacing the aristocracy and bourgeoisie politically, such a revolution would only "indirectly" threaten the bourgeoisie's social power. It would therefore give rise to a very unstable regime. Thus, Engels sought to capture the real complexities of this new situation. As long as the workers and peasants retained weapons, this revolution would soon place in question the bourgeoisie's power to exploit; the dynamic of this real movement would turn swiftly toward socialism.

Marx's December editorials "The Bourgeoisie and the Counterrevolution" sought to heighten popular sentiment for a red republic. Here he peremptorily dismissed the German bourgeoisie's longed-for solution—a constitutional monarchy—and defined the only realistic alternatives as "a feudal absolutist counterrevolution or a *social republican revolution*." [50]

Though these arguments again indicate that Marx and Engels advocated socialism in Germany during 1848, some scholars have questioned this point. In *Karl Marx: Man and Fighter*, Nicolaievsky and Maenchen-Helfen contend that Marx defended a "united front against absolutism *at all costs*" as if June

49. Marx and Engels, *Revolution of 1848–49*, p. 136.
50. Ibid., p. 202.

had never occurred. They eliminate the tension in Marx's strategy and suggest that he meant by red republic no more than an ordinary bourgeois republic, comparable to the French February one, which would make some concessions to the workers. Engels's account of communist policy in "Marx and the *Neue Rheinische Zeitung*" (1884) lends some authority to this interpretation. In retrospect, the potential for socialism in 1848 lost its vividness for Engels. Painting the revolution "gray on gray," he stressed only the possibility of energetic democratic struggle and omitted his and Marx's advocacy of socialism:

> When we founded a great newspaper in Germany, our banner was . . . that of a democracy which everywhere emphasized in every point the *specific proletarian character which it could not yet inscribe once for all on its banner* . . . if we did not want to take up the movement, adhere to its already existing, most advanced, actually proletarian side and to push it further, then there was nothing left for us to do but to preach communism in a little provincial sheet and to found a tiny sect instead of a great party of action.[51]

Yet even in their strictly democratic emphasis in early 1848, as Engels suggested, they still strengthened the movement's "proletarian character" and vehemently criticized the vacillating parliamentarians. This energetic revolutionary policy never collapsed into a "united front at all costs," trailing with trepidation in the footsteps of a still more timid bourgeoisie. As 1848–1849 wore on, however, Marx and Engels introduced a communist perspective. Marx's final editorial in the NRZ stated that by social or red republic, he meant exactly what the Parisian workers had fought for in June: socialism as it existed as a practical goal in 1848.

Seeking to arrest and expel Marx from Prussia, the authorities claimed that the NRZ had only recently espoused the goal of socialism. Thus, they alleged, the Prussian government had failed to oust this red agitator earlier not out of its own weakness, but because he had allegedly stayed within

51. Nicolaievsky and Maenchen-Helfen, *Karl Marx*, pp. 181–182. Auguste Cornu, *Karl Marx et la révolution de 1848*, pp. 17, 43, agrees with the Nicolaievsky and Maenchen-Helfen interpretation. Engels, "Marx and the *Neue Rheinische Zeitung* (1848–1849)," *MESW*, 2:330–331. The Third International's 1935 policy of pursuing a united front against fascism with the "progressive bourgeoisie" illustrates a united front at all costs. The Comintern abandoned advocacy of socialism and even dissolved the "red fractions" in the unions. This policy is prefigured with qualifications in speeches later printed in Georgi Dimitroff, *United Front against Fascism*.

some prescribed nonsocialist bounds (the government forgot that it had already put Marx on trial for sedition). Countering this accusation, Marx asserted that the *NRZ* had long pursued a determined socialist policy:

> And the "social republic"? Have we proclaimed it only in the "latest pieces" in the *Neue Rheinische Zeitung*?

> Did we not speak plainly and clearly enough for those dullards who failed to see the "red" thread running through all our comments and reports on the European movement? [52]

Marx then cited the main portion of the editorial of November 7, which called for "revolutionary terror" to overthrow the old society. "Is that clear, gentlemen?" During a polemic with the judiciary, Marx had argued, "the real opposition of the '*Neue Rheinische Zeitung*' will begin only in the tricolor republic" and continued, "We summed up the old year, 1848, in the following words . . . 'the only alternatives are either a feudal absolutist counter-revolution or a *social republican revolution*.' " Marx concluded, "The essence of the June revolution was the essence of our paper." [53] The *NRZ* had started as an "organ of democracy"; yet its final number, printed entirely in red, took leave solely of the revolutionary workers. Nicolaievsky and Maenchen-Helfen mistakenly reduce Marx's vision of a red republic to no more than an ordinary bourgeois one.

With this change of goal, Marx increasingly indicted the bourgeoisie not for vacillating in the democratic revolution but for exploiting the proletariat. Marx's editorial of January 5, 1849, entitled "A Bourgeois Document," attacked the English workhouses where the unemployed had "committed the crime of having ceased to be an object of exploitation yielding a profit": "To bring home to them [the unemployed] the full magnitude of their crime, they are deprived of everything that is granted to the lowest criminal— association with their wives and children, recreation, talk—everything." [54] This savage oppression, decorated with the euphemism of "charity," maintained a "reserve army" of the unemployed whom the bourgeoisie could use when prosperity returned.

52. Marx, "Suppression of the *Neue Rheinische Zeitung*" in Marx and Engels, *Revolution of 1848–49*, p. 252.

53. Ibid., pp. 252–254.

54. Marx and Engels, *Revolution of 1848–49*, pp. 206–207.

Marx considered the Prussian bourgeoisie much weaker industrially, more provincial politically, and "more humble" spiritually than the English. In only one respect, however, the Prussian bourgeoisie neared its "British ideal," namely in "its shameless maltreatment of the working class." Marx noted that the German bourgeoisie carried out its exploitation on a provincial and municipal rather than a national scale. Yet, "in these forms it confronts the working class even more ruthlessly than the English bourgeoisie." Marx described the worker's card instituted by the city of Cologne for proletarians engaged on municipal works. Its provisions included strict supervision, expandable hours, and numerous fines. In a final flourish, the card required the city to inform the police if it discharged a worker. Marx commented: "But gentlemen, if you dismiss a worker . . . what on earth has the *police* to do with this cancellation of a *civil agreement?* Is the municipal worker a convict?" Marx underlined the special combination of bourgeois exploitation with feudal oppression in Germany. He urged that "this model law shows *what sort of Charter our bourgeoisie,* if it stood at the helm of state, *would impose on the people.*" [55] Marx no longer abstained from attacking capitalism until the democratic movement had conquered the princes, but denounced bourgeois and feudal exploitation together.

In January, Marx still hoped for a renewal of the democratic revolution and urged the Worker Society to back democratic candidates. He and Engels engaged in socialist agitation mainly in the Worker Society itself. (In September, Marx had also spoken to the Vienna German Workers' Educational Society on the significance of June and delivered "Wage Labor and Capital.")[56] But the vivid experience of the bourgeoisie's counterrevolutionary role and the weakness of democracy led to a much more radical approach. In a second phase of Marx's revolutionary strategy, socialist themes permeated his activity in the democratic revolution as well.

By the anniversary of the March uprising, Marx would only participate in a large democratic meeting (5,000 to 6,000 people) in Gürzenich because it explicitly endorsed the red republic. In the spring, Marx, Schapper, and Wilhelm Wolff all resigned from the Rhineland District Democratic Committee to underline their allegiance to the workers' cause.[57] Marx intended not merely to "lead" a movement in a narrow organizational sense, but to

55. Ibid., pp. 207–210.

56. *Werke,* 5:490–491.

57. See "Bankett auf dem Gürzenich" and "Erklärung," *Werke,* 6:583, 426. Anneke also resigned from the Rhineland Democratic Committee.

imbue it with the revolutionary socialist insight needed to gain and hold power.

After September, Moll, who had escaped arrest, moved to London and reconstituted the Communist League. In 1849, Moll returned to Cologne and asked Marx to join. Though sympathizing with Moll's purpose, Marx apparently did not envision the Communist League as the most useful vehicle for advocating socialism among the masses. Reconstituting the League would have turned the energies of the small number of communists temporarily inward; Marx sought to turn those energies outward to galvanize a socialist outlook within a still existing mass working-class movement.[58] Under Marx's influence, the Worker Society called for the formation of a "purely social party" that would "resolutely support the principles of social democracy." A broad group of Rhenish Worker Societies convened in Cologne on May 6 in preparation for a projected Leipzig meeting to found a nationwide workers' party. Faced with a strengthened counterrevolution, delegates of the Cologne Workers Congress also met with representatives of a simultaneous democratic congress.[59] Though Marx's new strategy stressed the red republic and the bourgeoisie's exploitative character, he did not seek to cut off the workers' movement from the democratic revolution.

From April 5–11, Marx also published "Wage Labor and Capital" in the *NRZ*. During the spring, the Cologne Worker Society discussed these lectures and proposed them for study to Worker Societies throughout Germany (at least the Mannheim Society took up this suggestion). "Wage Labor" delineated the irreconcilable antagonism between bourgeoisie and proletariat, and the "unnatural" character of capitalist productive activity which, as already noted, reduced the diverse motivations for engaging in the manifold kinds of work to a uniform striving to survive. "Wage Labor" stressed the vital significance of proletarian revolution for the entire European move-

---

58. On the basis of indirect, elliptical, and suspect evidence (the later testimony of Röser who had turned informer), Na'aman, McLellan, and Hunt overstate the severity and misinterpret the character of the disagreement between Moll and Marx at this time. Contrary to McLellan's and Hunt's view, Marx's approach of publicly advocating socialism seems bolder and more radical than Moll's. Werner Blumenberg, "Zur Geschichte des Bundes der Kommunisten," pp. 90–91. Shlomo Na'aman, "Zur Geschichte des Bundes der Kommunisten in Deutschland in der zweiten Phase seines Bestehens," pp. 31–32. David McLellan, *Karl Marx*, p. 218. Hunt, *Political Ideas*, p. 240.

59. "Beschlüsse der General-Versammlung vom 23. April 1849" and "Mitteilung über die Einberufung des Kongresses der Arbeitervereine," *Werke*, 6:587–588, 584. *CW*, 9:506–507.

ment: "Every revolutionary upheaval, however remote from the class struggle its goal may appear to be, must fail until the revolutionary working class
is victorious . . . every social reform remains a utopia until the proletarian
revolution and the feudalistic counterrevolution measure swords in a *world
war.*" [60] In 1848–1849, proletarian revolution and the red republic had become the themes of the *NRZ*.

At the outset of 1848, Marx had emphasized democratic revolution more
strongly than socialism; in 1849, within the democratic revolution, he insisted that communists must present socialist politics in a far bolder and
more striking fashion. His new argument and activity prefigured the vivid
strategic formulations of his *Address of the Central Committee to the Communist
League* in March 1850. In the twentieth century, communist movements in
Russia and China would also have to choose between relentlessly instilling
hostility toward the bourgeoisie and pushing it to make some limited revolutionary contribution or remain neutral. Like Marx himself, these communists would favor relatively gradual expropriation once revolution had occurred. Yet they would still need to work out terms of expropriation and
compensation with the remaining bourgeoisie, to decide what role former
managers and capitalists would play in production, and to learn how quickly
and thoroughly the masses of workers (and peasants) could organize the new
society for themselves. As Marx would foresee in his examination of the Paris
Commune, these societies would experience the danger of a reversal of socialism and the creation of a new form of exploitative system. Marx's approach
of 1848–1849 left these decisive problems to be worked out. Given the lack
of actual socialist experience, Marx's new conclusions provided only the
most provisional insight into these future conflicts.

10–8. Radical Republican and Proletarian Government

IN 1848, Marx called for the "smashing up" of the old feudal monarchy by
revolutionary and dictatorial means. But would this "smashing up" place the
bourgeoisie in command, enable it to secure a new state structure to defend
its interests, and require the future destruction of this bourgeois state? While
Marx did not analyze this question in exactly these terms, borrowed from his
later conception of the Paris Commune, some aspects of his projected re-

60. *MESW*, 1:79–80, 96–98.

publican structure strongly resemble his future dictatorship of the proletariat.

Following the "Seventeen Demands," Marx stressed the abolition of a standing army and of a highly paid officialdom even in a democratic revolution. In Marx's first article in the *NRZ* (June 1, 1848), he attacked the proposal of the Prussian aristocrat Hüser, which "strives to disarm all civil guards . . . to destroy gradually the whole arming of the people . . . and to deliver us defenselessly into the hands of an army consisting mostly of foreign elements either easily assembled or already prepared." [61] In July, the Prussian government proposed a "Civic Militia Bill" which limited working-class membership and created an elaborate system of appointed officers. Engels's sarcastic response flowed from a fundamental Aristotelian criterion of republican participation:

> If the citizen at the very beginning of the bill matures toward the "nature of his function," "the protection of constitutional freedom," by ceasing to be what according to Aristotle is the function of man—a "*zoon politikon*," a "political animal"—then he only completes his vocation by surrendering his freedom as a citizen to the discretion of a colonel or corporal.[62]

In Aristotle's *Politics,* when the hares clamored for equality, the lions answered: where are your claws and teeth? Unarmed citizens became unequal beings. Thus, a standing army not only served an oppressive class; it deprived men of control of their political life, "denatured" them, and rendered their association apolitical. As for an elite officialdom, in an article on the Prussian judiciary (December 24), Marx contended that "the French Convention (1792–95) is and remains the lighthouse of all revolutionary epochs. It inaugurated the Revolution in that it removed all officials by decree." [63]

Marx's *Eighteenth Brumaire* would enumerate as the main characteristics of the "parasite state" the standing army and the bureaucracy. Marx's conception of a proletarian revolution, drawing on the French Revolution as a lighthouse, always involved the destruction of these two institutions. These dramatic institutional changes suggested that a fundamental democratic revolution might lead directly to a proletarian red republic in 1848 without

---

61. Marx, "Hüser" in *On Revolution*, p. 429.
62. Engels, "Der Bürgerwehrgesetzentwurf," *Werke*, 5:251.
63. Aristotle, *Politics*, 1284a 14–17, 1268a 16–20. Marx, "The Prussian Counterrevolution and the Prussian Judiciary" in *On Revolution*, p. 482.

intervening political forms. If the communist-led worker-peasant alliance could gain these victories, it might dispossess the bourgeoisie without re-modeling the state further. Revolutionizing the political structure rather than nationalizing industry provided the key to this transition.

The concepts of a people's army and citizen officials stretched back in French republican thinking to Montesquieu and Rousseau. These ideas lived on in the political traditions of French nineteenth-century social republi-canism, and Marx took them up from the 1840s on.[64] In analyzing the subse-quent experience of the Paris Commune, Marx would integrate these institu-tional changes into a more complete conception of proletarian rule.

10–9. The Role of Insurrection

THE INABILITY OR UNWILLINGNESS of the Assembly to oppose the provoca-tions of absolutism or to act on behalf of the people posed the issue of mass armed insurrection as the vehicle to forge this new state. Though Marx and Engels assessed particular opportunities for insurrection cautiously, they rec-ognized, in general, that only such an uprising could reinvigorate German democracy.

Following an economic determinist interpretation of Marx, Avineri holds that Marx simply opposed insurrection (when conditions ripen, the revolu-tion will take care of itself; workers and peasants should not act "prema-turely"). He argues, for example, "Despite his [Marx's] seeing in the politi-cal upheavals of this year a chance to create the circumstances of a socialist revolution, he consistently opposes all radical attempts at armed insur-rection." [65] Avineri reduces all armed struggle during 1848 to futile, "merely political," "Jacobin-Blanquist *émeutes.*"

To support Avineri's case, one could cite examples of attempted putsches that Marx discouraged in 1848. For instance, in Paris in March, Marx op-posed Herwegh's republican legion which would attempt to "liberate" Ger-many from without. Marx condemned this particular military maneuver only

---

64. The concept of a people's army as one essential component of the dictatorship of the proletariat would live on in Lenin and in the communist movements in China and Vietnam. Marx's argument about a relatively peaceful transition from a presocialist government to a fully developed socialist one required a nonparasite state with a limited standing army and bureaucratic apparatus like that of mid-nineteenth-century England. Lenin, *State and Revolu-tion*, p. 34.

65. Avineri, *Social and Political Thought*, p. 194.

because he thought that revolutionary violence must flow from a mass German revolution and not from an isolated, returning army of exiles seeking artificially to inspire such a movement. The sorry fate of this expedition bore out Marx's caution. The French republican minister Lamartine betrayed the legion's plans to the German princes, and Herwegh met defeat at the border.[66]

Marx also opposed an insurrection in Cologne during the September crisis around Schleswig-Holstein. After the Malmö armistice, a minor insurrection occurred in Frankfurt, and considerable sentiment for an uprising existed in Cologne. But at this time, 40,000 Prussian troops ringed the city. On September 25, the magistrates issued warrants for Schapper, Moll, Wilhelm Wolff, Bürgers, Becker, Wachter, and Engels on the charge of "conspiracy aimed at revolution" during the Worringen rally; at 6:00 A.M., the police began a roundup.[67] By these arrests, Marx realized, the authorities intended to provoke a "little June battle" which they could easily crush. On September 25, Rhenish democrats had planned to convene their second congress in Cologne. Given this threatening situation, Marx quickly went to the meeting hall, discussed the situation with other democrats, and persuaded them to call off the congress. He then visited the Worker Society headquarters to discourage any premature attempt at insurrection. But Marx opposed insurrection at that moment only because he believed that a massive uprising, stimulated by a nationwide issue, must start from Berlin and sweep the country. When the Berliners rebelled, Cologne should rise to their defense. On October 12, Marx summed up his opposition to an abortive "Cologne Revolution" of September 25:

> But at that point, *where there was no important question to drive the whole population to battle* and hence every rising was bound to fail, this insurrection was the more senseless in that it disabled men for battle on the eve of decision, at a time when tremendous events could occur in a few days. When the ministry in Berlin hazarded a counterrevolution, that was the day for the people to hazard a revolution.[68]

66. Nicolaievsky and Maenchen-Helfen, *Karl Marx*, pp. 148–154. "Brief an Etienne Cabet–Erklärung gegen die Deutsche demokratische Gesellschaft in Paris," *Werke*, 5:6–7, 505–506.

67. As Marx had applied for a renewal of his Prussian citizenship, he did not take part in the rally. Thus, on this occasion, the authorities did not issue a warrant for his arrest.

68. Marx, *On Revolution*, p. 446. Emphasis added.

Marx thought that radicals should unleash an insurrection under the proper political circumstances, prompted by a nationwide issue, and that such circumstances might crystallize "in a few days."

Marx not only advocated mass insurrection when he thought it would work, but took organizational steps to help guarantee it. On September 11 in Cologne, soldiers from the Saxon regiment had insulted a young woman, provoked a clash with several citizens, and gone on a rampage. The Cologne civic guard had stopped these soldiers. Members of the Democratic Society and the Worker Society demanded that the city council keep the civic guard mobilized against any repetition of the incident (the civic guard included at least one "red company" commanded by Karl Wachter and composed of democrats and Worker Society members such as Schapper; Engels, Dronke, and Weerth, editors of the NRZ, also served as platoon leaders).[69] Marx and his colleagues proposed a direct election, based on universal suffrage, of a Committee of Public Safety. Marx drew the name from the Jacobin Committee that directed the terror and led the fight against counterrevolutionary invaders. As the city council and the leadership of the civic guard feared such a committee, Marx and his colleagues organized a rally of 5,000 to 6,000 people on September 13, which created the committee by acclamation and elected thirty members. If the monarchy should dissolve the Prussian constitutional assembly, the rally resolved, then the delegates should defend their seats "with bayonets." The bourgeoisie denounced this new organization.[70]

The East German historian Becker notes that this committee represented the only revolutionary governmental organization in 1848 composed of the people themselves alongside the existing oppressive state apparatus. As the name indicated, Marx intended to fashion a vehicle to carry out the revolution "in plebeian fashion" like the French. If the objective situation made vigorous leadership possible, Marx sought to lead the revolution directly. But the existing revolutionary ground swell could not sustain this organization. The majority of the committee soon felt compelled to deny its revolutionary character and reinterpret it as a public association to represent propertyless citizens. The committee no longer played any effective public role. Contrary to Lichtheim who envisions Marx as a Jacobin in 1848, Marx and the other communists did not allow the spellbinding republican imagery of

69. "Report of Platoon Leader Mentés of the Cologne Civic Militia," CW, 7:574.
70. "Volksversammlung und Sicherheitsausschuss," Werke, 5:493–494.

the French Revolution to cloud their political judgment and ultimately dissolved this committee.[71]

Nonetheless, Marx kept up his advocacy of armed revolution. During the November crisis, when the Prussian monarch disbanded the Berlin Assembly, Marx joined the Assembly in a call for refusal to pay taxes. In the special November 15 edition of the *NRZ,* however, he went beyond this call for passive resistance:

FROM MANY PARTS OF THE COUNTRY, ARMED MEN ARE RUSHING TO DEFEND THE NATIONAL ASSEMBLY. THE GUARDS ARE REFUSING OBEDIENCE. THE SOL-DIERS FRATERNIZING WITH THE PEOPLE. SILESIA AND THURINGIA ARE IN FULL REVOLT.[72]

During this period, he called for answering "force with force."

In Engels's *Revolution and Counterrevolution in Germany* of 1851–1852, he analyzed what the Frankfurt Assembly should have done to inspire insurrection in the spring of 1849 (Marx sent these articles, which were written by Engels, to the *New York Tribune* under his own name).[73] According to Engels, the appropriate conditions for armed insurrection existed. Everything depended on the conduct of the Assembly. Would it call for insurrection or not? Would it depose the German imperial lieutenant and create a "strong, active, unscrupulous executive to call insurgent troops to Frankfurt" or not? The Assembly did none of these things. As a contrast, Engels summarized the art of insurrection, hailing Danton and the French Revolution as examples:

Now, insurrection is an art quite as much as war or any other, and subject to certain rules of proceeding, which, when neglected, will produce the ruin of the party neglecting them. Those rules . . . are so plain and simple that the short experience of 1848 had made the Germans pretty well acquainted with them. Firstly, never play with insurrection unless you are fully prepared to face the consequences of your play. Insurrection is a calculus with very indefinite magnitudes, the values of which may change every day; the forces opposed to

71. Becker, *Marx and Engels,* pp. 122–125. *EB,* pp. 247–250. Lichtheim, *Marxism,* pp. 126–127, 129.

72. Marx, "The Ministry under Indictment" in *On Revolution,* p. 453.

73. The currently fashionable but oversimplified distinction between Marx and Engels is particularly out of place on the issue of insurrection.

you have all the advantage of organization, discipline, and habitual authority; unless you bring strong odds against them, you are defeated and ruined. Secondly, the insurrectionary career once entered upon, act with the greatest determination, and on the offensive. The defensive is the death of every armed rising; it is lost before it measures itself with its enemies. Surprise your antagonists while their forces are scattering, prepare new successes, however small, but daily; keep up the moral ascendency which the first successful rising has given you; rally those vacillating elements to your side which always follow the stronger impulse, and which always look out for the safer side; force your enemies to a retreat before they can collect their strength against you; in the words of Danton, the greatest master of revolutionary policy yet known, *de l'audace, de l'audace, encore de l'audace!* [74]

As the *NRZ* happily reported, Engels brought "boxes of cartridges" to the insurrectionists in Elberfeld and participated in the uprising. Engels advocated the dismissal of the Elberfeld civil militia, the distribution of its weapons among the workers, particularly those of Solingen, and a compulsory tax to maintain these worker-soldiers. He later argued, "This step would have broken decisively with all the slackness that had hitherto characterized the [Elberfeld] Committee of Public Safety, given the proletariat new life, and crippled the 'neutral' districts' capacity for resistance." Frightened by these proposals, the bourgeoisie harassed Engels and forced him to withdraw.[75] Engels subsequently fought under Willich in the Rhine-Palatinate army; the Prussians killed Joseph Moll at the battle of the Murg. Thus, the German communists took part in the last military engagements of the revolution even though these armies demanded merely an imperial constitution. Though the communists still hoped to renew the democratic movement, even under so strategically timid a banner, the very class tensions that they had increasingly recognized defeated this uprising. The insurrectionaries would neither energetically mobilize the masses of workers and peasants to fight nor inspire them with any bold republican, let alone socialist, slogans. Defensive in every respect, these uprisings soon collapsed.

Avineri's claim to the contrary, Marx and Engels stressed the role of armed insurrection, even for relatively small democratic gains, in 1848–1849. Lenin

---

74. Engels, *Revolution and Counterrevolution*, p. 90.

75. *NRZ* article "Elberfeld" and Engels, "Die deutsche Reichsverfassungskampagne," *Werke*, 6:500; 7:128–130. *CW*, 9:580.

would invoke their arguments on the "art of insurrection" in the Russian revolutions of 1905 and 1917.[76]

10–10. Marx's Achievements in 1848

IN THE RHINELAND IN 1848, Marx forged a revolutionary movement around the "Seventeen Demands." Given the overall situation in Germany and internationally, however, his strategy achieved only limited results. The European revolution moved not in an "ascending line" of progressive radicalization as Marx had hoped, but in a "descending line" of reaction culminating in the temporary destruction of the revolutionary movement.

Yet Marx has some significant accomplishments to his credit. Despite the Frankfurt and Berlin parliaments' opposition to peasant demands, Marx and his colleagues built up a considerable movement to ally the city with the countryside in the Rhineland and in Silesia. This beginning unity contrasts with the division of French radical workers and peasants between 1848 and 1851. While German parliamentarians acquiesced in many of the revived monarchies' outrages, Marx demanded resolute armed action, for instance, during the November tax boycott. He even advocated and helped create a revolutionary Committee of Public Safety, led by the most radical democratic and communist forces. Without Marx's vehement combatting of other radical tendencies and his recruiting of organizers like Moll, Schapper, and Wilhelm Wolff, his growing influence in the Cologne Worker Society or the forging of a worker-peasant alliance in Worringen could not have occurred.

In the mirror of the broader historic counterrevolutionary movement,

76. In Lenin's controversy with the Mensheviks during the 1905 revolution, he recalled Marx's arguments of 1848: "If the revolution gains a decisive victory—then we shall settle accounts with tsarism in the Jacobin, or, if you like, in the plebeian way. 'The Terror in France,' wrote Marx in 1848 in the famous *Die Neue Rheinische Zeitung*, 'was nothing else than a plebeian method of settling accounts with the enemies of the bourgeoisie. . .' Have those who, in a period of democratic revolution, tried to frighten the Social-Democratic workers in Russia with the bogey of 'Jacobinism' ever given thought to the significance of these words of Marx?" V. I. Lenin, *Two Tactics of Social-Democracy in the Democratic Revolution, Collected Works*, 9:58–59.

Lenin also distinguished Jacobin republicanism from the Bolsheviks who called for a more radical "revolutionary democratic dictatorship of the workers and peasants." But on this important point—mass revolutionary violence to destroy the aristocracy and the old regime—the French revolutionaries, Marx, and Lenin concurred. See also "Marxism and Insurrection" in Lenin, *Selected Works*, vol. 2.

Marx's political role has seemed negligible to some historians. They have minimized or overlooked his achievements and the potential of his strategy and organizing. Yet an examination of Marx's activities in 1848, particularly in comparison with Lenin's in 1905 and 1917, suggests the enormous revolutionary potential in Marx's approach. Keenly aware of Marx's activity, Lenin summarized the similarities between their views in *Two Tactics of Social-Democracy in the Democratic Revolution*:

1. The uncompleted German revolution differs from the completed French Revolution in that the German bourgeoisie betrayed not only democracy in general, but also the peasantry in particular.
2. The creation of a free class of peasants is the foundation for the consummation of a democratic revolution.
3. The creation of such a class means the abolition of feudal services, the destruction of feudalism, but does not yet mean a socialist revolution.
4. The peasants are the "most natural" allies of the bourgeoisie, that is to say, of the democratic bourgeoisie, which without them is "powerless" against reaction.

With the proper allowances for concrete national peculiarities and with serfdom substituted for feudalism, all these propositions are fully applicable to the Russia of 1905.[77]

An important difference between Marx in 1848 and Lenin in 1905, it should be noted, was that Marx saw the German democratic revolution as the "immediate" prelude to a socialist one, whereas Lenin believed that Russia must undergo a period of capitalist development, conjoined to a radical democratic regime, before the workers and peasants could opt for socialism. Paradoxically for the conventional stereotype, Marx, the "economic determinist," held a more left-wing and less economic determinist view on the potentials of a German revolution in 1848 than Lenin, the "Blanquist" politician, did on Russia in 1905.

In the *NRZ*, Marx called the Jacobin Convention the "lighthouse of all revolutionary epochs." His analysis of this great revolutionary movement molded his views on energetic revolutionary leadership, on the peasants, on insurrection, on republicanism and red republicanism, and on world war. In 1848–1849, Marx constantly referred to the images and lessons of the French Revolution. In this sense, we might encapsulate his strategy for German

---

77. Lenin, *Two Tactics, Collected Works*, 9:135–136.

revolution in 1848 in the phrase: the French Revolution radicalized. Marx admired the vigorous citizenship of the early French revolutionary republicans, their intense political awareness, and sought to instill a similar sharp sense of the common interest in German democrats and communists. His outlook transformed French republicanism and sought to remedy its "merely political" defects; yet his communism built upon a political world that revolutionary French citizens had once inhabited.

As the German bourgeoisie proved itself more and more counterrevolutionary, Marx revised his earlier strategic estimate and advocated a "red republican" revolution, fusing the ideas of Babeuf with a worker-peasant alliance. In the pre-1848 Communist League and in Marx's subsequent (1850) *Address* to the reconstituted League, Marx argued that democratic revolution must precede the workers' revolution. Yet at times during 1848, he appeared to think that the peasants and petite bourgeoisie under working-class leadership could fuse the two revolutions and take power directly in a red republic. During 1848–1849 Marx changed his strategy under the impact of revolutionary experience. At the outset, he emphasized the common interests of the bourgeoisie and workers in overthrowing absolutism. He criticized the bourgeoisie's vacillation in destroying absolutism rather than its exploitation of the proletariat. As the revolution unfolded, however, Marx increasingly argued that a communist-led worker-peasant alliance must drive the revolution forward because the exploiters would not. In this second phase of his political activity, he sought to organize a "purely social" working-class party. Whether or not Marx thought that the workers could take power directly is not the decisive issue. As the workers organized independently and became more conscious of their situation, they would initiate a strong movement for socialism at least as soon as the democratic movement had concluded. Hence, fostering this consciousness and organization for a "future" socialism within the struggle for democracy became Marx's primary goal.

Marx elaborated a very well thought out and flexible strategy for democratic and proletarian revolution in 1848–1849. He failed (and these revolutions failed) not for any lack of political skill or hesitancy about insurrection, but because overall European conditions did not permit the most revolutionary elements in Germany to come to power.

PART THREE

Reevaluations after the Revolution

— XI —

Marx and the Peasants

11–1. *The Class Struggles in France*:
Peasants as Workers

MARX FORGED HIS STRATEGY of the worker-peasant alliance through a study
of the French Revolution and implemented it in 1848–a movement from
French practice to theory (Marx's new strategy for democracy and socialism
in Germany) and once again to practice (Marx's activity in 1848). In the
Manifesto's first sections, Marx had given a conservative albeit still dialectical
estimate of peasant political potential. The peasants would play a "reactionary" role insofar as they tried to "roll back the wheel of history." They would
embrace revolution only when they lost their small property and distinctive
viewpoint and became proletarians.[1] In the *Manifesto*'s strategic section,
however, Marx looked to Polish and German peasants to play a far more
significant role in democratic and socialist revolution than his first formulation suggested. Given Marx's subsequent political experience and his study
of post-1848 peasant politics in France, he refined his analysis of a worker-
peasant alliance in *The Class Struggles in France* (1850) and *The Eighteenth
Brumaire of Louis Napoleon* (1852). In these studies of France, Marx stressed
the many-sided fashion in which capitalism sucked the life out of apparently
independent small property, subjecting it to usury, mortgages, and taxation.
He then argued that peasant interests as small property holders coincided
with those of urban workers and even likened small holders to proletarians.
When peasant support for the second Bonaparte outweighed rural radicalism, Marx offered a subtle analysis of the contradictory economic and political forces, including Napoleonic traditions, that engendered these opposed
political currents.

In *Class Struggles*, Marx began his analysis of peasant radicalism in France
with the wine tax. At the end of 1848, the peasantry had voted for the second
Napoleon to become president. A year later the National Assembly (and the
president) restored the wine tax. This reversal stirred peasant anger: "When

1. *CM*, p. 44.

the French peasant paints the devil, he paints him in the guise of a tax collector. From the moment when Montalembert [a leading religious and conservative parliamentarian] elevated taxation to a god, the peasant became god-
less, atheist, and threw himself into the arms of the devil, of *socialism*." [2]
In exile on St. Helena, the first Napoleon had declared that reintroducing
the wine tax triggered his downfall by alienating him from the peasants of
southern France. Generations of rural families had passed on the message
that governments typically deceived the peasants by promising abolition of
this tax and, then, once they had secured peasant support, retaining it. In this
tax, "the peasant tests the bouquet of the government." [3]

Peasant hatred spurred a vigorous petition campaign eliciting millions of
signatures against the renewed tax. If the peasants had "discovered" the second Bonaparte, Marx argued, the petitions retracted this support. A gradual
"revolutionizing" of the peasantry occurred; they elected more radical candidates: a *Montagnard* in the department of the Gironde and a "red" in the
Gard, the former center of reaction. Yet Marx overstressed the peasants'
alienation from Napoleon. Peasant anger focused mainly on the republic.
Without socialist organizing in the countryside, many peasants blamed urban republicanism and not Napoleon for their misery.

Though taxes inflamed peasant discontent, far deeper causes, Marx argued,
also drove them to rebel. After the burning of the châteaus and the defeat of
feudalism in 1789, the first postrevolutionary generations owned small, genuinely independent plots. But population grew; the peasants subdivided the
land, and its price soared; fathers encumbered later generations with increasing debt. As the former serfs had paid duties to the lord, so peasants paid
interest to the new lord, the capitalist loan shark. As privileges had accumulated on the medieval estate, so mortgages accumulated on the modern small
plot. An admirer of Balzac's novel *Les Paysans* (1844), Marx in his analysis
echoed old Fourchon's debunking of peasant "freedom": "Liberated, are
we? . . . The hoe, our only property, has not left our hands. Whether it is
the *seigneur* or the tax collector who takes the best part of our labors, we still
have to spend our life in sweat." [4]

2. *CS*, p. 213.

3. Ibid., p. 215. Albert Soboul, *Problèmes paysans de la révolution (1789–1848)*, pp. 285, 322,
329.

4. *CS*, pp. 215–216. Honoré de Balzac, *Les Paysans*, pp. 132–133. By the final scene, the
peasants had succeeded in dividing the Montcornet estate into a thousand tiny plots (pp.
372–373). Though Balzac elegized the passing of the aristocracy, Marx admired his merciless

In Marx's view, this new system plunged the French peasant into a misery like that of the famished Irish tenant. Marx underlined the capitalist character of this suffering: "The French peasant cedes to the capitalist, in the form of *interest* on the *mortgages* . . . not only the ground rent, not only the industrial profit, in a word, not only the *whole net profit*, but even *a part of the wages* . . . all under the pretense of being a private proprietor." [5] Though the *form* of this exploitation differed, Marx envisioned the peasants almost as workers: "The exploiter [*Exploiteur*] is the same: *capital*. The individual capitalists exploit the individual peasants through *mortgages and usury;* the capitalist class exploits the peasant class through state taxes." [6] In their political attitudes, Marx argued, the peasants still leaned toward the capitalists as the representatives of private property. Like a "talisman," ownership of a small plot enthralled the peasant and set him against the industrial proletariat.[7] Yet the peasant's new economic interests should impel an alliance with the workers.

Division of land into tiny parcels, Marx argued, diminished the productivity of the soil and rendered modern methods of production (the use of machinery, canals, and the like) prohibitively expensive. In the French setting, state ownership and common cultivation of the land could easily compete with small holdings; these new arrangements could rescue the majority of peasants and rural laborers from misery. But communists would have to convince the small holders of this alternative. In Marx's *Address of the Central Committee to the Communist League* of March 1850, he urged this course in France and Germany as a revolutionary antidote to the cycle of French capitalist impoverishment and the democrats' plan of further land division. For Marx, nationalization of land would give the principle of common ownership "a firm basis in the midst of the tottering bourgeois production relations." [8] Agriculture became the opening wedge for collective ownership and cultivation rather than the most backward branch of industry.

In *Class Struggles*, Marx stressed the political as well as the economic causes of increasing peasant radicalism. While the Party of Order instituted crip-

---

depiction of the entire network of French social relationships. Marx and Engels, *Sur la littera-ture et l'art*, pp. 319–321. George Lukacs, *Studies in European Realism*, ch. 1.

5. *CS*, p. 216.

6. Ibid., p. 217. T. J. Clark, *Image of the People*, pp. 95–96.

7. *CS*, p. 217.

8. Ibid., pp. 215–216. Marx and Engels, *Address* in *MESW*, 1:114.

pling taxes, it howled against socialism and stimulated peasant interest in this "forbidden fruit." In a blatant contradiction, the February Republic had given the peasant the vote; yet its parliamentary acts served the peasants' enemies. As in the revolution of 1789, the antagonism between political equality (universal suffrage) and social exploitation grew: "Most understandable was the language of the actual experience that the peasant class had gained from the use of the suffrage, were the disillusionments overwhelming him, blow upon blow with revolutionary speed." During democratic revolutions, the political experience of class struggle itself rather than a new development of productive forces inspired a radical outlook among the masses.[9]

Though this economic and political experience laid the groundwork for revolution, Marx emphasized the political role of French radicals in translating the peasants' interests into an alliance with urban workers to secure the red republic: "The scale rises or falls, according to the votes that the peasant casts into the ballot box. He himself has to decide his fate. So spoke the socialists in pamphlets, almanacs, calendars and leaflets of all kinds." [10] Reversing age-old hierarchies, the *Almanach du Village* hailed the peasants as the arbiters of French destiny: "Peasants, you are the masters, the kings of the country. It is up to you to change the face of France." For Marx, consistent revolutionary political activity, not just spontaneous peasant revolt, would forge the worker-peasant alliance. Fearing this potential, Marx noted, the French bourgeoisie sought to quell socialist organizing by passing laws to harass radical teachers in rural communities and to reinforce the Church's influence in education.[11]

Nonetheless, as Roger Price, Albert Soboul, and T. J. Clark have shown, a widespread democratic-socialist movement sprang up among the peasants focusing on the year 1852. The peasants aimed to dispossess the declining aristocrats and the rising usurers and to reclaim what they regarded as rightfully their own. The *procureur général* at Aix complained, perhaps exaggeratedly, "There is not a peasant who does not regard the rich man or the bourgeois as the oppressor of the poor and who does not believe that the workers should be masters of France because they are the only producers." As Tocqueville noted, the rural bourgeoisie had united against June; these aristocrats, rich peasant moneylenders, merchants, bankers, and wealthier members of liberal

---

9. *CS*, p. 217. Marx's conception prefigured the development of revolutionary socialist sentiment in Russia between February and October 1917.

10. Ibid.

11. Ibid., pp. 217–218. Clark, *Image*, pp. 88–99. Price, *French Second Republic*, p. 302.

professions drove formerly stable poor peasant families to desperation (in lower Languedoc, after the insurrection against Napoleon's coup, eight-ninths of the deported peasants were fathers of families).[12] Popular songs rang out with social hatred:

> Misery has reappeared
> The harvest approaches and the peasants
> Will come to reap among the tyrants
> Hunger chases them from the village
> They must eat: Jesus has said so.
> Misery produces a rage,
> And if they [the peasants] complain, they are cursed.
> Let them have cause to curse us!
> The end must come, as soon as possible
> So that the bailiff will not seize it
> Carry the straw to the château.[13]

The peasant carmagnole from the Doubs demanded the return of the peasants' stolen goods and the hanging of all usurers.[14]

In 1851, the peasants staged a widespread revolt against Napoleon's coup. Rural democratic-socialist secret societies mobilized large numbers of fighters, 4,000 to 5,000 in the Drôme and 15,000 in the Basses-Alpes. On trial after the uprising, peasant witnesses still averred that "in 1852 property will be shared out," and the most defiant declared: "What is occurring is the war of the poor against the rich. There will be much blood spilt. . . . It is time that all this finished." [15] The political dynamic of republican revolution had transformed the citizen pageants depicted by David into the unceasing labor and hardship of peasant life. The republican promise had dramatized peasant

12. Price, *Second Republic*, p. 297. Tocqueville, *Recollections*, pp. 195–196. Soboul, *Problèmes paysans*, pp. 329, 332, 291.

13. Price, *Second Republic*, p. 298, cites this song.

14. Clark, *Image*, pp. 96, 93. Another song called for revolutionary terror:

> Amis vignerons et paysans
> Que l'Aristo a exploités
> Enfin pour en finir
> Aux armes il faut courir
> Dansons la Carmagnole . . .

15. Price, *Second Republic*, pp. 301, 299.

exploitation. This rural political atmosphere charged Gustave Courbet's paintings of 1850, "The Stonebreakers" and "Burial at Ornans," with revolutionary significance.[16] In *Class Struggles*, Marx identified this strong radical current among French peasants.

Price and Soboul trace not only the spread of usury but the overturning of peasants' common rights, such as the right to cut wood in the aristocrats' forests, as a source of revolt. Their argument confirms the role of what other scholars today have called an emerging "objective exploitation" in peasant radicalism. The shifting, increasingly burdensome economic, social, and political relationship between lords and peasants impelled rural revolt.[17] In this regard, Marx's own account does not rely on a narrow or technical condemnation of exploitation (the extraction of unpaid or surplus labor from the immediate producers). Instead, Marx stressed a broad combination of economic and political factors, deriving from exploitation and including the new forms of capitalist oppression, the contradictions of republicanism, and the role of democratic-socialist organizing, which goaded the peasants to rebel.

Yet the revolution in city and country moved in different phases. Though highly critical of the *Montagnards'* temporizing and urban pacifism, Marx admired the vigor of the *Montagnard*-led peasant movement. Many French radicals, however, ignored or underestimated the peasantry's radical potential. Blanqui, for example, formulated the concept of the "dictatorship of Paris" over the "unenlightened" and reactionary countryside and held his conspiracy aloof from peasant movements.[18] Socialist organizing in the countryside did not go nearly as far as Marx had hoped.

11–2. *The Eighteenth Brumaire*:
The Peasants and "Napoleonic Hallucinations"

IN 1851, despite the rural radical current, Louis Napoleon, supported by a majority of peasants, became emperor. His victory flatly contradicted Marx's

16. In the 1860s, Courbet planned a painting of Martin Bidouré, a peasant leader of the uprising against the *coup d'état* in the Var, whom the new empire executed. Clark, *Image*, pp. 94, 97.

17. Price, *Second Republic*, p. 308. Soboul, *Problèmes paysans*, pp. 276–281, 333–334. Moore, *Social Origins of Dictatorship and Democracy*, pp. 470–471, 473. Scott, *Moral Economy of the Peasant*, ch. 6. Sydel F. Silverman, "Exploitation in Rural Central Italy," p. 329.

18. Despite the weaknesses of Blanqui's general position, he nevertheless identified the source of increasing peasant misery and revolt. Thus, he scathingly condemned the forty-five-

prediction in *Class Struggles* of a predominant peasant socialism, but in Marx's judgment, did not refute his general theory. Instead, Marx emphasized those aspects of his general theory that explained peasant conservatism. He also added one political auxiliary statement, stressing the role played by memories of past Napoleonic glories in shifting the revolt against the republic mainly to the right rather than to the left.

In reassessing the peasants' economic situation, Marx highlighted their mutual isolation rather than their exploitation by the usurer, their privacy or, as he called it in the *Manifesto*, "the idiocy of rural life" rather than their links to the larger society, as the decisive factor conditioning their outlook:

> A small holding, a peasant, and his family; alongside them another small holding, another peasant and another family. A few score of these make up a village, and a few score of villages make up a Department. In this way, the great mass of the French nation is formed by simple addition of homologous magnitudes, much as potatoes in a sack form a sack of potatoes.[19]

The economic conditions of these families "separate[d] their mode of life, their interests and their culture" from other classes, and to this extent made the peasants a class. Yet these conditions also divided the peasants internally. They had only a "local interconnection" and lacked the wealth of social ties, knowledge of science, "diversity of individual talents," and political organization which for Marx characterized the revolutionary proletariat. Given this economic and social isolation, Marx argued, the peasants lacked the ability to act as a class. Peasant support for the Napoleon of a new empire as opposed to the previous Napoleon of the republic, illustrated their incapacity to "enforce their class interests." [20] This argument restated the *Manifesto*'s general characterization of the small property holder as "reactionary insofar as he tries to roll back the wheel of history." But Marx's explanation also stressed a new and more decisive element, the role of Napoleonic traditions, which, combined with the peasants' economic situation, "like a sack of potatoes," engendered a second Bonaparte who reigned in the peasants' name but

---

centime tax which turned many peasants against the republic. *Werke*, 7:568. Yet Blanqui isolated his conspiracy from this peasant movement as he did from the strikes whose militancy he admired.

19. *CM*, p. 38. *EB*, p. 334.
20. *EB*, p. 334.

against their interests. But Marx overstated his case on the separation of the peasants. In *Class Struggles*, Marx had rightly discerned the force of collective traditions and politics in the making of agrarian radicalism; the reactionary Napoleonic tradition reflected the peasantry's collective life and outlook at least as much as it indicated their mutual isolation.

Marx pointed to widespread Napoleonic ideas as the decisive factor in explaining Bonaparte's triumph. Recalling the era of the original Napoleon, many peasants dreamed of restoring their small holdings. Marx contended dialectically that this "Napoleonic form of property," a condition of the independence and liberation of French peasants in the early nineteenth century, had turned "into the law of their enslavement and pauperization." The bourgeois order had revealed its true physiognomy as a "vampire"; the Napoleonic Code had become "a codex of distraints, forced sales and compulsory auctions." Despite peasant fantasies, restoring Napoleon would not forestall this exploitation.[21]

The peasants' Napoleonic ideas also included "strong and unlimited government," featuring a "well-galloonned and well-fed bureaucracy." But this flourishing government meant an increase in the hated taxation that already impoverished the peasant. The first Napoleon had conquered the Continent and repaid the taxes. In fact, Marx suggested, those taxes had spurred the peasants' industry. But the new "Napoleonic" taxes had the opposite result: "They rob his industry of its last resources and complete his inability to resist pauperism." [22]

A new Napoleonic era would strengthen the priests as "an instrument of government." But, Marx argued, the new heaven of the mid-nineteenth century held no salvation for the small peasant: "Heaven was quite a pleasing accession to the narrow strip of land just won, more particularly because it makes the weather; it becomes an insult as soon as it is thrust forward as a substitute for the small holding. The priest then appears as only the anointed bloodhound of the earthly police." [23] Furthermore, revived Napoleonism meant war and a domineering army. Under the first Napoleon, the peasants had fought passionately to defend their newly won property. Subsequently, however, capitalism and usury had undermined the source of their patriotism: "The small holding lies no longer in the so-called fatherland but

21. Ibid., pp. 336–338.
22. Ibid., p. 338.
23. Ibid., p. 339.

in the register of mortgages." [24] The mid-nineteenth-century peasants defended their titles of property not against a foreign enemy but against the tax collector.

Marx's historical analysis of peasant Napoleonism illustrated Heraclitus's aphorism: one cannot step in the same river twice. The original Napoleonic ideas ideologically ornamented the small holding in the "freshness of its youth"; in 1852, they shrouded its "death struggle" with absurd "hallucinations." In this argument, the *Eighteenth Brumaire* incorporated and transformed the analysis in *Class Struggles*. Marx still viewed the peasants' living conditions as ferociously oppressive. The small holding had metamorphosed into the chain of the peasants' enslavement rather than the surety of their independence. And yet—the majority of peasants clung to "Napoleonic illusions" and restored a counterfeit Napoleon.

Marx's general theory partially explained the peasants' vacillation between reaction and revolution. Held by the talisman of their small plots, peasants looked to the conservative representatives of private property. Capitalist mortgages and usury, however, drove them toward a radical alliance with the workers. Yet, in the actual clash, the weight of a specific political tradition— the vision of a resuscitated Napoleon—exerted decisive and for Marx unexpected influence. French experience had illustrated the dramatic potentials for opposed political elaborations growing out of the dual economic interests of the peasants.

Economic determinist scholars generally identify Marx's interpretation of the peasants with that of Balzac's urban journalist Emile Blondet. Stumbling across old Fourchon, Blondet saw him as a "barbarian in the midst of civilization." [25] This view loses the subtlety and complexity of Marx's analysis of the peasantry. In the *Eighteenth Brumaire*, Marx reiterated that the majority of peasants could still become revolutionary and make an alliance with the urban workers:

> The Bonaparte dynasty represents not the revolutionary, but the conservative peasant . . . not the country folk, who, linked up with the towns, want to overthrow the old order through their own energies, but on the contrary, those who, in stupefied seclusion within this old order, want to see themselves and their small holding saved and favored by the ghost of the empire. It repre-

24. Ibid., pp. 339–340.

25. "Here are the redskins of Cooper, he [Blondet] said to himself. There's no need to go to America to observe savages." Balzac, *Paysans*, pp. 84–85.

sents not the enlightenment, but the superstition of the peasant; not his judgment, but his prejudice; not his future, but his past; not his modern Cevennes but his modern Vendée.[26]

In 1851, many French peasants confused conservative and revolutionary attitudes. The bourgeoisie had turned the peasants against the National Assembly; the peasants regarded the false Napoleon as an opponent of this republic of the rich. Hence, the "reddest Departments" among the peasants also voted for Bonaparte. "In some parts the peasants even entertained the grotesque notion of a convention side by side with Napoleon." [27] Furthermore, many peasants participated in the widespread insurrection against Napoleon's coup. If the peasants clarified their interests, Marx argued, they would move toward revolution. Upon his disillusionment with Napoleon, "the French peasant will part with his belief in his small holding, the entire state edifice erected on this small holding will fall to the ground, and *the proletarian revolution will obtain that chorus without which its solo song becomes a swan song in all peasant countries.*" [28]

Class Struggles and the *Eighteenth Brumaire* illustrate the striking relationship between prediction and explanation in the development of Marx's theory. Faced with the failure of a predicted worker-peasant alliance, Marx did not alter his general theory but changed an auxiliary statement concerning Napoleonic survivals. Such ideologies take the revolutionary sting out of peasant misery and turn it in a conservative direction. These Napoleonic ideas would not die through industrialization alone. This new explanation, based on French experience, reinforced Marx's general strategy for revolutionary political organizing among the peasantry "in all peasant countries." [29] Furthermore, Marx's explanation seems more sensitive to changing political circumstances than many of today's analyses of the "objective exploitation" of the peasants. Marx captured the dual potential for increasing

26. *EB*, p. 335. Protestant peasants staged an uprising calling for "No taxes" and "Freedom of conscience" at Cevennes at the beginning of the eighteenth century. The Vendée was the center of reaction during the French Revolution.

27. Ibid., p. 336. See also Price, *Second Republic*, p. 320.

28. *EB*, p. 340, n. 1. See also Dieter Hertz-Eichenrode, "Karl Marx über das Bauerntum und die Bündnisfrage," pp. 387–388.

29. Jerrold Seigel ignores the continuity in Marx's analysis of the capitalist exploitation of the French peasants between the *Class Struggles* and the *Eighteenth Brumaire*. For Marx's alteration of specific economic and political auxiliary statements or dialectic of prediction and explanation, Seigel substitutes an eschatological play between an expected "revelation" of basic

capitalist oppression within any one country to drive the peasants either to the left or to the right. Overall conservative and revolutionary political activity, not a conjunction of social circumstances alone, played a decisive part. In stressing the dialectical character of Marx's materialism against charges of economic reductionism in the 1890s, Engels rightly praised the *Eighteenth Brumaire* as a model of Marx's historical analysis.[30]

11–3. Engels on Radical Politics and the Peasant War

ENGELS'S *The Peasant War in Germany*, written in 1850, drew striking parallels between the peasant revolt of 1525 and the revolution of 1848. Both movements revealed the timidity of the urban middle classes, their fear of an aroused peasantry, and their consequent eagerness to unite with the princes; both illustrated the crippling impact of provincialism and decentralization on peasant uprisings, which the princes could put down one by one. Most important, Engels highlighted the role that a radical religious outlook, a "proletarian-plebeian asceticism," played in breaking down peasant isolation as well as in making the peasant war possible, and by implication, underlined a similar potential for political activity in the nineteenth century.

Engels emphasized the Catholic Church's ideological and political dominion in the sixteenth century. The supremacy of theology among intellectual activities mirrored the social and political situation of the Church "as the most general force coordinating and sanctioning existing feudal domination." In those conditions, all revolutionary indictments of feudalism inevi-

---

class forces on the surface of history (*Class Struggles*) and an alleged utter "masking" or "reveiling" of such forces (*Eighteenth Brumaire*). In considering *Class Struggles*, Seigel overlooks the existence of rural democratic-socialist secret societies; in the case of the *Eighteenth Brumaire*, he ignores the widespread peasant uprisings against Napoleon's *coup d'état*. John M. Merriman, *Agony of the Republic*, chs. 7–8. Though Seigel notes Marx's later advocacy of a worker-peasant alliance during the Paris Commune, he obscures the substance of Marx's historical argument and the complexities of peasant politics with a bewitching if slightly histrionic metaphor. Seigel, *Marx's Fate*, pp. 201–203, 212–213, 246.

30. Engels to Bloch, September 21, 1890, Engels to Schmidt, October 27, 1890, and Engels to Borgius, January 25, 1894, in Marx and Engels, *Selected Works*, pp. 693, 699, 706. For instance, Barrington Moore seems to regard the political direction of peasant revolt within a country as determined by the overall path of its industrialization and the specific economic character of agrarian change.

tably appeared as theological heresies. Such indictments had to strip prevailing arrangements "of their aureole of sanctity." Thus, Luther's translation of the Bible into German armed the peasant and plebeian movement with a powerful weapon.[31]

At this time, the lords exercised a terrible domination over the peasant, including not merely labor services but a variety of physical tortures. Despite the hatred for the lords that this treatment induced, the peasants could not easily unite in revolt.

> Being spread over large areas, it was highly difficult for them to come to a common understanding; the old habit of submission inherited from generation to generation, the lack of practice in the use of arms in many regions, the unequal degree of exploitation depending on the personality of the master all combined to keep the peasant quiet.[32]

Under these conditions, peasants launched local insurrections, but no Germany-wide rebellions, until the peasant war. What made this unusual, general peasant rising possible? Partly the severity of their oppression, Engels asserted, partly their alliance with plebeian elements in the city. As the central feature of his explanation, however, Engels stressed a radical, communal egalitarian ideology as the dynamic force in the peasant war and "in the beginning of every proletarian movement up to 1850." Describing Hans the Piper's revolt, Engels asserted: "All the prophets of rebellion started with appeals against sin, because, in fact, only a violent exertion, a sudden renunciation of all habitual forms of existence could bring into motion a disunited, widely scattered generation of peasants grown up on blind submission." [33] This religious and political outlook heightened peasant awareness of common oppression and overcame the divisions to which Engels and Marx attributed peasant reaction, inactivity, or impotence then and in the mid-nineteenth century. Like the *Eighteenth Brumaire*, Engels's *Peasant War* accentuated the role of political efforts in his and Marx's explanations and strategies.

In the *Peasant War*, Engels celebrated Thomas Münzer who had provided genuine theoretical leadership to a broader peasant movement than such ear-

31. Engels, *PW*, pp. 52, 62.
32. Ibid., pp. 47–48.
33. Ibid., pp. 74–76. Engels defined the plebeians as the growing urban dispossessed class, lacking both land and tools.

lier local conspiracies as Union Shoe and Poor Konrad. According to Engels, Münzer elaborated a new philosophy, a pantheism, or even an atheism which he tactically cloaked in Christian phrases. For Münzer, the Bible gave no infallible revelation. Men should follow their own reason and seek heaven in this world. They should "smite the ungodly"—the rich—who prevented them from attaining it:

> The source of the evil of usury, thievery and robbery . . . [was] the princes and the masters who had taken all creatures into their private possession—the fishes in the water, the birds in the air, the plants in the soil. And the usurpers, he said, still preached to the poor the commandment, "Thou shalt not steal," while they grabbed everything, and robbed and crushed the peasant and artisan. "When, however, one of the latter commits the slightest transgression," he said, "he has to hang, and Dr. Liar says to all this: Amen." The masters themselves created a situation, he argued, in which the poor man was forced to become their enemy. . . . "Oh, my dear gentlemen, how the Lord will smite with an iron rod all these old pots!" [34]

Münzer, Engels contended, transcended the general movement of his time in seeking communal property rather than land division, and a unified republic rather than a monarchy. Thus, Engels suggested ironically, biblical phraseology played a less significant role in Münzer's thinking than it did "for many a disciple of Hegel in modern times." [35]

Münzer did not restrict himself to an abstract philosophical enterprise. He not only denounced the "middle class reformation," led by Luther, that "easy-living flesh of Wittenburg," but also worked as a political agitator. Though forbidden to by the princes, he published radical pamphlets, sent forth emissaries to spur peasant organization, and founded a peasant union (conspiracy) in Altstedt. When the authorities drove Münzer from Altstedt, he joined with the Anabaptists, a sect united around egalitarian asceticism and antagonism to the princes, which propagated his ideas throughout the peasant movement. Münzer's "revolutionary energy and decisiveness" helped to instigate the peasant war. He forged an "advanced faction of the plebeians and peasants," distinct from the broader movement in that it shared Münzer's energy and outlook. According to Engels, radical political ideas, culminating in vigorous revolutionary organizing, played as vital a role in

34. Ibid., p. 68.
35. Ibid., pp. 65–67.

the peasant war as they had in 1848. As Marx had envisioned Babeuf in the French Revolution as the "voice of the proletariat," so Engels identified Münzer and later Marat as precursors of Marx and the German communists.[36]

Since Münzer saw "beyond his time," his outlook exemplified the uneven development of theory and history. His theory did not represent a "task" which medieval mankind could set itself and realize. Instead, Engels argued, only a bourgeois democratic revolution might have succeeded. Yet given the limited extent of the world market and the weak bourgeoisie in German towns, Engels concluded that even a bourgeois revolution would probably have failed. For Engels, economic obstacles (low level of production) and political wants (lack of a revolutionary bourgeoisie or working class, to a lesser extent absence of a fully developed democratic or communist revolutionary theory) forestalled democratic revolution at that time.

Engels then drew an inexact and problematic contrast between the fate of Münzer, executed by the princes, and that of Louis Blanc, minister of labor in the French February Republic:

> The worst thing that can befall a leader of an extreme party is to be compelled to take over a government in an epoch when the movement is not yet ripe for the domination of the class he represents and for the realization of the measures which that domination would imply. . . . What he *can* do is in contrast to all his actions as hitherto practiced, to all his principles and to the present interests of his party; what he *ought* to do cannot be achieved. In a word, he is compelled to represent not his party or his class, but the class for whom conditions are ripe for domination. . . . Whoever puts himself in this awkward position is irrevocably lost.[37]

This analogy confused the relationship between Blanc, Münzer, and Marx and Engels in 1848. When Blanc took an isolated "socialist" seat in the post-February French government, the once vigorous plain republicanism of the original French Revolution had exhausted its progressive role. The French

36. Ibid., pp. 67–73. Luther called for smiting the rebellious peasants as ungodly. *CM*, p. 61. Engels, "Marx and the *Neue Rheinische Zeitung (1848–1849)*," *MESW*, 2:334.

37. *PW*, pp. 135–136. Marx also employed this analogy to Louis Blanc in his bitter exchange with Schapper at the final September 15, 1850, meeting of the London-based Central Committee of the Communist League. Marx, *The Cologne Communist Trial*, p. 253.

working class had begun to fight directly for a realizable socialist goal. In this context, Blanc deflected the real movement and collaborated in a government that shot down the workers in June.

In Münzer's Germany, a successful democratic revolution, even without a subsequent communist one, would have represented an enormous advance, preceding the Puritan Revolution by a century and a quarter and the French Revolution by two centuries and a half. In fact, Münzer's program for a unified republic foreshadowed the first demand of the German communists in 1848 and would have improved upon the German constitutions of 1850. If such a revolution could have succeeded, should Münzer and his followers simply have abstained from leadership? Economic circumstances, especially the limited world market, might not have permitted a victorious revolution. But were English circumstances in the 1640s so much more propitious? In comparing Blanc and Münzer, Engels substituted a general economic determinist argument for his subtle analysis of the specific economic and political factors involved in the peasant war.

In the much more advanced European circumstances of 1848, Marx and Engels had envisioned a potential link between German democracy and socialism. They had organized to propel the democratic revolution to its conclusion and fuse these two revolutions. If a vigorous republican war against Russia had ensued, should they (and the revolutionary committees of public safety) have refused to lead it and bowed to the hesitant Frankfurt parliament? In a dynamic republican revolution, the communists could have mobilized the masses from within and without the new government and built upon its citizen army and democratic officialdom to make the revolution "permanent." Engels's brief analogy, implying a policy of extreme opposition in a democratic revolution, contradicted his and Marx's actual and projected activity in 1848. Engels's use of Louis Blanc and general economic tendencies seems particularly ironic in the midst of an argument that so clearly stressed the decisive role of politics in this medieval social movement.

Engels argued that the medieval countryside and not the city ignited the peasant war. He characterized the urban plebeian movement, left to itself, as "reactionary," "a shouting, rapacious tail-end to the middle class opposition." Only peasant leadership spurred it in a radical direction: "The revolt of the peasants . . . transformed them [the plebeians] into a party, and even then they were almost everywhere dependent upon the peasants both in demands and in action—a striking proof of the fact that the cities of that time were greatly dependent upon the country." [38] Despite Engels's book, Bakunin later perversely identified Marx and Engels with Lassalle's opposition to the peasant war. Lassalle would praise the crushing of the peasants which coincided, in his view, with the rise of a strong state. In his play *Franz von Sickingen*, Lassalle eulogized the aristocrats Sickingen and Ulrich von Hutten and intimated that their leadership would have been beneficial to the insurgent peasant movement. But Marx and Engels hailed the peasant rebels and Münzer as the real revolutionary forces of that time.[39]

Engels never extended this view of revolutionary initiative from the countryside in the Middle Ages into the new historical circumstances of the nineteenth century. In fact, Engels in his *Revolution and Counterrevolution in Germany* of 1851–1852, contended that "in all modern countries" the city must lead the countryside:

> The agricultural population, in consequence of its dispersion over a great space, and of the difficulty of bringing about an agreement among any considerable portion of it, never can attempt a successful independent movement; they require the initiatory impulse of the more concentrated, more enlightened, more easily moved people of the towns.[40]

Though this argument appears ironic in light of *The Peasant War*, written only a year earlier, Engels relied mainly on recent European, especially French, revolutionary experience. In that context, it made sense. Factory workers and even artisans, more concentrated and more easily organized than the nineteenth-century rural proletariat or peasantry, initiated the major rebellions; the peasants followed or, as in France in 1851, pursued their own course. Contrary to economic determinist stereotypes, Engels's *Peasant War* emphasized the revolutionary aspect of the peasantry, the importance of radical politics in furthering an alliance between city and countryside, and the potential, under specific historical circumstances, for the peasantry to play a predominant role.

38. *PW*, p. 46.

39. Michael Bakunin, *Etatisme et anarchie*, p. 321. See David Riazanov, introduction and Engels's evaluation of Hutten and Sickingen, *PW*, pp. 8, 95–99. Marx and Engels wrote to Lassalle, criticizing his play, *SC*, pp. 116–120.

40. Engels, *Revolution and Counterrevolution*, p. 8.

11–4. Marx's Later Conception of the Worker-Peasant Alliance

SOME SCHOLARS, notably Lichtheim, have argued that after 1848 Marx abandoned his alleged Jacobinism, that is, his advocacy of a worker-peasant alliance strategy. Yet Marx examined and reexamined this possibility on the basis of subsequent experience. On April 16, 1856, Marx wrote to Engels that a "new edition of the peasant war" must back a proletarian revolution in Germany. "Then the affair will be splendid." [41] In 1871, Marx argued that the Paris Commune defended the peasants' "living interests" in terms reminiscent of *The Class Struggles in France*. The French bourgeoisie at Versailles sought to shift the five-milliard Prussian indemnity from its own shoulders onto those of the peasants:

> The Commune . . . declared that the true originators of the war would be made to pay its cost. The Commune would have delivered the peasant of the blood tax [conscription]–would have given him a cheap government–transformed his present blood-suckers, the notary, advocate, executor, and other judicial vampires, into salaried communal agents, elected by, and responsible to, himself. It would have freed him of the tyranny of the . . . gendarme and the prefect; would have put enlightenment by the schoolmaster in the place of stultification by the priest. . . . Such were the great immediate boons which the rule of the Commune–and that rule alone–held out to the French peasantry. [42]

If the Commune had broken out of its military isolation, Marx argued, three months of free communication with the provinces would have inspired "a general rising of the peasants." The Versaillese spared no effort to prevent this "spread of the rinderpest" from the city to the countryside. In 1850, Marx had compared the "secondary exploitation" of the French peasantry to that of the starving Irish tenant; he now likened it to the capitalist bleeding of the "Hindu ryot," robbed even of part of his wage. Yet the "insulated" existence of the rural producer, accompanied by a whole social and political outlook, differed from the "world" of large-scale urban factory production.

41. Lichtheim, *Marxism*, p. 129. *SC*, p. 92.

42. Marx, *The Civil War in France* in *Writings on the Paris Commune*, p. 79. Engels's 1870 introduction to the *Peasant War* also called upon German socialists to unite with agricultural proletarians as "their most urgent task." *PW*, pp. 20–21.

Marx reaffirmed the *Eighteenth Brumaire*: "What separates the peasant from the proletariat is, therefore, no longer his real interest, but his delusive prejudice." [43]

In 1875, Marx defended a worker-peasant alliance against both Social Democrats and anarchists. The Eisenach Social Democrats had just fused with the Lassalleans. Their joint Gotha Program dismissed the German peasants as part of "one reactionary mass" opposed to the proletariat. Marx responded: "Has one proclaimed to the artisans, small manufacturers, etc., and *peasants* during the last elections: Relatively to us you, together with the bourgeoisie and feudal lords form only one reactionary mass?" [44]

Bakunin's *Statism and Anarchy* (1873) had asserted that Marx and his cohorts opposed all peasant uprisings. In Marx's notes on this attack, he reiterated the political alternatives in continental Europe where the peasants constituted a majority: "Either the peasant prevents or . . . dooms to failure every workers' revolution as he has done up to now in France, or the proletariat functioning as the government must take steps that will directly improve his position and thus win him over to the revolution." The policies of a workers' government must appeal at least as strongly to the peasantry as those of the original French Revolution. Beyond land division however, these measures must ease the transition to collective ownership and convince the peasant "of his own accord on economic grounds." French defeats had taken their toll on Marx's optimism in *Class Struggles* about the force of a sheerly economic push toward socialism. Capitalist exploitation of the peasant did not produce a proletarian response; instead, the peasant's "delusive prejudice" predominated: "Even where he [the peasant] does belong to it [the proletariat] by reason of his position, he does not consider himself as belonging to it." [45]

Marx noted that despite Bakunin's rhetorical fervor about the peasantry, he promulgated a profoundly counterproductive program: the abolition of inheritance. Bakunin's ideas did not strike at the root of capitalism in the countryside and would offend a small peasantry that strove to make its tiny property heritable.[46]

---

43. Marx, *Civil War* and *First Draft* in *Writings on the Paris Commune,* pp. 80, 155–158.

44. Marx, *Critique of the Gotha Program, MESW,* 2:25–26.

45. Marx, "Konspekt von Bakunins 'Staatlichkeit und Anarchie,' " *Werke,* 18:632–633.

46. Ibid., 18:633. See Temma Kaplan, *Anarchists of Andalusia,* chs. 6–7, for an analysis of the remarkable propagation of an anarchist outlook among Spanish peasants and artisans in the late nineteenth century. The community strikes she describes closely resemble Marx's

Contrary to the Social Democrats' Gotha Program and to Bakunin, a socialist party or proletarian government would have to evolve a skillful policy to unite with the peasantry. Thus, political experience had profoundly influenced even the nuances of Marx's theory and strategy. Throughout his political career, Marx continually stressed the forging of a worker-peasant alliance "in all peasant countries." He never argued that the triumph of socialism in any particular country required that the proletariat be a majority (as opposed to a sizable portion) of the population. Instead, he searched painstakingly for those conditions in which workers could join with other oppressed classes to take political power and initiate the further protracted transformation to communism.[47]

conception of radical unionism in the resolutions of the Geneva Congress of the IWA, though the anarchists differed with Marx's larger conception of socialism. General Council of the IWA, *Minutes*, 1:348–349.

47. Marx, *First Draft* in *Writings on the Paris Commune*, p. 154.

— XII —

Marx and the State

12–1. *Class Struggles* and the Bourgeois Republic

IN 1848, MARX PARTICIPATED in a great though unsuccessful revolutionary movement. Previously, he had offered a general view of the capitalist state and of the revolutionary workers' government that would replace it. Between 1848 and 1851, Marx's *Class Struggles* and *Eighteenth Brumaire* reevaluated and refined his earlier conceptions in the light of new experience.

Class Struggles seemed to confirm Marx's earlier view that the executive branch of a republic simply "manage[s] the common affairs of the whole bourgeoisie" and victimizes the workers.[1] Yet though Marx foresaw a red republic, a strange and unexpected Second Empire, manned at its heights by the lumpenproletariat, emerged from the fierce conflict following June. This empire silenced the bourgeoisie which had only recently stepped into the spotlight of political rule; the emperor's drunken soldiery even shot down individual bourgeois "fanatics for order" on their balconies. Did this transmogrified "parasite state" still illustrate the *Manifesto*'s claim that a state serves one class as an instrument of violence in oppressing another?

In *Class Struggles*, Marx contended that before the February Revolution, the factions of the French ruling class battled for supremacy. The Orleanist July Monarchy depended on the finance aristocracy. According to Marx: "When the liberal banker Lafitte led his companion, the Duke of Orléans . . . in triumph to the *Hôtel de Ville*, he let fall the words: '*From now on the bankers will rule.*'" Marx defined this ruling faction to include bankers, stock exchange kings, railway kings, owners of coal and iron mines and forests, and a part of the landed proprietors. He contrasted this group with the industrial bourgeoisie. The finance aristocracy ruled in its own person. "It sat on the throne, it dictated laws in the Chambers, it distributed public office, from cabinet portfolios to tobacco bureau posts."[2]

1. *CM*, pp. 36, 54.
2. *CS*, pp. 139–140.

During this period, the official opposition consisted of the industrial bourgeoisie as a minority in the legislature, and the ideological representatives (lawyers, doctors, and the like) of the petite bourgeoisie and peasants. The monarchy, however, completely excluded these classes from political power. Fearing the new working-class movement, the industrial bourgeoisie at first moved cautiously against the monarchy. When the regime drowned the proletarian "mutinies" of 1832, 1834, and 1839 in blood and seemingly ensured the industrialists' social domination, however, the industrialists sought to gain political power and fell upon the finance aristocracy.[3]

The finance aristocracy held the state debt. It used its political clout to encourage a rising deficit and promoted its own "parasitic" existence at the expense of industrial production. The industrialists countered with the slogan "cheap government." Joining with the petite bourgeoisie, they indicted the corrupt financiers in pamphlets like "The Rothschild Dynasty" and "Usurers, Kings of the Epoch." Borrowing this language, Marx likened the finance aristocracy to debauched criminals; this aristocracy exhibited "the same prostitution, the same shameless cheating, the same mania to get rich . . . not by production but by pocketing the already available wealth of others." Marx identified the finance aristocracy as *"nothing but the rebirth of the lumpenproletariat on the heights of bourgeois society."* [4]

This division within the bourgeoisie triggered the February Revolution of 1848. In 1850, Marx pinpointed the specific economic causes of the revolt, namely the potato blight and crop failures of 1845 to 1847 and the reverberations of the commercial and industrial crisis in England, which made the financiers' rule unbearable: "As against the shameless orgies of the finance aristocracy, the struggle of the people for the prime necessities of life! At Buzançais, hunger rioters executed; in Paris, oversatiated *escrocs* [swindlers] snatched from the courts by the royal family." [5] Death and starvation drove the people to revolt; the devastation of trade impelled the industrial bourgeoisie. Proletarians and capitalists struck together against the old monarchy and brought it down. The industrial bourgeoisie would have preferred its own monarchy, the Bourbons. But the workers, led by Raspail and Blanqui, stormed an early meeting, threatened renewed revolt, and forced the provisional government to declare a republic. As Marx had concluded in the *NRZ,*

3. Ibid., p. 140.
4. Ibid., pp. 142–143.
5. Ibid., p. 143.

the pressure of the masses generated this "energetic" revolutionary measure. Thus, the new provisional government embodied a temporary compromise between workers and capitalists despite their "antagonistic" interests. The bourgeoisie's representatives together with those of the petite bourgeoisie and the dynastic Bourbon opposition predominated. When 20,000 workers marched on the Hôtel de Ville to demand a Ministry of Labor, the provisional government appointed two workers' representatives, Louis Blanc and Albert, to set one up at the Luxemburg Palace.[6]

From the outset, the February Republic maintained a precarious existence. Having compelled the bourgeoisie to form this new regime, the workers expected its "citizen" leaders to represent them. As Marx put it, the February Revolution had proclaimed "a republic surrounded by social institutions." But the workers had won no real social institutions, Marx argued; they had merely forced the bourgeoisie to rule openly. In such a republic, the workers would no longer confuse the consequences of capitalist exploitation with monarchical oppression; in the words of the NRZ, the bourgeoisie had lost its "scapegoat." Thus, the republic completed bourgeois rule by permitting all sections of the propertied classes, not just the financiers, to "enter the orbit of political power"; yet this public role simultaneously exposed and endangered the bourgeoisie. Therefore, each bourgeois faction yearned for a nonbourgeois "representative" or protector to bear the brunt of popular outrage. Despite their mutual antipathy, the need to hold the workers in check (and later the peasantry and the petite bourgeoisie) drove these warring factions together. As Marx sarcastically put it, each faction taken separately advocated its own brand of royalism, but "the product of their chemical combination had necessarily to be republican . . . the white and the blue monarchy had to neutralize each other in the tri-color republic." [7]

In the February government, the workers' representatives stood out only by their ineffectuality. In *Class Struggles*, Marx contended that workers could not reform a bourgeois republic from within. The provisional government had originally pledged to guarantee jobs as well as to enforce "the right to work" and the "organization of labor." Its proletarian Ministry of Labor, led by Blanc and Albert, had a portfolio but no power. "Unlike any profane state power, they had no budget, no executive authority at their disposal." As capitalism thrived off exploitation, a proletarian or ostensibly nonexploita-

---

6. Ibid., pp. 145–147.
7. Ibid., pp. 146–147, 189–190.

tive Ministry of Labor in a capitalist government had a certain gravity-defying unreality about it:

> *Organize labor!* But wage labor, that is the existing, the bourgeois organization of labor. Without it there is no capital, no bourgeoisie, no bourgeois society. *A Special Ministry of Labor!* But the Ministries of Finance, of Trade, of Public Works—are not these the *bourgeois* Ministries of Labor? And *alongside* these a *proletarian* Ministry had to be a ministry of impotence, a ministry of pious wishes, a Luxemburg Commission.[8]

This bourgeois government adopted the national ateliers as a weapon to discredit socialism, to divide the workers from the petite bourgeoisie: "In the half naive, half intentional confusion of the Paris bourgeoisie, in the artificially molded opinion of France and of Europe, these workhouses were the first realization of socialism, which was put in the pillory with them." Gradually, the bourgeoisie gathered sufficient boldness to attack the social measures of the February Revolution and pinpointed the ateliers as their main target. They incited small businessmen and artisans to diagnose their own misery not as a consequence of bourgeois control of taxation and credit, but as a result of sums squandered on "proletarian loafers." [9] They called upon the petite bourgeoisie to ally themselves with their larger competitors rather than the workers and to blame their oppression on those more victimized than themselves. Divided from the peasantry and the petite bourgeoisie, the proletariat rebelled in June and suffered defeat. Dialectically, the attempt to reform the bourgeois republic from within through a socialist ministry of labor had turned into its opposite. The seemingly socialist "right to work" proved to be nothing but an instrument to exploit the workers and to isolate them politically.

According to Marx, June exposed capitalist politics, even in its republican form, as a "dictatorship of the bourgeoisie" accompanied by the "slavery of labor." For Marx, this bourgeois dictatorship extended its sway over the peasants and petite bourgeoisie as well. Yet even though the bourgeoisie retained its oppressive social power, the republic granted the oppressed classes the vote. The new constitution, drafted after June, strikingly manifested this

---

8. Ibid., pp. 147–148.

9. Ibid., pp. 156, 152–154. Price, *French Second Republic,* p. 182. The use of the issue of welfare to divide employed from unemployed workers in the United States today strikingly resembles this old bourgeois tactic.

contradiction: "While in theory it [the Assembly] accurately marked off the forms in which the rule of the bourgeoisie found republican expression, in reality it held its own only by the abolition of all formulas, by force *sans phrase*, by the *state of siege.*" The constitution demanded that the proletarians not move forward "from political to social emancipation"; it required that the bourgeoisie should not retreat "from social to political restoration." [10] This contradiction engendered a fundamental instability characteristic of newly forged republican rule in revolutionary situations. Throughout this period, Marx persistently emphasized this phenomenon.

Marx believed that universal suffrage exacerbated the contradiction inherent in this phase of French republicanism, but could not resolve it. In the *Eighteenth Brumaire*, Marx would describe how, following an electoral victory by a June insurgent, de Flotte, and the strengthening of the petit-bourgeois opposition under the leadership of Ledru-Rollin, the National Assembly excluded roughly one-third of those previously eligible to vote. "The majority of the people had passed through the school of development which is all that universal suffrage can serve for in a revolutionary period. It had to be set aside by a revolution or by the reaction." Marx briefly recounted the economic and political factors preventing a proletarian uprising to retain suffrage or gain the red republic: an army of 150,000 in Paris, the government's delay of the decision on the suffrage, the conciliatory attitude of the bourgeois press and of the Mountain, and finally, the return of commercial prosperity.[11] Though he would qualify this argument for England as we shall see, Marx's writings on France categorically limited the role of universal suffrage to exposure of the bourgeoisie. Only a violent revolutionary movement that had learned its lessons in this school could achieve socialism.

After June, Marx argued, the Party of Order still had considerable resources at its disposal: money, the allegiance of most of the old society's ideologists, control of a huge governmental apparatus, and allies among the nonrevolutionary petite bourgeoisie and peasantry who looked to "the high dignitaries of property" to represent them.[12] Yet the constant threat of renewed revolt from below crippled the bourgeoisie's capacity to rule. It therefore resorted to war as a classic means to acquire political support.

Victorious in the February Revolution, many French republicans sym-

10. *CS*, pp. 162–163, 170–172.
11. Ibid., p. 233.
12. Ibid., p. 190.

pathized with radical republicanism elsewhere. Even the French constitution explicitly "forbade" any attack on the liberty of foreign peoples. But the Italian revolt, according to Marx, menaced the French bourgeoisie. It endangered the power of the pope and undermined the spell of Catholicism over the French peasants. Thus it undercut the peasantry's political acquiescence in its increasing impoverishment: "The mortgage that the peasant has on heavenly possessions guarantees the mortgage that the bourgeois has on peasant possessions. The Roman revolution was an attack on property, on the bourgeois order, dreadful as the June revolution." [13]

In May 1849, therefore, Bonaparte, the new president, launched an invasion of republican Rome. The Roman revolutionaries had common interests with the French democrats; yet this invasion united the French Republic "with the Holy Alliance, with Naples and with Austria." [14] Like the German bourgeoisie whom Marx had condemned in 1848, the French bourgeoisie could maintain its power in the post-June republic only by pursuing a reactionary foreign policy.

In the *Manifesto*, Marx had contended that the state serves an oppressing class. His argument seemed almost restrictively to focus on violence or repression as the state's fundamental function. Yet Marx also discerned a secondary cultural or ideological role for the state. The French government promoted patriotism and religion along with the international violence of war to win its internal political battle against radical republicanism and socialism (the Second Empire, Marx would argue, also reinforced peasant "Napoleonic" ideas). In Marx's analysis, state action fostered reactionary political ideas to help maintain itself. This argument contained the embryo of a Marxian interpretation of Weber's concept of legitimacy; it also foreshadowed Gramsci's notion of hegemony.

Like the pompous Frankfurt parliamentarians, Marx noted, the French democrats had relied on the "ideal" force of constitutional provisions instead of mass revolutionary violence to oppose the Roman invasion. The Mountain, led by Ledru-Rollin, tried to impeach Bonaparte. With Humpty-Dumptyesque logic, the Party of Order responded that the French army had crushed the "despotism of anarchy" in Rome, not "liberty," and that no violation of the constitution had occurred. More important, the Party of Order controlled the guns. As Marx put it, "The interpretation of the consti-

13. Ibid., pp. 196, 187.
14. Ibid., p. 187.

tution did not belong to those who had made it, but only to those who had accepted it . . . its bourgeois meaning was its only viable meaning." Neither universal suffrage nor impeachment would defeat the bourgeoisie. Only a vast European revolutionary movement and ultimately world war, Marx argued in *Class Struggles,* could sweep away the Holy Alliance and its French republican ally.

> The workers . . . thought they would be able to consummate a proletarian revolution within the national walls of France, side by side with the remaining bourgeois nations. But French relations of production are conditioned by the foreign trade of France . . . how was France to break them without a European revolutionary war, which would strike back at the despot of the world market, England? [15]

Just as Marx saw the connection between the foreign policy of the French bourgeois republic and international reaction, so he envisioned the link between a potential proletarian dictatorship in France and the destiny of the European revolutionary movement. He opposed any limited proletarian citizenship in a red republic; no merely patriotic socialism could stamp out its external enemies.

Where the *Manifesto* had described proletarian rule as an unheard-of democracy for the vast majority of workers and a despotism over the bourgeoisie, *Class Struggles* first employed a new concept for this regime: the dictatorship of the proletariat. As in his writings in the *NRZ,* Marx expected this new form of rule to flow out of the real French movement for the red republic. He suggested that the network of Parisian workers' clubs (by no means fully Marxian in outlook) embodied this new state in embryonic form:

> And the clubs—what were they but a coalition of the whole working class against the whole bourgeois class, *the formation of a workers' state against a bourgeois state?* Were they not just so many constituent assemblies of the proletariat and just so many military detachments of revolt in fighting trim? [16]

Marx already surmised that the new political units of the proletarian regime would fuse military and deliberative functions; communism would integrate political life and the proletariat. Once again, Marx decried utopian fantasies

15. Ibid., pp. 196, 148, 163.
16. Ibid., p. 185.

that "dream of the peaceful achievement of . . . socialism—allowing, perhaps, for a second February revolution lasting a brief day or so." Instead, Marx conceived the revolution that would uproot classes entirely as a violent and protracted one:

> The *proletariat* rallies more and more round *revolutionary socialism,* round *communism,* for which the bourgeoisie has itself invented the name of *Blanqui.* This socialism is the *declaration of the permanence of the revolution,* the *class dictatorship* of the proletariat as the necessary transit point to the *abolition of class distinctions generally,* to the abolition of all the social relations that correspond to these relations of production, to the revolutionizing of all the ideas that result from these social relations.[17]

Contrary to Avineri and Hunt, Marx wholeheartedly favored the demolition of the bourgeoisie, as did Blanqui. If in the real movement the enemy had cursed proletarian revolution with the name "Blanqui," then Marx himself would adopt this name for socialism. But Marx also thought that this "practical-critical" movement must go beyond Blanqui. He opposed isolated putsches or the rule of elite conspiratorial "illuminati," and maintained that the masses of workers and peasants, led by communists, would themselves take over the exercise of state power. As in the *Theses on Feuerbach,* he emphasized that the revolutionary masses must educate themselves through their own experience. Where Blanqui utterly dismissed the peasants, Marx's embryonic dictatorship of the proletariat encompassed them: "Only the fall of capital can raise the peasant; only an anti-capitalist, a proletarian government can break his economic misery, his social degradation. The *constitutional republic* is the dictatorship of his united exploiters; *the social democratic, the Red* republic is the dictatorship of his allies." [18] In *Class Struggles,* Marx vividly portrayed the social alliance that would sustain a proletarian dictatorship. But beyond broad indications such as the role of the Paris clubs, Marx had yet to discern the political form of this new regime within the real movement.

12–2. The Parasite State

In *Class Struggles,* MARX HAD EMPHASIZED that the bourgeoisie's crushing of June, like the sorcerer's apprentice, had unleashed forces that a republic could

17. Ibid., pp. 222, 223, 162.
18. Ibid., p. 217.

not contain and predicted a strong socialist response. In 1851, however, the new Napoleonic empire reaped the benefit of this dynamic. In the *Eighteenth Brumaire,* Marx had to modify his earlier prediction and explain this new phenomenon. Given this reactionary development, he linked his analysis of the "parasite state" to a clearer picture of its opposite, proletarian rule.

In the *Eighteenth Brumaire,* Marx again underlined the republic's oppressiveness. Even before June, Marx noted, Blanqui and his comrades organized a large demonstration to regain the proletariat's influence over the republic and forced their way into the Assembly. Afterward, the republic arrested the leaders. Following June, the Party of Order continued this jailing and exiling of proletarian organizers. While recovering from June, the workers merely took part in the movements of other classes, particularly of the petite bourgeoisie. The new radical peasant movement had not strongly stimulated the proletariat, which had neither an overt program nor an organization of its own. On June 13, 1849, the Mountain staged a peaceful demonstration against the Roman invasion to declare the president "outside the law"; the national guard dispersed the demonstration, and the Mountain's leaders fled into exile.[19] Following the Mountain, the proletariat had gone down to a new defeat.

As the classes oppressed by this bourgeois republic could offer no alternative political leadership, an ever-narrowing circle of direct rulers bridled and crushed every suggestion of reform. Even the slogans of the Party of Order suddenly backfired against it:

> The high priests of the "religion of order" themselves are driven with kicks from their Pythian tripods, hauled out of their beds in the darkness of night, put in prison-vans, thrown into dungeons or sent into exile. . . . Bourgeois fanatics for order are shot down on their balconies . . . in the name of property, of the family, of religion and of order.[20]

With an almost Proudhonian irony, the mantle of defender of order fell upon thieves; the imitation Napoleon, surrounded by his lumpenproletarian entourage, ascended to imperial power. If the great French Revolution had traced an "ascending line" in which each party had relied on a more progressive party to gain power only to be thrown aside by it, the revolution of 1848 moved in a decadent, "descending line" in which the more reactionary par-

19. Ibid., pp. 253–254, 276–277.
20. *EB,* pp. 256, 330.

ties scrambled over one another until Napoleon triumphed. Again, the instability of a parliamentary republic played a vital role in Marx's explanation: "The parliamentary regime leaves everything to the decision of majorities; how shall the great majorities outside parliament not want to decide? When you play the fiddle at the top of the state, what else is to be expected but that those down below dance?" [21]

Believing that capitalism would rapidly place unbearable pressure on the workers, Marx's comment overestimated the instability of parliamentary republics in general. Yet he carefully defined the historical conditions in which this bewitching fiddle music of political egalitarianism would announce the social dance. He compared Europe and the United States. In the old societies, a "developed formation of classes" existed; "the work of centuries" had dissolved traditional ideas, and the republic signified "in general . . . the political form of revolution of bourgeois society." As June had demonstrated, the European republic soon initiated a red carmagnole. In the United States, however, the new republic embodied a "conservative form of life." A fluid social interchange of members of not yet fixed classes and a "feverish," dizzying development of modern means of production under the impetus of relatively few "heads and hands" had "left neither time nor opportunity for abolishing the old spirit world." Unlike Marx, Avineri neglects these historical conditions and asserts: "Bourgeois society will do anything—even prostrate itself before Louis Bonaparte—to prevent universal suffrage from achieving its [*sic*] ends." [22]

If the bourgeoisie could no longer rule directly, did this new empire oppose its fundamental social interests? Paradoxically, Marx suggested, "the individual bourgeois can continue to exploit the other classes . . . only on condition that their class be condemned along with the other classes to like political nullity." Yet the lumpenproletariat had not broken the bourgeoisie's political power simply to protect its social power; it exacted a price. Beyond the indulgence of shooting individual bourgeois, Napoleon plundered the bourgeoisie's collective wealth through increased taxes. Still, the

---

21. Ibid., pp. 294–297, 288.

22. Ibid., p. 255. Avineri, *Social and Political Thought,* pp. 212–213. Avineri notes that, in general, historical conditions or "social contexts" are important; as he fails to explore such conditions specifically, however, he creates the impression that for Marx universal voting by itself had some mysterious, self-transcending quality. In a flight of Hegelian fancy, he reinforces this impression by attributing purposes and actions to universal suffrage.

empire revealed the internal political secret of the conservative republic, its defense of exploitation and its creation of a gigantic state apparatus:

> No Circe, by means of black magic, has distorted that work of art, the bourgeois republic, into a monstrous shape. That republic has lost nothing but the semblance of respectability. Present-day France was contained in a finished state within the parliamentary republic. It only required a bayonet thrust for the bubble to burst and the monster to spring forth before our eyes.[23]

In backing the absolute monarchy and then making revolution, the French bourgeoisie had forged this state apparatus, consisting of a huge standing army and bureaucracy. The state's repressive side, the army, defended the bourgeoisie's "political interests," its capacity to exploit, against the Lyons uprisings and June. The state's "material side," the elaborate edifice of offices, soaked up the surplus bourgeois population. Though headed by the lumpenproletariat, this state apparatus retained its distinctively bourgeois support and functions. "This executive power," Marx contended, "with a host of officials numbering half a million, besides an army of another half million, this appalling parasitic body . . . enmeshes the body of French society like a net and chokes all its pores." [24] Thus, a life-sucking, symbiotic state structure grew out of the bourgeoisie's corrupt social dominance.

Marx's references to the executive of this parasite state as by turns "independent" and "seemingly independent" of the classes of bourgeois society recalled the analysis of the Jacobins and the first Napoleon in *The Holy Family*. But although the empire played a role over and above society and cut down individual bourgeois leaders, Napoleon could not defy the laws of gravity of the capitalist epoch. Napoleon announced his paradoxical mission as safeguarding the very "bourgeois order" whose political power he had defeated. The emperor's new railroad and construction contracts nurtured the bourgeoisie and revived its political influence even as his repressive measures strove to prevent this consequence from following the cause. "He is somebody solely due to the fact that he has broken the political power of the middle class and daily breaks it anew. . . . But by protecting its material power, he generates its political power anew." Thus, Napoleon constantly attempted to "perfect the executive," to pit an independent state against

23. *EB*, pp. 288, 330–331.
24. Ibid., pp. 284–285, 332.

society, and to enmesh with parasitic growths every live social stirring. This new experience made the essence of the old capitalist regime stand out:

> Every *common* interest was straightway severed from society, counterposed to it as a higher, *general* interest, snatched from the activity of society's members themselves and made an object of government activity, from a bridge, a schoolhouse and the communal property of a village community to the railways, the national wealth and the national university of France.[25]

In explaining this "independent" development of the state, Marx had emphasized the role of conservative peasants who, gulled by Napoleonic "hallucinations," allowed this oppressive regime to represent them from on high. This new auxiliary statement revealed that dead political experience could dominate living men. But the Napoleonic phenomenon had even wider ramifications for Marx's theory. It pressed to the limit the range of potential "bourgeois" states and cast a sudden, general light on the political character of proletarian rule. The exploitative state arrogated the "common interests" of society to itself. Through its "perfected" twin instruments of standing army and officialdom, the empire (and the class it served) monopolized and corrupted any genuine political life. A proletarian revolution, Marx asserted, must "destroy" these instruments and forge the new institutions already suggested in the "Seventeen Demands": worker-officials, stripped of any bureaucratic aureole of sanctity and special pay, and a citizen army. The workers and peasants themselves must take over the common tasks from the local bridge or schoolhouse to the national university and army. In the *Eighteenth Brumaire*, Marx went beyond the *Manifesto*, the experiences of 1848, and *Class Struggles*, to glimpse the political outlines of a regime that would appear full-fledged in the Commune as the "political form at last discovered in which to work out the economic emancipation of labor." Thus, fresh experience and a new explanation refined Marx's general theory of the state and contributed to Marx's strategy, before and after proletarian revolution, for building a new kind of political community.

Given the Napoleonic victory, Marx characterized the complex, continuous, self-critical or "practical-critical" character of proletarian revolution:

> Bourgeois revolutions . . . storm swiftly from success to success; their dramatic effects outdo each other; men and things seem set in sparkling bril-

25. Ibid., pp. 340–341, 332–333.

liants; ecstacy is the everyday spirit; but they are short-lived; soon they have attained their zenith, and a long crapulent depression lays hold of society before it learns soberly to assimilate the results of its storm-and-stress period . . . proletarian revolutions . . . criticize themselves constantly, interrupt themselves continually in their own course, come back to the apparently accomplished in order to begin it afresh . . . seem to throw down their adversary only in order that he may draw new strength from the earth and rise again, more gigantic, before them, recoil . . . from the indefinite prodigiousness of their own aims, until a situation has been created which makes all turning back impossible, and the conditions themselves cry out: *Hic Rhodus, hic salta!* [26]

Marx's increasingly refined analysis of the French Revolution, June, and the Paris Commune, and the subsequent, not always successful efforts of Marxian socialist parties to imbue future proletarian movements with this new understanding provide a striking example of the process Marx had in mind.

Recent writers, notably Avineri and Hunt, have played down the role of energetic dictatorship of the proletariat which Marx expected would dismantle the old state and suppress the bourgeoisie. In 1852, in a letter to his fellow communist Weydemeyer, Marx pointed out that he had inherited (and adapted) the idea of history characterized by class struggle from previous writers; he had contributed the idea of proletarian dictatorship leading to communism:

> What I did that was new was to prove: (1) that the *existence of classes* is only bound up with *particular historical phases* in the development of production; (2) that the class struggle necessarily leads to the *dictatorship of the proletariat*; (3) that this dictatorship itself only constitutes the transition to the *abolition of all classes* and *a classless society*.[27]

Marx's analysis of the Commune and his *Critique of the Gotha Program* (1875) would underline the enduring importance of this conception.

12–3. Marx's Theory of the State: Successive Approximations to the Truth

IN RESPONSE TO THE SECOND NAPOLEON, Marx's new theory of the capitalist state fused two distinct elements: the notion of an independent bureaucracy

26. Ibid., pp. 250–251.
27. Letter of March 5, 1852, *SC*, p. 69. Gilbert, "Salvaging Marx from Avineri," pp. 25–31.

which soars above society as an alienated expression of its perverted common power, and the concept of an instrument of violence which serves one class at the expense of others. Why did Marx continue to use the term "state," meaning a government dominated by the bourgeoisie (that is, a state only in the second sense) to describe so eccentric a form? Mightn't one view this Napoleonic apparatus as a new, wholly independent social force that contradicted Marx's theory and required either a fundamental change in the meaning of the term state or some new designation?

As the Second Empire defended the social power of the bourgeoisie, albeit in a peculiar fashion, it shared a nontrivial feature with the more clearly bourgeois Second Republic or July Monarchy (in *The Civil War in France*, Marx later referred to the Second Empire as the "ultimate" and "most prostitute" form of "bourgeois" rule on the European continent).[28] Thus, Marx's conception of all these states, despite their diversity of composition, had a common core. In addition, Marx's theory of presocialist states as defenders of exploitative classes captured a fundamental aspect of the repressive reality of Napoleonism.

On the basis of his investigation of the natural sciences and his knowledge of Marx's social theory, Engels made an argument that prefigured a modern realistic account of the relation of concepts and reality. In 1895 in a letter to Engels, Conrad Schmidt had described Marx's concept of value in *Capital* as simply a useful "fiction." If this were true, Engels replied, then one would have to consider all general concepts, including the notion of wages or of feudalism, as fictions, since such concepts never exhaust particular realities and contain some untrue or inadequate elements. Instead, Engels proposed, scientific concepts approximate reality though often in a "circuitous fashion." Turning to the practice of the natural sciences, Engels noted that the concept fish "includes life under water and breathing through gills"; yet the lungfish, a transitional form between fish and amphibian, no longer lived under water and breathed air (from the point of view of the *Eighteenth Brumaire*, it was a kind of odd Napoleonic fish). Despite structural similarities, some ostensibly universal features of the notion fish did not hold for the lungfish. Yet, Engels argued, that did not make the concept fish a "fiction." The scientific practice of the time considered the lungfish a (modified form of) fish.[29]

28. Marx, *Writings on the Civil War in France*, pp. 72, 150. Engels, "The Housing Question," *MESW*, 1:605–606.

29. Letter of March 12, 1895, *SC*, p. 484.

As Hilary Putnam restates Engels's point in his essay "Explanation and Reference," "to stick to the letter of the definition in applying the concept fish would be bad science." Similarly, Marx fairly viewed the "parasite state" as a class state in the sense defined in his theory. Putnam makes another point about the reference of scientific concepts to reality that casts light on Marx's refinement of his theories. A concept like fish continually changes "as a result of the impact of scientific discoveries, but that does not mean that it ceases to correspond to the same natural kind (which is itself, of course, always changing)." [30] In Marx's analysis of the state, the reality changed (the proletariat's first uprising, the ensuing class struggles, and the triumph of the Second Empire); Marx then altered his theory to encompass the "parasite state" as a paradoxical form of bourgeois rule and to discern the main features of its mortal enemy, the proletarian dictatorship. In other words, one might view Marx's original theory of the state as a first approximation and his subsequent refinements, given historical experience, as a more finely structured analysis of its varying forms.

I should note, however, two important qualifications to the analogy between Marx's conception of the parasite state and a Darwinian conception of lungfish. First, evolutionary theory investigated the lungfish as an interesting but peripheral phenomenon, but Marx saw the Napoleonic state as typical of the development of late nineteenth-century European capitalism. Furthermore, with due attention to different historical circumstances, one might want to compare the Napoleonic parasite state and later fascist governments (in the Nazi case, these circumstances would include the rise of imperialism and the defeat of Germany in World War I; the international impact of the Russian Revolution and the political and economic decline of capitalism; the more developed German working-class socialist and communist movements; and the role of modern eugenics or racist ideology). [31] Second, Putnam suggests that natural kinds are perpetually changing. While his remark holds true of Darwinism, Putnam would probably have qualified it with regard to other fields, for instance atomic physics where scientific understanding has deepened remarkably but the underlying reality has remained the same.

30. Putnam, *Collected Philosophical Papers*, 2:196–197.
31. Ralph Miliband, *The State in Capitalist Society*, pp. 93–94, draws this analogy but omits those decisive historical features that explain the genocidal character of Nazism and differentiate it from the rule of the second Bonaparte. On the modern racist response to class conflict in the United States and Germany, see Leon Kamin, *The Science and Politics of I.Q.*; Stephan L. Chorover, *From Genesis to Genocide*; Garland E. Allen, "Genetics, Eugenics and Class Struggle."

12–4. Reform and Revolution: The Shorter Work Week and Universal Suffrage

IN THE *Manifesto*, MARX OUTLINED separate strategies for England where the proletariat constituted a majority, and for Germany and France where peasants still outnumbered workers. In England, the workers would conduct a direct struggle for socialism; on the Continent, workers and peasants would attempt to link a republican revolution against autocracy with a proletarian one. After 1851, Marx concluded that the European class struggle would result in a parasite state which the workers would have to destroy (Engels would also argue in *The Housing Question* that Bonapartism and the restored and strengthened Prussian monarchy increasingly resembled one another).[32] Where such a gigantic state structure and a mainly rural population existed, as in much of Europe, Marx considered violent revolution the necessary course of development. In England, however, he projected a potential exceptional course characterized by a less violent transition to socialism by means of universal suffrage.

At this time, Marx and Engels's stress on universal suffrage in England accompanied a peculiar (for them) deprecation of other reform struggles, notably the battle for the shorter working day. In 1850 in two articles in the *Neue Rheinische Zeitung, Politisch-Ökonomische Revue*, Engels condemned the English Ten Hours Bill of 1847. According to Engels, the "social development" of England flowed from the "progress of industry." "Reactionary" and "impermanent" institutions, including the Ten Hours Bill of 1847, hindered this progress; the further unfolding of capitalism pushed them aside. In these articles, Engels ignored the previous independent workers' movement for shorter hours and contended instead that the workers had simply trailed after the Tories, led by Sadler, Oastler, and Ashley.[33] Hence the capitalists had easily undermined this frail Ten Hours Bill.

Yet, Engels argued, capitalism had physically "driven" this generation of English workers "into the ground." These workers desperately needed a shorter working day. He then distinguished a "real workers' ten hours bill" linked to universal suffrage and realizable only under socialism from the "reactionary" Ten Hours Bill of 1847.[34] But Engels's articles seemed lukewarm

---

32. *MESW*, 2:605–606.
33. *Werke*, 7:240–241. Thompson, *Making of the English Working Class*, p. 349.
34. *Werke*, 7:241.

toward a renewed ten hours movement. His main economic determinist argument endorsed the untrammeled development of capitalist industry and undercut any mass movement to hold back capitalist production or exploitation. Engels's argument contradicted the *Poverty of Philosophy* and the *Manifesto* in which Marx and Engels had contended that the workers should engage in reform movements like the one for shorter hours. The workers' party, argued the *Manifesto*, "compels the legislative recognition of the political interests of the workers by taking advantage of the divisions among the bourgeoisie itself. Thus, the ten hours' bill in England was carried." In addition, Engels's argument in 1850 contradicted the later thrust of Marx's and his own organizing in the IWA which centered on international strike support and the fight for a shorter work week. As an alternative in 1850, Engels contended that the English workers should fight mainly for universal suffrage. In England, where "the industrial proletariat is two-thirds of the population, universal suffrage is the open political domination of the working class with all the revolutionary transformations of social conditions which are inseparable from it." [35]

In 1850 for the first and only time in his life, Marx also veered toward a condemnation of reform struggles and defended the position that only revolution made any difference. In *Class Struggles*, he introduced the concept of dictatorship of the proletariat with an exaggerated antireform argument: "Only its [the Paris proletariat's June] defeat convinced it of the truth that the slightest improvement in its position remains a *utopia within the bourgeois republic*, a utopia that becomes a crime as soon as it wants to become a reality." [36] In *Capital*, Marx later argued that the workers could win certain reforms and significantly raise the social definition of subsistence under capitalism, but the bourgeoisie would continuously oppose these efforts and strive to reverse the workers' gains. In *Class Struggles*, Marx specifically referred to demands for the "right to work" and the "organization of labor" that legitimized the oppressive workhouses. Yet he formulated this position—"the slightest improvement . . . remains a utopia"—as an attack on reform struggles in general. But Marx also identified the primary English mass movement as the battle for universal suffrage, led by the Chartists. Even

35. *CM*, p. 43. *Werke*, 7:241.

36. *CS*, p. 162. Franz Mehring, *Karl Marx*, pp. 149–150, rightly emphasizes Marx's and Engels's temporary opposition to reform struggles, though he inappropriately reads it back into the pre-1848 period.

when Marx and Engels briefly advanced a sectarian (divorced from the mass movement) argument on reforms, they still attempted to learn from the practice of the workers and to participate in the main contemporary movement. In 1852 in an article in the *New York Tribune*, "The Chartists," Marx argued that universal suffrage would mean social and political domination by the English workers. They had already waged "a long though often underground civil war" and had infused the carrying of universal suffrage with "a far more socialist spirit than any measure that is honored with this name on the Continent." Universal suffrage would inevitably lead to "the political supremacy of the working class." [37]

Marx did not contend, however, that the workers could win universal suffrage without force. Describing an election rally for the Chartist Ernest Jones, Marx left the strong impression that universal suffrage would not come easily. To the repeated applause and eventual acclamation of the crowd of 20,000 workers, Jones denounced limited suffrage. A mere 500 legal voters would return his opponents, capitalists or their supporters, to Parliament on the next day though 20,000 workers wanted something different. Thus two systems clashed. The Tory candidate and the "Manchestermen" represented capitalism in which the businessman "buys cheap and sells dear." Analyzing this idea, Jones explained that the capitalist buys the workers' labor cheap; he sells dear to other workers what the workers produce. Jones therefore advocated socialism. Because he was a fighter for universal suffrage, the authorities had jailed him (hardly an indication of the peaceful prospects for winning universal suffrage); he identified the cause of socialism with that of the suffrage. In Marx's view, if the masses who applauded his speech had their say, they would have done away with the capitalism of the Tories and Whigs. [38]

Given this intense antagonistic contradiction between 20,000 workers denied real citizenship and 500 voters, Marx probably thought that the workers would need at least a brief violent revolution, as he had suggested in the *Manifesto*, to achieve or enforce universal suffrage. In an article written for the American radical but noncommunist press, Marx may have moderated his view. Or perhaps, given the comparative absence in England of a parasite state structure like the one in France, he may have thought that the workers could take over the state apparatus through universal suffrage without much

37. Marx, *Politische Schriften*, 1:398.
38. Ibid., 1:401–402, 404–406.

violent conflict. After the Commune, however, Marx would point out that a peaceful electoral victory for socialism in England would probably occasion "new slaveowners' rebellions." [39] In any case, in 1852, Marx greatly emphasized the role of universal suffrage in England in comparison with his earlier argument in the *Manifesto*. At this time, he saw it as the central focus of the English revolutionary movement and the main lever for achieving workers' rule.

39. Interview of R. Landor with Karl Marx, July 3, 1871, in Marx, *On the First International*, pp. 324–325.

— XIII —

Revolutionary Party
versus Conspiracy

13–1. The Strategy of Marx's *Address* of 1850

EXILED FROM GERMANY IN 1849, Marx emigrated first to France and then to England where he would spend the rest of his life. Most of the other leaders of the Communist League except Moll, who had died at the battle of the Murg, had already gathered in London and reconstituted the League. During this time, Heinrich Bauer had remained in Germany and successfully rebuilt the organization there. Attempting to recruit German radicals to a democratic organization, Karl Schurz reported that most activists had already joined the League. Marx's experiences in the democratic revolution had underlined the need for independent, revolutionary working-class activity; only a "purely social" political party could coordinate local actions and propel the real movement forward. Upon his arrival in London Marx rejoined the League. In March 1850, the Central Committee issued its famous *Address*, drafted by Marx, on how communists might transform a democratic revolution originally led by the petite bourgeoisie into a socialist one.

The *Address* opened by arguing that the experience of 1848–1849 had vindicated the League's strategic emphasis on the democratic revolution, as proclaimed by the *Manifesto*, and noted that its members had participated "energetically" in this conflict: "In the press, on the barricades and in the battlefields, they stood in the front ranks of the only decidedly revolutionary class, the proletariat." Yet the *Address* also criticized Marx's own position at the outset of 1848. In the revolution, the League's former organization had slackened, and a large part of its members had "believed the time for secret societies to have gone by and public activities alone sufficient." [1] Though the *Address* did not mention Marx specifically, he had dissolved the League in 1848. As the *Address* indicated, Marx still insisted on participation in the democratic revolution rather than pure conspiratorial isolation in the midst

---

1. *Address*, p. 106.

of conflict. But given the democratic movement's upshot, Marx placed another consideration alongside this one. Without a workers' party, he and his
colleagues had not sufficiently galvanized even the struggle for democracy to
ensure its success. While organization alone could not guarantee revolution
in the absence of favorable conditions, communist strategy, agitation, and
mobilization would decide among the political alternatives when a revolutionary situation existed. Lacking previous organization, the workers had
fallen under the leadership of petit-bourgeois democrats; a revolutionary
countercurrent had emerged only in 1849. To counteract the democrats'
influence, the workers must forge their own revolutionary party.

The March Revolution catapulted the bourgeoisie to power. But as the
NRZ had emphasized, the bourgeoisie quickly capitulated to the monarchy
and the Junkers. Even under the counterrevolution, Marx argued, the bourgeoisie held title to the state debt, would soon capture predominant
influence, and would ensure its social power. Given the bourgeoisie's political subordination, it would bear less obvious responsibility for repression
against the workers, the petite bourgeoisie, and the peasantry. In any uprising, however, the bourgeoisie would continue to cleave to the Monarchy.[2]
Accordingly, a new revolutionary upheaval would bring the petit-bourgeois
democrats to power. This democratic party consisted of three groups: the
"most advanced elements of the big bourgeoisie," particularly the Berliners
who had participated in the tax resistance movement; the democratic consti-
tutionalist petite bourgeoisie who sought a federal republic; and the republican petite bourgeoisie and small capitalists who detested their large capitalist
competitors. According to Marx, this last group, which sometimes called
itself "red and social-democratic," posed a greater danger to the workers than
the old liberal one. If, beguiled by its rhetoric, the workers followed these
republicans, they would lose their "independent, laboriously achieved position" and sink to an "appendage of official bourgeois democracy." For Marx,
the prevailing capitalist and feudal ideas would not simply fall away, especially when a competing "radical" leadership with such a sophisticated
camouflage strove to maintain them. Only determined socialist efforts would
forge a serious revolutionary movement:

> The workers and above all the League, must exert themselves to establish an
> independent, secret and public organization of the workers' party alongside of

2. Ibid., p. 107.

the official democrats and make each section the central point and nucleus of workers' societies in which the attitude and interests of the proletariat will be discussed independently of bourgeois influences.[3]

Given the rapid changes in any revolutionary conflict, these worker societies should unite in one nationwide movement to act swiftly upon a common purpose. Independent meetings and discussions would generate a mutual understanding; centralization would provide more vigorous leadership throughout Germany than Marx and his colleagues had exerted in the Rhineland in 1848. At the outset of a new democratic uprising, the Central Committee would "betake itself to Germany," convene a congress, and propose the centralization of the workers' clubs. In the *Address,* Marx stressed the strategy and program of such a movement. But once agreed upon, only a concerted organizational effort would give these politics decisive influence.[4]

Though the workers would provide the main fighting force on the barricades, the newly triumphant democrats would immediately strive to bridle them. Unlike the French proletarians of February 1848, the German workers must not allow themselves to become "intoxicated" by democratic victory. Even with relatively clear proletarian insight into the democrats' limitations, however, the communists could not simply overthrow them on the morrow of their accession to power because the new leadership would not have sufficiently discredited itself among the masses of the peasants and petite bourgeoisie. The communist movement must therefore press the government at every turn and expose the democrats' false revolutionary promises:

It is in their [the workers'] power to make it difficult for them [the petite bourgeoisie] to gain the upper hand against the armed proletariat, and to dictate such conditions to them that the rule of the bourgeois democrats will from the outset bear within it the seeds of their own downfall.[5]

Playing a stronger political role than the sans-culottes, the workers must force the democrats to "carry out their present terrorist phrases."

The workers, Marx argued, should pursue acts of vengeance against their worst oppressors to maintain the movement's initiative and "revolutionary excitement. . . . Far from opposing so-called excesses, instances of popular

3. Ibid., p. 111.
4. Ibid., p. 113.
5. Ibid., p. 112.

revenge against hated individuals or public buildings that are associated only with hateful recollections, such instances must not only be tolerated but leadership of them taken in hand." [6] This tactic recalled the satire in the *NRZ* of the reactionary leader Prince von Lichnowski whom Georg Weerth rechristened the "Knight Schnapphahnski." It prefigured the symbolism of the crash of Napoleon's statue in the *Eighteenth Brumaire* and the actual dismantling of the Vendôme column during the Paris Commune.[7]

Beyond its militancy, however, the proletariat must advance its own demands alongside those of the "reformist" democrats in order to "transform . . . [their demands] into direct attacks on private property." Here Marx vividly depicted the steps by which a democratic revolution might move in an "ascending line" to achieve a communist conclusion:

> If the petty-bourgeoisie propose purchase of the railways and factories, the workers must demand that these railways and factories shall simply be confiscated by the state without compensation as being the property of reactionaries. If the democrats propose proportional taxes, the workers must demand progressive taxes; if the democrats themselves put forward a moderately progressive tax, the workers must insist on a tax with rates that rise so steeply that big capital will be ruined by it; if the democrats demand the regulation of state debts, the workers must demand state bankruptcy. Thus the demands of the workers must everywhere be governed by the concessions and measures of the democrats.[8]

Though the workers would not at first propose "directly communistic measures," they would compel the democrats "to interfere in as many spheres as possible of the hitherto existing social order, to disturb its regular course and to compromise themselves as well as to concentrate the utmost possible productive forces, means of transportation, factories, railways, etc., in the hands of the state." [9] On the basis of post-*Manifesto* revolutionary experience, Marx

6. Ibid.

7. *EB*, p. 344.

8. *Address,* p. 116. In an article in Harney's journal, *The Friend of the People,* J. G. Eccarius, Marx's ally on the League Central Committee, suggested a similar strategy against English "financial reform": "As friends or allies, we can only form the tail of a deceitful and treacherous head. . . . If on the contrary, we help as foes and have a good organization for our own class interests, we can drive them [the bourgeoisie] farther than they wish to go themselves." John Saville, ed., *The Red Republican and the Friend of the People,* 2:50, 27–28.

9. *Address,* p. 116.

proposed a far more exact relationship between communists and democrats than he had in the *Manifesto*.

Still a minority of the population, the workers must press these revolutionary measures not only in their own interests, but also in those of the rural proletariat and the peasantry. As I noted above, Marx emphasized a demand for common property rather than the land division that had ruined the French peasants. As in 1848, he envisioned a socialist potential in the German peasantry. Only unity between the workers, peasants, and petite bourgeoisie could lead to a majority-supported, "permanent" revolution. Following the "Seventeen Demands," the workers would also fight for a single, indivisible republic, not for a federated one (in 1885, Engels would remark that at this time, he and Marx had misinterpreted the political form adopted by the Convention in the French Revolution and looked to an overly centralized republic; Engels would urge more provincial self-government along with unification).[10]

As the revolution progressed, the workers would create a "dual" government alongside the existing structure. This government, consisting of broad "municipal councils or committees" as well as "workers' clubs," would involve nonproletarian political forces. These independent governmental bodies, comparable to the Cologne Committee of Public Safety, would supervise and threaten the authorities.[11]

Unless the workers obtained weapons, however, these committees could not achieve their revolutionary purpose. Marx argued that the workers should form their own military organizations and resist the formation of nonproletarian armed forces. In effect, the armed workers and municipal committees would become the real power. Though the formal state structure would remain in the hands of the democrats, this state would lose its cutting edge and dwindle into a political shadow. If the proletariat could not yet gain such predominance, it should form separate detachments under elected commanders within the state army or under the authority of the revolutionary committees:

> The arming of the whole proletariat with rifles, muskets, cannon and munitions must be put through at once, the revival of the old Citizens' Guard directed against the workers must be resisted. . . . Arms and ammunition

10. Ibid., pp. 114–115 and Engels's addition of 1885, ibid., p. 115, n. 2.
11. Ibid., p. 112.

must not be surrendered on any pretext; any attempt at disarming must be frustrated, if necessary by force.[12]

Once again, Marx defended the concept of a proletarian political community that controlled its own committees and weapons and forcibly displaced an existing oppressive political structure. In Engels's words, the workers would become the genuine modern *"political* animals." Tactically, in a revolutionary situation, resistance to the disarming of a proletarian military unit could play an explosive role. Marx's argument foreshadowed Thiers's attempt in 1871 to strip the Paris national guard of its weapons which triggered the Commune. Marx offered these tactical and organizational suggestions for a revolutionary period. In more stable times, such "proletarian commanders" might turn into military Louis Blancs, impotent figureheads for a power lodged in a reactionary general staff.

Revamping his strategy of 1848, Marx contended in the *Address* that in a revolutionary setting, communists should participate in every election, advocate their own program, and expose the vacillating democrats. While Marx had previously supported "plain" democratic candidates, he argued in 1850 that such an approach would impede even the republican revolution:

> In this connection they [the workers] must not allow themselves to be seduced by such arguments . . . as, for example, that by doing so [putting up their own candidates] they are splitting the democratic party and making it possible for the reactionaries to win. The ultimate intention of all such phrases is to dupe the proletariat. The advance which the proletarian party is bound to make by such independent action is infinitely more important than the disadvantage that might be incurred by the presence of a few reactionaries in the representative body.[13]

In any case, Marx argued that communists should not settle accounts with reactionaries by voting; instead, they should encourage the democratic movement to deal with counterrevolutionaries "resolutely and terroristically" from the beginning.[14]

Marx's stress on open communist participation in elections exemplified his continuous reevaluation of theory on the basis of practical experience and clarified the *Manifesto's* broad conception of a dual democratic and socialist

12. Ibid., p. 113.
13. Ibid., p. 114.
14. Ibid.

role for communists in the German revolution. Marx substituted a vision of systematic propagation of a communist outlook and indictment of the exploitative bourgeoisie for his earlier criticism of parliamentarians as vacillating democrats.

In general, Marx's changing views on the role of the German bourgeoisie between 1843 and 1850 show how deeply political experience influenced his strategic estimates. In 1843, he looked to a radical social revolution that would overthrow the bourgeoisie along with the old order. Between 1845 and 1848, he envisioned the political experience of a democratic revolution as a necessary prelude to a proletarian one and thought that the bourgeoisie must play some role, probably a hesitant one, in the struggle for a republic. In 1848, as a leader of the left wing of the democratic movement, he criticized the bourgeoisie for lack of energetic revolutionary measures. From the autumn of 1848 through the spring of 1849, given the bourgeoisie's counterrevolutionary policies, he called for a "social-republican revolution," led by a new "purely social" party, and indicted the capitalists as an exploiting class. In his *Address* of 1850, reassessing this revolutionary experience, he further specified the role of a proletarian party, which would propel democracy to victory and build for socialism independently of the bourgeoisie. Given the vicissitudes of class struggle, Marx's theory of capitalism could lead to varying political conclusions. Historical materialism provided a basic framework for evaluating fresh experience. One cannot understand the changes in Marx's political position without attention to the underlying theory. But the reverse also holds: the general theory provided no excuse for ignoring or denying novel historical circumstances or political events.

Without mentioning world war (which he discussed in *Class Struggles*), Marx's *Address* cautioned against the expectation that a "revolution in permanence" could triumph quickly:

> If the German workers are not able to attain power . . . without going through a lengthy revolutionary development, they at least know for a certainty that the first act of this approaching revolutionary drama will coincide with the direct victory of their own class in France and will be very much accelerated by it.[15]

15. Ibid., p. 116. Marx projected a protracted revolution in the *Address* as well as in his later exchange with Willich and Schapper. Hunt ignores all the evidence both in 1848 and later that Marx advocated this radical strategy, interprets the *Address* as a "compromise," and attempts to read this document out of "the political doctrines of classical Marxism." Hunt, *Political Ideas*, pp. 243–248.

Marx never conceived socialist revolution as a sudden insurrectionary out-
burst. Instead, he saw it as a complex, protracted political struggle which
would culminate in violent proletarian seizure of power. Three criteria
would guide this extended political effort: destruction of the bourgeois democrats' influence upon the workers through a vigorous communist presence;
independent, armed workers' organizations; and the enforcement of demands "as difficult and compromising as possible upon the inevitable momentary rule of the bourgeois democracy." [16] A communist party pursuing
such policies bears no resemblance to the isolated conspiracy of the bistros
which Marx would shortly criticize. Though European circumstances seemed
less propitious for democratic or proletarian revolution than they had in the
1840s, Marx never changed his mind about furthering "permanent revolution" within a democratic movement.

13–2. Marx against "The Great Men of Exile"

IN MARX AND ENGELS'S PERIODICAL THE *Neue Rheinische Zeitung, Politisch-
Ökonomische Revue* for November 1850, they analyzed the resurgence of capitalist prosperity, stimulated and symbolized by the California gold rush,
throughout Europe and North America. The productive forces suddenly
flourished "as exuberantly as they can under bourgeois conditions" and temporarily ruled out any "real revolution." Marx and Engels asserted that an
economic and commercial crisis, deriving from a conflict between relations
and forces of capitalist production, had triggered the revolutions of 1848.
Only renewed crisis could foster the next revolutionary upsurge: "A [prole-
tarian] revolution is only possible in a period when these *two factors, the modern forces of production* and the bourgeois forms of production come into contradiction with each other." [17] This analysis of the need for an underlying
revolutionary period complemented their previous arguments on complex
European class structures, the role of war, the ramifications of political strategy, and the implications of uprisings like the June insurrection. Faced with
this rebirth of capitalism, however, they drastically revised their tactics and
discounted all plans for insurrection in the near future. Instead, they envisioned a long-term political effort in the circumstances of a further unfolding
of capitalism, "class and national wars," to forge a revolutionary workers'
movement.

16. *Address,* p. 113.
17. Marx and Engels, "Revue, Mai bis October 1850," *Werke,* 7:440.

Many European democrats and communists disagreed with Marx and Engels's materialist assessment of politics. For them, the true moral view, a revolutionary "will" to battle, and tight organization would suffice. Mazzini (Italy), Ledru-Rollin (France), Darasz (Poland), and Ruge (Germany) formed a European republican central committee to coordinate new uprisings. This committee's manifesto proclaimed that the democratic revolution had foundered solely on its leaders' petty jealousies and ambitions. Somehow, the members of this central committee would escape these passions. Marx opposed this posturing by the "great men of exile" and contrasted their moralist point of view with his material analysis of the class struggle. Offering only "Lamartinish phrases about brotherhood," the democrats uged the workers to neglect their own interests and accept bourgeois leadership. In the absence of revolutionary conditions, Marx suggested, the central committee offered an intellectually and politically impotent republican litany: "Progress–Association–Moral Law–Freedom–Equality–Brotherhood–Family, Community, State–Holiness of Property–Credit–Education–God and People–*Dio e Popolo.*" As Marx saw it, this incantation would not summon forth a revolutionary movement. In contrast, Marx looked to future class conflict to bring the proletariat to the fore and undermine the democrats' "holiness of property." [18]

During this period, Marx broke not only with these democratic leaders, but also with the Blanquists and other conspirators within the Communist League. In April 1850, Marx, Engels, and Willich cooperated with Harney, representing the Chartists, and the Blanquists Vidil and Adam to form a Universal Society of Revolutionary Communists. This organization had statutes but no activities and soon lapsed entirely. Shortly thereafter, Marx and Engels adopted their new strategic outlook. In addition, the Blanquists supported Marx and Engels's opponents in the Communist League, the Willich-Schapper faction. When the Blanquists contacted Marx, Engels, and Harney about reactivating this society, Marx and his colleagues responded with a humorous invitation to an official burning of the defunct organization's statutes at Engels's residence on the following Sunday. [19]

In the *Neue Rheinische Zeitung, Politisch-Ökonomische Revue,* Marx reviewed Chenu's *Les Conspirateurs,* which traced the history of proletarian insurrec-

18. *Werke,* 7:459–465.
19. *Werke,* 7:415, 553–554, 616. Nicolaievsky and Maenchen-Helfen, *Karl Marx,* pp. 208–209.

tionary societies in France. Marx distinguished between occasional conspirators, that is, "workers who practiced conspiracy as a side issue, merely attended meetings and held themselves in readiness for the order of the chiefs to assemble at an appointed place," and professional conspirators, that is, former workers or lumpenproletarians who devoted full time to the organization and lived off it. Marx depicted the curious life-style of these professionals. Lacking regular jobs, relying on the conspiracy for survival, these conspirators led a decadent, bohemian existence "with its only fixed posts the *bistros* of the *marchands de vin.*" By their life-style, the professionals isolated themselves from other workers.[20] Instead of patient activity linked to union organizing, strikes, and communist agitation among the workers, this bistro atmosphere furthered a continual sense of danger and artificial excitement. Such conspirators engaged in sometimes praiseworthy though often "foolhardy" actions during insurrections:

> It is they who throw up and command the barricades, organize the resistance, plunder the arsenals, lead in the seizure of arms and munitions in homes, and in the midst of the insurrection carry out those daring coups which so often cause disarray in the government ranks. In a word, they are officers of the insurrection.[21]

Furthermore, the bistro atmosphere transformed the "morose" and austere conspirator of the secret gatherings into a full-fledged rake, living for the moment, a "widely known *habitué* who knows how to appreciate wine and the female sex." [22]

In place of a real working-class movement, these technocrats of revolution believed in the potency of mere organization and the magic of weaponry. "They seize on new discoveries which are supposed to achieve revolutionary miracles; incendiary bombs, demolition machines . . . riots that are to be the more miraculous and surprising the less rational ground they have." These conspirators instigated uprisings "artificially" when the conditions for revolution did not exist. Through lack of judgment of the sentiments of the workers, they constantly forestalled genuine revolutionary movements (here Marx foresaw the fate of Blanqui's coups, out of phase with mass uprisings,

---

20. Marx, *On Revolution,* p. 54.
21. Ibid., p. 55.
22. Ibid., pp. 54–55.

which landed him in jail during the Paris Commune). Marx called them the "alchemists of revolution." [23]

The conspirators scorned intellectuals like Marx who engaged in the "theoretical clarification" of communist politics. As in the case of Weitling, Willich, and later the Proudhonists and Bakunin, Marx referred to a distinctively plebeian, not proletarian "anger at the *habits noirs,* the more or less educated persons who join their side of the movement as official representatives and of whom they [the plebeians] cannot become entirely independent." [24] Marx too easily foresaw an absence of tension between workers and intellectuals in future socialist and communist movements. Yet Marx captured the conspirators' peculiar, sterile hostility to any real debate over the rulers' conceptions. The truly "enlightened" already belonged to the conspiracy; the conspirators looked down on the masses of workers and avoided any serious political education among the noncommitted. In their political passivity, the conspirators, like the later economic determinists, left the prevailing ideas unchallenged.

Given the absence of any other political activity, the struggle against the police consumed the conspirators' daily lives. Frequenters of the bistros themselves, the police tolerated conspiracies in order to keep watch over revolutionaries, to engage the conspirators in futile actions, and finally to recruit spies. As the professionals also plotted against the police, they sometimes deliberately became spies to gain inside information. In this atmosphere of intrigue, no one really knew whether the police tricked the conspirators or the reverse. Yet as Marx emphasized, even conspiratorial success in these adventures yielded no gains for a real revolutionary movement.

Goaded by misery and imprisonment, many conspirators made "the small jump" from professional to police spy. Given the conspirators' quixotic lives, Marx argued, their entrapment by the police depended mainly on circumstances and reflected more "a quantitative than a qualitative difference in

23. Ibid., p. 55. Bernstein notes that Blanqui saw the hopelessness of the putsch of August 14, 1870, yet ordered it anyway under the artificial pressure of his organization. Bernstein, *Auguste Blanqui and the Art of Insurrection,* pp. 314–315. Blanqui spent over thirty years of his adult life in jail for attempting to overthrow the French government and won considerable influence among Paris workers. Though guarded in his relations with Blanqui and an opponent of his conspiratorial strategy, Marx always admired his revolutionary ardor.

24. Marx, *On Revolution,* p. 55. At the 1866 Geneva Congress of the IWA, the Proudhonists proposed a resolution to restrict the membership of the General Council to manual workers. Freymond, ed., *La Première International,* 1:56.

strength of character." The conspiracies breathed an atmosphere of distrust. Very often the professionals suspected loyal conspirators of spying and identified police agents as genuine conspirators.[25]

Marx's article marked his sharpest break with the conspiratorial communists, particularly the Willich-Schapper faction inside the Communist League. In the absence of a revolutionary movement in Germany, Willich and Schapper transformed the mass approach of the March *Address* into feverish plotting among a handful of exiles. Willich's zeal to participate in "great events" overrode any perception of political realities. Reverting to Gottschalk's (and his own) former position, he argued that a well-organized conspiracy would establish socialism in Germany without a preceding democratic revolution.

Though the majority of the League's Central Committee supported Marx and Engels, the London branch and the German Workers' Educational Society supported Willich. Many League members hesitated to conclude that they faced semipermanent exile from their homeland. An additional, though less decisive factor, was that Marx lived at a remove with his family, and many saw him simply as an interesting lecturer on the dynamics of capitalism. The unmarried Willich, on the other hand, lived in a cooperative arrangement with other League members. As Nicolaievsky and Maenchen-Helfen put it, "Marx was respected but Willich was popular."[26]

At the final Central Committee meeting on September 15, 1850, Marx delineated the fundamental differences between them:

> In place of a critical attitude, the minority set up a dogmatic one, in place of a materialistic attitude, an idealistic one. . . . While we say to the workers, you have fifteen or twenty or fifty years of civil and national wars to go through, not just to alter conditions but to alter yourselves and qualify for political power—you on the contrary say: we must obtain power at once or we might as well lay ourselves down to sleep.[27]

In the workers' movements during these "civil and national wars," Marx's strategies would play an essential part. As I have noted, in criticizing this sheerly political republican or communist viewpoint, Marx and Engels occasionally fostered a potentially deceptive, nondialectical dichotomy between

25. Marx, *On Revolution*, p. 56.
26. Nicolaievsky and Maenchen-Helfen, *Karl Marx*, p. 217.
27. Ibid., pp. 217–218.

economics and politics, materialism and will. Put differently, the "will" of a few isolated conspirators, determined to have their way regardless of circumstances would accomplish nothing; it led to the empty putschism of a Willich or Weitling, which Marx opposed. But in the appropriate circumstances, the will of a mass radical movement to break with the past and take power would play a decisive role. A movement that lacked such a will, despite the presence of many other favorable conditions for revolution, would fail for this reason alone.[28]

The communist tailor J. G. Eccarius agreed with Marx and Engels's materialist outlook at the Central Committee meetings. In the *Neue Rheinische Zeitung, Politisch-Ökonomische Revue,* he analyzed the competition between big and small capital in the London tailoring industry where many German artisans worked. As opposed to other artisans like Weitling (or officers like Willich) who demanded instant uprising and envisioned the resurrection of an ideal, almost medieval egalitarian socialism, Eccarius hailed the progressive role of machinery and modern industry and looked to a protracted Marxian proletarian revolution.[29] Though socialism did not loom on the immediate political horizon, Marx continued to locate artisan and working-class supporters for his approach.

Furthermore, in combatting the Blanquists as well as Willich and Schapper, Marx still defended his fundamental revolutionary position. On February 24, 1851, Willich, Schapper, Vidil, Adam, and Louis Blanc convened a "banquet of the equal" in commemoration of the French February Revolution from which they physically excluded two of Marx's colleagues, Pieper and Schramm. The convenors solicited toasts from German communist workers (they received none) and from Blanqui imprisoned at Belle-Île-en-Mer. Yet they refused to read Blanqui's toast which defended armed revolution and condemned the provisional government including Ledru-Rollin, the European Central Committee, and Louis Blanc as sinister "bourgeois disguised as champions of the people" who had led the revolution to bloody defeat. Marx and Engels translated Blanqui's toast, and the Cologne Com-

---

28. The policies of the Italian Communist Party in leading the resistance (at least following United States withdrawal) and in the peasant uprising of 1949–1952 seem to reveal a lack of revolutionary will. Tarrow, *Peasant Communism in Southern Italy.* Lenin's position in October 1917—in contrast to that of many other Bolshevik leaders—provides a vigorous positive example.

29. Marx and Engels, "Redaktionelle Anmerkung zu dem Artikel 'Die Schneiderei in London oder der Kampf des grossen und des kleinen Capitals' von J. G. Eccarius," *Werke,* 7:416.

munist League printed some 30,000 copies. Marx and Engels also sent Blanqui's message, accompanied by their own comment on Louis Blanc, to the London *Times,* but the *Times* rejected it. In the toast, Blanqui argued that the republic's imposition of the forty-five-centime tax had alienated the French peasantry and denounced the retention of "royalist" officers, magistrates, and laws. The toast specially stressed that "rulers would be traitors if, raised to power on the workers' shoulders," they did not at once disarm the bourgeois guards and organize and arm the workers. In Blanqui's eloquent phrase, "unarmed crowds are swept away like chaff. France bristling with workers in arms, that is the coming of socialism." [30] If circumstances permitted (and here Marx's analysis differed fundamentally from Blanqui's), Marx also advocated the mass armed overthrow of the old state structure.

In the aftermath of 1848, Marx had altered his strategy dramatically. He no longer looked mainly to a democratic revolution, though he still thought such a revolution might precede socialism in Germany. Instead, he insisted much more strongly on the continuous political organization of the working class. He carried forward this emphasis on the working-class movement in 1864 when he became the driving force in the IWA.

At its meeting on September 15, 1850, the Central Committee had shifted the League's headquarters from London to Cologne. Living in Germany, the Cologne branch had a stronger sense of the immediate impracticability of revolution and supported Marx's caution. Given the inauspicious conditions combined with extreme police harassment, the organization soon died. This transfer of the location of the Central Committee paralleled in miniature the shift of the IWA headquarters from London to New York arranged at the 1872 Hague conference to forestall the attempt of Bakunin's forces to seize control and promulgate views similar to Willich's. Throughout his career, Marx tailored organization to political strategy. When circumstances altered, he never clung to organizational forms that had outlived their usefulness.

After this meeting, Marx and Engels withdrew from the Workers' Educational Society, and the Willich-Schapper faction left the Communist League. Willich then plunged into a variety of fantastic projects for immediate revolution and sent feverish messages to the Cologne communists. A conflict

---

30. Marx and Engels, "Vorbemerkung zur deutschen Übersetzung des Toastes von L.-A. Blanqui (Mit dem Text des Toastes)" and Engels, "Brief an den Redakteur der 'Times,'" *Werke,* 7:568–570, 466–467, 626.

between Prussia and Austria loomed. The monarchy had called up the reserves. Willich recommended that the communists seize the Cologne city hall, confiscate all private property, ban all newspapers but one, and institute a dictatorship. Willich would arrive, gather revolutionary troops for a march to Paris, boot out Louis Napoleon, and return in glory to proclaim a united Germany. The Cologne communists ignored him.[31]

The Prussian police, however, hoped to complete the restoration by wiping out the political opposition, particularly the communists. In 1851, a communist messenger from London en route to Cologne fell into their hands, and the police arrested the whole branch (eleven members). They then staged a "monster" communist trial. Even in the overbearing atmosphere of triumphant counterrevolution, the authorities could not count on a Rhineland jury to deliver an easy conviction of the communists. Thus, the Prussian police sought to procure damning evidence against them.

Though the police fantasized about Marx the fervent terrorist training assassins to kill the Prussian monarch, the post-1849 Communist League under Marx's leadership advocated socialist agitation among the workers and eschewed terrorism as well as immediate insurrection. Undaunted, the police, led by Stieber, set a small apparatus of spies—Hirsch, Fleury, and Greif—in motion in London to forge a minute book of the "Marx Society." This book fused Willich's schemes with sheer fabrications. Exemplifying the honor of the Prussian monarchy, these minutes provided the "factual" basis for the subsequent convictions.

In 1852, Marx and other League members worked ceaselessly to expose this minute book. They acquired evidence of forgery, analyzed in detail the book's lies and inconsistencies, and despite attempts to intercept and censor their mail, got these proofs to the trial.[32] Though the communists made a vigorous case, the government obtained convictions of seven of the eleven defendants. The prosecutor exhausted the theme that the defendants led "a dreadful communist conspiracy got up in order to subvert everything sacred," and a conservative jury (six nobles, two government officials) returned the verdict. Marx contended, however, that even this jury voted to convict

31. Marx and Engels, "Erklärung über den Austritt aus dem Deutschen Bildungsverein für Arbeiter in London," *Werke*, 7:414, 614. Nicolaievsky and Maenchen-Helfen, *Karl Marx*, p. 218.

32. Nicolaievsky and Maenchen-Helfen, *Karl Marx*, pp. 221–223.

mainly because the Prussian government had stigmatized acquittal as a direct challenge to its rule.[33]

During the trial, Marx grew increasingly bitter toward Willich and Schapper who had provided such inflammatory and silly material for the police to elaborate upon in order to discredit German communism. In Marx's *Revelations about the Communist Trial in Cologne,* he again posed the differences between the two groups and argued that the Communist League had no conspiratorial ambitions. He characterized it as "a secret organization of the proletarian party, while the German proletariat is officially interdicted from *igni et aqua,* writing, speech, and association. If such a society conspires, it happens only in the sense that steam and electricity also conspire against the status quo."[34] According to Marx, this society intended to constitute an "opposition party of the future," not an opposition "of the present," an enemy of the capitalist class itself, not an instigator of democratic revolution against the monarchy.

This argument came perilously close to the position of "true socialism." It contradicted Marx's activity in 1848 and his *Address* of March 1850. In 1848, Marx had advocated violent revolution and mass terrorism. In 1852, under the circumstances of counterrevolution, he and his colleagues urged political agitation as the main thrust of communist activity. Yet this tactical argument would hardly have convinced an upper-class jury. Furthermore, Marx vigorously opposed the conspiracies of that time. These two considerations, constructing a workable defense and discouraging conspiracy, influenced Marx's brief and peculiar vision of communism as "the opposition party of the future."

Yet Marx and Engels may temporarily have held this view more strongly. In the *Peasant War,* as we have seen, Engels decried the "tragedy" of revolutionaries' seizing power before their time. Playing down the importance of reforms, Marx and Engels in 1850 advocated only the mass movement for suffrage in England. Furthermore, in 1851, Engels drew up a rough, never published essay "Conditions and Prospects of War of the Holy Alliance against France," which contrasted the Jacobin *levée en masse* unfavorably with Napoleonic warfare. Contrary to his and Marx's expectation in 1848, Engels

---

33. Engels, *Revolution and Counterrevolution,* p. 107. In newspaper interview in 1853, Hirsch confirmed his recruitment as a police spy and the falsification of the minute book. Marx, *Politische Schriften,* 1:519–532.

34. Marx, *Politische Schriften,* 1:508. *Werke,* 8:602–603.

contended that a Holy Alliance, learning from Napoleon's methods, could suppress a revolutionary army generated by a new uprising in France.[35] In this context, Marx's and Engels's concept of the "opposition party of the future" may have stemmed from a temporary general retreat from mass struggle (democratic revolution, union reforms, and the like) in reaction to the defeat of revolution and to harebrained conspiratorial scheming. If so, this retreat occasioned Marx's only genuine economic determinist formulations about communist political activity. But Marx and Engels soon returned to their earlier, more realistic political position.

Recalling these events in 1875, Marx commented on the "powerful after-effect of a revolution" on participants suddenly exiled from their homelands. This "shock" made "able personalities for a shorter or longer period of time so to speak, irresponsible." Thus, Willich, Schapper, and others could not see that "history had changed direction" and engaged in conspiratorial "games" which compromised them and the revolutionary movement.[36] Yet, Marx noted, Willich soon regained his political grasp and served with distinction as a Northern officer in the American Civil War. Previously a leader of the League of the Just, then of the Communist League and of revolutionary activity in Cologne in 1848, Schapper also soon resumed his "lifelong" effort to advance the workers' cause.

Considering this shock effect, Marx regretted some of his earlier bitterness toward them. This same aftereffect of receding revolution might also explain some of Marx's tactical formulations of 1850–1852. Yet such an explanation could easily understate Marx's fundamental consistency, his desire to participate wherever possible in a mass movement, and his militant advocacy of internationalism and proletarian dictatorship.

35. *Werke*, 7:468–493.
36. Marx, *Politische Schriften*, 1:533.

— XIV —

Conclusion

MARX FOUGHT ABOVE ALL ELSE for the principles of proletarian internationalism and socialist revolution. As he envisioned it, his general theory, underpinning these principles, would perform a dual role in the working-class movement. It would provide a deeper understanding of the overall process of revolution, of the national as well as international contradictions in capitalism that would instigate class struggle. In addition, in "gripping" the workers, the theory would contribute directly to their political emancipation. Thus, Marx did not conceive of his theory as a shadowy or abstract philosophical picture of revolution, taking flight only at dusk like Hegel's owl of Minerva. Instead, workers and their allies, bridging the division between mental and manual labor, would adopt and transform these ideas. Marx's theory always emphasized the expansion of capitalism and the existence of a working-class movement as prerequisites for socialist revolution. In this sense, the theory entailed a productive forces or mode of production determinism. But within this framework, the emergence of novel political movements in changing historical circumstances spurred Marx to fresh advances in his theory and strategy. Marx's theory exhibited a dialectical resiliency or flexibility that an economic determinist conception at its best only faintly caricatures.

Some might still say: a contextual analysis of Marx's theory and activity between 1844 and 1853 may be an interesting historical study, but it casts no light on the future development of Marxian movements or on the long-term economic insights of Marxian theory. "We" may safely dismiss Marx's worker-peasant alliance or revolutionary union strategies as parochial responses to that particular time.

This objection echoes a general criticism that the contextual analysis of any philosopher loses the overall force, coherence, or interest of the argument in a narrow consideration of the writer's local intentions and environment.[1] But as Quentin Skinner has retorted, this complaint often serves as an

---

1. John Dunn, *The Political Thought of John Locke*, p. 208.

excuse for offering an absurd reconstruction of a philosopher's general argument, tailored anachronistically to modern prejudices or problems, in place of an accurate account of the argument in its historical setting.[2] On the most general level, contextualism can provide a fresh probing of the philosopher's intentions as well as the effect on his or her immediate audience and a point of access to a deeper understanding of the philosopher's overall argument. In studies of Marx, for instance, economic determinist prejudices have created unnecessary confusion and obscured Marx's theoretical approach to historical explanation and the formulation of strategy. Lichtheim, to take an extreme example, patches together a peculiar Marx who confusedly defended the Paris Commune, but who, given the ineluctable trends of the "modern" labor movement, "had to" support a gradualist "democratic socialism."[3] By an act of intellectual prestidigitation, Marx's reasoning in behalf of the Commune vanishes and Lichtheim's preferences, transformed into alleged historical trends, usurp Marx's place. But Lichtheim, not Marx, exhibits the confusion here. This study has attempted to restore the vigor and revolutionary insight of Marx's politics as well as to explore the complex relations between Marx's theory and activity.

Like Marx, Skinner attempts to study political theorists in the context of clashing political ideologies and class interests. His analysis, drawing upon Weber, of the role of Puritanism in legitimizing capitalist interests closely resembles a dialectical Marxism. His subtle account of the use of Catholic theories of resistance by Protestant writers before the Puritan Revolution can be interpreted as perhaps even nearer to a Marxian than a Weberian view. Considered in its historical context rather than as an ideal type, Puritanism did not break irrevocably with previous arguments and "create" the drive toward capitalism and revolution; rather, the Calvinist theorists of revolution selected those arguments of their Catholic predecessors that they could

2. Quentin Skinner, "Meaning and Understanding in the History of Ideas," pp. 2–39. Dunn, *Political Thought*, chs. 15–17.

3. Lichtheim, *Marxism*, pp. 126–129, 99. Lichtheim also suggests: "The Marx of 1864 was the theorist of a *labor* movement and *therefore* committed to democratic socialism, however much this circumstance was clouded in his own mind by the continuing struggle to overthrow the old regime."

Similarly, Hunt's mistaken view of Marx's strategy in the *Communist Manifesto* flows from his concern to prove that Marx and Engels were not, in a peculiar post–World War II phrase, "totalitarian democrats" (roughly, chiliastic revolutionaries aiming to achieve a "harmonious and perfect scheme of things"). Hunt, *Political Ideas*, pp. 4, 13–14. Subtract this concern, and the need for Hunt's arcane interpretation of the evidence vanishes.

best turn against the old order to justify their cause. Though Skinner recognizes the complexities of philosophical argument (or what one might call in Marxian terms, the uneven development of philosophy and class conflict), his account underlines the interests of social classes and parties that affect this choice of argument and govern its ultimate political impact.[4] Analogously, the philosophical and political debates between Marx and artisans and intellectuals in the German communist movement of the 1840s cannot be understood through the application of some simple external class, status, or psychological criterion. But despite the intricacies of the argument, Engels, Moll, Bauer, Schapper, and Wolff eventually adhered to Marx's strategy as the best way to advance and justify a proletarian socialist movement in the context of democratic revolution. This strategy in turn had its political impact because of the needs and purposes of workers, peasants, and artisans in 1848 and afterward. Theory and strategy would shape the working-class movement, but the movement made choices in theory and strategy real.

A dialectical contextualism, especially apt in a study of Marx, differs from the general contextualism of Skinner, J. G. A. Pocock, or John Dunn. The analyst does not apply this methodology externally to Marx's activity; rather, Marx studied other political thinkers and movements contextually. For instance, Babeuf's communism, according to Marx, resulted from his attempts to deal with the problems of his political environment, particularly from insights into the failure of political egalitarianism to alleviate the capitalist oppression of the proletariat. Furthermore, Marx's politics displays an explicit internal dialectic of this kind. From the *Theses on Feuerbach* on, Marx invoked a continuous attention to fresh practical experience, that is, a sort of contextualism, as one of the central facets of his theory.[5] Marx would alter and deepen even such fundamental concepts as internationalism (consider the impact of English colonialism in Ireland) or the dictatorship of the prole-

---

4. Quentin Skinner, "Some Problems in the Analysis of Political Thought and Action," pp. 292–301, 291. Skinner, "The Principles and Practice of Opposition: The Case of Bolingbroke versus Walpole," pp. 110–113, 124–128. Skinner, *The Foundations of Modern Political Thought,* 1:x–xiii; 2:322–323.

5. By a dialectical contextualism, I mean one that stresses the interplay of theory and practice and not the mistaken attempt, criticized by Skinner, to reduce a writer's intentions to an expression of circumstances alone. Skinner, "Meaning and Understanding," pp. 42–48. For the purposes of this argument, I use the term to refer to Marx's method of analyzing other theorists, the internal relationship of Marx's theory to his political activity, and my approach to studying Marx.

tariat (the *Eighteenth Brumaire,* the Paris Commune) through reflection upon his own participation in Germany and England as well as on the class struggles in France. Only a contextual examination can ferret out the crucial, relatively constant elements in Marx's theory and strategy, spell out the contradictions or tensions within it, and specify Marx's own reasons for changing it.[6] Given Marx's theoretical emphasis on practice as well as his extensive activity and influence, the prevalent overwhelmingly noncontextual approach to Marx's theory stands in special need of justification.

Unlike a Marxian or dialectical contextualism, however, Skinner's or Pocock's approach seems strongly relativistic. Despite Skinner's objections to relativism, he argues that the history of political philosophy mainly teaches us the divergence of the past from the present and enables us to discern the contingency of many aspects of contemporary society that might otherwise be viewed as "necessary." Skinner properly mocks certain attempts at transhistorical application, for instance of Plato's teaching about political participation—the alleged "perennial" disqualification of those who work with their hands. While Skinner does not rule out learning from past theorists, he does not offer a clear account of what insights—except relativistic ones arising from recognition of differences ("the essential variety of viable moral and political commitments")—one might hope to gain.[7]

In his methodological essays, Pocock, relying on T. S. Kuhn, goes further in this regard. Roughly, as the various conventions of political language of an epoch change or as theorists alter these conventions, the world seems to change as well.[8] This type of contextualism tends to make the world radically mind or language dependent. Thus, a natural scientific or political theory does not refer, well or badly, to a world outside it, and a new theory, however revolutionary in its formulation and impact, does not provide a better (more accurate) story about the world. Whatever the merits of an antirealist view of science or of moral and political philosophy, a Marxian contextualism requires a much less relativistic account.[9] Applied to Marx's own activity,

6. Ibid., pp. 17–22.

7. Ibid., pp. 51–52.

8. J. G. A. Pocock, *Politics, Language and Time,* pp. 13–19. T. S. Kuhn, *The Structure of Scientific Revolutions,* pp. 110–111. Skinner, "Some Problems," pp. 280–281, has expressed reservations about Pocock's essay.

9. I cannot take up these issues here. For a good account, see Richard N. Boyd, *Realism and Scientific Epistemology* and "Metaphor and Theory Change: What Is 'Metaphor' a Metaphor for?" See also David-Hillel Ruben, *Marxism and Materialism.*

this contextualism contends that Marx altered his theory to approximate changing reality with greater precision. Thus, the theory's accuracy in gauging reality–despite its unpopularity among many other radicals–enabled Marx to cut against the grain of the bourgeois-led democratic movement and inspire a significant worker-peasant alliance in Germany in 1848. Similarly, the brilliant dialectic of strategy and explanation in Marx's study of the French peasantry illuminates the theory's explanatory power and a self-healing quality that can exist (though it often has not) within Marxism.

If this materialist or realist depiction of the relation between theory and the world is true, then a dialectical contextualism may open up new avenues of research into later Marxian movements and theorists. We might now investigate whether such movements followed Marx in altering the theory to understand class conflict and to move it in a more revolutionary direction. Such an approach could identify genuine advances in as well as departures from Marx's theory and strategy and reveal the threads that link Marx to subsequent Marxian revolutionary activity. This method would cast aside the dreary, reified distinctions, unhappily visited upon every student of the social sciences, between Marx the economic determinist theorist or esoteric philosopher, Lenin the Blanquist politician who tried to "force history" before it had "ripened," Mao "the peasant nationalist," and other fantastic characters rumored to exist in the stereotypical mill of noncontextual scholarship on Marx.[10]

Intellectuals often conceive of the power and attractiveness of Marx's theory (or the lack of it) simply within the context of their own disciplines–what has been kept of Marx, inappropriately translated into a different theoretical idiom, or, more rarely, a fresh alternative to a prevailing paradigm. They attribute the influence of the theory mainly to its internal elegance and to the norms of scholarly objectivity, which have allowed it to be studied. In reality, universities in capitalist societies have been singularly inhospitable to any lively form of Marxism. Radical movements, reflecting the insights of the theory, have been the primary force in making Marxism an academic issue and sophisticated study of Marx and later Marxists an academic possibility.[11] Far from exhibiting parochialism, Marx's strategies of the 1840s and

10. For instance, this contextualism would insist on Lenin's application and transformation of Marx's theory and redescribe his practical activity which was hardly Blanquist.

11. David Caute, *The Great Fear*, pp. 403–430. Richard W. Miller, "Reason and Commitment in the Social Sciences," pp. 263–266.

their practical successes have ultimately generated the enormous political and intellectual influence of Marxism in the twentieth century. These strategies have retained their relevance, sometimes as a critical standard, for assessing subsequent revolutionary movements. They help to clarify Marx's crucial conception of political alternatives.

For instance, Marx's vision of a worker-peasant alliance casts important light on the radicalism of the Russian revolutions of 1905 and 1917. It highlights the conservatism and failure of German Social Democrats and communists to win the cooperation of peasants in the attempt to head off Nazism. It illuminates the radical potential of the peasant uprisings in southern Italy between 1949 and 1952 as well as the reactionary role of the Italian Communist Party in forestalling socialist worker-peasant unity.[12] Between 1927 and 1949, under special historical conditions including the existence of the Soviet Union as a socialist power, the emergence of a third international communist movement, the history of Chinese peasant revolts, and the impact of imperialism, fascism, and war, the Chinese Communist Party forged an even more radical peasant movement than anything Marx or Engels envisioned in the nineteenth century. Chinese experience contradicted the universal or univocal force of Marx's statement of tendencies in the first part of the *Manifesto.* Yet if, as Engels argued in 1850, peasants could take the leading role in the radicalism of the Middle Ages, no general historical tendency of capitalism to undermine the existence of independent, small-holding peasants could prevent them from playing a similar part under all modern circumstances. With sufficient attention to these historical conditions, a Marxian analysis might encompass such a movement rather than treat it as a counterexample. This analysis, while more overtly political and more explicit about historical variability than some of Marx's general formulations, would still emphasize the particular mode of production and social forces of China.[13]

Similarly, Marx's strategy of radical unionism and his own activity reinforced the internationalism of the IWA and inspired the Bolsheviks whose organization, contrary to stereotype, focused on revolutionary groups in the unions. Marx's strategy highlights, by contrast, the militancy without advo-

---

12. Tarrow, *Peasant Communism in Southern Italy.*

13. Even if the masses of peasants as well as urban workers supported socialism, the functioning of small property holders under backward conditions of production would present important obstacles to a socialist regime. A Marxian strategy would have to specify the steps by which peasants and workers might overcome these obstacles and conflicts in the course of subsequent cooperative or collective development.

cating socialism of the American Communist Party when it galvanized the sit-down strikes of the 1930s. It conflicts utterly with the conservative role of union leaders in German Social Democracy as well as that party's lack of political organizing on the shop floor and with the French Communist Party's opposition to the strike of 14 million workers and students in May 1968.[14] Given these varying experiences, perhaps the failure of socialists and communists to put forward internationalism and socialism over the long haul has played a more decisive part in the defeat of radicalism (so far) in advanced capitalist societies than any economic determinist notion can permit. In assessing the prospects of movements over periods of ten, twenty-five, or fifty years, Marx's argument suggests, radicals cannot achieve more than they attempt. Either they exhibit sufficient confidence in the masses to argue persistently for their ideas among them—and then other workers may take up these ideas, develop them further, and drive the movement into acute conflict with the capitalists—or they eschew this political effort on the spurious grounds that "economic conditions are not ripe" and that the majority of workers and peasants are "too backward." Thus, as opposed to economic determinist stereotypes, Marx's approach and that of his most prominent followers like Lenin and Mao was profoundly antielitist.[15]

In 1848, Marx initiated this process of advancing revolutionary ideas within the class struggle. In every strike, mutiny, peasant revolt, or battle for socialism, this first experience, its lessons and ambiguities, would remain relevant. Tactics of course might vary as Marx's own did. Yet persistent advocacy of the strategic core, of internationalism and socialism, exerts independent historical weight and differentiates Marx from many later "Marxists." [16] Those interpreters who view Marx's activity between 1843 and 1852—the practical orientation of his theory and strategy—as parochial or as "contradictory to his basic'insights" miss what Marxism is about.

G. A. Cohen's *Marx's Theory of History: A Defense* offers a sophisticated productive forces determinism based on Marx's *Preface* of 1859. His argument differs from the common economic determinism that denies any role to

14. James R. Prickett, "Communists and the Communist Issue in the American Labor Movement, 1920–1950." Carl E. Schorske, *German Social Democracy 1905–1917*, pp. 108–109. Lucien Rioux and René Backmann, *L'explosion de mai*, chs. 11, 13, 18, 20.

15. Mao Tse-tung, "Investigation of the Peasant Movement in Hunan" in *Selected Works*, vol. 1. William Hinton, *Fanshen*.

16. For some contemporary illustrations, see Gilbert, "Marx on Internationalism and War," pp. 362–369.

politics and permits no variation of historical paths of development. Cohen shows that Marx rightly regarded the advance of human productive powers as the decisive force in the class struggle over whole historical epochs. Cohen also envisions an important dialectical role for class struggle and the super-structure in realizing advances of the productive forces.[17] Yet Cohen gener-ally ignores Marx's own activity as well as subsequent socialist experience. Does Cohen's sophisticated productive forces argument contradict Marx's activity?

If one attributes, as Cohen does, a significant dialectical role to politics, then he could easily defend a general need for a communist movement or party to break down the main divisions among workers and combat the pre-dominant reactionary ideas. Yet Cohen fails to articulate the specific political character of Marx's historical explanations. As I noted in Chapter 1, the ex-pansion of capitalism and the existence of a working class could have made socialism possible, on Marx's view, in England in the 1860s. In accordance with Cohen, one might call this need for some development of modern in-dustry and a proletariat a productive forces determinism (no socialism, for Marx, could have emerged out of the medieval Wat Tyler-led peasant re-volt). Yet as Marx saw it, the international hold of English colonialism upon Ireland and the influence of racist divisions between English and Irish laborers—political and ideological factors—blunted or undermined a socialist movement. A more sophisticated, highly practice-influenced dialectic of eco-nomics and politics characterized Marx's analysis of the decline of English socialism than Cohen suggests. Similarly, given the historical development of capitalism in one country—England—and its impact on world affairs, a socialist revolution might unfold under the specific conditions of Germany in the 1840s (perhaps in conjunction with or quickly followed by an English one). Again, the new mode of production, embodied in English and to a lesser extent German capitalism, played an important role, but for Marx, a variety of political circumstances also shaped this unusual possibility. Though Cohen does not consider Marx's explanations and strategies (what I have called Marx's second type of theorizing), his argument, suitably modified to investigate the international situation, specific political tradi-tions, and the like, might encompass these analyses.

On a more general level, however, Cohen overstresses Marx's account of the role of human productive powers (he treats material productive powers

17. G. A. Cohen, *Marx's Theory of History*, pp. 160–166, 231–234, 240–245.

as too easily separable from the relations of production) and tends to decouple Marx's theory from class struggle and revolutionary politics. He weakens (and even fails to discuss) Marx's decisive revolutionary principles—internationalism, a state modeled on the Paris Commune, the role of political experience in the development of the theory—and, despite the vigor and clarity of his interpretation, gives a serious misimpression of what Marx's argument is about. As opposed to Marx, Cohen's account treats the theory more as a tool for historians than as a vehicle to change the world.[18] Yet Cohen's reservations about some of Marx's positions point in the direction that Marx took in modifying the theory.

According to Cohen, Marx's general formulations about the prerequisites of socialism require an exploitative class structure which forces a sufficient surplus out of the immediate producers to open up new more cooperative possibilities. As Cohen phrases the crucial argument, "Class oppression is necessary to bring society to stage four [postclass society characterized by massive surplus] of productive development" because "no group of producers will impose . . . conditions like those which prevail in large-scale industry on themselves." [19] Marx never explicitly stated this condition in this way. In *The German Ideology,* however, Marx and Engels opposed a premature revolution in which, given destitution and a "struggle for necessities," "all the old filthy business" would reassert itself (note that this conception of a premature revolution did not rule out socialism in backward Germany in the 1840s).[20] Some argument such as Cohen's—no group of even destitute producers would volunteer to create the conditions of large-scale industry—must sustain Marx's conception.

For Cohen, subsequent socialist experience suggests that Marx overemphasized the necessity of class oppression. Greater potential for cooperation in necessary production exists than some of Marx's general formulations indicate.[21] Yet Cohen ignores the role of practice in Marx's alterations of his theory. For instance, Marx regarded the rule of worker-officials in the Commune, acting not to secure monetary reward but to forge a cooperative society for its own sake, as a great step forward. With more socialist experience, Marx might have envisioned similar possibilities in production and amended

---

18. Cohen, however, shares Marx's belief in "human liberation." Ibid., pp. 204, 325.
19. Ibid., p. 214.
20. *GI,* pp. 48–49.
21. Cohen, *Marx's Theory,* pp. 206–207, 214, 323–325. Marx, *Capital,* 3:799–800.

his general theoretical argument to take them into account. He might have contended, for instance, that the initial capitalist development and its accompanying international impact had to occur in an alienated form since, as Cohen argues, workers would not impose industrial conditions on themselves to ward off unknown dangers or to achieve unknown potentials. Marx might even have extended this argument to the emergence of capitalism in several countries. But once the new capitalist system could be clearly recognized and analyzed, once its productive powers had penetrated at least to some degree in many countries, once a communist theory existed that the masses could take up, new possibilities for socialism, perhaps under unusual and backward conditions, might emerge. Furthermore, faced with subsequent capitalist oppression–depression, war, and fascism, for example–as well as the appearance of large socialist movements, workers and ultimately peasants in many countries might entertain the idea of a more cooperative reorganization of production and collective (politically decided) sacrifices to achieve a common good as opposed to an exploitative industrialization for the benefit of a small ruling class. Such a movement might display adequate initiative in overcoming the economic obstacles to socialism.[22] This argument would alter or qualify one of Marx's general formulations, a change in the basic theory rather than a modification of auxiliary statements; yet it would be consistent with Marx's attention to practice and willingness to draw new theoretical conclusions.

Thus, to paraphrase Hegel, in the dialectical bacchanal of history, all the dancers are at once drunken (do the unexpected) and yet also at rest (exist in a pattern or historical sequence in which each grows out of and responds to

22. In the first draft of the *Civil War in France,* Marx already saw the Paris Commune as the political form of a conflict-ridden system and suggested that socialism must pass through "different phases of class struggle," peaceful and violent: "The communal organization once firmly established on a national scale . . . might still have to undergo . . . sporadic slaveholders' insurrections, which, while for a moment interrupting the work of peaceful progress, would only accelerate the movement by putting the sword into the hand of the Social Revolution." Marx, *Writings on the Commune,* pp. 154–155.

Revolutionaries in a less economically developed country would face some peculiar obstacles to socialism–accentuating these conflicts–though they might gain some specific advantages as well. Mao for instance argued that whatever the negative role of precapitalist ideology, such a country might lack two or three centuries of "poisoning" with bourgeois ideology. Mao, *Critique of Soviet Political Economy,* p. 50. The ultimate triumph of reactionary regimes in both Russia and China, however, suggests that the conflicts in socialism are far more serious than anything that Marx or his later followers envisioned.

the experience of its predecessors).[23] Historical laws (more accurately tendencies) capture reality for a time. A new situation arises, and the historical actors sometimes take account of and attempt to change the laws. Then theorists must frequently modify the laws, at least in their range. Socialism, for example, could not exist in ancient Greece or sixteenth-century India, but might come to exist, at least for a time, in twentieth-century Szechwan.

Lenin's scathing response in 1923 to the Menshevik Sukhanov on the possibility of socialist revolution in Russia captures Marx's own attitude toward historical variation:

> "The development of the productive forces of Russia has not attained the level that makes socialism possible," [Sukhanov argued.] . . . But why could we not first create such prerequisites of civilization in our country as the expulsion of the landowners and the Russian capitalists and then start moving toward socialism? Where, *in what books,* have you read that such variations on the *customary* historical order of events are impermissible or impossible? [24]

In fact, the Bolshevik conception represents a rather less dramatic leaping of historical stages than Marx's flirtation with a development of communism— under the circumstances of a proletarian revolution in Western Europe—out of the primitive Russian agricultural commune, the *mir* (of course the Bolsheviks did not have the advantage of a European revolution to accompany their less dramatic leap). Though apparently sympathetic to this type of argument, Cohen ignores the complex, heavily experience-influenced way in which Marx reached or altered his practical conclusions, auxiliary statements, and general theory.

When some element of his theory conflicted with practical radical experience, Marx always chose to modify the theory rather than to ignore reality. As he would say of unusual Russian possibilities in the 1870s, he did not envision the theory as laying down a "superhistorical path" that all nations must tread. Marx ruled out an empty politics of the will of an individual, a conspiracy, or clique; he also disdained waiting upon "objective forces" to achieve socialism. On a continuum between these extremes, however, his conclusions veered toward the side of politics, not as determined by the iso-

23. Hegel, *Phenomenology of Spirit,* p. 27 (a debatable translation of *Phänomenologie des Geistes,* p. 39).
24. Lenin, "Our Revolution (Apropos of N. Sukhanov's Notes)," *Collected Works,* 33:480, 476–478.

lated individual will but by the actions of masses of workers in definite situations. Thus, Marx traced a dialectic of economic forces and politics, of social being and consciousness, in which material conditions provided the underpinning and yet in which innovative political activity had a wide latitude of influence. In the complex, three-tiered interplay of general theory, analysis of specific historical configurations, and new forms of class struggle, political movements played a decisive part.

When Marx changed his older arguments, one might still ask, did he (or later Marxists) adhere to the same basic theory or had he adopted a fundamentally different one? To establish a criterion for assessing such changes, we might look at cases of major transformations in other theories in which scientists nonetheless recognize that the core theory has remained the same. For instance Newton, in common with other seventeenth-century mechanists, interpreted gravity as a mechanical force and rejected the concept of action at a distance. He opposed the theorists of "occult forces or qualities" who attributed the specific motion of any body to the operation of such a power. Toward the end of his life, however, Newton abandoned the attempt to interpret gravity mechanically and recognized the possibility of action at a distance. He allowed *one* nonmechanical force specifically interpreted through his theory of universal gravitation and the evidence for it (Kepler's laws, tides), as opposed to the many elusive occult forces that nonmechanists accepted. Though strengthening his own theory (action at a distance was more plausible than various mechanical solutions pertaining to the physical action of an aether), he also made a minor concession to the "occult" theorists. Despite this change, the fundamental thrust of Newton's theory remained intact. His acceptance of gravitational action at a distance did not require him to abandon his opposition to alternative conceptions of causation in terms of occult powers.[25]

As another example, evolutionary biologists today consider themselves Darwinians. Yet when Darwin proposed his theory of natural selection, he also entertained the possibilities that acquired characteristics might be inherited and that the crossing of two features might result in a genetic "blend-

25. Richard S. Westfall, *The Construction of Modern Science*, pp. 28–29, 140–141. In Query 31 of the *Opticks*, Newton replied to the charge that he had reinstated occult powers: "These Principles I consider, not as occult Qualities, supposed to result from the specifick Forms of Things, but as general Laws of Nature, by which the Things themselves are formed; their Truth appearing to us by Phaenomena, though their Causes be not yet discovered. For these are manifest Qualities, and their causes only are occult. To tell us that every Species of Things

ing." With the acceptance of Mendel's theory in the early twentieth century, biologists could discern the genetic mechanism underlying natural selection. Yet Mendel's theory rejected both the inheritance of acquired characteristics and blending. Why therefore did twentieth-century evolutionary biologists consider themselves Darwinians? Before Darwin, "creationism" with its idealized or "fixed" species and teleological explanations for adaptive features had been the dominant biological theory. Paley's *Natural Theology* (1802) had persuasively compared the complexity of the human eye to the work of a skilled watchmaker. Darwin's evolutionary theory showed how species could change over time and how design could exist in nature without a designer. Despite significant changes, the eventual synthesis of natural selection and Mendelian genetics maintained the fundamental thrust of Darwin's theory against its creationist and teleological rivals.[26]

From the practice of scientists in these two cases, we might elicit the following criterion for assessing whether theorists have made a change within a single theory or whether they have abandoned it: if a theory retains, while rendering more plausible, the thrust of its earlier argument against its chief competitors of the time, scientists consider it to be the same basic theory. Correspondingly, if a changed theory takes over central features of its main opponent, scientists would agree that the rival theory has become predominant. The theory that has proven true (to be exact, more nearly or approximately true) typically retains or reinterprets the grain of truth in its competitors, as in Newton's argument on gravitational action at a distance or Darwin's on the complexity of the human eye.

Some socialists and communists have attempted to delete from Marx's general theory the importance of class conflict and revolution and to adapt Marxism to a process of gradual economic evolution and peaceful reform. By the above criterion, these attempts would abandon fundamental features of

---

is endowed with an occult specifick Quality by which it acts and produces manifest Effects, is to tell us nothing: But to derive two or three general Principles of Motion from Phaenomena, and afterwards to tell us how the Properties and Actions of all corporeal Things follow from those manifest Principles, would be a very great step in Philosophy, though the Causes of those Principles were not yet discovered: And therefore I scruple not to propose the Principles of Motion above-mentioned, they being of very general Extent, and leave their Causes to be found out." Cited in Westfall, *Construction*, p. 158.

26. William B. Provine, *The Origins of Theoretical Population Genetics*, pp. 6–9, chs. 4–5. Garland E. Allen, *Life Science in the Twentieth Century*, chs. 1, 5.

Marxian theory and allow its liberal competitors to replace it. In contrast, modifications of the theory that render class conflict (and its basis in exploitative modes of production) more comprehensible, highlight new possibilities of peasant radicalism or even socialism, and stress the primary political consequences of the theory such as internationalism fit in with Marx's original project and make no important concessions to rival theories.[27]

As we have seen, Marx's use of auxiliary statements did not conflict with his general theory but rather permitted his explanations to approximate reality more closely. Yet although Marx studied the specifics of each situation, he saw the internal tensions in capitalism as sufficiently strong to give rise to a socialist movement that would "ultimately" overcome all these local political problems and make revolution. Given the practical obstacles to socialism, however, Marx's new explanations increasingly emphasized the need for revolutionary political activity. If an ultimate tension exists between Marx's two types of theorizing, it lies in the degree to which economic tensions directly engender mortal revolutionary combat.

Once again, a practical exception to the projected path of development, say a socialist revolution in Germany in 1848 or in Russia in 1917, need not throw the productive or economic dynamic of Marx's pattern into question. But a persistent failure of revolution in the more industrialized capitalist societies, despite a considerable degree of oppression, must lead to questions within Marx's own framework about an ultimate determining role for economic contradictions.

Oppression, often violent class conflict over unions, the formation of significant socialist and communist parties, and the emergence of three international workers' movements have marked European and American history in the nineteenth and twentieth centuries. In Putnam's terms, the exist-

---

27. Marx provided an alternative explanation of and remedy for the central phenomenon that troubled liberals and anarchists: the suffocating growth of the parasite state. He thought that all socialist revolutions would transform the old exploitative state. As I have noted (see section 12–4), even an unusual road to socialism through universal suffrage in democracies with relatively small state apparatuses would involve a long underground and later overt civil war, a creation of a new state modeled on the Paris Commune and composed primarily of a citizen-army and worker-officials, and suppression of a new "slaveowners' revolt." In contrast, the notion of a gradual reform of twentieth-century parasite state structures, advocated by Bernstein, later Social Democracy, and contemporary Eurocommunism, abandons the distinguishing features of Marx's argument. Furthermore, Marx's formulation of his theory of surplus value in the late 1850s deepened his historical materialism. Gilbert, "Social Theory and Revolutionary Activity in Marx," pp. 531–536.

ence of such movements constitutes a striking predictive success for Marx's general theory of capitalism's internal conflicts. Such movements show that capitalism creates a potential for working-class socialism. But proletarian revolution turned out, even in Marx's lifetime, to be a far trickier political proposition than Marx or Engels envisioned. Taken as a whole, Marx's constant refinements of explanation and strategy, especially on the role of English colonialism and the peasants, accentuate the importance of political choices or alternatives and would seem to require modification of Marx's general theory of class struggle in an even more overtly political direction. Oppression, war, and even large radical movements do not lead inevitably to the overthrow of capitalism.

In the twentieth century, as I have noted, socialist and communist movements have taken up some aspects of Marx's theory and strategy and discarded others. Scholars who have poorly understood Marx's strategy and theory may have overlooked the ultimate consequences of these political choices; they may have glossed over the difference between changes that maintain the radicalism of the theory and those that undermine it. Marx's strategies themselves exhibit a constant tension between the present of the movement and its future, between furthering a movement for reform and a protracted appeal to workers, peasants, and intellectuals on a more revolutionary and internationalist basis. Interpretation of Marx's theory by later radicals has also bifurcated into a predominant productive forces emphasis and a harder stress on class conflict. The latter points toward a discerning of alternatives through political action of the sort discussed throughout this book; the former can be misinterpreted to supply a priori strictures against genuine revolutionary movements. In this context, misuse of Marx's general theory may often have curtailed the revolutionary aspect of modern socialism and communism. Furthermore, to use Marx's own corrective, a willingness to learn from the political experience of mass movements, requires timely and innovative theoretical skill.

Thus, variations of emphasis within Marx's general theory as well as tensions between Marx's two types of theorizing and within his strategies themselves may have generated all sorts of problems for radical movements both before and after proletarian revolution. As Marxian movements have shaken Europe and the world since 1848, so the specter of more radical possibilities has often pursued Marxists. The conflicts between formal democratic citizenship and social equality, between patriotism and internationalism, between a further development of capitalism and the possibility of socialism have haunted radical-led anticapitalist, antifascist, anticolonialist, and antiimperialist movements. The very first contradiction in social republicanism, that of citizens and communists, has profoundly influenced subsequent Marxian politics. Following Hegel and seeking to criticize these experiences internally, we might restore a decisive aspect of the dialectic between politics or strategy and social forces, rubbed away, until recently, by economic determinist misinterpretation.

Appendix: Demands of
the Communist Party in Germany

"Workers of all countries unite!"

1. All Germany will be declared a single, indivisible republic.

2. Every German who is twenty-one years old is a voter and eligible for election, provided that he has never been convicted of a crime.

3. The people's representatives will be paid so that workers, too, may sit in the German parliament.

4. Universal arming of the people. Armies will in future also be worker-armies so that the troops will not merely consume as in the past but also produce more than the cost of their maintenance.

    This is, in addition, a vehicle for the organization of labor.

5. The administration of justice will be free.

6. All feudal burdens, all duties, corvée, tithes, and the like, that have hitherto weighed on the rural people will be abolished without compensation.

7. Princely and other feudal estates, all mines, pits, and the like, will be converted into state property. On these estates, agriculture will be conducted on a large scale and with the most modern scientific techniques for the common good.

8. Mortgages on peasant lands will be declared state property. Interest on these mortgages will be paid by the peasants to the state.

SOURCE: *Bund Dokumente,* pp. 739–741. For another translation, see Marx, *On Revolution,* pp. 427–428.

9. In districts where the tenant system has developed, the ground rent or tenant dues will be paid as a tax to the state.

   All the measures indicated in 6, 7, 8, and 9 aim to decrease the public and other burdens on the peasants and small tenants without diminishing the resources necessary to defray state costs and without endangering production itself.

   The actual landowner, who is neither peasant nor tenant, has no part in production. His consumption is, therefore, a mere abuse.

10. In place of all private banks will be a state bank whose paper currency will be the legal means of exchange.

    This measure makes it possible to regulate credit in the interest of the *entire* people and thereby undermines the domination of the big money men. While it replaces gold and silver with paper money by degrees, it cheapens the indispensable means of bourgeois commerce, the universal means of exchange, and allows gold and silver to be used for foreign trade. Finally, this measure is necessary to fasten the interests of the conservative bourgeoisie tightly to the new regime.

11. The state will take in hand all means of transportation: railroads, canals, steamboats, roads, the posts, and the like. They will be converted into state property and placed free at the disposal of the impoverished classes.

12. In the salary of all civil servants, there will be no differential except that those with a family, therefore with more needs, will receive higher pay than others.

13. Complete separation of church and state. The clergy of every denomination will only be paid voluntarily by their congregations.

14. Restriction of the right of inheritance.

15. Introduction of steep progressive taxation and abolition of sales taxes.

16. Founding of national ateliers. The state will guarantee a livelihood to all workers and provide for those unable to work.

17. Universal, free education.

It is in the interest of the German proletariat, the petite bourgeoisie, and the peasantry to work energetically to achieve the foregoing measures. For only through the realization of these demands can the millions, who have hitherto been exploited in Germany by a small number who will strive to keep them in subjection, attain their rights and achieve the power that rightly belongs to them as the producers of all wealth.

The committee: Karl Marx, Karl Schapper, H. Bauer, F. Engels, J. Moll, W. Wolff.

Chronology

1838	Weitling publishes *Menschheit, wie sie ist und wie sie sein sollte* for the League of the Just.
1839	Abortive revolutionary uprising in Paris led by Barbès's Société des Saisons. Schapper, Bauer, and Moll, leaders of the League of the Just, emigrate to London, Weitling to Switzerland.
1839–1841	Marx completes his doctoral dissertation, "Difference between the Democritean and Epicurean Philosophy of Nature" in Berlin.
1840	Proudhon publishes *What Is Property?*
1841	Feuerbach, *The Essence of Christianity*.
1842	Marx becomes editor of the *Rheinische Zeitung* and moves to Cologne. Publishes articles on the law on the thefts of wood (October 1842) and the Moselle winegrowers (January 1843). Weitling edits *Die junge Generation* and *Der Hülferuf der deutschen Jugend* in Switzerland.
1842	Marx and Engels meet for first time in offices of *Rheinische Zeitung*.
1843	Feuerbach, *Principles of the Philosophy of the Future*. Hess, "Socialismus und Kommunismus," "Philosophie der That." Weitling, *Garantien der Harmonie und Freiheit*.
March 17, 1843	Marx resigns from the *Rheinische Zeitung* (closed by the Prussian censor on April 1).
Summer 1843	Marx, *Critique of Hegel's Philosophy of Right* and "On the Jewish Question" (published in February 1844).
September 16, 1843	Zurich court sentences Weitling for inciting to riot and blasphemy.
October 1843	Marx moves to Paris.
1844	Marx, economic and philosophical manuscripts (unpublished during his lifetime).
April 16, 1844	Prussian government issues order for Marx's arrest on charges of lese majesty and high treason if he reenters Prussia.

June 4–6, 1844	Silesian weavers' revolt.
August 7–10, 1844	Marx's article against Ruge in *Vorwärts*, "Critical Marginal Notes on the Article 'The King of Prussia and Social Reform. By a Prussian.'"
August 28, 1844	Marx and Engels meet again and begin their lifelong friendship and collaboration.
September 1844	Marx begins to meet with artisan communist groups in Paris.
September 22, 1844	International gathering of communists and democrats in London to greet Weitling.
November 1844–March 1845	Engels, *The Condition of the Working Class in England.*
January 1845	Marx expelled from Paris, moves to Brussels.
February 1845	Marx and Engels, *The Holy Family.*
February 18, 1845–January 14, 1846	Discussions of Schapper, Bauer, Moll, and Weitling in London.
Spring 1845	Marx writes but does not publish *Theses on Feuerbach.*
September 22, 1845	Festival of Nations in London commemorating the founding of the first French Republic and establishing the international society of Fraternal Democrats.
September 1845–summer 1846	Marx and Engels write but do not publish *The German Ideology.*
November–December 1845	Marx gives up Prussian citizenship.
1846	Proudhon, *Système des contradictions économiques ou philosophie de la misère.* Marx and Engels found Communist Correspondence Committee in Brussels.
February 22, 1846	Uprising and declaration of Polish republic in Cracow (suppressed in March).
March 30, 1846	Marx's confrontation with Weitling in Brussels.
April 1, 1846	Marx meets Wilhelm Wolff.
May 11, 1846	Brussels Committee's "Circular against Kriege."
August 1846	Engels goes to Paris to work in German Workers' Educational Society and the League of the Just.
1847	Ten Hours Bill in England.
January 3, 1847–February 1848	Marx's articles for *Deutsche Brüsseler Zeitung.*
Spring 1847	Moll journeys to Brussels to meet with Marx and Engels.

June 1847	First congress of Communist League. Marx and Engels organize League branch in Brussels. Marx's *Poverty of Philosophy* published in Paris.
August 1847	Marx and Engels help found German Workers' Educational Association in Brussels.
September 1847	First and only issue of the *Kommunistische Zeitschrift.*
October 1847	Hess, "Die Folgen einer Revolution des Proletariats."
October–November 1847	Engels's draft of a communist "Catechism."
November 1847	Marx elected vice-president of Brussels Democratic Association. Marx and Engels participate in meeting of Fraternal Democrats in London.
November 29–December 8, 1847	Marx and Engels participate in London Congress of Communist League which commissions them to draw up the final version of its manifesto.
Late December 1847	Marx's lectures "Wage Labor and Capital" delivered to German Workers' Educational Association in Brussels.
January–February 1848	Completion and publication of *Manifesto.*
February 22–24, 1848	Republican revolution in France.
February 26, 1848	National ateliers set up in Paris.
March 1848	Marx and other German communists expelled from Belgium; Marx invited by French provisional government to return to Paris.
March 3, 1848	Demonstration of Cologne democrats at city hall led by Gottschalk.
March 13, 1848	Revolution in Vienna.
March 18–19, 1848	Barricade fighting in Berlin.
March 21–29, 1848	Marx and Engels draft "Demands of the Communist Party in Germany" in Paris.
Late March 1848	Polish uprising in grand duchy of Posen.
April 11, 1848	Marx and Engels arrive in Cologne.
April 13, 1848	First meeting of Cologne Worker Society.
April 25, 1848	First meeting of Cologne Democratic Society.
June 1, 1848	First issue of the *Neue Rheinische Zeitung.*
June 12–13, 1848	Uprising in Prague.
June 23–26, 1848	Workers' insurrection in Paris.
July 6, 1848	Moll and Schapper elected president and vice-president of Cologne Worker Society.

July 24–27, 1848	Debate over the Prussian reannexation of Poland in Frankfurt National Assembly (Engels's articles in NRZ, August 7–September 6).
August 3, 1848	Marx denied citizenship by Prussia.
August 26, 1848	Prussian-Danish armistice over Schleswig-Holstein signed at Malmö.
September 13, 1848	Rally of 5,000–6,000 forms Committee of Public Safety in Cologne.
September 17, 1848	Rally of 10,000 workers and peasants in Worringen.
Mid-September 1848	Uprising against Schleswig-Holstein armistice in Frankfurt.
September 26–October 5, 1848	Martial law in Cologne; NRZ suspended.
October 31, 1848	Fall of Vienna to the counterrevolution.
November 1848	Disbanding of Berlin Assembly by monarch; NRZ's campaign to withhold taxes.
November–December 1848	Marx indicted on charges of lese majesty and incitement to rebellion; February 1849 trial and acquittal by Cologne jury.
December 10, 1848	Louis Napoleon elected president of France.
1849–1850	Emergence of democratic-socialist peasant movement in France.
March 1849	Marx's NRZ editorial on French peasant movement for return of the milliard. Articles by Wilhelm Wolff, "Silesian Billion," March 12–April 25.
April 5–11, 1849	NRZ publishes "Wage Labor and Capital."
May 3–8, 1849	Insurrections in Dresden and Leipzig triggered by Saxon king's refusal to accept the Reich constitution.
May 6, 1849	Congress of Rhenish Worker Societies in Cologne.
May 13, 1849	Mass demonstration in Baden; army goes over to side of people.
May 16, 1849	Monarchy orders expulsion of Marx from Prussia.
May 19, 1849	Last issue of NRZ.
Spring–August 1849	Revolution in Hungary against Austria, finally defeated with aid of Russian troops.
June 3, 1849	Marx arrives in Paris; expelled July 19.
June 12–July 12, 1849	Prussian troops suppress revolutionary forces in Baden and Palatinate.
August 1849	Marx moves to London, helps to reconstitute the Commu-

nist League, and joins German Workers' Educational Society.

December 1849–November 1850 Marx and Engels publish the *Neue Rheinische Zeitung, Politisch-Ökonomische Revue,* including Marx's *The Class Struggles in France* and Marx and Engels's review of Chenu's *Les Conspirateurs.*

1850 Engels, *The Peasant War in Germany.*

March 1850 Marx, *Address of the Central Committee to the Communist League.*

April 1850 Founding of short-lived Universal Society of Revolutionary Communists by Marx, Engels, Harney, Willich, Vidil, and Adam.

September 15, 1850 Last meeting of Central Committee in London; Marx's clash with Willich and Schapper.

1851–1852 Engels, *The Revolution and Counterrevolution in Germany,* published under Marx's name in the *New York Daily Tribune.*

December 2, 1851 Napoleon's coup.

January–May 1852 Marx, *The Eighteenth Brumaire of Louis Napoleon,* published in Weydemeyer's New York German-language journal, *Die Revolution.*

October 4–November 12, 1852 Cologne communist trial.

November 1852 Dissolution of the Communist League.

January 1853 Marx, *Revelations about the Cologne Communist Trial.*

1857–1858 Marx writes but does not publish *Grundrisse.*

1864 Marx participates in the founding of the International Workingmen's Association and writes its *Inaugural Address* and *General Rules.*

1865 Marx delivers "Wages, Price and Profit" to General Council of IWA.

1867 Marx, *Capital,* vol. 1.

1870 General Council resolutions on Ireland.

March–May 1871 Paris Commune; Marx's *The Civil War in France.*

1872 Hague Congress of IWA.

1875 Marx writes but does not publish *Critique of the Gotha Program* and *Conspectus of Bakunin's Statism and Anarchy.*

List of Historical Figures*

Adam. French tanner. Member of Blanqui's secret societies under July Monarchy and in exile in London in 1850.

Albert (Martin, Alexandre) (1815–1895). Leader of French revolutionary secret societies under July Monarchy and member of the provisional government after the February Revolution of 1848.

Friedrich Anneke (1818–1872). Army officer, discharged for his political views. Supported Gottschalk in Cologne Communist League. Member of Rhineland District Democratic Committee.

Pavel V. Annenkov (1812–1887). Russian writer and landowner. Present during clash of Weitling and Marx at Brussels Communist Correspondence Committee, 1846.

Ernst Moritz Arndt (1769–1860). Historian and philologist. Began to advocate resurrection of heroic German people during wars against Napoleon.

Ashley (Anthony Ashley Cooper, Earl of Shaftesbury) (1801–1855). Tory parliamentarian. Advocated Ten Hours Bill of 1847.

François Noel Babeuf, called Gracchus (1760–1797). Leader of the first communist movement, the conspiracy of equals, in the French Revolution. Keeper of the manorial rolls in the town of Roye in Picardy until the revolution. Imprisoned as a radical during the greater part of the Terror and arrested again under Thermidor. Projected a second communal and egalitarian revolution in 1795. Arrested in 1796, tried and executed in 1797.

Mikhail Bakunin (1814–1876). Russian journalist and anarchist. Despised Marx's Communist Correspondence Committee in Brussels. Participated in the Dresden insurrection of 1849. Chief theoretical and political opponent of Marx in the International Workingmen's Association, 1868–1872.

Armand Barbès (1809–1870). Leader of the Société des Saisons which launched an unsuccessful communist putsch in Paris in 1839. Participated in May 15, 1848, demonstration that forced the declaration of the Second Republic; sentenced to life imprisonment. Pardoned in 1854 and emigrated to Belgium.

Heinrich Bauer (born 1813). Shoemaker. London leader of the League of the Just and Communist League who eventually became a supporter of Marx. Reorganized the Communist League in Germany in 1850. Emigrated to Australia in 1851.

* This list covers mainly nineteenth-century historical figures.

August Bebel (1840–1913). Leader of German Social Democracy. Elected deputy to North German Reichstag in 1867. Opposed war credits for Prussia during Franco-Prussian war; imprisoned for two years.

Hermann Heinrich Becker (1820–1885). Lawyer and journalist. Leader of Association of Workers and Employers in Cologne and member of Rhineland District Democratic Committee in 1848. Joined Communist League in 1850.

Jean Joseph Louis Blanc (1811–1882). French socialist and advocate of "organization of work." One of two workers' representatives in the French provisional government of 1848 and president of Luxemburg Commission.

Louis Auguste Blanqui (1805–1881). Main leader of nineteenth-century French communism. Organized conspiracies of artisans and intellectuals; led unsuccessful putsches in 1834, 1839, and 1870 as well as the demonstration that forced declaration of the Second Republic on May 15, 1848. Imprisoned for revolutionary activity by the French government for over thirty years of his adult life.

Stephan Born (1824–1898). Printer. Member of Communist League. In 1848 in Berlin, founded unions–the Workers' Brotherhood–and abstained from participation in the democratic revolution. Along with Marx, his newspaper *Das Volk* supported the June insurrection. Commanded Dresden insurrection in 1849.

Friedrich Wilhelm von Brandenburg (1792–1850). Prussian general and statesman. Head of counterrevolutionary ministry (November 1848–November 1850).

John Bray (1809–1895). American economist. While residing in England, became Ricardian socialist and follower of Robert Owen. Author of *Labour's Wrongs and Labour's Remedy* (1839). Returned to the United States and advocated farmer-labor cooperation and banking reform; became vice-president of the American Labor Reform League.

John Bright (1811–1889). English manufacturer. Leader of Free Traders and founder of Anti-Corn Law League.

Filippo Michele Buonarroti (1761–1837), Italian revolutionary. Became commissioner to Maritime Alps of Jacobin republic. Participated in Babeuf's conspiracy in 1796; imprisoned. Attempted to lead insurrection in Grenoble (1812). Author of *Babeuf's Conspiracy for Equality* (1828).

Heinrich Bürgers (1820–1870). Cologne journalist. Wrote for *Rheinische Zeitung*. Member of Communist League. Leader of September 1848 rally at which Committee of Public Safety elected. Sentenced to six years in prison at Cologne communist trial of 1852.

Etienne Cabet (1788–1856). Teacher and lawyer from Dijon. After revolution of 1830, appointed attorney general in Corsica, but discharged for criticizing July Monarchy's failure to institute social reforms. Sat in chamber as deputy for the Côte-d'Or. Condemned for articles published in his journal, *Le Populaire*, and in 1834, fled to England. After amnesty permitted his return to France, published *Voyage en Icarie* (1840). In 1848, led 1,500 emigrants to found a real Icaria in the

New World. Beset by sickness and insolvency, the community disbanded. Cabet died in St. Louis in 1856.

Ludolf Camphausen (1803–1890). Cologne banker. Leading liberal politician who became Prussian prime minister, March–June 1848.

Marc Caussidière (1801–1861). French democrat. Participated in Lyons uprising of 1834. Became Paris prefect of police after February Revolution and deputy to National Assembly. Emigrated to England in June 1848.

Louis Eugène Cavaignac (1802–1850). French general. Directed conquest of Algeria in 1830 and suppression of June insurrection in 1848.

Adolphe Chenu (b. 1816). Participated in pre-1848 French communist secret societies. Police agent. Author of *Les Conspirateurs* (1850).

Richard Cobden (1804–1865). English manufacturer. Founder of the Anti-Corn Law League.

Gustave Courbet (1819–1877). French painter whose realistic portrayal of peasants shocked the salon audiences of 1849–1851. Participated in the Paris Commune.

Friedrich Dahlmann (1785–1860). During September 1848 crisis over Schleswig-Holstein, appointed to form a Prussian ministry to continue the war. Reported to Frankfurt parliament that he could not form such a ministry which led to a narrow acceptance of the Malmö armistice.

Roland Daniels (1819–1855). Cologne doctor. Member of Communist League and ally of Marx. Arrested in 1850 by Prussian government and jailed for eighteen months awaiting trial. Acquitted but died in 1855 of tuberculosis contracted in prison.

Georges-Jacques Danton (1759–1794). Jacobin revolutionary. Leader of the "Indulgents" (opposed dechristianization). Executed during the Terror.

Albert Darasz (1808–1852). Participated in Polish uprising of 1830–1831. Member of Central Committee of European Democracy in exile in London, 1850.

Jacques-Louis David (1748–1825). French painter. Participated vigorously in the French Revolution. Painted "The Oath of the Tennis Court" (1791) and "The Death of Marat" (1793). Imprisoned after fall of Robespierre.

Théodore Dézamy (1803–1850). French communist. Author of *Code de la Communauté*.

John Doherty. Most influential union leader among Manchester spinners. Emigrated from Ireland to England in 1817. Organized movement against combination laws and first national union in England—Grand General Union of All the Operative Spinners of the United Kingdom. Launched a general union for all trades in 1830.

Ernst Dronke (1822–1891). Writer. Editor of *Neue Rheinische Zeitung* and ally of Marx in Cologne Worker Society. Emigrated to England after 1848.

J. G. Eccarius (1818–1889). Tailor. Member of League of the Just. Later ally of

Marx in Communist League in 1850 and member of General Council of International Workingmen's Association.

Karl Ludwig Johann d'Ester (1811–1859). Doctor. Ally of Brussels Communist Correspondence Committee in Cologne. Elected deputy to Berlin Assembly in 1848. Became head of Democratic Central Committee to which Marx urged all withheld taxes be sent during the November crisis. Participated in Baden-Palatinate uprising in 1849 and then emigrated to Switzerland.

August Hermann Ewerbeck (1816–1860). German doctor. Leader of League of the Just and Communist League in Paris until 1850.

Ludwig Andreas Feuerbach (1804–1872). Philosopher who moved from defender to materialist critic of Hegel. His *The Essence of Christianity* (1841) and *Principles of the Philosophy of the Future* (1843) strongly influenced Marx, Engels, and Hess. Advocated republicanism and communism but did not participate in the revolution of 1848.

Charles Fleury (b. 1824). Merchant. Prussian police agent in London.

Ferdinand Flocon (1800–1866). French democratic politician and journalist. Editor of *La Réforme.*

Paul-Louis-François-René de Flotte (1817–1860). French naval officer, democrat, and communist. A supporter of Blanqui who participated in the May 15 storming of the National Assembly and the June insurrection in 1848. Elected deputy to National Assembly in 1851.

François Marie Charles Fourier (1772–1837). Son of Besançon cloth merchant. Lost fortune; became minor clerk in a business house. Master satirist of frauds, monotony, and vices of "civilized" society. Dreamed of a new "Combined Order" which would exalt the passions. Its unit, the phalanstery, would be composed of all psychological types, assigned tasks attractive to their diverse temperaments.

Friedrich Karl (1801–1883). Prince of Prussia, general.

Friedrich Wilhelm IV (1795–1861). King of Prussia, 1840–1861.

Benjamin-Sigismond Frossard (1754–1830). Protestant pastor at Lyons and anti-slavery organizer. Member of Société des Amis des Noirs. Author of an influential two-volume attack on slavery, *La Cause des esclaves nègres et des habitants de la Guinée portée au tribunal de la raison, de la politique et de la religion* (1788). During the French Revolution, made dean of the faculty of theology at Montauban. During the reaction of 1815, deprived of his posts at Montauban and as pastor.

Philippe Charles Gigot (1819–1860). Paleographist in Belgian Ministry of Interior. Cooperated with Marx in Brussels Communist Correspondence Committee and Communist League.

Andreas Gottschalk (1815–1849). Doctor. Member of Cologne Communist League. Led March 3, 1848, demonstration at city council and founded Cologne Worker Society. Opposed republic; advocated either uprising for socialism or red monarchy. Vehement opponent of Marx.

Greif. Prussian police spy in London in 1850.

Karl Grün (1817–1887). University of Berlin philosophy student at same time as Marx. Disciple of Feuerbach and "true socialist" writer. Collaborated with Proudhon in Paris. Deputy to Prussian National Assembly in 1848.

David Justus Hansemann (1790–1864). Cologne merchant. Prussian finance minister, March–September 1848.

George Julian Harney (1817–1897). Left-wing Chartist leader and editor of the *Northern Star*. Participated in the Fraternal Democrats and published the first English translation of the *Manifesto* in his journal, the *Red Republican* (1850).

Friedrich Karl Franz Hecker (1811–1881). German democrat. Leader of republican uprising in Baden in April 1848.

Louis Heilberg (1818–1852). Journalist. Member of Brussels Communist Correspondence Committee. Participant in German revolution of 1848. Emigrated to London in 1851.

Heinrich Heine (1797–1856). Satiric poet and friend of Marx. Brilliantly defended republicanism and communism in the 1840s in such works as "The Weavers" and "Germany: A Winter's Tale."

Karl Heinzen (1809–1880). German journalist and democrat. Engaged in bitter exchanges with Engels and Marx in Brussels in 1847. Participated in Baden-Palatinate uprising of 1849. Emigrated to United States in 1850.

Tony Hepburn. Leader of coal miners' movements in Northumberland and Durham in 1830–1831. Campaigned for reform of suffrage.

Georg Friedrich Herwegh (1817–1875). German democrat and poet. Recruited a legion composed primarily of artisans in Paris in 1848 to march into Germany and declare a republic. Defeated at border.

Moses Hess (1812–1875). Communist philosopher and journalist. His writings influenced Engels and Marx and the "true socialists." Collaborated with Marx and Engels on *The German Ideology*. Joined Communist League. Adopted Marx's general materialist theory but hesitated to support democratic revolution in Germany. After 1850, collaborated with Willich-Schapper group in the Communist League. Emigrated to Switzerland, Holland, and France. In the 1860s, participated in the General Association of German Workers led by Lassalle and in the IWA. His essay "Rom und Jerusalem" foreshadowed the Zionist movement.

Wilhelm Hirsch. Clerk from Hamburg. Prussian police spy in London in 1850.

Thomas Hodgskin (1783–1869). English naval officer and Ricardian socialist. Published *Labor Defended against the Claims of Capital* (1825). Supported the new unions but looked to a society of equal independent property holders rather than a cooperative one. Helped to found a college for workers, the London Mechanics' Institute. Later became an editorial writer for the *Economist* in its early years.

Ulrich von Hutten (1488–1523). Aristocrat, poet, advocate of Reformation, and participant in knights' uprising of 1522–1523.

Friedrich Ludwig Jahn (1778–1852). Professor at University of Berlin in early nineteenth century. Founded the fraternity movement and association of German gymnasts to propagate "Germanic culture" and encourage young Germans to fight Napoleon. In 1817, the fraternities convened at Wartburg castle to burn "foreign books" which had allegedly poisoned the culture of the German people.

Count Josef Jellachich (1801–1859). Austrian general. Participated in suppression of Vienna uprising (1848) and Hungarian revolution (1848–1849).

Ernest Charles Jones (1819–1859). Lawyer. Joined Chartists in 1846 and became left-wing leader. Imprisoned for two years for advocating uprisings following parliamentary rejection of Charter in 1848. Continued to campaign for Charter through his journals, *Notes of the People* and *The People's Paper,* 1851–1858.

Martin Jude. Led miners of northeast and Yorkshire in forming the Miners' Association of Great Britain in 1841, which joined Chartist strikes of 1842. The owners broke this union in the late 1840s.

Adolf Friedrich Junge. German worker, member of League of the Just and Communist League. Emigrated to United States early in 1848.

Gustav Adolf Köttgen (1805–1882). Poet. Took part in German communist movement of 1840s in Elberfeld.

Hermann Kriege (1802–1850). Westphalian journalist. Ally of Weitling in League of the Just. Emigrated to New York and edited the *People's Tribune* which advocated a sentimental humanism and alliance of the workers with the rich. Vehemently criticized in circular of Brussels Communist Correspondence Committee in 1846.

Georg Kühlmann (b. 1812). Austrian police agent, "true socialist" publicist in Switzerland.

Marie Joseph Paul Yves Roch Gilbert du Motier, Marquis de La Fayette (1757–1834). Leader of moderate constitutionalists (*Feuillants*) in the French Revolution. Fled to Holland in 1793.

Jacques Laffitte (1767–1844). French banker and prime minister under July Monarchy (1830–1831).

Alphonse Maria Louis de Lamartine (1790–1869). French poet, historian, republican politician. Minister of foreign affairs after the February Revolution.

Felicité Robert de Lamennais (1782–1854). French priest and Christian socialist. Author of *Paroles d'un Croyant* (1833).

Ferdinand Lassalle (1825–1864). Lawyer, philosopher, playwright, and communist politician. Participated as a representative of Düsseldorf radicals in the Worringen rally in 1848. Jailed for six months for inciting resistance to government officials. Advocated Prussian state socialism that would give economic aid to workers' cooperatives; founded General Association of German Workers in 1863.

Alexandre Auguste Ledru-Rollin (1807–1874). Leader of the *Montagne* (democratic-socialist) party during the revolution of 1848–1849; editor of *La Réforme;*

minister of the interior in the post-February provisional government. Proposed censure of Louis Napoleon for intervention against the Italian republicans; led peaceful demonstration which was dispersed by Napoleon's troops on June 13, 1849. Member of Central Committee of European Democracy in exile in London in 1850.

Prince Felix Maria von Lichnowski (1814–1848). Prussian officer. Right-wing deputy to Frankfurt Assembly. Prototype for Georg Weerth's satirical series in the *Neue Rheinische Zeitung,* "Life and Deeds of the Knight Schnapphahnski." Killed in Frankfurt September uprising.

Louis Philippe I (1773–1850). Duke of Orléans, king of France (1830–1848).

Otto Lüning (1818–1868). Physician and "true socialist" writer. Editor of *Westphälische Dampfboot.*

Jean-Paul Marat (1743–1793). His newspaper, *L'Ami du Peuple,* spoke for the sans-culottes in the French Revolution and made the social question a central issue. Assassinated in the heart of Paris by a royalist, Charlotte Corday, in 1793.

Rudolph Matthäi. "True socialist" journalist. Author of "Socialistische Bausteine" in *Rheinische Jahrbücher* (1845). Criticized by Marx and Engels in *The German Ideology.*

Giuseppe Mazzini (1805–1872). Leader of the Italian democratic movement. Head of provisional government of Roman Republic (1849). Organizer of Central Committee of European Democracy in exile in London in 1850.

Christian Friedrich Mentel (b. 1812). Tailor. Member of League of the Just with "true socialist" leanings. When arrested by Prussian authorities, became an informer. Emigrated to the United States.

Karl Joseph Moll (1813–1849). Watchmaker. Leader of League of the Just and Communist League. Ally of Marx in Cologne Worker Society and briefly its president. Killed at the Battle of the Murg in 1849.

Charles Montalembert (1810–1870). Writer, leader of conservative French Catholics.

Thomas Münzer (c. 1490–1525). Radical opponent of Luther and leader of the German peasant war of 1525. Advocate of communal holding of land.

Louis Napoleon (1808–1873). Nephew of the original Napoleon. President of France (1848–1851), emperor (1852–1870).

Count Karl Vasilyevich Nesselrode (1780–1862). Russian foreign minister (1816–1856), chancellor of state (1845–1862).

Peter Nothjung (1821–1880). Cologne tailor and communist. Sentenced to three years' imprisonment at Cologne communist trial of 1852. Joined General Association of German Workers in 1863.

Richard Oastler (1789–1861). English Tory politician and advocate of Ten Hours Bill.

Feargus O'Connor (1794–1855). Radical Chartist leader whose strongest support came from factory workers of the North and Midlands; editor of *Northern Star*.

Robert Owen (1771–1858). Textile manufacturer in Scotland. Introduced exemplary conditions in his own factory and advocated cooperative communities. Founded New Harmony, Indiana, community (1825–1828). Edited the Chartist journal, *The New Moral World*.

Baron Erasmus Robert von Patöw (1804–1890). Minister of trade, industry, and public works under Camphausen (April–June 1848).

Wilhelm Pieper (1826–1899). German philologist, journalist, and communist. Tried for lese majesty in 1849. Emigrated to London. Ally of Marx in Communist League in London in 1850.

Wilhelm Prinz. Member of Cologne Worker Society and editor of its newspaper. Ally of Gottschalk.

Pierre-Joseph Proudhon (1809–1865). Printer. Leading French anarchist theorist and politician of nineteenth century. Author of many influential works including *What Is Property?* (1840) and *Philosophie de la misère* (1846). Advocated an egalitarian or mutualist association of small property holders; opposed unions and participation in parliamentary politics. Nonetheless, elected representative from the Doubs to the National Assembly of 1848. His followers would oppose Marx in the early years of the International Workingmen's Association.

François Raspail (1794–1878). French naturalist, journalist, communist. Participated in revolutions of 1830 and 1848 and became deputy to 1848 National Assembly.

Franz Raveaux (1810–1851). Cigar maker and democrat. Cologne deputy to Frankfurt National Assembly, 1848–1849. Member of the provisional government in Baden in 1849. Emigrated to Switzerland.

Maximilien-Marie-Isidore Robespierre (1758–1794). Leader of the Jacobin Committee of Public Safety in the French Revolution.

Jacques Roux (d. 1794). Priest. Radical leader of sans-culottes; demanded maximum on grain prices and dechristianization.

Arnold Ruge (1802–1880). Young Hegelian philosopher and republican. Cooperated with Marx on the *Deutsch-Französische Jahrbücher* of 1843. Opposed the Silesian weavers' revolt of 1844 and clashed with Marx. Deputy to Frankfurt Assembly in 1848. Member of Central Committee of European Democrats in exile in London in 1850. After 1866, became a National Liberal and supporter of Bismarck.

Michael Thomas Sadler (1780–1830). English economist. Tory advocate of Ten Hours Bill.

Antoine Louis Léon de Richebourg de Saint-Just (1767–1794). Jacobin leader in the French Revolution.

Claude Henri de Saint-Simon (1760–1825). A nobleman who renounced his title during the French Revolution, denounced the "unproductive" classes, and became the exponent of an industrial society based on the development of human capacities and dedicated to increased production. Though imprisoned for a time during the Revolution, acquired immense wealth through land speculation. Fell on evil days of poverty and madness, ignored by the Napoleonic establishment, but became a publicist for bankers and entrepreneurs under the restoration. After his publication of "A Parable" and the assassination of the duc de Barry, Saint-Simon was tried, and though acquitted, branded dangerous. In his last years, cast his doctrine in the form of a religion, "the new Christianity," and attracted a group of disciples who founded the Saint-Simonian school.

George Sand (pen name of Amandine Lucie Aurore Dupin, baronne Dudevant) (1804–1876). French novelist and democrat.

Karl Schapper (1812–1870). Forestry student from Nassau. Leader of League of the Just and Communist League. Ally of Marx in Cologne Worker Society in 1848 and its president (February–May 1849). In 1850, joined with Willich to advocate immediate communist uprising in Germany and oppose Marx in London Communist League. Member of General Council of International Workingmen's Association.

Konrad Schramm (1822–1858). German worker. Member of Communist League. Manager of *Neue Rheinische Zeitung, Politisch-Ökonomische Revue* in London, 1850.

Levin Schücking (1814–1883). Contributor to *Kölnische Zeitung* in 1848.

Karl Schurz (1829–1906). German democrat. Participant in Baden-Palatinate uprising in 1849. Emigrated to Switzerland, then to United States where he became a Republican politician. Led volunteers from Wisconsin against slavery in Civil War. Elected senator (1869); later campaigned for civil service reform.

Johann Baptist Schweitzer (1833–1873). Lassallean editor of *Sozial-Demokrat* (1864–1867) and president of General Association of German Workers. Supported Bismarck's unification of Germany from above.

Sebastian Seiler (1810–1890). Swiss journalist. Contributor to *Rheinische Zeitung*. Member of Brussels Communist Correspondence Committee and of Communist League.

Friedrich Hermann Semmig (1820–1897). "True socialist" journalist. Author of "Communismus, Socialismus, Humanismus" in *Rheinische Jahrbücher* (1845). Criticized by Marx and Engels in *The German Ideology*.

Franz von Sickingen (1481–1523). German nobleman who joined Reformation and led knights' uprising in 1522–1523.

Baron Heinrich vom Stein (1757–1831). Prussian politician. Helped initiate early nineteenth-century agrarian reforms.

Joseph Rayner Stephens (1805–1879). Methodist minister. Chartist advocate of use of physical force by workers against capitalists in Lancashire, 1837–1839.

Wilhelm Stieber (1818–1882). Chief of Prussian political police, 1850–1860. Organizer of and principal witness at Cologne communist trial of 1852. Author of *Die Communisten-Verschwörungen des 19. Jahrhunderts.*

Gustav von Struve (1805–1870). Journalist and democrat. Leader of Baden uprising of 1848 and Baden-Palatinate uprising of 1849.

Nikoláy Nikoláyevich Sukhanov (b. 1882). Historian. Became a member of Russian Socialist Revolutionary Party (1903–1904), joined Mensheviks (1909). After February Revolution of 1917, member, executive committee of Petrograd soviet. Wrote *Notes on the Russian Revolution.*

Louis-Adolphe Thiers (1797–1877). French historian and politician. Prime minister (1836, 1840). Deputy to National Assembly, 1848. Brutal suppressor of Paris Commune and president of Third Republic, 1871–1873.

François Dominique Toussaint-L'Ouverture (1743–1803). Leader of slave rebellion in Haiti against Spanish and English domination at the time of the French Revolution.

Wat Tyler (d. 1381). Leader of English peasant revolt of 1381.

Jules Vidil. French officer. Emigrated to England in 1849. Member of Blanquist secret society in London in 1850.

Karl Wachter. Radical democrat. Commander of "red company" in Cologne civic guard in 1848.

Georg Weerth (1822–1856). Representative of German commercial firm and revolutionary poet. Collaborated with Marx on the *Neue Rheinische Zeitung.*

Edgar von Westphalen (1819–1890). Marx's brother-in-law. Participated in meeting of Brussels Communist Correspondence Committee at which Marx and Weitling clashed.

Wilhelm Weitling (1808–1871). Tailor. Ideological and political leader of League of the Just in 1830s. Author of League's program, *Menschheit, wie sie ist und wie sie sein sollte,* and of *Garantien der Harmonie und Freiheit* and *The Poor Sinner's Gospel.* Organized branches of League in Switzerland in early 1840s. Jailed by Swiss government for blasphemy, 1843. After his release, journeyed to London. Clashed with leaders of the League of the Just, and in Brussels, with Communist Correspondence Committee, 1845–1846. Emigrated to the United States. Returned to Germany in 1848, but played no significant role in the revolution. Advocate of immediate communist uprising, spurred on by the "thieving proletariat."

Joseph Weydemeyer (1818–1866). Prussian officer. Ally of Marx in Communist Correspondence Committee in Brussels and Westphalia. After 1848, emigrated to the United States. Founded American Worker Society composed of German immigrants, which led strikes in New York and opposed the expansion of slavery. Published Marx's *Eighteenth Brumaire* in his journal, *Die Revolution.* Colonel in Northern army and commanded defense of St. Louis in Civil War.

August Willich (1810–1878). Officer. Ally of Gottschalk in Cologne Communist

League. Leader of Baden-Palatinate uprising in 1849. In 1850 in London, advocated immediate communist uprising in Germany and clashed with Marx in Communist League. Served as officer in American Civil War.

Prince Alfred zu Windischgrätz (1787–1862). Austrian field marshal. Commanded army that crushed the Prague and Vienna uprisings in 1848 as well as the Hungarian revolution of 1848–1849.

Franz Anton von Wolfers. Member of editorial board of *Kölnische Zeitung* in 1848.

Ferdinand Wolff (1812–1895). Journalist, editor of *Neue Rheinische Zeitung*. Sided with Marx in Communist League in London in 1850.

Wilhelm Wolff (1809–1864). From a Silesian peasant family. Studied at University of Breslau and became a teacher. Ally of Marx in Brussels Communist Correspondence Committee. Wrote "Silesian Billion" for the *Neue Rheinische Zeitung* in 1848. Marx dedicated first volume of *Capital* to this "intrepid, faithful, noble protagonist of the proletariat."

Count Friedrich Heinrich Ernst von Wrangel (1784–1877). Prussian general. Took part in counterrevolutionary *coup d'état* in Berlin and in dispersing the Prussian National Assembly in November 1848.

Vera Ivanovna Zasulich (1849–1919). Prominent in Narodnik and later Social Democratic movement in Russia. Participated in organizing Emancipation of Labor group.

Wilhelm Zimmerman (1807–1878). German historian of peasant wars and democrat. Deputy to Frankfurt National Assembly in 1848.

Bibliography

The bibliography consists mainly of works cited in the text. For more complete bibliographies of Marx's writings and books and articles on Marx, the reader should consult Maximilien Rubel, *Bibliographie des oeuvres de Karl Marx avec en appendice un repertoire des oeuvres de Friedrich Engels* (Paris: Marcel Rivière, 1956) with a *Supplément* (1960); David McLellan, *Karl Marx: His Life and Thought* (New York: Harper and Row, 1973), pp. 469–489; and Terrell Carver, "A Guide to Further Reading" in Isaiah Berlin, *Karl Marx: His Life and Environment,* 4th rev. ed. (Oxford: Oxford University Press, 1978), pp. 208–222.

The first attempt at a complete collection of the works of Marx and Engels in the original languages, Marx and Engels, *Gesamtausgabe,* edited by D. Rjazanov (Berlin: Marx-Engels Verlag, 1927–1935), was left unfinished. A German-language edition, Marx and Engels, *Werke* (Berlin: Dietz Verlag), begun in 1956, is now complete in thirty-nine volumes with two supplementary volumes and a two-volume index. A fuller English version of Marx and Engels, *Collected Works,* was started by International Publishers, New York and Progress Publishers, Moscow, in 1975; ten volumes had appeared by 1980. Volumes 7–9, which unfortunately appeared too late for use in this book, include a translation of Marx's and Engels's articles from the *Neue Rheinische Zeitung.* Dietz Verlag has begun to issue a definitive edition of the Marx and Engels *Gesamtausgabe* in the original languages with textual variants, projected for 100 volumes (Berlin, 1972–   ).

Writings of Marx and Engels

Marx, Karl; Engels, Friedrich; and Lenin, V. I. *Anarchism and Anarchosyndicalism.* New York: International Publishers, 1972.

Marx, Karl, and Engels, Friedrich. *The Birth of the Communist Manifesto.* Edited by Dirk Struik. New York: International Publishers, 1971.

————. *The Civil War in the United States.* 3rd ed. New York: International Publishers, 1969.

————. *Collected Works.* 10 vols. so far. New York: International Publishers, 1975–   . Cited as *CW.*

————. *The Communist Manifesto of Marx and Engels.* Edited by David Ryazanoff. New York: Russell & Russell, 1963.

————. *The German Ideology.* Edited by S. Ryazanskaya. Moscow: Progress Publishers, 1964.

————. *Gesamtausgabe.* Edited by David Rjazanov. 11 vols. Berlin: Marx-Engels Verlag, 1927–1935.

————. *Ireland and the Irish Question.* Edited by R. Dixon. New York: International Publishers, 1972.

————. *The Revolution of 1848–49: Articles from the Neue Rheinische Zeitung.* Translated by S. Ryazanskaya and edited by Bernard Isaacs. New York: International Publishers, 1972.

————. *Selected Correspondence.* 2d rev. ed. Moscow: Progress Publishers, 1965. Cited as *SC.*

————. *Selected Works.* 2 vols. Moscow: Foreign Languages Publishing House, 1962. Cited as *MESW.*

————. *Selected Works.* New York: International Publishers, 1974.

————. *Sur la literature et l'art.* Paris: Editions sociales, 1954.

————. *Werke.* 39 vols. with a supplemental volume in 2 parts. Berlin: Dietz Verlag, 1956–1968. Cited as *Werke.*

————. *Writings on the Paris Commune.* Edited by Hal Draper. New York: Monthly Review Press, 1971.

Writings of Engels

Engels, Friedrich. *The Condition of the Working Class in England.* Edited and translated by W. D. Henderson and W. H. Chaloner. Stanford: Stanford University Press, 1968. Cited as *Condition.*

————. *The Peasant War in Germany.* Translated by Moissaye J. Olgin. New York: International Publishers, 1966. Cited as *PW.*

————. *Revolution and Counterrevolution in Germany.* Translated by Eleanor Marx Aveling. New York: Capricorn Books, 1971.

Writings of Marx

Marx, Karl. *Capital.* Translated by Samuel Moore and Edward Aveling. 3 vols. Moscow: Foreign Languages Publishing House, 1957–1962.

————. *The Cologne Communist Trial.* Translated by Rodney Livingstone. New York: International Publishers, 1971.

―――. *Frühe Schriften.* Edited by Hans-Joachim Lieber and Peter Furth. Stuttgart: Cotta Verlag, 1971.

―――. *Grundrisse.* Translated by Martin Nicolaus. New York: Vintage Books, 1973.

―――. *Karl Marx on Colonialism and Modernization.* Edited by Shlomo Avineri. New York: Doubleday & Co., 1969.

―――. *Letters to Kugelmann.* New York: International Publishers, 1934.

―――. *On the First International.* The Karl Marx Library. Edited by Saul K. Padover. New York: McGraw-Hill, 1973.

―――. *On Revolution.* The Karl Marx Library. Edited by Saul K. Padover. New York: McGraw-Hill, 1970.

―――. *Politische Schriften.* Edited by Hans-Joachim Lieber. 2 vols. Stuttgart: Cotta Verlag, 1960.

―――. *The Poverty of Philosophy.* New York: International Publishers, 1963.

―――. *Theories of Surplus Value.* Translated by G. A. Bonner and Emile Burns. New York: International Publishers, 1952.

―――. *Writings of the Young Marx on Philosophy and Society.* Translated and edited by Loyd D. Easton and Kurt H. Guddat. New York: Doubleday & Co., 1967.

Other Writings

Allen, Garland E. "Genetics, Eugenics and Class Struggle." *Genetics* 79(1975): 29–45.

―――. *Life Science in the Twentieth Century.* Wiley History of Science Series, edited by George Basalla and William Coleman. New York: John Wiley & Sons, 1975.

Althusser, Louis. *Lire le Capital.* 2 vols. Paris: Maspero, 1965.

―――. *Pour Marx.* Paris: Maspero, 1965.

Andreas, Bert, ed. *Gründungsdokumente des Bundes der Kommunisten (Juni bis September 1847).* Hamburg: Ernest Hauswedell, 1969.

Arendt, Hannah. *The Human Condition.* Chicago: University of Chicago Press, 1974.

―――. *On Revolution.* New York: Viking Press, Viking Compass Books, 1965.

Aristotle. *Politics.* Translated by H. Rackham. Cambridge, Mass.: Harvard University Press, 1969.

Avineri, Shlomo. "How to Save Marx from the Alchemists of Revolution." *Political Theory* 4(1976): 35–44.

―――. *The Social and Political Thought of Karl Marx.* Cambridge: Cambridge University Press, 1970.

Bakunin, Michael. *Etatisme et anarchie.* Translated by Marcel Body. Leiden: E. J. Brill, 1967.

Balzac, Honoré de. *Illusions perdues.* Paris: Garnier Flammarion, 1961.

―――. *Les Paysans.* Paris: Garnier Flammarion, 1970.

Bayle, Pierre. *Ouevres diverses.* Paris: Editions sociales, 1971.

Becker, Gerhard. *Karl Marx und Friedrich Engels in Köln 1848–1849.* Berlin: Rütten und Loening, 1963.

Beik, Paul H., ed. *The French Revolution.* The Documentary History of Western Civilization. London: Macmillan, 1970.

Berlin, Isaiah. *Karl Marx: His Life and Environment.* 4th rev. ed. Oxford: Oxford University Press, 1978.

Bernstein, Samuel. *Auguste Blanqui and the Art of Insurrection.* London: Lawrence and Wishart, 1971.

Blanqui, Louis Auguste. *Critique Sociale.* 2 vols. Paris: Félix Alcan, 1885.

———. *Textes choisies.* Edited by V.-P. Volguine. Paris: Editions sociales, 1955.

Blumenberg, Werner. *Portrait of Marx.* Translated by Douglas Scott. New York: Herder and Herder, 1972.

———. "Zur Geschichte des Bundes der Kommunisten. Die Aussagen des Peter Gerhardt Röser." *International Review of Social History* 9(1964):89–122.

Bober, Martin. *Karl Marx's Interpretation of History.* 2d ed. Cambridge, Mass.: Harvard University Press, 1948.

Boyd, Richard N. "Metaphor and Theory Change: What Is 'Metaphor' a Metaphor for?" In *Metaphor and Thought,* edited by Andrew Ortony, pp. 356–408. Cambridge: Cambridge University Press, 1979.

———. *Realism and Scientific Epistemology.* Cambridge: Cambridge University Press, forthcoming.

Briggs, Asa, ed. *Chartist Studies.* London: Macmillan, 1959.

Buonarroti, Philippe. *Babeuf's Conspiracy for Equality.* Translated by Bronterre O'Brien, 1836. Reprint. New York: A. M. Kelley, 1965.

Carr, Edward Hallett. *Karl Marx: A Study in Fanaticism.* London: J. M. Dent, 1934.

———. *Michael Bakunin.* London: Macmillan, 1937.

Caute, David. *The Great Fear: The Anti-Communist Purge under Truman and Eisenhower.* New York: Simon and Schuster, 1978.

Chang, Sherman H. M. *The Marxian Theory of the State.* Philadelphia: John Spencer, 1931.

Chorover, Stephan L. *From Genesis to Genocide: The Meaning of Human Nature and the Power of Behavior Control.* Cambridge, Mass.: Massachusetts Institute of Technology Press, 1979.

Clapham, J. H. *Economic Development of France and Germany 1815–1914.* 4th ed. Cambridge: Cambridge University Press, 1966.

Clark, T. J. *Image of the People.* Greenwich, Conn.: New York Graphic Society, 1973.

Cohen, G. A. *Marx's Theory of History: A Defense.* Princeton: Princeton University Press, 1978.

Cole, G. D. H. *A Short History of the British Working Class Movement 1789–1947.* 3rd rev. ed. London: George Allen and Unwin, 1966.

Cornu, Auguste. *Karl Marx et Friedrich Engels: leur vie et leur oeuvre.* 4 vols. Paris: Presses Universitaires de France, 1948– .

———. *Karl Marx et la révolution de 1848.* Paris: Presses Universitaires de France, 1948.

Cornu, Auguste, and Mönke, Wolfgang, eds. *Moses Hess, Philosophische und Sozialistische Schriften 1837–1850: eine Auswahl.* Berlin: Akademie Verlag, 1961.

Diderot, Denis. *Oeuvres philosophiques.* Edited by Paul Vernière. Paris: Garnier Flammarion, 1964.

———. *Rameau's Nephew and Other Works.* Translated by Jacques Barzun and Ralph H. Bowen. Indianapolis: Bobbs-Merrill, The Library of Liberal Arts, 1956.

Dimitroff, Georgi. *The United Front against Fascism.* New York: New Century, 1950.

Dolgoff, Sam, ed. *Bakunin on Anarchy.* New York: Knopf, 1972.

Dowe, Dieter. *Aktion und Organisation: Arbeiterbewegung, sozialistische und kommunistische Bewegung in der preussischen Rheinprovinz 1820–1852.* Hanover: Verlag für Literatur und Zeitgeschehen, 1970.

Draper, Hal. *Karl Marx's Theory of Revolution.* 2 vols. so far. New York: Monthly Review Press, 1977.

———. "A Note on the Father of Anarchism." *New Politics* 8(1969):79–93.

Droz, Jacques. *Les Révolutions allemandes de 1848.* Paris: Presses Universitaires de France, 1957.

Dunn, John. *The Political Thought of John Locke.* Cambridge: Cambridge University Press, 1969.

Edwards, Stewart, ed. *Selected Writings of Pierre-Joseph Proudhon.* London: Macmillan, 1969.

Feuerbach, Ludwig. *The Essence of Christianity.* Translated by George Eliot. New York: Harper and Row, 1957.

———. *Kleine Schriften.* Edited by Hans Blumenberg, Jürgen Habermas, Dieter Henrich, and Jacob Taubes. Frankfurt: Suhrkamp Verlag, 1966.

———. *Lectures on the Essence of Religion.* Translated by Ralph Mannheim. New York: Harper and Row, 1967.

Förder, Herwig. *Marx und Engels am Vorabend der Revolution.* Berlin: Akademie Verlag, 1960.

Förder, Herwig; Hundt, Martin; Kandel, Jefim; and Lewiowa, Sofia, eds., *Der Bund der Kommunisten: Dokumente und Materialen, 1836–49.* Berlin: Dietz Verlag, 1970. Cited as *Bund Dokumente.*

Fourier, Charles. *Textes choisies.* Edited by F. Armand. Paris: Editions sociales, 1953.

Freymond, Jacques, ed. *La Première International, Recueil de documents.* 4 vols. Geneva: E. Droz, 1962.

General Council of the International Workingmen's Association. *Minutes.* 5 vols. London: Lawrence and Wishart, 1964.

Gilbert, Alan. "Historical Theory and the Structure of Moral Argument in Marx." In press, *Political Theory*, 1981.

———. "Marx on Internationalism and War." *Philosophy and Public Affairs* 7(1978):346–369.

———. "Marx on Internationalism, War and Exploitation." *Proceedings of the American Political Science Association*. Ann Arbor: University of Michigan Press, 1977.

———. "Salvaging Marx from Avineri." *Political Theory* 4(1976):9–34.

———. "Social Theory and Revolutionary Activity in Marx." *American Political Science Review* 73(1979):521–538.

Hamerow, Theodore S. *Restoration, Revolution, Reaction*. Princeton: Princeton University Press, 1958.

———. *The Social Foundations of German Unification 1858–71*. Princeton: Princeton University Press, 1972.

Hammen, Oscar J. "Marx and the Agrarian Question." *American Historical Review* 77(1972):679–704.

———. *The Red '48ers: Karl Marx and Friedrich Engels*. New York: Scribner's, 1969.

Hanfi, Zawar, ed. and trans. *The Fiery Brook: Selected Writings of Ludwig Feuerbach*. New York: Doubleday & Co., 1972.

Hegel, Georg Wilhem Friedrich. *Phänomenologie des Geistes*. Edited by Johannes Hoffmeister. 6th ed. Hamburg: Verlag von Felix Meiner, 1952.

———. *Phenomenology of Spirit*. Translated by A. V. Miller. Oxford: Oxford University Press, 1977.

———. *The Philosophy of History*. Translated by J. Sibree. New York: Dover Publications, 1956.

———. *The Philosophy of Right*. Translated by T. M. Knox. Oxford: Clarendon Press, 1962.

———. *Science of Logic*. Translated by A. V. Miller. London: George Allen and Unwin, 1969.

Heine, Heinrich. *Deutschland, Ein Wintermärchen*. Stuttgart: Philipp Reclam, 1975.

Hempel, Carl. *Philosophy of Natural Science*. Foundations of Philosophy Series. Englewood Cliffs, N.J.: Prentice-Hall, 1966.

Hertz-Eichenrode, Dieter. "Karl Marx über das Bauerntum und die Bündnisfrage." *International Review of Social History* 11(1966):382–402.

Hess, Moses. *Briefwechsel*. Edited by Edmund Silberner. The Hague: Mouton, 1959.

Hinton, William. *Fanshen: A Documentary of Revolution in a Chinese Village*. New York: Vintage Books, 1968.

Hobsbawm, E. J. *The Age of Revolution, 1789–1848*. New York: New American Library, Mentor, 1962.

———. *Industry and Empire*. The Making of Modern English Society, vol. 2, 1750 to the Present Day. New York: Pantheon Books, 1968.

Hobsbawm, E. J., and Rudé, George. *Captain Swing.* New York: Pantheon Books, 1968.

Hook, Sidney. *From Hegel to Marx: Studies in the Intellectual Development of Karl Marx.* Ann Arbor: University of Michigan Press, Ann Arbor Paperbacks for the Study of Communism and Marxism, 1971.

Hunt, Richard N. *The Political Ideas of Marx and Engels: Marxism and Totalitarian Democracy.* Pittsburgh: University of Pittsburgh Press, 1974.

Jantke, Carl, and Hilger, Dietrich, eds. *Die Eigentumslosen: der deutsche Pauperismus und die Emanzipationskrise in Darstellungen und Deutungen der zeitgenössischen Literatur.* Munich: K. Alber, 1965.

Johnson, Christopher H. "Etienne Cabet and the Problem of Class Antagonism." *International Review of Social History* 11(1966):403–443.

Johnson, Douglas, ed. *French Society and the Revolution.* Cambridge: Cambridge University Press, 1976.

Kägi, Paul. *Genesis des historischen Materialismus: Karl Marx und die Dynamik der Gesellschaft.* Vienna: Europa Verlag, 1965.

Kamenka, Eugene. *The Ethical Foundation of Marxism.* London: Routledge & Kegan Paul, 1962.

Kamin, Leon. *The Science and Politics of I.Q.* New York: John Wiley & Sons, 1974.

Kandel, E. P., ed. *Marx und Engels und die ersten proletarischen Revolutionäre.* Berlin: Dietz Verlag, 1965.

Kaplan, Temma. *Anarchists of Andalusia.* Princeton: Princeton University Press, 1977.

Kowalski, Werner, ed. *Vom Kleinbürgerlichen Demokratismus zum Kommunismus: Zeitschriften aus der Frühzeit der deutschen Arbeiterbewegung, 1834–1847.* Berlin: Akademie Verlag, 1967.

———. *Vorgeschichte und Entstehung des Bundes der Gerechten.* Berlin: Rütten und Loening, 1962.

Krupskaya, Nadesdha K. *Memories of Lenin.* 2 vols. London: Lawrence and Wishart, 1930.

Kuhn, Thomas S. *The Structure of Scientific Revolutions.* Chicago: University of Chicago Press, Phoenix Books, 1967.

Lenin, V. I. *Collected Works.* 45 vols. Moscow: Progress Publishers, 1972.

———. *State and Revolution.* New York: International Publishers, 1974.

Lewis, John. *The Life and Teaching of Karl Marx.* New York: International Publishers, 1965.

Lichtheim, George. *Marxism: An Historical and Critical Study.* New York: Praeger, 1965.

———. *The Origins of Socialism.* New York: Praeger, 1969.

Lowy, Michael. *La Théorie de la révolution chez le jeune Marx.* Paris: Maspero, 1970.

Lozovsky, A. *Marx and the Trade Unions.* New York: International Publishers, 1935.

Lukacs, George. *Studies in European Realism.* London: Hillway, 1959.

McLellan, David. *Karl Marx: His Life and Thought.* New York: Harper and Row, 1973.

———. *Marx before Marxism.* New York: Harper and Row, 1970.

McMurtry, John. *The Structure of Marx's World-View.* Princeton: Princeton University Press, 1978.

Mao Tse-tung. *Critique of Soviet Political Economy.* Translated by Moss Roberts. New York: Monthly Review Press, 1977.

———. *Selected Readings.* Peking: Foreign Languages Press, 1967.

———. *Selected Works,* 5 vols. Peking: Foreign Languages Press, 1965.

Marat, Jean Paul. *Textes choisies.* Edited by Michel Vovelle. Paris: Editions sociales, 1963.

———. *Writings.* Edited by Paul Friedländer. 2 vols. New York: International Publishers, 1927.

Masters, Roger D., ed. *Jean-Jacques Rousseau: The First and Second Discourses.* Translated by Roger D. and Judith R. Masters. New York: St. Martin's Press, 1964.

———, ed. *Jean-Jacques Rousseau: On the Social Contract with Geneva Manuscript and Political Economy.* Translated by Judith R. Masters. New York: St. Martin's Press, 1978.

Meek, Ronald L. *Economics and Ideology and Other Essays.* London: Chapman and Hall, 1967.

Mehring, Franz. *Karl Marx: The Story of His Life.* Translated by Edward Fitzgerald. Ann Arbor: University of Michigan Press, Ann Arbor Paperbacks for the Study of Communism and Marxism, 1962.

Merriman, John M. *The Agony of the Republic: The Repression of the Left in Revolutionary France 1848–1851.* New Haven: Yale University Press, 1978.

Mewes, Horst. "On the Concept of Politics in the Early Works of Karl Marx." *Social Research* 43(1976):276–294.

Miliband, Ralph. *Marxism and Politics.* Oxford: Oxford University Press, 1977.

———. *The State in Capitalist Society.* New York: Basic Books, 1969.

Miller, Richard W. "Aristotle and Marx: The Unity of Two Opposites." *Proceedings of the American Political Science Association.* Ann Arbor: University of Michigan Press, 1978.

———. "The Consistency of Historical Materialism." *Philosophy and Public Affairs* 4(1975):390–409.

———. "Reason and Commitment in the Social Sciences." *Philosophy and Public Affairs* 8(1979):241–266.

Mitrany, David. *Marx against the Peasant: A Study in Social Dogmatism.* Chapel Hill: University of North Carolina Press, 1951.

Molnár, Erik. *La Politique d'alliances du Marxisme (1848–1889).* Budapest: Akadémai Kiadó, 1967.

Montesquieu, Charles Louis de Secondat, baron de la Brède et de. *De l'esprit des lois.* Edited by Gonzague Truc. 2 vols. Paris: Garnier Flammarion, 1961.

Moore, Barrington, Jr. *Social Origins of Dictatorship and Democracy: Lord and Peasant in the Making of the Modern World.* Boston: Beacon Press, 1966.

Moore, Stanley. "Marx and Lenin as Historical Materialists." *Philosophy and Public Affairs* 4(1975):171–194.

Moss, Bernard H. *The Origins of the French Labor Movement: The Socialism of Skilled Workers.* Berkeley: University of California Press, 1976.

Na'aman, Shlomo. "Zur Geschichte des Bundes der Kommunisten in Deutschland in der zweiten Phase seines Bestehens." *Archiv für Sozialgeschichte* 5(1965):5–82.

Nicolaievsky, Boris, and Maenchen-Helfen, Otto. *Karl Marx: Man and Fighter.* Translated by Gwenda David and Eric Mosbacher. London: Methuen, 1936.

Noyes, P. H. *Organization and Revolution: Working Class Associations in the German Revolution of 1848–1849.* Princeton: Princeton University Press, 1966.

Oakeshott, Michael. *On Human Conduct.* Oxford: Clarendon Press, 1975.

Obermann, Karl. *Zur Geschichte des Bundes der Kommunisten 1849–52.* Berlin: Dietz Verlag, 1955.

Ollman, Bertell. *Alienation: Marx's Conception of Man in Capitalist Society.* Cambridge: Cambridge University Press, 1971.

Padover, Saul K. *Karl Marx: An Intimate Biography.* New York: McGraw-Hill, 1978.

Plamenatz, John. *German Marxism and Russian Communism.* London: Longmans, Green, 1954.

Plekhanov, G. F. *Selected Philosophical Works.* Translated by Andrew Rothstein and R. Dixon. 5 vols. London: Lawrence and Wishart, 1961.

Pocock, J. G. A. *Politics, Language and Time: Essays on Political Thought and History.* New York: Atheneum, 1971.

Price, Roger, ed. *1848 in France.* Documents of Revolution. Translated by C. M. Smith. Ithaca: Cornell University Press, 1975.

———. *The French Second Republic.* Ithaca: Cornell University Press, 1972.

———, ed. *Revolution and Reaction: 1848 and the Second French Republic.* New York: Barnes and Noble, 1976.

Prickett, James R. "Communists and the Communist Issue in the American Labor Movement, 1920–1950." Ph.D. dissertation, University of California. Ann Arbor: University Microfilms, 1975.

Proudhon, Pierre-Joseph. *Carnets.* Edited by Pierre Haubtman. 4 vols. Paris: Marcel Rivière, 1961–

———. *Confessions d'un révolutionnaire.* Paris: Marcel Rivière, 1929.

———. *De la capacité politique des classes ouvrières.* Paris: Marcel Rivière, 1924.

———. *De la justice dans la révolution et dans l'église.* 4 vols. Paris: Marcel Rivière, 1935.

————. *General Idea of the Revolution in the Nineteenth Century.* Translated by John Beverly Robinson. London: Freedom Press, 1923.

————. *Système des contradictions économiques ou philosophie de la misère.* 2 vols. Paris: Marcel Rivière, 1923.

Provine, William B. *The Origins of Theoretical Population Genetics.* Chicago: University of Chicago Press, 1971.

Putnam, Hilary. *Collected Philosophical Papers.* 2 vols. Cambridge: Cambridge University Press, 1975.

Rabinowitch, Alexander. *The Bolsheviks Come to Power.* New York: Norton, 1976.

Rawidowicz, S. *Ludwig Feuerbachs Philosophie.* Berlin: deGruyter, 1964.

Reeves, Nigel. *Heinrich Heine: Poetry and Politics.* Oxford: Oxford University Press, 1974.

Reichard, Richard W. *Crippled from Birth: German Social Democracy 1844–70.* Ames: Iowa State University Press, 1969.

Rioux, Lucien, and Backmann, René. *L'explosion de mai: histoire complète des 'événements'.* Paris: Laffont, 1968.

Rosdolsky, Roman. "Friedrich Engels und das Problem der 'Geschichtlosen Völker' (Die Nationalitätenfrage in der Revolution 1848–49 im Lichte der 'Neuen Rheinischen Zeitung')". *Archiv für Sozialgeschichte* 4(1964):87–282.

Ruben, David-Hillel. *Marxism and Materialism: A Study in Marxist Theory of Knowledge.* Sussex: Harvester, 1977.

Rudé, George. *The Crowd in the French Revolution.* Oxford: Oxford University Press, 1971.

Ryazanoff, David. *Karl Marx and Friedrich Engels.* New York: International Publishers, 1972.

Saville, John, ed. *The Red Republican and the Friend of the People, 1850–1851.* 2 vols. London: Merlin, 1966.

Schieder, Wolfgang. *Anfänge der deutschen Arbeiterbewegung: die Auslandsvereine im Jahrzehnt nach der Julirevolution von 1830.* Stuttgart: Klett, 1963.

Schorske, Carl E. *German Social Democracy 1905–1917: The Development of the Great Schism.* New York: Harper and Row, Harper Torchbooks, 1972.

Schraepler, Ernst. *Handwerkerbünde und Arbeitervereine, 1830–53.* Berlin: deGruyter, 1972.

Schwartz, Michael. *Radical Protest and Social Structure: The Southern Farmers' Alliance and Cotton Tenancy.* Studies in Social Discontinuity, edited by Charles Tilly. New York: Academic Press, 1976.

Scott, James. *The Moral Economy of the Peasant: Rebellion and Subsistence in Southeast Asia.* New Haven: Yale University Press, 1976.

Scriven, Michael. "Explanation and Prediction in Evolutionary Theory." In *The Nature and Scope of Social Science: A Critical Anthology,* edited by Leonard I. Krimerman, pp. 117–125. New York: Appleton-Century-Crofts, 1969.

Seidel-Hoppner, Waltraud. *Wilhelm Weitling—der erste deutsche Theoretiker und Agitator des Kommunismus.* Berlin: Dietz Verlag, 1961.

Seigel, Jerrold. *Marx's Fate: The Shape of a Life.* Princeton: Princeton University Press, 1978.

Shaw, William H. *Marx's Theory of History.* Stanford: Stanford University Press, 1978.

Silverman, Sydel F. "Exploitation in Rural Central Italy." *Comparative Studies in Society and History* 12(1970):327–339.

Skinner, Quentin. *The Foundations of Modern Political Thought.* 2 vols. Cambridge: Cambridge University Press, 1978.

———. "Meaning and Understanding in the History of Ideas." *History and Theory* 8(1969):3–53.

———. "The Principles and Practice of Opposition: The Case of Bolingbroke versus Walpole." In *Historical Perspectives: Studies in English Thought and Society in Honor of J. H. Plumb,* edited by N. McKendrick. London: Europa Publications, 1974.

———. "Some Problems in the Analysis of Political Thought and Action." *Political Theory* 2(1974):277–303.

Soboul, Albert. *The French Revolution 1787–1799: From the Storming of the Bastille to Napoleon.* Translated by Alan Forrest and Colin Jones. 2 vols. London: New Left Books, 1974.

———. *Problèmes paysans de la révolution (1789–1848).* Paris: Maspero, 1976.

———. *The Sans-Culottes: The Popular Movement and Revolutionary Government 1793–1794.* Translated by Remy Inglis Hall. New York: Doubleday & Co., 1972.

———. *A Short History of the French Revolution, 1789–1799.* Translated by Geoffrey Symcox. Berkeley: University of California Press, 1965.

Stadelmann, Rudolph. *Social and Political History of the German 1848 Revolution.* Translated by James G. Chastain. Athens: Ohio University Press, 1975.

Tarrow, Sidney. *Peasant Communism in Southern Italy.* New Haven: Yale University Press, 1967.

Thompson, Dorothy, ed. *The Early Chartists.* History in Depth, edited by G. A. Williams. Columbia: University of South Carolina Press, 1971.

Thompson, Edward P. *The Making of the English Working Class.* New York: Vintage Books, 1966.

———. "The Moral Economy of the English Crowd in the Eighteenth Century." *Past and Present* 50(1971):76–136.

Tilly, Charles; Tilly, Louise; and Tilly, Richard. *The Rebellious Century: 1830–1930.* Cambridge, Mass.: Harvard University Press, 1975.

Tocqueville, Alexis de. *Recollections.* Translated by Alexander Teixeira de Mattos and edited by J. P. Mayer. London: Harvill Press, 1948.

Tucker, Robert C. *The Marxian Revolutionary Idea.* New York: Norton, 1970.

Ward, J. T. *Chartism.* London: B. T. Batsford, 1973.

Wartofsky, Marx W. *Feuerbach.* Cambridge: Cambridge University Press, 1977.

Wehler, Hans-Ulrich. *Sozialgeschichte Heute: Festschrift für Hans Rosenberg zum 70. Geburtstag.* Gottingen: Vandenhoeck und Ruprecht, 1974.

Weitling, Wilhelm. *Garantien der Harmonie und Freiheit.* Berlin: Akademie Verlag, 1955.

———. *The Poor Sinner's Gospel.* Translated by Dinah Livingstone. London: Sheed and Ward, n.d.

Westfall, Richard S. *The Construction of Modern Science: Mechanisms and Mechanics.* Wiley History of Science Series, edited by George Basalla and William Coleman. New York: John Wiley & Sons, 1971.

Wittke, Carl. *The Utopian Communist: A Biography of Wilhelm Weitling, Nineteenth Century Reformer.* Baton Rouge: Louisiana State University Press, 1950.

Wood, Allen W. "The Marxian Critique of Justice." *Philosophy and Public Affairs* 1(1972):244–283.

Index

*For more information on participants,
see List of Historical Figures*